ŚRĪ CAITANYA-CARITĀMṚTA

BOOKS by
His Divine Grace A.C. Bhaktivedanta Swami Prabhupāda

Bhagavad-gītā As It Is
Śrīmad-Bhāgavatam, Cantos 1-5 (15 Vols.)
Śrī Caitanya-caritāmṛta (17 Vols.)
Teachings of Lord Caitanya
The Nectar of Devotion
Śrī Īśopaniṣad
Easy Journey to Other Planets
Kṛṣṇa Consciousness: The Topmost Yoga System
Kṛṣṇa, The Supreme Personality of Godhead (3 Vols.)
Transcendental Teachings of Prahlād Mahārāja
Kṛṣṇa, the Reservoir of Pleasure
The Perfection of Yoga
Beyond Birth and Death
On the Way to Kṛṣṇa
Rāja-vidyā: The King of Knowledge
Elevation to Kṛṣṇa Consciousness
Kṛṣṇa Consciousness: The Matchless Gift
Back to Godhead Magazine (Founder)

A complete catalogue is available upon request

International Society for Krishna Consciousness
3764 Watseka Avenue
Los Angeles, California 90034

All Glory to Śrī Guru and Gaurāṅga

ŚRĪ CAITANYA-CARITĀMṚTA

of Kṛṣṇadāsa Kavirāja Gosvāmī

Madhya-līlā
Volume Four

"The Lord's Return to Jagannātha Purī"

with the original Bengali text, Roman transliterations, synonyms, translation and elaborate purports

by

HIS DIVINE GRACE

A.C. Bhaktivedanta Swami Prabhupāda

Founder-Ācārya of the International Society for Krishna Consciousness

THE BHAKTIVEDANTA BOOK TRUST
New York · Los Angeles · London · Bombay

Readers interested in the subject matter of this book
are invited by the International Society for Krishna Consciousness
to correspond with its Secretary.

International Society for Krishna Consciousness
3764 Watseka Avenue
Los Angeles, California 90034

Library of Congress Catalogue Card Number: 73-93206
International Standard Book Number: 0-912776-66-8

First printing, 1975: 20,000 copies

Printed in the United States of America

Contents

Introduction

Śrī Caitanya-caritāmṛta is the principal work on the life and teachings of Śrī Kṛṣṇa Caitanya. Śrī Caitanya is the pioneer of a great social and religious movement which began in India a little less than five hundred years ago and which has directly and indirectly influenced the subsequent course of religious and philosophical thinking not only in India but in the recent West as well.

Caitanya Mahāprabhu is regarded as a figure of great historical significance. However, our conventional method of historical analysis—that of seeing a man as a product of his times—fails here. Śrī Caitanya is a personality who transcends the limited scope of historical settings.

At a time when, in the West, man was directing his explorative spirit toward studying the structure of the physical universe and circumnavigating the world in search of new oceans and continents, Śrī Kṛṣṇa Caitanya, in the East, was inaugurating and masterminding a revolution directed inward, toward a scientific understanding of the highest knowledge of man's spiritual nature.

The chief historical sources for the life of Śrī Kṛṣṇa Caitanya are the *kaḍacās* (diaries) kept by Murāri Gupta and Svarūpa Dāmodara Gosvāmī. Murāri Gupta, a physician and close associate of Śrī Caitanya's, recorded extensive notes on the first twenty-four years of Śrī Caitanya's life, culminating in his initiation into the renounced order, *sannyāsa*. The events of the rest of Caitanya Mahāprabhu's forty-eight years are recorded in the diary of Svarūpa Dāmodora Gosvāmī, another of Caitanya Mahāprabhu's intimate associates.

Śrī Caitanya-caritāmṛta is divided into three sections called *līlās,* which literally means "pastimes"—*Ādi-līlā* (the early period), *Madhya-līlā* (the middle period) and *Antya-līlā* (the final period). The notes of Murāri Gupta form the basis of the *Ādi-līlā,* and Svarūpa Dāmodara's diary provides the details for the *Madhya-* and *Antya-līlās.*

The first twelve of the seventeen chapters of *Ādi-līlā* constitute the preface for the entire work. By referring to Vedic scriptural evidence, this preface establishes Śrī Caitanya as the *avatāra* (incarnation) of Kṛṣṇa (God) for the age of Kali—the current epoch, beginning five thousand years ago and characterized by materialism, hypocrisy and dissension. In these descriptions, Caitanya Mahāprabhu, who is identical with Lord Kṛṣṇa, descends to liberally grant pure love of God to the fallen souls of this degraded age by propagating *saṅkīrtana*—literally, "congregational glorification of God"—especially by organizing massive public chanting of the *mahā-mantra* (Great Chant for Deliverance). The esoteric purpose of Lord Caitanya's appearance in the world is revealed, his co-*avatāras* and principal devotees are described and his teachings are summarized. The remaining portion of *Ādi-līlā,* chapters thirteen through seventeen, briefly recounts his divine birth and his life until he accepted the renounced order. This includes his childhood miracles, schooling, marriage and early philosophical confrontations, as well as his organization of a widespread *saṅkīrtana* movement and his civil disobedience against the repression of the Mohammedan government.

The subject of *Madhya-līlā,* the longest of the three divisions, is a detailed narration of Lord Caitanya's extensive and eventful travels throughout India as a renounced mendicant, teacher, philosopher, spiritual preceptor and mystic. During this period of six years, Śrī Caitanya transmits his teachings to his principal disciples. He debates and converts many of the most renowned philosophers and theologians of his time, including Śaṅkarites, Buddhists and Muslims, and incorporates their many thousands of followers and disciples into his own burgeoning numbers. A dramatic account of Caitanya Mahāprabhu's miraculous activities at the giant Jagannātha Cart Festival in Orissa is also included in this section.

Antya-līlā concerns the last eighteen years of Śrī Caitanya's manifest presence, spent in semiseclusion near the famous Jagannātha temple at Jagannātha Purī in Orissa. During these final years, Śrī Caitanya drifted deeper and deeper into trances of spiritual ecstasy unparalleled in all of religious and literary history, Eastern or Western. Śrī Caitanya's perpetual and ever-increasing religious beatitude, graphically described in the eyewitness accounts of Svarūpa Dāmodara Gosvāmī, his constant companion during this period, clearly defy the investigative and descriptive abilities of modern psychologists and phenomenologists of religious experience.

The author of this great classic, Kṛṣṇadāsa Kavirāja Gosvāmī, born in the year 1507, was a disciple of Raghunātha dāsa Gosvāmī, a confidential follower of Caitanya Mahāprabhu. Raghunātha dāsa, a renowned ascetic saint, heard and memorized all the activities of Caitanya Mahāprabhu told to him by Svarūpa Dāmodara. After the passing away of Śrī Caitanya and Svarūpa Dāmodara, Raghunātha dāsa, unable to bear the pain of separation from these objects of his complete devotion, traveled to Vṛndāvana, intending to commit suicide by jumping from Govardhana Hill. In Vṛndāvana, however, he encountered Rūpa Gosvāmī and Sanātana Gosvāmī, the most confidential disciples of Caitanya Mahāprabhu. They convinced him to give up his plan of suicide and impelled him to reveal to them the spiritually inspiring events of Lord Caitanya's later life. Kṛṣṇadāsa Kavirāja Gosvāmī was also residing in Vṛndāvana at this time, and Raghunātha dāsa Gosvāmī endowed him with a full comprehension of the transcendental life of Śrī Caitanya.

By this time, several biographical works had already been written on the life of Śrī Caitanya by contemporary and near-contemporary scholars and devotees. These included *Śrī Caitanya-carita* by Murāri Gupta, *Caitanya-maṅgala* by Locana dāsa Ṭhākura and *Caitanya-bhāgavata.* This latter text, a work by Vṛndāvana dāsa Ṭhākura, who was then considered the principal authority on Śrī Caitanya's life, was highly revered. While composing his important work, Vṛndāvana dāsa, fearing that it would become too voluminous, avoided elaborately describing many of the events of Śrī Caitanya's life, particulary the later ones. Anxious to hear of these later pastimes, the devotees of Vṛndāvana requested Kṛṣṇadāsa Kavirāja Gosvāmī, whom they respected as a great saint, to compose a book to narrate these episodes in detail. Upon this request, and with the permission and blessings of the Madana-mohana Deity of Vṛndāvana, he began compiling *Śrī Caitanya-caritāmṛta,* which, due to its biographical excellence and thorough exposition of Lord Caitanya's profound philosophy and teachings, is regarded as the most significant of biographical works on Śrī Caitanya.

He commenced work on the text while in his late nineties and in failing health, as he vividly describes in the text itself: "I have now become too old and disturbed in invalidity. While writing, my hands tremble. I cannot remember anything, nor can I see or hear properly. Still I write, and this is a great wonder." That he nevertheless completed, under such debilitating conditions, the greatest literary gem of medieval India is surely one of the wonders of literary history.

This English translation and commentary is the work of His Divine Grace A. C. Bhaktivedanta Swami Prabhupāda, the world's most distinguished teacher of Indian religious and philosophical thought. His commentary is based upon two Bengali commentaries, one by his teacher Śrīla Bhaktisiddhānta Sarasvatī Gosvāmī, the eminent Vedic scholar who predicted, "The time will come when the people of the world will learn Bengali to read *Śrī Caitanya-caritāmṛta,*" and the other by Śrīla Bhaktisiddhānta's father, Bhaktivinoda Ṭhākura.

His Divine Grace A. C. Bhaktivedanta Swami Prabhupāda is himself a disciplic descendant of Śrī Caitanya Mahāprabhu, and he is the first scholar to execute systematic English translations of the major works of Śrī Caitanya's followers. His consummate Bengali and Sanskrit scholarship and intimate familiarity with the precepts of Śrī Kṛṣṇa Caitanya are a fitting combination that eminently qualifies him to present this important classic to the English-speaking world. The ease and clarity with which he expounds upon difficult philosophical concepts lures even a reader totally unfamiliar with Indian religious tradition into a genuine understanding and appreciation of this profound and monumental work.

The entire text, with commentary, presented in seventeen lavishly illustrated volumes by the Bhaktivedanta Book Trust, represents a contribution of major importance to the intellectual, cultural and spiritual life of contemporary man.

—The Publishers

His Divine Grace
A. C. Bhaktivedanta Swami Prabhupāda
Founder-Ācārya of the International Society for Krishna Consciousness

Śrīdhāma Māyāpur
The birthplace of the Supreme Lord Śrī Kṛṣṇa Caitanya in the province of Gauḍa in Bengal.

In Māyāpur, a reconstruction of the house of Advaita Ācārya, the incarnation of Lord Caitanya as a devotee.

The Rāmeśvara temple in southern Mathurā (Mādurā), where Caitanya Mahāprabhu bestowed His mercy upon a great devotee of Lord Rāmacandra. (*p.7*)

The Mīnākṣī-Devī temple in Mādurā. *(p.7)*

The Rāmeśvara temple in Setubandha, where Lord Caitanya took possession of the original manuscript of the *Kūrma Purāṇa*. (p.17)

A monument commemorating the site where Caitanya Mahāprabhu first saw the Jagannātha Purī temple.

PLATE ONE

Śrī Ṣaḍbhuja, the six-armed form of the Supreme Lord, was revealed by Śrī Caitanya Mahāprabhu during His stay on this planet. In two of His hands He holds a bow and arrow, the symbols of Lord Rāmacandra; two hands hold a flute, the symbol of Lord Kṛṣṇa; and two hands hold a *daṇḍa* and waterpot, the symbols of Caitanya Mahāprabhu. By manifesting this form, Lord Caitanya conclusively proves that he is Bhagavān, the original Supreme Personality of Godhead.

PLATE TWO

"It was in Śrī Śaila that Lord Śiva and his wife Durgā lived in the dress of *brāhmaṇas,* and when they saw Śrī Caitanya Mahāprabhu, they became very pleased. Lord Śiva, dressed like a *brāhmaṇa,* gave alms to Śrī Caitanya Mahāprabhu and invited Him to spend three days in a solitary place. Sitting there together, they talked very confidentially. After talking with Lord Śiva, Śrī Caitanya Mahāprabhu took his permission to leave." (*pp.5-6*)

PLATE THREE

"Śrīmatī Sītādevī is the mother of the three worlds and the wife of Lord Rāmacandra. Among chaste women, she is supreme, and she is the daughter of King Janaka. When Rāvaṇa came to kidnap mother Sītā and she saw him, she took shelter of the fire-god, Agni. The fire-god covered the body of mother Sītā, and in this way she was protected from the hands of Rāvaṇa. The fire-god, Agni, took away the real Sītā and brought her to the place of Pārvatī, goddess Durgā. An illusory form of mother Sītā was then delivered to Rāvaṇa, and in this way Rāvaṇa was cheated. After Rāvaṇa was killed by Lord Rāmacandra, Sītādevī was brought before the fire. When the illusory Sītā was brought before the fire by Lord Rāmacandra, the fire-god made the illusory form disappear and delivered the real Sītā to Lord Rāmacandra." (*pp.18-20*)

PLATE FOUR

"Śrīpāda Madhvācārya is the fifth *ācārya* in the disciplic succession bearing his name (the Mādhva-gauḍīya-sampradāya). His devotion to the Lord and his erudite scholarship are known throughout India. After traveling all over India, Madhvācārya went to Badarikāśrama, where he met Vyāsadeva and explained his commentary on *Bhagavad-gītā* before him. Thus he became a great scholar by studying before Vyāsadeva. Aside from his great spiritual power, it is also said that there was no limit to his bodily strength, and he performed many astonishing pastimes testifying to this fact. His disciple Padmanābha Tīrtha followed him in the disciplic succession." (*pp.41-44*)

PLATE FIVE

"Śrī Caitanya Mahāprabhu then visited a place within the forest called Saptatāla. All the trees there were very old, very bulky and very high. After seeing the seven palm trees, Śrī Caitanya Mahāprabhu embraced them. As a result, they all returned to Vaikuṇṭhaloka, the spiritual world. After the seven palm trees departed for the Vaikuṇṭhas, everyone was astonished to see them gone. The people then began to say, 'This *sannyāsī* called Śrī Caitanya Mahāprabhu must be an incarnation of Lord Rāmacandra. Only Lord Rāmacandra has the power to send seven palm trees to the spiritual Vaikuṇṭha planets.' " (*pp.81-82*)

PLATE SIX

" 'Fulfilling my desire and sacrificing His own promise, He got down from the chariot, took up its wheel, and ran toward me hurriedly, just as a lion goes to kill an elephant. He even dropped His outer garment on the way.'

Kṛṣṇa promised not to fight in the Battle of Kurukṣetra, but in order to break Kṛṣṇa's promise, Bhīṣma attacked Arjuna in such a vigorous way that Kṛṣṇa was obliged to take up a chariot wheel and attack Bhīṣma. The Lord did this to show that His devotee was being maintained at the sacrifice of His own promise." (*p.196*)

PLATE SEVEN

"Śrī Caitanya Mahāprabhu, accompanied by His personal associates, met all the Vaiṣṇavas on the road with great jubilation. First Advaita Ācārya offered prayers to the lotus feet of the Lord, and the Lord immediately embraced Him in ecstatic love. After this, all the devotees, headed by Śrīvāsa Ṭhākura, offered prayers to the lotus feet of the Lord, and the Lord embraced each and every one of them in great love and ecstasy. The Lord addressed all the devotees one after another and took all of them with Him into the house. Since the residence of Kāśī Miśra was insufficient, all the assembled devotees were very overcrowded. Śrī Caitanya Mahāprabhu made all the devotees sit at His side, and with His own hand He offered them garlands and sandalwood pulp." (*pp.277-280*)

PLATE EIGHT

"After this, Śrī Caitanya Mahāprabhu went to meet Haridāsa Ṭhākura, and He saw him engaged in chanting the *mahā-mantra* with ecstatic love. Haridāsa chanted, 'Hare Kṛṣṇa, Hare Kṛṣṇa, Kṛṣṇa Kṛṣṇa, Hare Hare/ Hare Rāma, Hare Rāma, Rāma Rāma, Hare Hare.' As soon as Haridāsa Ṭhākura saw Śrī Caitanya Mahāprabhu, he immediately fell down like a stick to offer Him obeisances, and Lord Śrī Caitanya Mahāprabhu raised him up and embraced him. Then both the Lord and His servant began to cry in ecstatic love. Śrī Caitanya took Haridāsa Ṭhākura within the flower garden, and there, in a very secluded place, He showed him his residence. The Lord requested: 'Remain here and chant the Hare Kṛṣṇa *mahā-mantra*. I shall personally come here to meet you daily. Remain here peacefully and look at the *cakra* on the top of the temple and offer obeisances. As far as your *prasāda* is concerned, I shall arrange to have that sent here.' " (*pp.305-311*)

CHAPTER 9

Lord Śrī Caitanya Mahāprabhu's Travels to the Holy Places

(continued from the previous volume)

TEXT 166

ঋষভ-পর্বতে চলি' আইলা গৌরহরি ।
নারায়ণ দেখিলা তাঁহা নতি-স্তুতি করি' ॥ ১৬৬ ॥

ṛṣabha-parvate cali' āilā gaurahari
nārāyaṇa dekhilā tāṅhā nati-stuti kari'

SYNONYMS

ṛṣabha-parvate—to the Ṛṣabha Hill; *cali'*—walking; *āilā*—arrived; *gaura-hari*—Lord Śrī Caitanya Mahāprabhu; *nārāyaṇa*—the Deity of Lord Nārāyaṇa; *dekhilā*—saw; *tāṅhā*—there; *nati-stuti kari'*—offering obeisances and prayers.

TRANSLATION

When the Lord arrived at Ṛṣabha Hill, He saw the temple of Lord Nārāyaṇa and offered obeisances and various prayers.

PURPORT

Ṛṣabha Hill is in southern Karṇāṭa in the district of Mādurā. Twelve miles north of Mādurā City is a place called Ānāgaḍa-malaya-parvata, which is situated within the forest of Kuṭakācala. Within this forest Lord Ṛṣabhadeva burned Himself to ashes. Now this place is known as Pālni Hill.

TEXT 167

পরমানন্দপুরী তাহাঁ রহে চতুর্মাস ।
শুনি' মহাপ্রভু গেলা পুরী-গোসাঞির পাশ ॥ ১৬৭ ॥

paramānanda-purī tāhāṅ rahe catur-māsa
śuni' mahāprabhu gelā purī-gosāñira pāśa

SYNONYMS

paramānanda-purī—Paramānanda Purī; *tāhāṅ*—there; *rahe*—remained; *catuḥ-māsa*—four months; *śuni'*—hearing; *mahāprabhu*—Śrī Caitanya Mahāprabhu; *gelā*—went; *purī*—Paramānanda Purī; *gosāñira*—the spiritual master; *pāśa*—near.

TRANSLATION

Paramānanda Purī was staying at Ṛṣabha Hill, and when Śrī Caitanya Mahāprabhu heard this, He immediately went to see him.

TEXT 168

পুরী-গোসাঞির প্রভু কৈল চরণ বন্দন ।
প্রেমে পুরী গোসাঞি তাঁরে কৈল আলিঙ্গন ॥১৬৮॥

purī-gosāñira prabhu kaila caraṇa vandana
preme purī gosāñi tāṅre kaila āliṅgana

SYNONYMS

purī-gosāñira—of Paramānanda Purī; *prabhu*—Śrī Caitanya Mahāprabhu; *kaila*—did; *caraṇa vandana*—worship of the lotus feet; *preme*—in ecstasy; *purī gosāñi*—Paramānanda Purī; *tāṅre*—unto Him; *kaila*—did; *āliṅgana*—embracing.

TRANSLATION

Upon meeting Paramānanda Purī, Śrī Caitanya Mahāprabhu offered him all respects, touching his lotus feet, and Paramānanda Purī embraced the Lord in ecstasy.

TEXT 169

তিনদিন প্রেমে দোঁহে কৃষ্ণকথা-রঙ্গে ।
সেই বিপ্র-ঘরে দোঁহে রহে একসঙ্গে ॥ ১৬৯ ॥

tina-dina preme doṅhe kṛṣṇa-kathā-raṅge
sei vipra-ghare doṅhe rahe eka-saṅge

SYNONYMS

tina-dina—three days; *preme*—in ecstasy; *doṅhe*—both; *kṛṣṇa-kathā*—discussing topics of Kṛṣṇa; *raṅge*—in jubilation; *sei vipra-ghare*—in the home of a *brāhmaṇa*; *doṅhe*—both of them; *rahe*—stayed; *eka-saṅge*—together.

TRANSLATION

Śrī Caitanya Mahāprabhu stayed with Paramānanda Purī in a brāhmaṇa's house where Paramānanda Purī was residing. Both of them passed three days there discussing topics of Kṛṣṇa.

TEXT 170

পুরী-গোসাঞি বলে,—আমি যাব পুরুষোত্তমে।
পুরুষোত্তম দেখি' গৌড়ে যাব গঙ্গাস্নানে ॥ ১৭০ ॥

purī-gosāñi bale,——āmi yāba puruṣottame
puruṣottama dekhi' gauḍe yāba gaṅgā-snāne

SYNONYMS

purī-gosāñi—Paramānanda Purī; *bale*—said; *āmi*—I; *yāba*—shall go; *puruṣottame*—to Jagannātha Purī; *puruṣottama dekhi'*—after visiting Jagannātha Purī; *gauḍe yāba*—I shall go to Bengal; *gaṅgā-snāne*—for bathing in the Ganges.

TRANSLATION

Paramānanda Purī informed Śrī Caitanya Mahāprabhu that he was going to see Puruṣottama at Jagannātha Purī. After seeing Lord Jagannātha there, he would go to Bengal to bathe in the Ganges.

TEXT 171

প্রভু কহে,—তুমি পুনঃ আইস নীলাচলে।
আমি সেতুবন্ধ হৈতে আসিব অল্পকালে ॥ ১৭১ ॥

prabhu kahe,——tumi punaḥ āisa nīlācale
āmi setubandha haite āsiba alpa-kāle

SYNONYMS

prabhu kahe—the Lord said; *tumi*—you; *punaḥ*—again; *āisa*—come; *nīlācale*—to Jagannātha Purī; *āmi*—I; *setubandha haite*—from Rāmeśvara; *āsiba*—shall return; *alpa-kāle*—very soon.

TRANSLATION

Śrī Caitanya Mahāprabhu then told him, "Please return to Jagannātha Purī, for I will return there very soon from Rāmeśvara [Setubandha].

TEXT 172

তোমার নিকটে রহি,—হেন বাঞ্ছা হয়।
নীলাচলে আসিবে মোরে হঞা সদয় ॥ ১৭২ ॥

tomāra nikaṭe rahi,——hena vāñchā haya
nīlācale āsibe more hañā sadaya

SYNONYMS

tomāra nikaṭe—with you; *rahi*—I may stay; *hena*—such; *vāñchā haya*—is My desire; *nīlācale*—to Jagannātha Purī; *āsibe*—please come; *more*—unto Me; *hañā*—being; *sa-daya*—merciful.

TRANSLATION

"It is My desire to stay with you, and therefore if you would return to Jagannātha Purī, you would show great mercy upon Me."

TEXT 173

এত বলি' তাঁর ঠাঞি এই আজ্ঞা লঞা।
দক্ষিণে চলিলা প্রভু হরষিত হঞা ॥ ১৭৩ ॥

eta bali' tāṅra ṭhāñi ei ājñā lañā
dakṣiṇe calilā prabhu haraṣita hañā

SYNONYMS

eta bali'—saying this; *tāṅra ṭhāñi*—from him; *ei ājñā lañā*—taking permission; *dakṣiṇe calilā*—departed for southern India; *prabhu*—Lord Śrī Caitanya Mahāprabhu; *haraṣita hañā*—being very pleased.

TRANSLATION

After talking in this way with Paramānanda Purī, the Lord took his permission to leave and departed for southern India. The Lord Himself was very pleased.

TEXT 174

পরমানন্দ পুরী তবে চলিলা নীলাচলে।
মহাপ্রভু চলি চলি আইলা শ্রীশৈলে ॥ ১৭৪ ॥

paramānanda purī tabe calilā nīlācale
mahāprabhu cali cali āilā śrī-śaile

SYNONYMS

paramānanda purī—Paramānanda Purī; *tabe*—then; *calilā nīlācale*—departed for Jagannātha Purī; *mahāprabhu*—Śrī Caitanya Mahāprabhu; *cali cali*—walking; *āilā*—came; *śrī-śaile*—to Śrī Śaila.

TRANSLATION

Thus Paramānanda Purī started for Jagannātha Purī, and Śrī Caitanya Mahāprabhu began walking toward Śrī Śaila.

PURPORT

Śrīla Bhaktisiddhānta Sarasvatī Ṭhākura remarks, "Which Śrī Śaila is being indicated by Kṛṣṇadāsa Kavirāja Gosvāmī is not clearly understood. There is no temple of Mallikārjuna in this area because the Śrī Śaila located in the district of Dhāravāḍa cannot possibly be there. That Śrī Śaila is on the southern side of Belagrāma, and the Śiva temple of Mallikārjuna is located there. (Refer to text fifteen of this chapter.) It is said that there on that hill Lord Śiva lived with Devī. Also Lord Brahmā lived there with all the demigods."

TEXT 175

শিব-দুর্গা রহে তাহাঁ ব্রাহ্মণের বেশে ।
মহাপ্রভু দেখি' দোঁহার হইল উল্লাসে ॥ ১৭৫ ॥

śiva-durgā rahe tāhāṅ brāhmaṇera veśe
mahāprabhu dekhi' doṅhāra ha-ila ullāse

SYNONYMS

śiva-durgā—Lord Śiva and his wife Durgā; *rahe tāhāṅ*—stayed there; *brāhmaṇera veśe*—in the dress of *brāhmaṇas; mahāprabhu dekhi'*—seeing Śrī Caitanya Mahāprabhu; *doṅhāra*—of both of them; *ha-ila*—there was; *ullāse*—great pleasure.

TRANSLATION

It was in Śrī Śaila that Lord Śiva and his wife Durgā lived in the dress of *brāhmaṇas*, and when they saw Śrī Caitanya Mahāprabhu, they became very pleased.

TEXT 176

তিন দিন ভিক্ষা দিল করি' নিমন্ত্রণ ।
নিভৃতে বসি' গুপ্তবার্তা কহে দুই জন ॥ ১৭৬ ॥

tina dina bhikṣā dila kari' nimantraṇa
nibhṛte vasi' gupta-vārtā kahe dui jana

SYNONYMS

tina dina—for three days; *bhikṣā dila*—offered alms; *kari' nimantraṇa*—inviting Him; *nibhṛte*—in a solitary place; *vasi'*—sitting together; *gupta-vārtā*—confidential talks; *kahe*—speak; *dui jana*—both of them.

TRANSLATION

Lord Śiva, dressed like a brāhmaṇa, gave alms to Śrī Caitanya Mahāprabhu and invited Him to spend three days in a solitary place. Sitting there together, they talked very confidentially.

TEXT 177

তাঁর সঙ্গে মহাপ্রভু করি ইষ্টগোষ্ঠী ।
তাঁর আজ্ঞা লঞা আইলা পুরী কামকোষ্ঠী ॥১৭৭॥

tāṅra saṅge mahāprabhu kari iṣṭagoṣṭhī
tāṅra ājñā lañā āilā purī kāmakoṣṭhī

SYNONYMS

tāṅra saṅge—with him; *mahāprabhu*—Śrī Caitanya Mahāprabhu; *kari iṣṭa-goṣṭhī*—discussing spiritual subject matter; *tāṅra*—his; *ājñā*—order; *lañā*—taking; *āilā*—came; *purī kāmakoṣṭhī*—to Kāmakoṣṭhī-purī.

TRANSLATION

After talking with Lord Śiva, Śrī Caitanya Mahāprabhu took his permission to leave and went to Kāmakoṣṭhī-purī.

TEXT 178

দক্ষিণ-মথুরা আইলা কামকোষ্ঠী হৈতে ।
তাহাঁ দেখা হৈল এক ব্রাহ্মণ-সহিতে ॥ ১৭৮ ॥

dakṣiṇa-mathurā āilā kāmakoṣṭhī haite
tāhāṅ dekhā haila eka brāhmaṇa-sahite

SYNONYMS

dakṣiṇa-mathurā—at southern Mathurā; *āilā*—arrived; *kāma-koṣṭhī haite*—from Kāmakoṣṭhī; *tāhāṅ*—there; *dekhā haila*—He met; *eka*—one; *brāhmaṇa-sahite*—with a *brāhmaṇa.*

TRANSLATION

When Śrī Caitanya Mahāprabhu arrived at southern Mathurā from Kāmakoṣṭhī, He met a brāhmaṇa.

PURPORT

This southern Mathurā, presently known as Mādurā, is situated on the banks of the Bhāgāi River. This place of pilgrimage is specifically meant for the devotees of Lord Śiva; therefore it is called Śaivakṣetra, that is, the place where Lord Śiva is worshiped. In this area there are mountains and forests. There are also two Śiva temples, one known as Rāmeśvara and the other known as Sundareśvara. There is also a temple to Devī called Mīnākṣī-Devī, which is a very great architectural achievement. It was built under the supervision of the kings of the Pāṇḍya Dynasty, and when the Mohammedans attacked this temple, as well as the temple of Sundareśvara, great damage was done. In the Christian year 1372, a king named Kampanna Udaiyara reigned on the throne of Mādurā. Long ago, Emperor Kulaśekhara ruled this area, and during his reign he established a colony of *brāhmaṇas*. A well-known king named Anantaguṇa Pāṇḍya is an eleventh generation descendant of Emperor Kulaśekhara.

TEXT 179

সেই বিপ্র মহাপ্রভুকে কৈল নিমন্ত্রণ ।
রামভক্ত সেই বিপ্র – বিরক্ত মহাজন ॥ ১৭৯ ॥

sei vipra mahāprabhuke kaila nimantraṇa
rāma-bhakta sei vipra——virakta mahājana

SYNONYMS

sei vipra—that *brāhmaṇa*; *mahāprabhuke*—unto Lord Śrī Caitanya Mahāprabhu; *kaila*—did; *nimantraṇa*—invitation; *rāma-bhakta*—devotee of Lord Rāmacandra; *sei*—that; *vipra*—*brāhmaṇa*; *virakta*—very detached; *mahājana*—a great devotee and authority.

TRANSLATION

The brāhmaṇa who met Śrī Caitanya Mahāprabhu invited the Lord to his home. This brāhmaṇa was a great devotee and authority on Lord Śrī Rāmacandra. He was always detached from material activities.

TEXT 180

কৃতমালায় স্নান করি' আইলা তাঁর ঘরে ।
ভিক্ষা কি দিবেন বিপ্র,—পাক নাহি করে ॥ ১৮০ ॥

kṛtamālāya snāna kari' āilā tāṅra ghare
bhikṣā ki dibena vipra,——pāka nāhi kare

SYNONYMS

kṛta-mālāya—in the Kṛtamālā River; *snāna kari'*—bathing; *āilā*—came; *tāṅra*—of the *brāhmaṇa; ghare*—to the home; *bhikṣā*—offering of alms; *ki dibena*—what shall give; *vipra*—the *brāhmaṇa; pāka*—cooking; *nāhi kare*—did not do.

TRANSLATION

After bathing in the River Kṛtamālā, Śrī Caitanya Mahāprabhu went to the brāhmaṇa's house, but before taking lunch, He saw that the food was unprepared because the brāhmaṇa had not cooked it.

TEXT 181

মহাপ্রভু কহে তাঁরে,—শুন মহাশয় ।
মধ্যাহ্ন হৈল, কেনে পাক নাহি হয় ॥ ১৮১ ॥

mahāprabhu kahe tāṅre,——śuna mahāśaya
madhyāhna haila, kene pāka nāhi haya

SYNONYMS

mahāprabhu kahe—Śrī Caitanya Mahāprabhu said; *tāṅre*—unto him; *śuna mahāśaya*—please hear, My dear sir; *madhya-ahna haila*—it is already noon; *kene*—why; *pāka nāhi haya*—you did not cook.

TRANSLATION

Seeing this, Śrī Caitanya Mahāprabhu said, "My dear sir, please tell me why you have not cooked. It is already noon."

TEXT 182

বিপ্র কহে,—প্রভু, মোর অরণ্যে বসতি ।
পাকের সামগ্রী বনে না মিলে সম্প্রতি ॥ ১৮২ ॥

vipra kahe,——prabhu, mora araṇye vasati
pākera sāmagrī vane nā mile samprati

SYNONYMS

vipra kahe—the *brāhmaṇa* replied; *prabhu*—O Lord; *mora*—my; *araṇye*—in the forest; *vasati*—residence; *pākera sāmagrī*—the ingredients for cooking; *vane*—in the forest; *nā mile*—are not available; *samprati*—at this time.

TRANSLATION

The brāhmaṇa replied, "My dear Lord, we are living in the forest. For the time being we cannot get all the ingredients for cooking.

TEXT 183

বন্য শাক-ফল-মূল আনিবে লক্ষ্মণ।
তবে সীতা করিবেন পাক-প্রয়োজন ॥ ১৮৩ ॥

vanya śāka-phala-mūla ānibe lakṣmaṇa
tabe sītā karibena pāka-prayojana

SYNONYMS

vanya—of the forest; *śāka*—vegetables; *phala-mūla*—fruits and roots; *ānibe*—will bring; *lakṣmaṇa*—Lakṣmaṇa; *tabe*—that time; *sītā*—mother Sītā; *karibena*—will do; *pāka-prayojana*—the necessary cooking.

TRANSLATION

"When Lakṣmaṇa brings all the vegetables, fruits and roots from the forest, Sītā will arrange the necessary cooking."

TEXT 184

তাঁর উপাসনা শুনি' প্রভু তুষ্ট হৈলা।
আস্তে-ব্যস্তে সেই বিপ্র রন্ধন করিলা ॥ ১৮৪ ॥

tāṅra upāsanā śuni' prabhu tuṣṭa hailā
āste-vyaste sei vipra randhana karilā

SYNONYMS

tāṅra—his; *upāsanā*—method of worship; *śuni'*—hearing; *prabhu*—Lord Śrī Caitanya Mahāprabhu; *tuṣṭa hailā*—was very much pleased; *āste-vyaste*—with great haste; *sei*—that; *vipra*—*brāhmaṇa*; *randhana karilā*—began to cook.

TRANSLATION

Śrī Caitanya Mahāprabhu was very satisfied to hear about the brāhmaṇa's method of worship. Finally the brāhmaṇa hastily made arrangements for cooking.

TEXT 185

প্রভু ভিক্ষা কৈল দিনের তৃতীয়প্রহরে।
নির্বিঘ্ন সেই বিপ্র উপবাস করে ॥ ১৮৫ ॥

prabhu bhikṣā kaila dinera tṛtīya-prahare
nirviṇṇa sei vipra upavāsa kare

SYNONYMS

prabhu—Lord Caitanya Mahāprabhu; *bhikṣā kaila*—took His luncheon; *dinera*—of the day; *tṛtīya-prahare*—at about three o'clock; *nirviṇṇa*—sorrowful; *sei*—that; *vipra*—*brāhmaṇa*; *upavāsa kare*—fasted.

TRANSLATION

Śrī Caitanya Mahāprabhu took His lunch at about three o'clock, but the brāhmaṇa, being very sorrowful, fasted.

TEXT 186

প্রভু কহে,—বিপ্র কাঁহে কর উপবাস।
কেনে এত দুঃখ, কেনে করহ হুতাশ ॥ ১৮৬ ॥

prabhu kahe,——vipra kāṅhe kara upavāsa
kene eta duḥkha, kene karaha hutāśa

SYNONYMS

prabhu kahe—Lord Śrī Caitanya Mahāprabhu said; *vipra*—My dear *brāhmaṇa*; *kāṅhe*—why; *kara upavāsa*—you are fasting; *kene*—why; *eta*—so much; *duḥkha*—unhappiness; *kene*—why; *karaha hutāśa*—you express so much worry.

TRANSLATION

While the brāhmaṇa was fasting, Śrī Caitanya Mahāprabhu asked him, "Why are you fasting? Why are you so unhappy? Why are you so worried?"

TEXT 187

বিপ্র কহে,—জীবনে মোর নাহি প্রয়োজন।
অগ্নি-জলে প্রবেশিয়া ছাড়িব জীবন ॥ ১৮৭ ॥

vipra kahe,——jīvane mora nāhi prayojana
agni-jale praveśiyā chāḍiba jīvana

SYNONYMS

vipra kahe—the *brāhmaṇa* said; *jīvane mora*—for my life; *nāhi*—there is not; *prayojana*—necessity; *agni*—in fire; *jale*—in water; *praveśiyā*—entering; *chāḍiba*—I shall give up; *jīvana*—life.

TRANSLATION

The brāhmaṇa replied, "I have no reason to live. I shall give up my life by entering either fire or water.

TEXT 188

জগন্মাতা মহালক্ষ্মী সীতা-ঠাকুরাণী ।
রাক্ষসে স্পর্শিল তাঁরে,—ইহা কানে শুনি ॥ ১৮৮ ॥

jagan-mātā mahā-lakṣmī sītā-ṭhākurāṇī
rākṣase sparśila tāṅre,——ihā kāne śuni

SYNONYMS

jagat-mātā—the mother of the universe; *mahā-lakṣmī*—the supreme goddess of fortune; *sītā-ṭhākurāṇī*—mother Sītā; *rākṣase*—the demon Rāvaṇa; *sparśila*—touched; *tāṅre*—her; *ihā*—this; *kāne śuni*—I have heard.

TRANSLATION

"My dear sir, mother Sītā is the mother of the universe and the supreme goddess of fortune. She has been touched by the demon Rāvaṇa, and I am troubled upon hearing this news.

TEXT 189

এ শরীর ধরিবারে কভু না যুয়ায় ।
এই দুঃখে জ্বলে দেহ, প্রাণ নাহি যায় ॥ ১৮৯ ॥

e śarīra dharibāre kabhu nā yuyāya
ei duḥkhe jvale deha, prāṇa nāhi yāya

SYNONYMS

e śarīra—this body; *dharibāre*—to keep; *kabhu*—ever; *nā*—not; *yuyāya*—deserve; *ei duḥkhe*—in this unhappiness; *jvale deha*—my body is burning; *prāṇa*—my life; *nāhi yāya*—does not go away.

TRANSLATION

"Sir, due to my unhappiness I cannot continue living. Although my body is burning, my life is not leaving."

TEXT 190

প্রভু কহে,—এ ভাবনা না করিহ আর ।
পণ্ডিত হঞা কেনে না করহ বিচার ॥ ১৯০ ॥

prabhu kahe,——e bhāvanā nā kariha āra
paṇḍita hañā kene nā karaha vicāra

SYNONYMS

prabhu kahe—the Lord said; *e bhāvanā*—this kind of thinking; *nā*—do not; *kariha*—do; *āra*—anymore; *paṇḍita hañā*—being a learned *paṇḍita; kena*—why; *nā karaha*—you do not make; *vicāra*—consideration.

TRANSLATION

Śrī Caitanya Mahāprabhu replied, "Please do not think this way any longer. You are a learned paṇḍita. Why don't you consider the case?"

TEXT 191

ঈশ্বর-প্রেয়সী সীতা—চিদানন্দমূর্তি ।
প্রাকৃত-ইন্দ্রিয়ের তাঁরে দেখিতে নাহি শক্তি ॥১৯১॥

īśvara-preyasī sītā——cid-ānanda-mūrti
prākṛta-indriyera tāṅre dekhite nāhi śakti

SYNONYMS

īśvara-preyasī—the dearmost wife of the Lord; *sītā*—mother Sītā; *cit-ānanda-mūrti*—spiritual blissful form; *prākṛta*—material; *indriyera*—of the senses; *tāṅre*—her; *dekhite*—to see; *nāhi*—there is not; *śakti*—power.

TRANSLATION

Śrī Caitanya Mahāprabhu continued, "Sītādevī, the dearmost wife of the Supreme Lord Rāmacandra, certainly has a spiritual form full of bliss. No one can see her with material eyes, for no one material has such power.

TEXT 192

স্পর্শিবার কার্য আছুক, না পায় দর্শন ।
সীতার আকৃতি-মায়া হরিল রাবণ ॥ ১৯২ ॥

sparśibāra kārya āchuka, nā pāya darśana
sītāra ākṛti-māyā harila rāvaṇa

SYNONYMS

sparśibāra—to touch; *kārya*—business; *āchuka*—let it be; *nā*—does not; *pāya*—get; *darśana*—sight; *sītāra*—of mother Sītā; *ākṛti-māyā*—the form made of *māyā; harila*—took away; *rāvaṇa*—the demon Rāvaṇa.

TRANSLATION

"To say nothing of touching mother Sītā, a person with material senses cannot even see her. When Rāvaṇa kidnapped her, he kidnapped only her material illusory form.

TEXT 193

রাবণ আসিতেই সীতা অন্তর্ধান কৈল ।
রাবণের আগে মায়া-সীতা পাঠাইল ॥ ১৯৩ ॥

rāvaṇa āsitei sītā antardhāna kaila
rāvaṇera āge māyā-sītā pāṭhāila

SYNONYMS

rāvaṇa—the demon Rāvaṇa; *āsitei*—as soon as he arrived; *sītā*—mother Sītā; *antardhāna kaila*—disappeared; *rāvaṇera āge*—before the demon Rāvaṇa; *māyā-sītā*—illusory material form of Sītā; *pāṭhāila*—sent.

TRANSLATION

"As soon as Rāvaṇa arrived before Sītā, she disappeared. It was just to cheat Rāvaṇa that she sent an illusory material form.

TEXT 194

অপ্রাকৃত বস্তু নহে প্রাকৃত-গোচর ।
বেদ-পুরাণেতে এই কহে নিরন্তর ॥ ১৯৪ ॥

aprākṛta vastu nahe prākṛta-gocara
veda-purāṇete ei kahe nirantara

SYNONYMS

aprākṛta—spiritual; *vastu*—substance; *nahe*—not; *prākṛta*—of matter; *gocara*—within the jurisdiction; *veda-purāṇete*—the *Vedas* and the *Purāṇas*; *ei*—this; *kahe*—say; *nirantara*—always.

TRANSLATION

"Spiritual substance is never within the jurisdiction of the material conception. This is always the verdict of the Vedas and Purāṇas."

PURPORT

As stated in *Kaṭha Upaniṣad* (2.3.9,12):

na saṁdṛśe tiṣṭhati rūpam asya
na cakṣuṣā paśyati kaścanainam
hṛdā manīṣā manasābhikḷpto
ya etad vidur amṛtās te bhavanti
naiva vācā na manasā
prāptuṁ śakyo na cakṣuṣā

"Spirit is not within the jurisdiction of material eyes, words or mind."

Similarly in *Śrīmad-Bhāgavatam* (10.84.13):

yasyātma-buddhiḥ kuṇape tri-dhātuke
sva-dhīḥ kalatrādiṣu bhauma-ijya-dhīḥ
yat-tīrtha-buddhiḥ salile na karhicij
janeṣv abhijñeṣu sa eva go-kharaḥ

Spiritual substance cannot be seen by the unintelligent because they do not have the eyes or the mentality to see spirit soul. Consequently they think that there is no such thing as spirit. However, followers of the Vedic injunctions take their information from Vedic statements, as found in *Śrīmad-Bhāgavatam* and *Kaṭha Upaniṣad.*

TEXT 195

বিশ্বাস করহ তুমি আমার বচনে ।
পুনরপি কু-ভাবনা না করিহ মনে ॥ ১৯৫ ॥

viśvāsa karaha tumi āmāra vacane
punarapi ku-bhāvanā nā kariha mane

SYNONYMS

viśvāsa karaha—believe; *tumi*—you; *āmāra*—My; *vacane*—in the words; *punarapi*—again; *ku-bhāvanā*—misconception; *nā kariha*—do not do; *mane*—in the mind.

TRANSLATION

Śrī Caitanya Mahāprabhu then assured the brāhmaṇa, "Have faith in My words and do not burden your mind any longer with this misconception."

PURPORT

This is the process of spiritual understanding. *Acintyā khalu ye bhāvā na tāṁs tarkeṇa yojayet.* We should not try to understand things beyond our material conception by argument and counter argument. *Mahājano yena gataḥ sa panthāḥ*: we have to follow in the footsteps of great authorities coming down in the *paramparā* system. If we approach a bona fide *ācārya* and keep faith in his words, spiritual realization will be easy.

TEXT 196

প্রভুর বচনে বিপ্রের হইল বিশ্বাস ।
ভোজন করিল, হৈল জীবনের আশ ॥ ১৯৬ ॥

prabhura vacane viprera ha-ila viśvāsa
bhojana karila, haila jīvanera āśa

SYNONYMS

prabhura vacane—in the words of Lord Śrī Caitanya Mahāprabhu; *viprera*—of the *brāhmaṇa*; *ha-ila*—was; *viśvāsa*—faith; *bhojana karila*—he took his lunch; *haila*—there was; *jīvanera*—for living; *āśa*—hope.

TRANSLATION

Although the brāhmaṇa was fasting, he had faith in the words of Śrī Caitanya Mahāprabhu and accepted food. In this way his life was saved.

TEXT 197

তাঁরে আশ্বাসিয়া প্রভু করিলা গমন ।
কৃতমালায় স্নান করি আইলা দুর্বশন ॥ ১৯৭ ॥

tāṅre āśvāsiyā prabhu karilā gamana
kṛtamālāya snāna kari āilā durvaśana

SYNONYMS

tāṅre āśvāsiyā—assuring him; *prabhu*—Śrī Caitanya Mahāprabhu; *karilā gamana*—departed; *kṛta-mālāya*—in the river known as Kṛtamālā; *snāna kari*—bathing; *āilā*—came; *durvaśana*—to Durvaśana.

TRANSLATION

After thus assuring the brāhmaṇa, Śrī Caitanya Mahāprabhu proceeded further into southern India and finally arrived at Durvaśana, where He bathed in the River Kṛtamālā.

PURPORT

Presently this Kṛtamālā River is known as the River Bhāgāi. This river has three tributaries, named Surulī, Varāhanadī and Baṭṭilla-guṇḍu. The River Kṛtamālā is also mentioned in *Śrīmad-Bhāgavatam* (11.5.39) by the sage Karabhājana.

TEXT 198

দুর্বশনে রঘুনাথে কৈল দরশন ।
মহেন্দ্র-শৈলে পরশুরামের কৈল বন্দন ॥ ১৯৮ ॥

durvaśane raghunāthe kaila daraśana
mahendra-śaile paraśurāmera kaila vandana

SYNONYMS

durvaśane—at Durvaśana; *raghu-nāthe*—Lord Rāmacandra; *kaila daraśana*—Śrī Caitanya Mahāprabhu visited; *mahendra-śaile*—on Mahendra-śaila; *paraśu-rāmera*—to Lord Paraśurāma; *kaila vandana*—offered prayers.

TRANSLATION

At Durvaśana Śrī Caitanya Mahāprabhu visited the temple of Lord Rāmacandra, and on the hill known as Mahendra-śaila, He saw Lord Paraśurāma.

PURPORT

In Durvaśana, or Darbhaśayana, there is a temple of Lord Rāmacandra, located seven miles east of Rāmanāda. The temple overlooks the ocean. The hill known as Mahendra-śaila is near Tinebheli, and at the end of this hill is a city known as Tricinaguḍi. West of Mahendra-śaila is the territory of Tribāṅkura. There is mention of Mahendra-śaila in the *Rāmāyaṇa.*

TEXT 199

সেতুবন্ধে আসি' কৈল ধনুস্তীর্থে স্নান ।
রামেশ্বর দেখি' তাহাঁ করিল বিশ্রাম ॥ ১৯৯ ॥

setubandhe āsi' kaila dhanustīrthe snāna
rāmeśvara dekhi' tāhāṅ karila viśrāma

SYNONYMS

setu-bandhe āsi'—coming to Setubandha; *kaila*—did; *dhanuḥ-tīrthe snāna*—bathing at the holy place known as Dhanustīrtha; *rāmeśvara dekhi'*—visiting the holy place Rāmeśvara; *tāhāṅ*—there; *karila viśrāma*—took rest.

TRANSLATION

Śrī Caitanya Mahāprabhu then went to Setubandha [Rāmeśvara], where He took His bath at a place called Dhanustīrtha. From there He visited the Rāmeśvara temple and then took rest.

PURPORT

The path through the ocean to the islands known as Maṇḍapam and Pambam consists partly of sand and partly of water. The island of Pambam is about eleven miles long and six miles wide. From the Pambam Harbor four miles to the north is a temple known as Rāmeśvara. It is said, *devī-pattanam ārabhya gaccheyuḥ setu-bandhanam*: "After visiting the temple of the goddess Durgā, one should go to the temple of Rāmeśvara." In this area there are twenty-four different holy places, one of which is Dhanustīrtha, located about twelve miles southeast of Rāmeśvara. It is near the last station of the South Indian Railway, a station called Rāmanāda. It is said that here, due to the request of Vibhīṣaṇa, the younger brother of Rāvaṇa, Lord Rāmacandra destroyed a small bridge with His bow upon returning to His capital. If one visits Dhanustīrtha, he is liberated from the cycle of birth and death. It is also said that if one bathes at Dhanustīrtha, he gets all the fruitive results of performing the *yajña* known as *agniṣṭoma*.

Setubandha is on the island of Pambam. There is a temple of Lord Śiva there called Rāmeśvara. This indicates that Lord Śiva is a great personality whose worshipable Deity is Lord Rāma. Thus the Lord Śiva found in the temple of Rāmeśvara is a great devotee of Lord Rāmacandra.

TEXT 200

বিপ্র-সভায় শুনে তাঁহা কূর্ম-পুরাণ ।
তার মধ্যে আইলা পতিব্রতা-উপাখ্যান ॥ ২০০ ॥

vipra-sabhāya śune tāṅhā kūrma-purāṇa
tāra madhye āilā pativratā-upākhyāna

SYNONYMS

vipra-sabhāya—among the assembly of *brāhmaṇas*; *śune*—hears; *tāṅhā*—there; *kūrma-purāṇa*—the *Kūrma Purāṇa*; *tāra madhye*—within that book; *āilā*—there was; *pati-vratā*—of the chaste woman; *upākhyāna*—narration.

TRANSLATION

There, among the brāhmaṇas, Śrī Caitanya Mahāprabhu heard the Kūrma Purāṇa, wherein was mentioned the chaste woman's narration.

PURPORT

Śrīla Bhaktisiddhānta Sarasvatī Ṭhākura remarks that in the *Kūrma Purāṇa* there are only two *khaṇḍas,* namely the *Pūrva-khaṇḍa* and *Uttara-khaṇḍa.* Sometimes it is said that the *Kūrma Purāṇa* contains six thousand verses, but originally the *Kūrma Purāṇa* contains seventeen thousand verses. According to *Śrīmad-Bhāgavatam,* there are seventeen thousand verses in the *Kūrma Purāṇa,* which is one of the eighteen *Mahā-purāṇas.* The *Kūrma Purāṇa* is considered the fifteenth of these *Mahā-purāṇas.*

TEXT 201

পতিব্রতা-শিরোমণি জনক-নন্দিনী ।
জগতের মাতা সীতা—রামের গৃহিণী ॥ ২০১ ॥

pativratā-śiromaṇi janaka-nandinī
jagatera mātā sītā——rāmera gṛhiṇī

SYNONYMS

pati-vratā—chaste woman; *śiromaṇi*—the topmost; *janaka-nandinī*—is the daughter of King Janaka; *jagatera*—of all the three worlds; *mātā*—the mother; *sītā*—Sītā; *rāmera*—of Lord Rāmacandra; *gṛhiṇī*—wife.

TRANSLATION

Śrīmatī Sītādevī is the mother of the three worlds and the wife of Lord Rāmacandra. Among chaste women, she is supreme, and she is the daughter of King Janaka.

TEXT 202

রাবণ দেখিয়া সীতা লৈল অগ্নির শরণ ।
রাবণ হৈতে অগ্নি কৈল সীতাকে আবরণ ॥ ২০২ ॥

rāvaṇa dekhiyā sītā laila agnira śaraṇa
rāvaṇa haite agni kaila sītāke āvaraṇa

SYNONYMS

rāvaṇa dekhiyā—after seeing Rāvaṇa; *sītā*—mother Sītā; *laila*—took; *agnira*—of fire; *śaraṇa*—shelter; *rāvaṇa*—Rāvaṇa; *haite*—from; *agni*—fire; *kaila*—did; *sītāke*—unto mother Sītā; *āvaraṇa*—covering.

TRANSLATION

When Rāvaṇa came to kidnap mother Sītā and she saw him, she took shelter of the fire-god, Agni. The fire-god covered the body of mother Sītā, and in this way she was protected from the hands of Rāvaṇa.

TEXT 203

‘মায়াসীতা’ রাবণ নিল, শুনিলা আখ্যানে ।
শুনি’ মহাপ্রভু হৈল আনন্দিত মনে ॥ ২০৩ ॥

'māyā-sītā' rāvaṇa nila, śunilā ākhyāne
śuni' mahāprabhu haila ānandita mane

SYNONYMS

māyā-sītā—false, illusory Sītā; *rāvaṇa*—the demon Rāvaṇa; *nila*—took; *śunilā*—heard; *ākhyāne*—in the narration of the *Kūrma Purāṇa*; *śuni'*—hearing this; *mahāprabhu*—Lord Śrī Caitanya Mahāprabhu; *haila*—became; *ānandita*—very happy; *mane*—within the mind.

TRANSLATION

Upon hearing from the Kūrma Purāṇa how Rāvaṇa had kidnapped the false form of mother Sītā, Śrī Caitanya Mahāprabhu became very satisfied.

TEXT 204

সীতা লঞা রাখিলেন পার্বতীর স্থানে ।
‘মায়াসীতা’ দিয়া অগ্নি বঞ্চিলা রাবণে ॥ ২০৪ ॥

sītā lañā rākhilena pārvatīra sthāne
'māyā-sītā' diyā agni vañcilā rāvaṇe

SYNONYMS

sītā lañā—taking away mother Sītā; *rākhilena*—kept; *pārvatīra sthāne*—with mother Pārvatī, or goddess Durgā; *māyā-sītā*—the false, illusory form of Sītā; *diyā*—delivering; *agni*—fire-god; *vañcilā*—cheated; *rāvaṇe*—the demon Rāvaṇa.

TRANSLATION

The fire-god, Agni, took away the real Sītā and brought her to the place of Pārvatī, goddess Durgā. An illusory form of mother Sītā was then delivered to Rāvaṇa, and in this way Rāvaṇa was cheated.

TEXT 205

রঘুনাথ আসি’ যবে রাবণে মারিল ।
অগ্নি-পরীক্ষা দিতে যবে সীতারে আনিল ॥ ২০৫ ॥

raghunātha āsi' yabe rāvaṇe mārila
agni-parīkṣā dite yabe sītāre ānila

SYNONYMS

raghu-nātha—Lord Rāmacandra; *āsi'*—coming; *yabe*—when; *rāvaṇe*—Rāvaṇa; *mārila*—killed; *agni-parīkṣā*—test by fire; *dite*—to give; *yabe*—when; *sītāre*—Sītā; *ānila*—brought.

TRANSLATION

After Rāvaṇa was killed by Lord Rāmacandra, Sītādevī was brought before the fire.

TEXT 206

তবে মায়াসীতা অগ্নি করি অন্তর্ধান।
সত্য-সীতা আনি' দিল রাম-বিদ্যমান ॥ ২০৬ ॥

tabe māyā-sītā agni kari antardhāna
satya-sītā āni' dila rāma-vidyamāna

SYNONYMS

tabe—at that time; *māyā-sītā*—the illusory form of Sītā; *agni*—the fire-god; *kari*—doing; *antardhāna*—disappearing; *satya-sītā*—real Sītā; *āni'*—bringing; *dila*—delivered; *rāma*—of Rāmacandra; *vidyamāna*—in the presence.

TRANSLATION

When the illusory Sītā was brought before the fire by Lord Rāmacandra, the fire-god made the illusory form disappear and delivered the real Sītā to Lord Rāmacandra.

TEXT 207

শুনিঞা প্রভুর আনন্দিত হৈল মন।
রামদাস-বিপ্রের কথা হইল স্মরণ ॥ ২০৭ ॥

śuniñā prabhura ānandita haila mana
rāmadāsa-viprera kathā ha-ila smaraṇa

SYNONYMS

śuniñā—hearing; *prabhura*—of Śrī Caitanya Mahāprabhu; *ānandita*—very pleased; *haila*—became; *mana*—the mind; *rāma-dāsa-viprera*—of the *brāhmaṇa* known as Rāmadāsa; *kathā*—words; *ha-ila smaraṇa*—He remembered.

TRANSLATION

When Śrī Caitanya Mahāprabhu heard this story, He was very pleased, and He remembered the words of Rāmadāsa Vipra.

TEXT 208

এ-সব সিদ্ধান্ত শুনি' প্রভুর আনন্দ হৈল ।
ব্রাহ্মণের স্থানে মাগি' সেই পত্র নিল ॥ ২০৮ ॥

e-saba siddhānta śuni' prabhura ānanda haila
brāhmaṇera sthāne māgi' sei patra nila

SYNONYMS

e-saba siddhānta—all these conclusive statements; *śuni'*—hearing; *prabhura*—of Lord Śrī Caitanya Mahāprabhu; *ānanda*—happiness; *haila*—there was; *brāhmaṇera sthāne*—from the *brāhmaṇas*; *māgi'*—asking; *sei*—those; *patra*—leaves; *nila*—took.

TRANSLATION

Indeed, when Śrī Caitanya Mahāprabhu heard these conclusive statements from Kūrma Purāṇa, He felt great happiness. After asking the brāhmaṇa's permission, He took possession of those manuscript scrolls. In this way Śrī Caitanya Mahāprabhu received the old manuscript of the Kūrma Purāṇa.

TEXT 209

নূতন পত্র লেখাঞা পুস্তকে দেওয়াইল ।
প্রতীতি লাগি' পুরাতন পত্র মাগি' নিল ॥ ২০৯ ॥

nūtana patra lekhāñā pustake deoyāila
pratīti lāgi' purātana patra māgi' nila

SYNONYMS

nūtana—new; *patra*—leaves; *lekhāñā*—getting written; *pustake*—the book; *deoyāila*—He gave; *pratīti lāgi'*—for direct evidence; *purātana*—the old; *patra*—leaves; *māgi'*—requesting; *nila*—He took.

TRANSLATION

Since the Kūrma Purāṇa was very old, the manuscript was also very old. Śrī Caitanya Mahāprabhu took possession of the original leaves in order to have direct evidence. The text was copied on to a new scroll in order that the Purāṇa be replaced.

TEXT 210

পত্র লঞা পুনঃ দক্ষিণ-মথুরা আইলা।
রামদাস বিপ্রে সেই পত্র আনি দিলা ॥ ২১০ ॥

patra lañā punaḥ dakṣiṇa-mathurā āilā
rāmadāsa vipre sei patra āni dilā

SYNONYMS

patra lañā—taking those leaves; *punaḥ*—again; *dakṣiṇa-mathurā*—to southern Mathurā; *āilā*—came; *rāma-dāsa vipre*—unto the *brāhmaṇa* known as Rāmadāsa; *sei patra*—those leaves; *āni*—bringing back; *dilā*—delivered.

TRANSLATION

Śrī Caitanya Mahāprabhu returned to southern Mathurā [Mādurā] and delivered the original manuscript of the Kūrma Purāṇa to Rāmadāsa Vipra.

TEXTS 211-212

সীতয়ারাধিতো বহ্নিশ্ছায়া-সীতামজীজনৎ।
তাং জহার দশগ্রীবঃ সীতা বহ্নিপুরং গতা ॥ ২১১ ॥
পরীক্ষা-সময়ে বহ্নিং ছায়া-সীতা বিবেশ সা।
বহ্নিঃ সীতাং সমানীয় তৎপুরস্তাদনীনয়ৎ ॥ ২১২ ॥

sītayārādhito vahniś
chāyā-sītām ajījanat
tāṁ jahāra daśa-grīvaḥ
sītā vahni-puraṁ gatā

parīkṣā-samaye vahniṁ
chāyā-sītā viveśa sā
vahniḥ sītāṁ samānīya
tat-purastād anīnayat

SYNONYMS

sītayā—by mother Sītā; *ārādhitaḥ*—being called for; *vahniḥ*—the fire-god; *chāyā-sītām*—the illusory form of mother Sītā; *ajījanat*—created; *tām*—her; *jahāra*—kidnapped; *daśa-grīvaḥ*—the ten-faced Rāvaṇa; *sītā*—mother Sītā; *vahni-puram*—to the abode of the fire-god; *gatā*—departed; *parīkṣā-samaye*—at the time of testing; *vahnim*—the fire; *chāyā-sītā*—the illusory form of Sītā; *viveśa*—entered; *sā*—she; *vahniḥ*—the fire-god; *sītām*—the original mother Sītā; *samānīya*—bringing back; *tat-purastāt*—in His presence; *anīnayat*—brought back.

TRANSLATION

"When he was petitioned by mother Sītā, the fire-god, Agni, brought forth an illusory form of Sītā, and Rāvaṇa, who had ten heads, kidnapped the false Sītā. The original Sītā then went to the abode of the fire-god. When Lord Rāmacandra tested the body of Sītā, it was the false illusory Sītā that entered the fire. At that time the fire-god brought the original Sītā from his abode and delivered her to Lord Rāmacandra."

PURPORT

These two verses are taken from the *Kūrma Purāṇa.*

TEXT 213

পত্র পাঞা বিপ্রের হৈল আনন্দিত মন ।
প্রভুর চরণে ধরি' করয়ে ক্রন্দন ॥ ২১৩ ॥

patra pāñā viprera haila ānandita mana
prabhura caraṇe dhari' karaye krandana

SYNONYMS

patra pāñā—getting the leaves; *viprera*—of the *brāhmaṇa*; *haila*—there was; *ānandita*—pleased; *mana*—mind; *prabhura caraṇe*—the lotus feet of Lord Śrī Caitanya Mahāprabhu; *dhari'*—taking; *karaye*—does; *krandana*—crying.

TRANSLATION

Rāmadasa Vipra was very pleased to receive the original scrolls of the Kūrma Purāṇa, and he immediately fell down before the lotus feet of Śrī Caitanya Mahāprabhu and began to cry.

TEXT 214

বিপ্র কহে,—তুমি সাক্ষাৎ শ্রীরঘুনন্দন ।
সন্ন্যাসীর বেষে মোরে দিলা দরশন ॥ ২১৪ ॥

vipra kahe,——tumi sākṣāt śrī-raghunandana
sannyāsīra veṣe more dilā daraśana

SYNONYMS

vipra kahe—the *brāhmaṇa* said; *tumi*—You; *sākṣāt*—directly; *śrī-raghunandana*—Lord Śrī Rāmacandra; *sannyāsīra veṣe*—in the dress of a mendicant; *more*—unto me; *dilā*—You gave; *daraśana*—audience.

TRANSLATION

After receiving the manuscript, the brāhmaṇa, being very pleased, said, "Sir, You are Lord Rāmacandra Himself and have come in the dress of a sannyāsī to give me audience.

TEXT 215

মহা-দুঃখ হইতে মোরে করিলা নিস্তার ।
আজি মোর ঘরে ভিক্ষা কর অঙ্গীকার ॥ ২১৫ ॥

mahā-duḥkha ha-ite more karilā nistāra
āji mora ghare bhikṣā kara aṅgīkāra

SYNONYMS

mahā-duḥkha—great unhappiness; *ha-ite*—from; *more*—me; *karilā nistāra*—You delivered; *āji*—today; *mora*—my; *ghare*—at home; *bhikṣā*—lunch; *kara*—do; *aṅgīkāra*—accept.

TRANSLATION

"My dear sir, You have delivered me from a very unhappy condition. I request that You take Your lunch at my place. Please accept this invitation.

TEXT 216

মনোদুঃখে ভাল ভিক্ষা না দিল সেই দিনে ।
মোর ভাগ্যে পুনরপি পাইলুঁ দরশনে ॥ ২১৬ ॥

mano-duḥkhe bhāla bhikṣā nā dila sei dine
mora bhāgye punarapi pāiluṅ daraśane

SYNONYMS

mano-duḥkhe—out of great mental distress; *bhāla bhikṣā*—good lunch; *nā dila*—could not give You; *sei dine*—that day; *mora bhāgye*—because of my fortune; *punarapi*—again; *pāiluṅ*—I have gotten; *daraśane*—visit.

TRANSLATION

"Due to my mental distress I could not give You a very nice lunch the other day. Now, by good fortune, You have come again to my home."

TEXT 217

এত বলি' সেই বিপ্র সুখে পাক কৈল ।
উত্তম প্রকারে প্রভুকে ভিক্ষা করাইল ॥ ২১৭ ॥

eta bali' sei vipra sukhe pāka kaila
uttama prakāre prabhuke bhikṣā karāila

SYNONYMS

eta bali'—saying this; *sei vipra*—that *brāhmaṇa;* *sukhe*—in great happiness; *pāka kaila*—cooked; *uttama prakāre*—very nicely; *prabhuke*—unto Lord Śrī Caitanya Mahāprabhu; *bhikṣā*—lunch; *karāila*—gave.

TRANSLATION

Saying this, the brāhmaṇa very happily cooked food, and a first-class dinner was offered to Śrī Caitanya Mahāprabhu.

TEXT 218

সেই রাত্রি তাহাঁ রহি' তাঁরে কৃপা করি' ।
পাণ্ড্যদেশে তাম্রপর্ণী গেলা গৌরহরি ॥ ২১৮ ॥

sei rātri tāhāṅ rahi' tāṅre kṛpā kari'
pāṇḍya-deśe tāmraparṇī gelā gaurahari

SYNONYMS

sei rātri—that night; *tāhāṅ*—there; *rahi'*—staying; *tāṅre*—unto the *brāhmaṇa;* *kṛpā kari'*—showing mercy; *pāṇḍya-deśe*—in the country known as Pāṇḍya-deśa; *tāmra-parṇī*—to the place named Tāmraparṇī; *gelā*—went; *gaura-hari*—Lord Śrī Caitanya Mahāprabhu.

TRANSLATION

Śrī Caitanya Mahāprabhu passed that night in the house of the brāhmaṇa. Then, after showing him mercy, the Lord started toward Tāmraparṇī in Pāṇḍya-deśa.

PURPORT

Pāṇḍya-deśa is situated in the southern part of India known as Kerala. In all these areas there were many kings with the title Pāṇḍya who ruled over places known as Mādurā and Rāmeśvara. In the *Rāmāyaṇa* the name of Tāmraparṇī is mentioned. Tāmraparṇī is also known as Puruṇai and is situated on the bank of the Tinebheli River. This river flows into the Bay of Bengal. Tāmraparṇī is also mentioned in *Śrīmad-Bhāgavatam* (11.5.39).

TEXT 219

তাম্রপর্ণী স্নান করি' তাম্রপর্ণী-তীরে ।
নয় ত্রিপতি দেখি' বুলে কুতুহলে ॥ ২১৯ ॥

tāmraparṇī snāna kari' tāmraparṇī-tīre
naya tripati dekhi' bule kutūhale

SYNONYMS

tāmra-parṇī—in the Tāmraparṇī River; *snāna kari'*—taking a bath; *tāmra-parṇī-tīre*—on the bank of the Tāmraparṇī River; *naya tripati*—the Deity named Naya-tripati; *dekhi'*—after seeing; *bule*—wandered on; *kutūhale*—in great curiosity.

TRANSLATION

There was also a temple of Lord Viṣṇu at Naya-tripati on the bank of the River Tāmraparṇī, and after bathing in the river, Lord Caitanya Mahāprabhu saw the Deity with great curiosity and wandered on.

PURPORT

This Naya-tripati is also called Ālovara Tirunagarī. It is a town about seventeen miles southeast of Tinebheli. There are nine temples there of Śrīpati, or Viṣṇu. All the Deities of the temples assemble together during a yearly festival in the town.

TEXT 220

চিয়ড়তলা তীর্থে দেখি' শ্রীরাম-লক্ষ্মণ ।
তিলকাঞ্চী আসি' কৈল শিব দরশন ॥ ২২০ ॥

ciyaḍatalā tīrthe dekhi' śrī-rāma-lakṣmaṇa
tilakāñcī āsi' kaila śiva daraśana

SYNONYMS

ciyaḍatalā—named Ciyaḍatalā; *tīrthe*—at the holy place; *dekhi'*—seeing; *śrī-rāma-lakṣmaṇa*—the Deity of Lord Rāma and Lakṣmaṇa; *tilakāñcī*—to Tilakāñcī; *āsi'*—coming; *kaila*—did; *śiva daraśana*—visiting the temple of Lord Śiva.

TRANSLATION

After this, Śrī Caitanya Mahāprabhu went to a holy place known as Ciyaḍatalā, where He saw the Deities of the two brothers, Lord Rāmacandra and Lakṣmaṇa. He then proceeded to Tilakāñcī, where He saw the temple of Lord Śiva.

PURPORT

Ciyaḍatalā is sometimes known as Cheratalā. It is near the city of Kaila, and there is a temple there dedicated to Lord Śrī Rāmacandra and His brother Lakṣmaṇa. Tilankāñcī is about thirty miles northeast of the city of Tinebheli.

TEXT 221

গজেন্দ্রমোক্ষণ-তীর্থে দেখি বিষ্ণুমূর্তি ।
পানাগড়ি-তীর্থে আসি' দেখিল সীতাপতি ॥ ২২১ ॥

gajendra-mokṣaṇa-tīrthe dekhi viṣṇu-mūrti
pānāgaḍi-tīrthe āsi' dekhila sītāpati

SYNONYMS

gajendra-mokṣaṇa-tīrthe—at the holy place named Gajendra-mokṣaṇa; *dekhi*—seeing; *viṣṇu-mūrti*—the Deity of Lord Viṣṇu; *pānāgaḍi-tīrthe*—to the holy place Pānāgaḍi; *āsi'*—coming; *dekhila*—saw; *sītā-pati*—Lord Śrī Rāmacandra and Sītādevī.

TRANSLATION

Lord Śrī Caitanya Mahāprabhu then visited the holy place named Gajendra-mokṣaṇa, where He went to a temple of Lord Viṣṇu. He then came to Pānāgaḍi, a holy place where He saw the Deities of Lord Rāmacandra and Sītā.

PURPORT

The Gajendra-mokṣaṇa temple is sometimes mistaken for a temple of Lord Śiva. It is about two miles south of the city of Kaivera. Actually the Deity is not of Lord Śiva but of Viṣṇu. Pānāgaḍi is about thirty miles south of the Tinebheli. Formerly the temple there contained the Deity of Śrī Rāmacandra, but later the devotees of

Lord Śiva replaced Lord Rāmacandra with a deity of Lord Śiva named Rāmeśvara or Rāmaliṅga Śiva.

TEXT 222

চাম্তাপুরে আসি' দেখি' শ্রীরাম-লক্ষ্মণ ।
শ্রীবৈকুণ্ঠে আসি' কৈল বিষ্ণু দরশন ॥ ২২২ ॥

cāmtāpure āsi' dekhi' śrī-rāma-lakṣmaṇa
śrī-vaikuṇṭhe āsi' kaila viṣṇu daraśana

SYNONYMS

cāmtāpure—to Cāmtāpura; *āsi'*—coming; *dekhi'*—seeing; *śrī-rāma-lakṣmaṇa*—Lord Rāmacandra and Lakṣmaṇa; *śrī-vaikuṇṭhe āsi'*—coming to Śrī Vaikuṇṭha; *kaila*—did; *viṣṇu daraśana*—seeing the temple of Lord Viṣṇu.

TRANSLATION

Later the Lord went to Cāmtāpura, where He saw the Deities of Lord Rāmacandra and Lakṣmaṇa. He then went to Śrī Vaikuṇṭha and saw the temple of Lord Viṣṇu there.

PURPORT

This Cāmtāpura is sometimes called Ceṅgānura and is located in the state of Tribāṅkura. A temple of Lord Rāmacandra and Lakṣmaṇa is located there. Śrī Vaikuṇṭha—about four miles north of Āloyāra Tirunagarī and sixteen miles southeast of Tinebheli—is situated on the bank of the Tāmraparṇī River.

TEXT 223

মলয়-পর্বতে কৈল অগস্ত্য-বন্দন ।
কন্যাকুমারী তাঁহাঁ কৈল দরশন ॥ ২২৩ ॥

malaya-parvate kaila agastya-vandana
kanyā-kumārī tāṅhāṅ kaila daraśana

SYNONYMS

malaya-parvate—in the Malaya Hills; *kaila*—did; *agastya-vandana*—obeisances to Agastya Muni; *kanyā-kumārī*—Kanyākumārī; *tāṅhāṅ*—there; *kaila daraśana*—visited.

TRANSLATION

Śrī Caitanya Mahāprabhu then went to Malaya-parvata and offered prayers to Agastya Muni. He then visited a place known as Kanyākumārī [presently Cape Comorin].

PURPORT

The range of mountains in South India beginning at Kerala and extending up to Cape Comorin is called Malaya-parvata. Concerning Agastya there are four opinions: (1) There is a temple of Agastya Muni in the village of Agastyam-pallī in the district of Tāñjor. (2) There is a temple of Lord Skanda on a hill known as Śivagiri, and it is supposed to have been established by Agastya Muni. (3) Some say that near Cape Comorin there is a hill known as Paṭhiyā, which was supposed to have served as Agastya Muni's residence. (4) There is another place known as Agastya-malaya, which is a range of hills on both sides of the Tāmraparṇī River. Cape Comorin itself is known as Kanyākumārī.

TEXT 224

আম্‌লিতলায় দেখি' শ্রীরাম গৌরহরি ।
মল্লার-দেশেতে আইলা যথা ভট্টথারি ॥ ২২৪ ॥

āmlitalāya dekhi' śrī-rāma gaurahari
mallāra-deśete āilā yathā bhaṭṭathāri

SYNONYMS

āmlitalāya—at Āmlitalā; *dekhi'*—seeing; *śrī-rāma*—the Deity of Rāmacandra; *gaura-hari*—Śrī Caitanya Mahāprabhu; *mallāra-deśete*—to Mallāra-deśa; *āilā*—came; *yathā*—where; *bhaṭṭathāri*—the Bhaṭṭathāri community.

TRANSLATION

After visiting Kanyākumārī, Śrī Caitanya Mahāprabhu came to Āmlitalā, where He saw the Deity of Śrī Rāmacandra. Thereafter He went to a place known as Mallāra-deśa, where a community of Bhaṭṭathāris lived.

PURPORT

North of Mallāra-deśa is South Kānāḍā. To the east is Kurga and Mahīśūra. To the south is Kocina, and to the west is the Arabian Sea. As far as the Bhaṭṭathāris are concerned, they are a nomadic community. They camp wherever they like and have no fixed place of residence. Outwardly they take up the dress of *sannyāsīs*, but their real business is stealing and cheating. They allure others to supply women for their camp, and they cheat many women and keep them within their community. In this way they increase their population. In Bengal also there is a similar community. Actually, all over the world there are nomadic communities whose business is simply to allure, cheat and steal innocent women.

TEXT 225

তমাল-কার্তিক দেখি' আইল বেতাপনি ।
রঘুনাথ দেখি' তাহাঁ বঞ্চিলা রজনী ॥ ২২৫ ॥

tamāla-kārtika dekhi' āila vetāpani
raghunātha dekhi' tāhāṅ vañcilā rajanī

SYNONYMS

tamāla-kārtika—the place named Tamāla-kārtika; *dekhi'*—seeing; *āila*—came; *vetāpani*—to Vetāpani; *raghu-nātha dekhi'*—seeing the temple of Lord Rāmacandra; *tāhāṅ*—there; *vañcilā rajanī*—passed the night.

TRANSLATION

After visiting Mallāra-deśa, Caitanya Mahāprabhu went to Tamāla-kārtika and then to Vetāpani. There He saw the temple of Raghunātha, Lord Rāmacandra, and passed the night.

PURPORT

Tamāla-kārtika is forty-four miles south of Tinebheli and two miles south of the Aramavallī mountain. It is located within the jurisdiction of Tobala. There is situated there a temple of Subrahmaṇya, or Lord Kārtika, the son of Lord Śiva. Vetāpani, or Vātāpāṇī, is north of Kaila in the Tribāṅkura state. It is known also as Bhūtapaṇḍi and is within the jurisdiction of the Tobala district. It is understood that formerly there was a Deity of Lord Rāmacandra there. Later the Deity was replaced with a deity of Lord Śiva known as Rāmeśvara or Bhūtanātha.

TEXT 226

গোসাঞির সঙ্গে রহে কৃষ্ণদাস ব্রাহ্মণ ।
ভট্টথারি-সহ তাহাঁ হৈল দরশন ॥ ২২৬ ॥

gosāñira saṅge rahe kṛṣṇadāsa brāhmaṇa
bhaṭṭathāri-saha tāhāṅ haila daraśana

SYNONYMS

gosāñira—the Lord; *saṅge*—with; *rahe*—there was; *kṛṣṇa-dāsa brāhmaṇa*—a *brāhmaṇa* servant named Kṛṣṇadāsa; *bhaṭṭathāri-saha*—with the Bhaṭṭathāris; *tāhāṅ*—there; *haila*—there was; *daraśana*—a meeting.

TRANSLATION

Śrī Caitanya Mahāprabhu was accompanied by His servant called Kṛṣṇadāsa. He was a brāhmaṇa, but he met with the Bhaṭṭathāris there.

TEXT 227

স্ত্রীধন দেখাঞা তাঁর লোভ জন্মাইল ।
আর্য সরল বিপ্রের বুদ্ধিনাশ কৈল ॥ ২২৭ ॥

strī-dhana dekhāñā tāṅra lobha janmāila
ārya sarala viprera buddhi-nāśa kaila

SYNONYMS

strī-dhana—women; *dekhāñā*—showing; *tāṅra*—his; *lobha*—attraction; *janmāila*—they created; *ārya*—gentleman; *sarala*—simple; *viprera*—of the *brāhmaṇa*; *buddhi-nāśa*—loss of intelligence; *kaila*—they made.

TRANSLATION

The Bhaṭṭathāris allured the brāhmaṇa Kṛṣṇadāsa, who was simple and gentle. By virtue of their bad association, they polluted his intelligence.

TEXT 228

প্রাতে উঠি' আইলা বিপ্র ভট্টথারি-ঘরে ।
তাহার উদ্দেশে প্রভু আইলা সত্বরে ॥ ২২৮ ॥

prāte uṭhi' āilā vipra bhaṭṭathāri-ghare
tāhāra uddeśe prabhu āilā satvare

SYNONYMS

prāte—in the morning; *uṭhi'*—rising from bed; *āilā*—came; *vipra*—the *brāhmaṇa* Kṛṣṇadāsa; *bhaṭṭathāri-ghare*—to the place of the Bhaṭṭathāris; *tāhāra uddeśe*—for him; *prabhu*—Lord Caitanya Mahāprabhu; *āilā*—came; *satvare*—very soon.

TRANSLATION

The allured Kṛṣṇadāsa went to their place early in the morning. Just to find him out, the Lord also went there very quickly.

TEXT 229

আসিয়া কহেন সব ভট্টথারিগণে ।
আমার ব্রাহ্মণ তুমি রাখ কি কারণে ॥ ২২৯ ॥

āsiyā kahena saba bhaṭṭathāri-gaṇe
āmāra brāhmaṇa tumi rākha ki kāraṇe

SYNONYMS

āsiyā—coming; *kahena*—He said; *saba*—all; *bhaṭṭathāri-gaṇe*—to the Bhaṭṭathāris; *āmāra*—My; *brāhmaṇa*—*brāhmaṇa* assistant; *tumi*—you; *rākha*—are keeping; *ki*—for what; *kāraṇe*—reason.

TRANSLATION

Upon reaching their community, Śrī Caitanya Mahāprabhu asked the Bhaṭṭathāris, "Why are you keeping My brāhmaṇa assistant?

TEXT 230

আমিহ সন্ন্যাসী দেখ, তুমিহ সন্ন্যাসী ।
মোরে দুঃখ দেহ,—তোমার 'ন্যায়' নাহি বাসি' ॥২৩০॥

āmi-ha sannyāsī dekha, tumi-ha sannyāsī
more duḥkha deha,—tomāra 'nyāya' nāhi vāsi

SYNONYMS

āmi-ha—I; *sannyāsī*—in the renounced order of life; *dekha*—you see; *tumi-ha*—you; *sannyāsī*—in the renounced order of life; *more*—unto Me; *duḥkha*—pains; *deha*—you give; *tomāra*—your; *nyāya*—logic; *nāhi vāsi*—I do not find.

TRANSLATION

"I am in the renounced order of life, and so are you. Yet you are purposefully giving Me pain, and I do not see any good logic in this."

TEXT 231

শুন' সব ভট্টথারি উঠে অস্ত্র লঞা ।
মারিবারে আইল সবে চারিদিকে ধাঞা ॥ ২৩১ ॥

suna' saba bhaṭṭathāri uṭhe astra lañā
māribāre āila sabe cāri-dike dhāñā

SYNONYMS

suna'—hearing; *saba*—all; *bhaṭṭathāri*—nomads; *uṭhe*—rise up; *astra*—weapons; *lañā*—taking; *māribāre*—to kill; *āila*—came; *sabe*—all; *cāri-dike*—all around; *dhāñā*—running.

TRANSLATION

Upon hearing Śrī Caitanya Mahāprabhu, all the Bhaṭṭathāris came running, with weapons in their hands, desiring to hurt the Lord.

TEXT 232

তার অস্ত্র তার অঙ্গে পড়ে হাত হৈতে ।
খণ্ড খণ্ড হৈল ভট্টথারি পলায় চারি ভিতে ॥ ২৩২ ॥

tāra astra tāra aṅge paḍe hāta haite
khaṇḍa khaṇḍa haila bhaṭṭathāri palāya cāri bhite

SYNONYMS

tāra astra—their weapons; *tāra aṅge*—on their bodies; *paḍe*—fall; *hāta haite*—from their hands; *khaṇḍa khaṇḍa*—cut into pieces; *haila*—became; *bhaṭṭathāri*—the nomads; *palāya*—run away; *cāri bhite*—in the four directions.

TRANSLATION

However, their weapons fell from their hands and struck their own bodies. When some of the Bhaṭṭathāris were thus cut to pieces, the others ran away in the four directions.

TEXT 233

ভট্টথারি-ঘরে মহা উঠিল ক্রন্দন ।
কেশে ধরি' বিপ্রে লঞা করিল গমন ॥ ২৩৩ ॥

bhaṭṭathāri-ghare mahā uṭhila krandana
keśe dhari' vipre lañā karila gamana

SYNONYMS

bhaṭṭathāri-ghare—at the home of the Bhaṭṭathāris; *mahā*—great; *uṭhila*—there arose; *krandana*—crying; *keśe dhari'*—catching by the hair; *vipre*—the *brāhmaṇa* Kṛṣṇadāsa; *lañā*—taking; *karila*—did; *gamana*—departure.

TRANSLATION

While there was much roaring and crying at the Bhaṭṭathāri community, Śrī Caitanya Mahāprabhu grabbed Kṛṣṇadāsa by the hair and took him away.

TEXT 234

সেই দিন চলি' আইলা পয়স্বিনী-তীরে ।
স্নান করি' গেলা আদিকেশব-মন্দিরে ॥ ২৩৪ ॥

sei dina cali' āilā payasvinī-tīre
snāna kari' gelā ādi-keśava-mandire

SYNONYMS

sei dina—on that very day; *cali'*—walking; *āilā*—came; *payasvinī-tīre*—to the bank of the Payasvinī River; *snāna kari'*—bathing; *gelā*—went; *ādi-keśava-mandire*—to the temple of Ādi-keśava.

TRANSLATION

That very night, Śrī Catianya Mahāprabhu and His assistant Kṛṣṇadāsa arrived at the bank of the Payasvinī River. They took their bath and then went to see the temple of Ādi-keśava.

TEXT 235

কেশব দেখিয়া প্রেমে আবিষ্ট হৈলা ।
নতি, স্তুতি, নৃত্য, গীত, বহুত করিলা ॥ ২৩৫ ॥

keśava dekhiyā preme āviṣṭa hailā
nati, stuti, nṛtya, gīta, bahuta karilā

SYNONYMS

keśava dekhiyā—after seeing the Deity of Lord Keśava; *preme*—in ecstasy; *āviṣṭa hailā*—became overwhelmed; *nati*—obeisances; *stuti*—prayer; *nṛtya*—dancing; *gīta*—chanting; *bahuta karilā*—performed in various ways.

TRANSLATION

When the Lord saw the Ādi-keśava temple, He was immediately overwhelmed with ecstasy. Offering various obeisances and prayers, He chanted and danced.

TEXT 236

প্রেম দেখি' লোকে হৈল মহা-চমৎকার ।
সর্বলোক কৈল প্রভুর পরম সৎকার ॥ ২৩৬ ॥

prema dekhi' loke haila mahā-camatkāra
sarva-loka kaila prabhura parama satkāra

SYNONYMS

prema dekhi'—seeing His ecstatic features; *loke*—people; *haila*—became; *mahā-camatkāra*—greatly astonished; *sarva-loka*—all people; *kaila*—did; *prabhura*—of Lord Śrī Caitanya Mahāprabhu; *parama satkāra*—great reception.

TRANSLATION

All the people there were greatly astonished to see the ecstatic pastimes of Śrī Caitanya Mahāprabhu. They all received the Lord very well.

TEXT 237

মহাভক্তগণসহ তাহাঁ গোষ্ঠী কৈল ।
'ব্রহ্মসংহিতাধ্যায়'-পুঁথি তাহাঁ পাইল ॥ ২৩৭ ॥

mahā-bhakta-gaṇa-saha tāhāṅ goṣṭhī kaila
'brahma-saṁhitādhyāya'-puṅthi tāhāṅ pāila

SYNONYMS

mahā-bhakta-gaṇa-saha—among highly advanced devotees; *tāhāṅ*—there; *goṣṭhī kaila*—discussed; *brahma-saṁhitā-adhyāya*—one chapter of *Brahma-saṁhitā; puṅthi*—scripture; *tāhāṅ*—there; *pāila*—found.

TRANSLATION

In the temple of Ādi-keśava, Śrī Caitanya Mahāprabhu discussed spiritual matters among highly advanced devotees. While there, He found a chapter of the Brahma-saṁhitā.

TEXT 238

পুঁথি পাঞা প্রভুর হৈল আনন্দ অপার ।
কম্পাশ্রু-স্বেদ-স্তম্ভ-পুলক বিকার ॥ ২৩৮ ॥

puṅthi pāñā prabhura haila ānanda apāra
kampāśru-sveda-stambha-pulaka vikāra

SYNONYMS

puṅthi pāñā—getting that scripture; *prabhura*—of Lord Śrī Caitanya Mahāprabhu; *haila*—there was; *ānanda*—happiness; *apāra*—unlimited; *kampa*—trembling; *aśru*—tears; *sveda*—perspiration; *stambha*—being stunned; *pulaka*—jubilation; *vikāra*—transformations.

TRANSLATION

Śrī Caitanya Mahāprabhu was greatly happy to find a chapter of that scripture, and symptoms of ecstatic transformation—trembling, tears, perspiration, trance and jubilation—were manifest in His body.

TEXTS 239-240

সিদ্ধান্ত-শাস্ত্র নাহি 'ব্রহ্মসংহিতা'র সম ।
গোবিন্দমহিমা জ্ঞানের পরম কারণ ॥ ২৩৯ ॥
অল্পাক্ষরে কহে সিদ্ধান্ত অপার ।
সকল-বৈষ্ণবশাস্ত্র-মধ্যে অতি সার ॥ ২৪০ ॥

siddhānta-śāstra nāhi 'brahma-saṁhitā'ra sama
govinda-mahimā jñānera parama kāraṇa

alpākṣare kahe siddhānta apāra
sakala-vaiṣṇava-śāstra-madhye ati sāra

SYNONYMS

siddhānta-śāstra—conclusive scripture; *nāhi*—there is not; *brahma-saṁhitāra sama*—like the scripture *Brahma-saṁhitā; govinda-mahimā*—of the glories of Lord Govinda; *jñānera*—of knowledge; *parama*—final; *kāraṇa*—cause; *alpa-akṣare*—briefly; *kahe*—expresses; *siddhānta*—conclusion; *apāra*—unlimited; *sakala*—all; *vaiṣṇava-śāstra*—devotional scriptures; *madhye*—among; *ati sāra*—very essential.

TRANSLATION

There is no scripture equal to the Brahma-saṁhitā as far as the final spiritual conclusion is concerned. Indeed, that scripture is the supreme revelation of the glories of Lord Govinda, for it reveals the topmost knowledge about Him. Since all conclusions are briefly presented in Brahma-saṁhitā, it is essential among all the Vaiṣṇava literatures.

PURPORT

The *Brahma-saṁhitā* is a very important scripture. Śrī Caitanya Mahāprabhu acquired the Fifth Chapter from the Ādi-keśava temple. In that Fifth Chapter, the philosophical conclusion of *acintya-bhedābheda-tattva* (simultaneous oneness and difference) is presented. The chapter also presents methods of devotional service, the eighteen-syllable Vedic hymn, discourses on the soul, the Supersoul and fruitive activity, an explanation of *kāma-gāyatrī, kāma-bīja* and the original Mahā-Viṣṇu, and a specific description of the spiritual world, specifically Goloka Vṛndāvana. *Brahma-saṁhitā* also explains the demigod Gaṇeśa, the Garbhodakaśāyī Viṣṇu, the origin of the Gāyatrī *mantra,* the form of Govinda and His transcendental position and abode, the living entities, the highest goal, the goddess Durgā, the meaning of austerity, the five gross elements, love of Godhead, impersonal Brahman, the initiation of Lord Brahmā, and the vision of transcendental love enabling one to see the Lord. The steps of devotional service are also explained. The mind, *yoga-nidrā,* the goddess of fortune, devotional service in spontaneous ecstasy, incarnations beginning with Lord Rāmacandra, Deities, the conditioned soul and its duties, the truth about Lord Viṣṇu, prayers, Vedic hymns, Lord Śiva, Vedic literature, personalism and impersonalism, good behavior and many other subjects are also discussed. There is also a description of the sun and the universal forms of the Lord. All these subjects are conclusively explained in a nutshell in this *Brahma-saṁhitā.*

TEXT 241

বহু যত্নে সেই পুঁথি নিল লেখাইয়া ।
'অনন্ত-পদ্মনাভ' আইলা হরষিত হঞা ॥ ২৪১ ॥

bahu yatne sei puṅthi nila lekhāiyā
'ananta padmanābha' āilā haraṣita hañā

SYNONYMS

bahu yatne—with great attention; *sei puṅthi*—that scripture; *nila*—took; *lekhāiyā*—having it copied; *ananta-padmanābha*—to Ananta Padmanābha; *āilā*—came; *haraṣita*—in great happiness; *hañā*—being.

TRANSLATION

Śrī Caitanya Mahāprabhu copied the Brahma-saṁhitā and afterwards, with great pleasure, went to a place known as Ananta Padmanābha.

PURPORT

Concerning Ananta Padmanābha, one should refer to *Madhya-līlā,* Chapter One, text 115.

TEXT 242

দিন-দুই পদ্মনাভের কৈল দরশন ।
আনন্দে দেখিতে আইলা শ্রীজনার্দন ॥ ২৪২ ॥

dina-dui padmanābhera kaila daraśana
ānande dekhite āilā śrī-janārdana

SYNONYMS

dina-dui—two days; *padma-nābhera*—of the Deity known as Padmanābha; *kaila daraśana*—visited the temple; *ānande*—in great ecstasy; *dekhite*—to see; *āilā*—came; *śrī-janārdana*—to the temple of Śrī Janārdana.

TRANSLATION

Śrī Caitanya Mahāprabhu remained for two or three days at Ananta Padmanābha and visited the temple there. Then, with great ecstasy, He went to see the temple of Śrī Janārdana.

PURPORT

The temple of Śrī Janārdana is situated twenty-six miles north of Trivāndrama near the Varkālā railway station.

TEXT 243

দিন-দুই তাহাঁ করি' কীর্তন-নর্তন ।
পয়স্বিনী আসিয়া দেখে শঙ্কর নারায়ণ ॥ ২৪৩ ॥

dina-dui tāhāṅ kari' kīrtana-nartana
payasvinī āsiyā dekhe śaṅkara nārāyaṇa

SYNONYMS

dina-dui—two days; *tāhāṅ*—there; *kari'*—performing; *kīrtana-nartana*—chanting and dancing; *payasvinī āsiyā*—coming to the bank of the Payasvinī; *dekhe*—sees; *śaṅkara nārāyaṇa*—the temple of Śaṅkara-nārāyaṇa.

TRANSLATION

Śrī Caitanya Mahāprabhu chanted and danced at Śrī Janārdana for two days. He then went to the bank of the Payasvinī River and visited the temple of Śaṅkara-nārāyaṇa.

TEXT 244

শৃঙ্গেরি-মঠে আইলা শঙ্করাচার্য-স্থানে ।
মৎস্য-তীর্থ দেখি' কৈল তুঙ্গভদ্রায় স্নানে ॥ ২৪৪ ॥

śṛṅgeri-maṭhe āilā śaṅkarācārya-sthāne
matsya-tīrtha dekhi' kaila tuṅgabhadrāya snāne

SYNONYMS

śṛṅgeri-maṭhe—to the Śṛṅgeri monastery; *āilā*—came; *śaṅkarācārya-sthāne*—at the place of Śaṅkarācārya; *matsya-tīrtha*—the holy place named Matsya-tīrtha; *dekhi'*—seeing; *kaila*—did; *tuṅgabhadrāya snāne*—bathing in the River Tuṅgabhadrā.

TRANSLATION

There He saw the monastery known as Śṛṅgeri-maṭha, the abode of Ācārya Śaṅkara. He then visited Matsya-tīrtha, a place of pilgrimage, and took a bath in the River Tuṅgabhadrā.

PURPORT

The monastery known as Śṛṅgeri-maṭha is situated in the province of Mysore (Mahīśūra) in the district of Śimogā. This monastery is located on the left bank of the River Tuṅgabhadrā, seven miles south of Harihara-pura. The real name of this place is Śṛṅga-giri or Śṛṅgavera-purī, and it is the headquarters of Śaṅkarācārya. Śaṅkarācārya had four principal disciples, and he established four centers under their management.

In North India at Badarikāśrama, the monastery named Jyotir-maṭha was established. At Puruṣottama, the Bhogavardhana or Govardhana monastery was established. In Dvārakā, the Sāradā monastery was established, and the fourth monastery, established in South India, is known as Śṛṅgeri-maṭha. In the Śṛṅgeri-maṭha, the *sannyāsīs* assume the designations Sarasvatī, Bhāratī and Purī. They are all *ekadaṇḍi-sannyāsīs,* distinguished from the Vaiṣṇava *sannyāsīs,* who are known as *tridaṇḍi-sannyāsīs*. The Śṛṅgeri-maṭha is situated in South India in a portion of the country known as Āndhra, Draviḍa, Karṇāṭa and Kerala. The community is called Bhūvibāra, and the dynasty is called Bhūr-bhuvaḥ. The place is called Rāmeśvara, and the slogan is "*Ahaṁ brahmāsmi.*" The Deity is Lord Varāha, and the energetic power is Kāmākṣī. The *ācārya* is Hastāmalaka, and the *brahmacārī* assistants of the *sannyāsīs* are known as Caitanya. The place of pilgrimage is called Tuṅgabhadrā, and the subject for Vedic study is the *Yajur Veda.*

The list of the disciplic succession from Śaṅkarācārya is available, and the names of the *ācāryas* and their dates according to the Śaka Era (or Śakābda) are as follows: Śaṅkarācārya, 622 Śaka; Sureśvarācārya, 630; Bodhanācārya, 680; Jñānadhanācārya, 768; Jñānottama-śivācārya, 827; Jñānagiri Ācārya, 871; Siṁhagiri Ācārya, 958; Īśvara Tīrtha, 1019; Narasiṁha Tīrtha, 1067; Vidyātīrtha Vidyāśaṅkara, 1150; Bhāratī-Kṛṣṇa Tīrtha, 1250; Vidyāraṇya Bhāratī, 1253; Candraśekhara Bhāratī, 1290; Narasiṁha Bhāratī, 1309; Puruṣottama Bhāratī, 1328; Śaṅkarānanda, 1350; Candraśekhara Bhāratī, 1371; Narasiṁha Bhāratī, 1386; Puruṣottama Bhāratī, 1394; Rāmacandra Bhāratī, 1430; Narasiṁha Bhāratī, 1479; Narasiṁha Bhāratī, 1485; Dhanamaḍi-narasiṁha Bhāratī, 1498; Abhinava-narasiṁha Bhāratī, 1521; Saccidānanda Bhāratī, 1544; Narasiṁha Bhāratī, 1585; Saccidānanda Bhāratī, 1627; Abhinava-saccidānanda Bhāratī, 1663; Nṛsiṁha Bhāratī, 1689; Saccidānanda Bhāratī, 1692; Abhinava-saccidānanda Bhāratī, 1730; Narasiṁha Bhāratī, 1739; Saccidānanda Śivābhinava Vidyā-narasiṁha Bhāratī, 1788.

Regarding Śaṅkarācārya, it is understood that he was born in the year 608 of the Śakābda Era in the month of Vaiśākha, on the third day of the waxing moon, in a place in South India known as Kālāḍi. His father's name was Śivaguru, and he lost his father at an early age. When Śaṅkarācārya was only eight years old, he completed his study of all scriptures and took *sannyāsa* from Govinda, who was residing on the banks of the Narmadā. After accepting *sannyāsa,* Śaṅkarācārya stayed with his spiritual master for some days. He then took his permission to go to Vārāṇasī and from there went to Badarikāśrama, where he stayed until his twelfth year. While there, he wrote a commentary on *Brahma-sūtra,* as well as ten *Upaniṣads* and *Bhagavad-gītā.* He also wrote *Sanat-sujātīya* and *Nṛsiṁha-tāpinī.* Among his many disciples, his four chief disciples are Padmapāda, Sureśvara, Hastāmalaka and Troṭaka. After departing from Vārāṇasī, Śaṅkarācārya went to Prayāga, where he met a great learned scholar called Kumārila Bhaṭṭa. Śaṅkarācārya wanted to discuss the authority of the scriptures, but Kumārila Bhaṭṭa, being on his deathbed, sent him to his disciple Maṇḍana, in the city of Māhiṣmatī. It was there that Śaṅkarācārya defeated Maṇḍana Miśra in a discussion of the *śāstras.* Maṇḍana had a wife named Sarasvatī, or Ubhaya-bhāratī, who served as mediator between Śaṅkarācārya and her husband. It is said that she wanted to discuss erotic principles and amorous love with Śaṅkarācārya, but Śaṅkarācārya had been a *brahmacārī* since birth and therefore had no experience in amorous love. He took a month's leave from Ubhaya-bhāratī and, by his mystic power, entered the body of a king who had recently died. In this way Śaṅkarācārya experienced the erotic principles. After attaining this experience, he wanted to discuss erotic principles with Ubhaya-bhāratī, but without hearing his discussion, she blessed him and assured the continuous existence of the Śṛṅgeri-maṭha. She then took leave of material life. Afterwards, Maṇḍana Miśra took the order of *sannyāsa* from Śaṅkarācārya and became known as Sureśvara.

Śaṅkarācārya defeated many scholars throughout India and converted them to his Māyāvāda philosophy. He left the material body at the age of thirty-three.

As far as Matsya-tīrtha is concerned, it was supposedly situated beside the ocean in the district of Mālābāra.

TEXT 245

মধ্বাচার্য-স্থানে আইলা যাঁহা 'তত্ত্ববাদী'।
উড়ুপীতে 'কৃষ্ণ' দেখি, তাহাঁ হৈল প্রেমোন্মাদী॥২৪৫

madhvācārya-sthāne āilā yāṅhā 'tattvavādī'
uḍupīte 'kṛṣṇa' dekhi, tāhāṅ haila premonmādī

SYNONYMS

madhva-ācārya-sthāne—at the place of Madhvācārya; *āilā*—arrived; *yāṅhā*—where; *tattva-vādī*—philosophers known as Tattvavādīs; *uḍupīte*—at the place known as Uḍupī; *kṛṣṇa*—the Deity of Lord Kṛṣṇa; *dekhi*—seeing; *tāhāṅ*—there; *haila*—became; *prema-unmādī*—mad in ecstasy.

TRANSLATION

Caitanya Mahāprabhu next arrived at the place of Madhvācārya, where the philosophers known as Tattvavādīs resided. He stayed there at a place known as Uḍupī, where he saw the Deity of Lord Kṛṣṇa and became mad with ecstasy.

PURPORT

Śrīpāda Madhvācārya took his birth at Uḍupī, which is situated in the South Kānāḍā district of South India, just west of Sahyādri. This is the chief city of the South Kānāḍā province and is near the city of Maṅgalore, which is situated to the south of Uḍupī. In the city of Uḍupī is a place called Pājakā-kṣetra, where Madhvācārya took his birth in a *śivāllī-brāhmaṇa* dynasty as the son of Madhyageha Bhaṭṭa, in the year 1040 of Śakābda. According to some, he was born in the year 1160 Śakābda.

In his childhood, Madhvācārya was known as Vāsudeva, and there are some wonderful stories surrounding him. It is also said that his father piled up many debts, and Madhvācārya converted tamarind seeds into actual coins to pay them off. When he was five years old, he was offered the sacred thread. One demon named Maṇimān lived near his abode in the form of a snake, and at the age of five Madhvācārya killed that snake with the toe of his left foot. When his mother was very disturbed, he would appear before her in one jump. He was a great scholar even in childhood, and although his father did not agree, he accepted *sannyāsa* at the age of twelve. After receiving *sannyāsa* from Acyuta Prekṣa, he received the name Pūrṇaprajña Tīrtha. After traveling all over India, he finally discussed scriptures with Vidyāśaṅkara, the exalted leader of Śṛṅgeri-maṭha. Vidyāśaṅkara was actually diminished in the presence of Madhvācārya. Accompanied by Satya Tīrtha, Madhvācārya went to Badarikāśrama. It was there that he met Vyāsadeva and explained his commentary on *Bhagavad-gītā* before him. Thus he became a great scholar by studying before Vyāsadeva.

By the time he came to the Ānanda-maṭha from Badarikāśrama, Madhvācārya had finished his commentary on *Bhagavad-gītā.* His companion Satya Tīrtha wrote down the entire commentary. When Madhvācārya returned from Badarikāśrama, he went to Gañjāma, which is on the bank of the River Godāvarī. He met there with two learned scholars named Śobhana Bhaṭṭa and Svāmī Śāstrī. Later these scholars became known in the disciplic succession of Madhvācārya as Padmanābha Tīrtha and Narahari Tīrtha. When he returned to Uḍupī, he would sometimes bathe in the ocean. On such an occasion he composed one prayer in five chapters. Once, while sitting beside the sea engrossed in meditation upon Lord Śrī Kṛṣṇa, he saw that a large boat containing goods for Dvārakā was in danger. He gave some signs by which the boat could approach the shore, and it was saved. The owners of the boat wanted to give him a present, and at the time Madhvācārya agreed to take some *gopī-candana.* He received a big lump of *gopī-candana,* and as it was being brought to him, it broke apart and revealed a large Deity of Lord Kṛṣṇa. The Deity had a stick in one hand and a lump of food in the other. As soon as Madhvācārya received the Deity of Kṛṣṇa in this way, he composed a prayer. The Deity was so heavy that not even thirty people could raise it. Madhvācārya personally brought this Deity to Uḍupī. Madhvācārya had eight disciples, all of whom took *sannyāsa* from him and became directors of his eight monasteries. Worship of the Lord Kṛṣṇa Deity is still going on at Uḍupī according to the plans Madhvācārya established.

Madhvācārya then for the second time visited Badarikāśrama. While he was passing through Mahārāṣṭra, the local king was digging a big lake for the public benefit. As Madhvācārya passed through that area with his disciples, he was also obliged to help in the excavation. After some time, when Madhvācārya visited the king, he engaged the king in that work and departed with his disciples.

Often in the province of Gāṅga Pradesh there were fights between Hindus and Mohammedans. The Hindus were on one bank of the river, and the Mohammedans on the other. Due to the community tension, no boat was available for crossing the river. The Mohammedan soldiers were always stopping passengers on the other side, but Madhvācārya did not care for these soldiers. He crossed the river anyway, and when he met the soldiers on the other side, he was brought before the king. The Mohammedan king was so pleased with him that he wanted to give him a kingdom and some money, but Madhvācārya refused. While walking on the road, he was attacked by some dacoits, but by his bodily strength he killed them all. When his companion Satya Tīrtha was attacked by a tiger, Madhvācārya separated them by virtue of his great strength. When he met Vyāsadeva, he received from him the *śālagrama-śilā* known as Aṣṭamūrti. After this, he summarized the *Mahābhārata.*

Madhvācārya's devotion to the Lord and his erudite scholarship are known throughout India. Because of this, the owners of the Śṛṅgeri-maṭha established by Śaṅkarācārya became a little perturbed. At that time the followers of Śaṅkarācārya were afraid of Madhvācārya's rising power, and they began to tease Madhvācārya's disciples in many ways. There was even an attempt to prove that the disciplic succession of Madhvācārya was not in line with Vedic principles. One person named Puṇḍarīka Purī, a follower of the Māyāvāda philosophy of Śaṅkarācārya, came before Madhvācārya to discuss the *śāstras.* It is said that all of Madhvācārya's books were taken away, but later they were found with the help of King Jayasiṁha, ruler of Kumla. In discussion, Puṇḍarīka Purī was defeated by Madhvācārya. A great personality named Trivikramācārya, who was a resident of Viṣṇumaṅgala, became Madhvācārya's disciple, and his son later became Nārāyaṇācārya, the composer of *Śrī Madhva-vijaya.* After the death of Trivikramācārya, the younger brother of Nārāyaṇācārya took *sannyāsa* and later became known as Viṣṇu Tīrtha.

At that time it was reputed that there was no limit to the bodily strength of Pūrṇaprajña, Madhvācārya. There was a person named Kaḍañjari who was famed for possessing the strength of thirty men. Madhvācārya placed the big toe of his foot upon the ground and asked the man to separate it from the ground, but the great strong man could not do so even after great effort. Śrīla Madhvācārya passed from this material world at the age of eighty while writing a commentary on the *Aitareya Upaniṣad.* For further information about Madhvācārya, one should read *Madhva-vijaya* by Nārāyaṇa Ācārya. The *ācāryas* of the Madhva-sampradāya established Uḍupī as the chief center, and the monastery there was known as Uttararāḍhī-maṭha. A list of the different centers of the Madhvācārya-sampradāya can be found at Uḍupī, and their *maṭha* commanders are (1) Viṣṇu Tīrtha (Śoda-maṭha), (2) Janārdana Tīrtha (Kṛṣṇapura-maṭha), (3) Vāmana Tīrtha (Kanura-maṭha), (4) Narasiṁha Tīrtha (Adamara-maṭha), (5) Upendra Tīrtha (Puttugī-maṭha), (6) Rāma Tīrtha (Śirura-maṭha), (7) Hṛṣīkeśa Tīrtha (Palimara-maṭha), and (8) Akṣobhya Tīrtha (Pejāvara-maṭha). The disciplic succession of the Madhvācārya-sampradāya is as follows: (1) Haṁsa Paramātmā; (2) Caturmukha Brahmā; (3) Sanakādi; (4) Durvāsā; (5) Jñānanidhi; (6) Garuḍa-vāhana; (7) Kaivalya Tīrtha; (8) Jñāneśa Tīrtha; (9) Para Tīrtha; (10) Satyaprajña Tīrtha; (11) Prājña Tīrtha; (12) Acyuta Prekṣācārya Tīrtha; (13) Śrī Madhvācārya, 1040 Śaka; (14) Padmanābha, 1120; Narahari, 1127; Mādhava, 1136; and Akṣobhya, 1159; (15) Jaya Tīrtha, 1167; (16) Vidyādhirāja, 1190; (17) Kavīndra, 1255; (18) Vāgīśa, 1261; (19) Rāmacandra, 1269; (20) Vidyānidhi, 1298; (21) Śrī Raghunātha, 1366; (22)

Rayuvarya (who spoke with Śrī Caitanya Mahāprabhu), 1424; (23) Raghūttama, 1471; (24) Vedavyāsa, 1517; (25) Vidyādhīśa, 1541; (26) Vedanidhi, 1553; (27) Satyavrata, 1557; (28) Satyanidhi, 1560; (29) Satyanātha, 1582; (30) Satyābhinava, 1595; (31) Satyapūrṇa, 1628; (32) Satyavijaya, 1648; (33) Satyapriya, 1659; (34) Satyabodha, 1666; (35) Satyasandha, 1705; (36) Satyavara, 1716; (37) Satyadharma, 1719; (38) Satyasaṅkalpa, 1752; (39) Satyasantuṣṭa, 1763; (40) Satyaparāyaṇa, 1763; (41) Satyakāma, 1785; (42) Satyeṣṭa, 1793; (43) Satyaparākrama, 1794; (44) Satyadhīra, 1801; (45) Satyadhīra Tīrtha, 1808.

After the sixteenth *ācārya* (Vidyādhirāja Tīrtha), there was another disciplic succession, including Rājendra Tīrtha, 1254; Vijayadhvaja; Puruṣottama; Subrahmaṇya; Vyāsa Rāya, 1470-1520. The nineteenth *ācārya*, Rāmacandra Tīrtha, had another disciplic succession, including Vibudhendra, 1218; Jitāmitra, 1348; Raghunandana; Surendra; Vijendra; Sudhīndra; Rāghavendra Tīrtha, 1545.

To date, in the Uḍupī monastery there are another fourteen Madhva-tīrtha *sannyāsīs.* As stated, Uḍupī is situated in South Kānāḍā, about thirty-six miles north of Maṅgalore. It is situated beside the sea. This information is available from the *South Kānāḍā Manual* and the *Bombay Gazette.*

TEXT 246

'নর্তক গোপাল দেখে পরম-মোহনে ।
মধ্বাচার্যে স্বপ্ন দিয়া আইলা তাঁর স্থানে ॥ ২৪৬ ॥

nartaka gopāla dekhe parama-mohane
madhvācārye svapna diyā āilā tāṅra sthāne

SYNONYMS

nartaka gopāla—dancing Gopāla; *dekhe*—saw; *parama-mohane*—most beautiful; *madhva-ācārye*—unto Madhvācārya; *svapna diyā*—appearing in a dream; *āilā*—came; *tāṅra*—his; *sthāne*—to the place.

TRANSLATION

While at the Uḍupī monastery, Śrī Caitanya Mahāprabhu saw "dancing Gopāla," a most beautiful Deity. This Deity appeared to Madhvācārya in a dream.

TEXT 247

গোপীচন্দন-তলে আছিল ডিঙ্গাতে ।
মধ্বাচার্য সেই কৃষ্ণ পাইলা কোনমতে ॥ ২৪৭ ॥

gopī-candana-tale āchila ḍiṅgāte
madhvācārya sei kṛṣṇa pāilā kona-mate

SYNONYMS

gopī-candana-tale—under heaps of *gopī-candana* (yellowish clay used for *tilaka*); *āchila*—came; *ḍiṅgāte*—in a boat; *madhva-ācārya*—Madhvācārya; *sei kṛṣṇa*—that Kṛṣṇa Deity; *pāilā*—got; *kona-mate*—somehow or other.

TRANSLATION

Madhvācārya had somehow or other acquired the Deity of Kṛṣṇa from a heap of gopī-candana that had been transported in a boat.

TEXT 248

মাধ্বাচার্য আনি' তাঁরে করিলা স্থাপন ।
অদ্যাবধি সেবা করে তত্ত্ববাদিগণ ॥ ২৪৮ ॥

madhvācārya āni' tāṅre karilā sthāpana
adyāvadhi sevā kare tattvavādi-gaṇa

SYNONYMS

madhva-ācārya—Madhvācārya; *āni'*—bringing; *tāṅre*—Him; *karilā sthāpana*—installed; *adya-avadhi*—to date; *sevā kare*—worship; *tattva-vādi-gaṇa*—the Tattvavādīs.

TRANSLATION

Madhvācārya brought this dancing Gopāla Deity to Uḍupī and installed Him in the temple. To date, the followers of Madhvācārya, known as Tattvavādīs, worship this Deity.

TEXT 249

কৃষ্ণমূর্তি দেখি' প্রভু মহাসুখ পাইল ।
প্রেমাবেশে বহুক্ষণ নৃত্য-গীত কৈল ॥ ২৪৯ ॥

kṛṣṇa-mūrti dekhi' prabhu mahā-sukha pāila
premāveśe bahu-kṣaṇa nṛtya-gīta kaila

SYNONYMS

kṛṣṇa-mūrti dekhi'—seeing the Deity of Lord Kṛṣṇa; *prabhu*—Lord Śrī Caitanya Mahāprabhu; *mahā-sukha*—great happiness; *pāila*—got; *prema-āveśe*—in ecstatic love; *bahu-kṣaṇa*—for a long time; *nṛtya-gīta*—dancing and singing; *kaila*—performed.

TRANSLATION

Śrī Caitanya Mahāprabhu received great pleasure in seeing this beautiful form of Gopāla. For a long time He danced and chanted in ecstatic love.

TEXT 250

তত্ত্ববাদিগণ প্রভুকে 'মায়াবাদী' জ্ঞানে।
প্রথম দর্শনে প্রভুকে না কৈল সম্ভাষণে ॥ ২৫০ ॥

tattvavādi-gaṇa prabhuke 'māyāvādī' jñāne
prathama darśane prabhuke nā kaila sambhāṣaṇe

SYNONYMS

tattva-vādi-gaṇa—the Tattvavādīs; *prabhuke*—Śrī Caitanya Mahāprabhu; *māyāvādī jñāne*—considering as a Māyāvādī *sannyāsī; prathama darśane*—in the first meeting; *prabhuke*—Śrī Caitanya Mahāprabhu; *nā*—did not; *kaila*—do; *sambhāṣaṇe*—addressing.

TRANSLATION

At first sight, the Tattvavādī Vaiṣṇavas considered Śrī Caitanya Mahāprabhu a Māyāvādī sannyāsī. Therefore they did not talk to Him.

TEXT 251

পাছে প্রেমাবেশ দেখি' হৈল চমৎকার।
বৈষ্ণব-জ্ঞানে বহুত করিল সৎকার ॥ ২৫১ ॥

pāche premāveśa dekhi' haila camatkāra
vaiṣṇava-jñāne bahuta karila satkāra

SYNONYMS

pāche—later; *prema-āveśa*—ecstatic love; *dekhi'*—seeing; *haila camatkāra*—became struck with wonder; *vaiṣṇava-jñāne*—understanding as a Vaiṣṇava; *bahuta*—much; *karila*—did; *satkāra*—reception.

TRANSLATION

Later, after seeing Śrī Caitanya Mahāprabhu in ecstatic love, they were struck with wonder. Then, considering Him a Vaiṣṇava, they gave Him a nice reception.

TEXT 252

'বৈষ্ণবতা' সবার অন্তরে গর্ব জানি' ।
ঈষৎ হাসিয়া কিছু কহে গৌরমণি ॥ ২৫২ ॥

'vaiṣṇavatā' sabāra antare garva jāni'
īṣat hāsiyā kichu kahe gauramaṇi

SYNONYMS

vaiṣṇavatā—Vaiṣṇavism; *sabāra*—of all of them; *antare*—within the mind; *garva*—pride; *jāni'*—knowing; *īṣat*—mildly; *hāsiyā*—smiling; *kichu*—something; *kahe*—says; *gaura-maṇi*—Lord Śrī Caitanya Mahāprabhu.

TRANSLATION

Śrī Caitanya Mahāprabhu could understand that the Tattvavādīs were very proud of their Vaiṣṇavism. He therefore smiled and began to speak to them.

TEXT 253

তাঁ-সবার অন্তরে গর্ব জানি গৌরচন্দ্র ।
তাঁ-সবা-সঙ্গে গোষ্ঠী করিলা আরম্ভ ॥ ২৫৩ ॥

tāṅ-sabāra antare garva jāni gauracandra
tāṅ-sabā-saṅge goṣṭhī karilā ārambha

SYNONYMS

tāṅ-sabāra—of all of them, *antare*—within the mind; *garva*—pride; *jāni*—knowing; *gaura-candra*—Śrī Caitanya Mahāprabhu; *tāṅ-sabā-saṅge*—with them; *goṣṭhī*—discussion; *karilā*—made; *ārambha*—beginning.

TRANSLATION

Considering them very proud, Caitanya Mahāprabhu began His discussion.

TEXT 254

তত্ত্ববাদী আচার্য—সব শাস্ত্রেতে প্রবীণ ।
তাঁরে প্রশ্ন কৈল প্রভু হঞা যেন দীন ॥ ২৫৪ ॥

tattvavādī ācārya——saba śāstrete pravīṇa
tāṅre praśna kaila prabhu hañā yena dīna

SYNONYMS

tattva-vādī ācārya—the chief preacher of the Tattvavāda community; *saba*—all; *śāstrete*—in revealed scriptures; *pravīṇa*—experienced; *tāṅre*—unto him; *praśna*—question; *kaila*—did; *prabhu*—Śrī Caitanya Mahāprabhu; *hañā*—becoming; *yena*—as if; *dīna*—very humble.

TRANSLATION

The chief ācārya of the Tattvavāda community was very learned in the revealed scriptures. Out of humility, Śrī Caitanya Mahāprabhu questioned him.

TEXT 255

সাধ্য-সাধন আমি না জানি ভালমতে ।
সাধ্য-সাধন-শ্রেষ্ঠ জানাহ আমাতে ॥ ২৫৫ ॥

sādhya-sādhana āmi nā jāni bhāla-mate
sādhya-sādhana-śreṣṭha jānāha āmāte

SYNONYMS

sādhya-sādhana—the aim of life and how to achieve it; *āmi*—I; *nā*—not; *jāni*—know; *bhāla-mate*—very well; *sādhya-sādhana*—the aim of life and how to achieve it; *śreṣṭha*—the best; *jānāha*—kindly explain; *āmāte*—unto Me.

TRANSLATION

Caitanya Mahāprabhu said, "I do not know very well the aim of life and how to achieve it. Please tell me of the best ideal for humanity and how to attain it."

TEXT 256

আচার্য কহে,—'বর্ণাশ্রম-ধর্ম, কৃষ্ণে সমর্পণ' ।
এই হয় কৃষ্ণভক্তের শ্রেষ্ঠ 'সাধন' ॥ ২৫৬ ॥

ācārya kahe,—'varṇāśrama-dharma, kṛṣṇe samarpaṇa'
ei haya kṛṣṇa-bhaktera śreṣṭha 'sādhana'

SYNONYMS

ācārya kahe—the ācārya said; *varṇa-āśrama-dharma*—the institution of four castes and four *āśramas*; *kṛṣṇe*—unto Kṛṣṇa; *samarpaṇa*—to dedicate; *ei haya*—this is; *kṛṣṇa-bhaktera*—of the devotee of Kṛṣṇa; *śreṣṭha sādhana*—the best means of achievement.

TRANSLATION

The ācārya replied, "When the activities of the four castes and the four āśramas are dedicated to Kṛṣṇa, they constitute the best means whereby one can attain the highest goal of life.

TEXT 257

'পঞ্চবিধ মুক্তি' পাঞা বৈকুণ্ঠে গমন ।
'সাধ্য-শ্রেষ্ঠ' হয়,—এই শাস্ত্র-নিরূপণ ॥ ২৫৭ ॥

'pañca-vidha mukti' pāñā vaikuṇṭhe gamana
'sādhya-śreṣṭha' haya,——ei śāstra-nirūpaṇa

SYNONYMS

pañca-vidha mukti—five kinds of liberation; *pāñā*—getting; *vaikuṇṭhe*—in the spiritual world; *gamana*—transference; *sādhya-śreṣṭha haya*—is the highest achievement of the goal of life; *ei*—this; *śāstra-nirūpaṇa*—the verdict of all revealed scriptures.

TRANSLATION

"When one dedicates the duties of varṇāśrama-dharma to Kṛṣṇa, he is eligible for five kinds of liberation. Thus he is transferred to the spiritual world in Vaikuṇṭha. This is the highest goal of life and the verdict of all revealed scriptures."

TEXT 258

প্রভু কহে,—শাস্ত্রে কহে শ্রবণ-কীর্তন ।
কৃষ্ণপ্রেমসেবা-ফলের 'পরম-সাধন' ॥ ২৫৮ ॥

prabhu kahe,——śāstre kahe śravaṇa-kīrtana
kṛṣṇa-prema-sevā-phalera 'parama-sādhana'

SYNONYMS

prabhu kahe—Lord Śrī Caitanya Mahāprabhu said; *śāstre kahe*—in the *śāstra* it is said; *śravaṇa-kīrtana*—the process of chanting and hearing; *kṛṣṇa-prema-sevā*—of loving service to Lord Kṛṣṇa; *phalera*—of the result; *parama-sādhana*—best process of achievement.

TRANSLATION

Śrī Caitanya Mahāprabhu said, "According to the verdict of the śāstras, the process of hearing and chanting is the best means to attain loving service to Kṛṣṇa.

PURPORT

According to the Tattvavādīs, the best process is to execute the duties of the four *varṇas* and *āśramas*. In the material world, unless one is situated in one of the *varṇas* (*brāhmaṇa, kṣatriya, vaiśya* and *śūdra*) one cannot manage social affairs properly to attain the ultimate goal. One also has to follow the principles of the *āśramas* (*brahmacarya, gṛhastha, vānaprastha* and *sannyāsa*), which are considered essential for the attainment of the highest goal. In this way the Tattvavādīs establish that the execution of the principles of *varṇa* and *āśrama* for the sake of Kṛṣṇa is the best way to attain the topmost goal. The Tattvavādīs thus established their principles in terms of human society. Śrī Caitanya Mahāprabhu, however, differed when He said that the best process is hearing and chanting about Lord Viṣṇu. According to the Tattvavādīs, the highest goal is returning home, back to Godhead, but in Śrī Caitanya Mahāprabhu's opinion the highest goal is attaining love of Godhead, either in the material or spiritual world. In the material world this is practiced according to śāstric injunction, and in the spiritual world the real achievement is already there.

TEXTS 259-260

শ্রবণং কীর্তনং বিষ্ণোঃ স্মরণং পাদসেবনম্ ।
অর্চনং বন্দনং দাস্যং সখ্যমাত্মনিবেদনম্ ॥ ২৫৯ ॥
ইতি পুংসার্পিতা বিষ্ণৌ ভক্তিশ্চেন্নবলক্ষণা ।
ক্রিয়েত ভগবত্যদ্ধা তন্মন্যেঽধীতমুত্তমম্ ॥ ২৬০ ॥

śravaṇaṁ kīrtanaṁ viṣṇoḥ
smaraṇaṁ pāda-sevanam
arcanaṁ vandanaṁ dāsyaṁ
sakhyam ātma-nivedanam

iti puṁsārpitā viṣṇau
bhaktiś cen nava-lakṣaṇā
kriyeta bhagavaty addhā
tan manye 'dhītam uttamam

SYNONYMS

śravaṇam—hearing of the holy name, form, qualities, entourage and pastimes, which must pertain to Lord Viṣṇu; *kīrtanam*—vibrating transcendental sounds pertaining to the holy name, form, qualities and entourage, and inquiring about them (these also should be only in relationship to Viṣṇu); *viṣṇoḥ*—of Lord Viṣṇu; *smaraṇam*—remembering the holy name, form and entourage, and inquiring about them, also only for Viṣṇu; *pāda-sevanam*—executing devotional service according to time, circumstances and situation, only in relationship with Viṣṇu; *ar-*

canam—worshiping the Deity of Lord Kṛṣṇa, Lord Rāmacandra, Lakṣmī-Nārāyaṇa or the other forms of Viṣṇu; *vandanam*—offering prayers to the Supreme Personality of Godhead; *dāsyam*—always thinking oneself an eternal servant of the Supreme Personality of Godhead; *sakhyam*—making friends with the Supreme Personality of Godhead; *ātma-nivedanam*—dedicating everything (body, mind and soul) for the service of the Lord; *iti*—thus; *puṁsā*—by the human being; *arpitā*—dedicated; *viṣṇau*—unto the Supreme Personality of Godhead, Viṣṇu; *bhaktiḥ*—devotional service; *cet*—if; *nava-lakṣaṇā*—possessing nine different systems, as above mentioned; *kriyeta*—one should execute; *bhagavati*—unto the Supreme Personality of Godhead; *addhā*—directly (not indirectly through *karma, jñāna* or *yoga*); *tat*—that; *manye*—I understand; *adhītam*—studied; *uttamam*—first class.

TRANSLATION

" 'This process entails hearing, chanting and remembering the holy name, form, pastimes, qualities and entourage of the Lord, offering service according to the time, place and performer, worshiping the Deity, offering prayers, always considering oneself the eternal servant of Kṛṣṇa, making friends with Him and dedicating everything unto Him. These nine items of devotional service, when directly offered to Kṛṣṇa, constitute the highest attainment of life. This is the verdict of revealed scriptures.'

PURPORT

Śrī Caitanya Mahāprabhu quoted these verses from *Śrīmad-Bhāgavatam* (7.5.23-24).

TEXT 261

শ্রবণ-কীর্তন হইতে কৃষ্ণে হয় 'প্রেমা'।
সেই পঞ্চম পুরুষার্থ—পুরুষার্থের সীমা ॥ ২৬১ ॥

śravaṇa-kīrtana ha-ite kṛṣṇe haya 'premā'
sei pañcama puruṣārtha——puruṣārthera sīmā

SYNONYMS

śravaṇa-kīrtana—hearing and chanting; *ha-ite*—from; *kṛṣṇe*—unto Lord Kṛṣṇa; *haya*—there is; *premā*—transcendental love; *sei*—that; *pañcama puruṣa-artha*—the fifth platform of perfection of life; *puruṣa-arthera sīmā*—the limit of goals of life.

TRANSLATION

"When one comes to the platform of loving service to Lord Kṛṣṇa by executing these nine processes, he has attained the fifth platform of success and the limit of life's goals.

PURPORT

Everyone is after success in religion, economic development, sense gratification and ultimately merging into the existence of Brahman. These are the general practices of the common man, but according to the strict principles of the *Vedas,* the highest attainment is to rise to the platform of *śravaṇam, kīrtanam*—chanting and hearing about the Supreme Personality of Godhead. This is confirmed in *Śrīmad-Bhāgavatam* (1.1.2):

dharmaḥ projjhita-kaitavo 'tra paramo nirmatsarāṇāṁ satāṁ
vedyaṁ vāstavam atra vastu śivadaṁ tāpa-trayonmūlanam
śrīmad-bhāgavate mahāmuni-kṛte kiṁ vā parair īśvaraḥ
sadyo hṛdy avarudhyate 'tra kṛtibhiḥ śuśrūṣubhis tat-kṣaṇāt

"Completely rejecting all religious activities which are materially motivated, this *Bhāgavata Purāṇa* propounds the highest truth, which is understandable by those devotees who are pure in heart. The highest truth is reality distinguished from illusion for the welfare of all. Such truth uproots the threefold miseries. This beautiful *Bhāgavatam,* compiled by the great sage Śrī Vyāsadeva, is sufficient in itself for God realization. As soon as one attentively and submissively hears the message of *Bhāgavatam,* he becomes attached to the Supreme Lord."

According to Śrīdhara Svāmī, the material conception of success (*mokṣa* or liberation) is desired by those in material existence. Not being situated in material existence, the devotees have no desire for liberation.

A devotee is always liberated in all stages of life because he is always engaged in the nine items of devotional service (*śravaṇam, kīrtanam,* etc.). Śrī Caitanya Mahāprabhu's philosophy holds that devotional service to Kṛṣṇa always exists in everyone's heart. It simply has to be awakened by the process of *śravaṇaṁ kīrtanaṁ viṣṇoḥ. Śravaṇādi śuddha-citte karaye udaya* (Cc. *Madhya* 22.107). When a person is actually engaged in devotional service, his eternal relationship with the Lord, the servant-master relationship, is awakened.

TEXT 262

এবংব্রতঃ স্বপ্রিয়নাম-কীর্ত্ত্যা
জাতানুরাগো দ্রুতচিত্ত উচ্চৈঃ ।
হসত্যথো রোদিতি রৌতি গায়-
ত্যুন্মাদবন্নৃত্যতি লোকবাহ্যঃ ॥ ২৬২ ॥

evaṁ-vrataḥ sva-priya-nāma-kīrtyā
jātānurāgo druta-citta uccaiḥ

hasaty atho roditi rauti gāyaty
unmādavan nṛtyati loka-bāhyaḥ

SYNONYMS

evam-vrataḥ—when one thus engages in a vow to chant and dance; *sva*—own; *priya*—very dear; *nāma*—holy name; *kīrtyā*—by chanting; *jāta*—in this way develops; *anurāgaḥ*—attachment; *druta-cittaḥ*—very eagerly; *uccaiḥ*—loudly; *hasati*—laughs; *atho*—also; *roditi*—cries; *rauti*—becomes agitated; *gāyati*—chants; *unmāda-vat*—like a madman; *nṛtyati*—dances; *loka-bāhyaḥ*—without caring for outsiders.

TRANSLATION

" 'When a person is actually advanced and takes pleasure in chanting the holy name of the Lord, who is very dear to him, he is agitated and loudly chants the holy name. He also laughs, cries, becomes agitated and chants just like a madman, not caring for outsiders.'

PURPORT

This verse is a quotation from *Śrīmad-Bhāgavatam* (11.2.40).

TEXT 263

কর্মনিন্দা, কর্মত্যাগ, সর্বশাস্ত্রে কহে ।
কর্ম হৈতে প্রেমভক্তি কৃষ্ণে কভু নহে ॥ ২৬৩ ॥

karma-nindā, karma-tyāga, sarva-śāstre kahe
karma haite prema-bhakti kṛṣṇe kabhu nahe

SYNONYMS

karma-nindā—condemnation of fruitive activities; *karma-tyāga*—renunciation of fruitive activities; *sarva-śāstre kahe*—is announced in every revealed scripture; *karma haite*—from fruitive activities; *prema-bhakti*—devotional service in ecstatic love; *kṛṣṇe*—for Kṛṣṇa; *kabhu nahe*—can never be achieved.

TRANSLATION

"In every revealed scripture there is condemnation of fruitive activity. It is advised everywhere to give up engagement in fruitive activity, for by it no one can attain the highest goal of life, love of Godhead.

PURPORT

In the *Vedas* there are three *kāṇḍas,* or divisions: *karma-kāṇḍa, jñāna-kāṇḍa,* and *upāsanā-kāṇḍa.* The *karma-kāṇḍa* portion stresses the execution of fruitive activities, although ultimately it is advised that one abandon both *karma-kāṇḍa* and *jñāna-kāṇḍa* (speculative knowledge) and accept only *upāsanā-kāṇḍa,* or *bhakti-kāṇḍa.* One cannot attain love of Godhead by executing *karma-kāṇḍa* or *jñāna-kāṇḍa.* However, by dedicating one's *karma,* or fruitive activities, to the Supreme Lord, one may be relieved from the polluted mind. But when one is actually free from mental pollution, one must be elevated to the spiritual platform. It is then that one needs the association of a pure devotee, for only by a pure devotee's association can one become a pure devotee of the Supreme Personality of Godhead, Kṛṣṇa. When one comes to the stage of pure devotional service, the process of *śravaṇaṁ kīrtanam* is very essential. By executing the nine items of devotional service, one is completely purified. *Anyābhilāṣitā-śūnyaṁ jñāna-karmādy-anāvṛtam* (B.r.s. 1.1.12). Only then is one able to execute the order of Kṛṣṇa.

man-manā bhava mad-bhakto
mad-yājī māṁ namaskuru
mām evaiṣyasi satyam te
pratijāne priyo 'si me

"Always think of Me and become My devotee. Worship Me and offer your homage unto Me. Thus you will come to Me without fail. I promise you this because you are My very dear friend." (Bg. 18.65)

sarva-dharmān parityajya
mām ekaṁ śaraṇaṁ vraja
ahaṁ tvāṁ sarva-pāpebhyo
mokṣayiṣyāmi mā śucaḥ

"Abandon all varieties of religion and just surrender unto Me. I shall deliver you from all sinful reaction. Do not fear." (Bg. 18.66)

In this way one develops his original constitutional position by which he can render loving service to the Lord. One cannot be elevated to the highest platform of devotional service by *karma-kāṇḍa* or *jñāna-kāṇḍa.* Pure devotional service can be understood and attained only through the association of pure devotees. In this regard, Śrīla Bhaktisiddhānta Sarasvatī Ṭhākura states that there are two types of *karma-kāṇḍa* activities—pious and impious. Pious activities are certainly preferred to impious activities, but even pious activities cannot assure one ecstatic love of God, Kṛṣṇa. Pious and impious activities can bring about material happiness or distress, but there is no possibility in one's becoming a pure devotee simply by acting piously or impiously. *Bhakti,* devotional service, means satisfying Kṛṣṇa. In every revealed scripture—whether *jñāna-kāṇḍa* or *karma-kāṇḍa* is stressed—the principle of renunciation is always praised. The ripened fruit of Vedic knowledge, *Śrīmad-Bhāgavatam,* is the supreme Vedic evidence. In *Śrīmad-Bhāgavatam* it is said:

naiṣkarmyam apy acyuta-bhāva-varjitaṁ
na śobhate jñānam alaṁ nirañjanam
kutaḥ punaḥ śaśvad abhadram īśvare
na cārpitaṁ karma yad apy akāraṇam

"Knowledge of self-realization, even though freed from all material affinity, does not look well if devoid of a conception of the Infallible [God]. What, then, is the use of fruitive activities, which are naturally painful from the very beginning and transient by nature, if they are not utilized for the devotional service of the Lord?" (*Bhāg.* 1.5.12) This means that even knowledge, which is superior to fruitive activity, is not successful if it is devoid of devotional service. In all scriptures—in the beginning, middle and end—*karma-kāṇḍa* and *jñāna-kāṇḍa* are condemned. In *Śrīmad-Bhāgavatam* it is said: *dharmaḥ projjhita-kaitavo 'tra.*

This is explained in the following verses taken from *Śrīmad-Bhāgavatam* (11.11.32) and *Bhagavad-gītā* (18.66).

TEXT 264

আজ্ঞায়ৈবং গুণান্ দোষান্ময়াদিষ্টানপি স্বকান্।
ধর্মান্ সন্ত্যজ্য যঃ সর্বান্মাং ভজেৎ স চ সত্তমঃ ॥ ২৬৪ ॥

ājñāyaivaṁ guṇān doṣān
mayādiṣṭān api svakān
dharmān santyajya yaḥ sarvān
māṁ bhajet sa ca sattamaḥ

SYNONYMS

ājñāya—knowing perfectly; *evam*—thus; *guṇān*—qualities; *doṣān*—faults; *mayā*—by Me; *ādiṣṭān*—instructed; *api*—although; *svakān*—own; *dharmān*—occupational duties; *santyajya*—giving up; *yaḥ*—anyone who; *sarvān*—all; *mām*—unto Me; *bhajet*—may render service; *saḥ*—he; *ca*—and; *sat-tamaḥ*—first-class person.

TRANSLATION

" 'Occupational duties are described in the religious scriptures. If one analyzes them, he can fully understand their qualities and faults and then give them up completely to render service unto the Supreme Personality of Godhead. A person who does so is considered to be a first-class man.'

TEXT 265

সর্বধর্মান্ পরিত্যজ্য মামেকং শরণং ব্রজ ।
অহং ত্বাং সর্বপাপেভ্যো মোক্ষয়িষ্যামি মা শুচঃ ॥ ২৬৫ ॥

sarva-dharmān parityajya
mām ekaṁ śaraṇaṁ vraja
ahaṁ tvāṁ sarva-pāpebhyo
mokṣayiṣyāmi mā śucaḥ

SYNONYMS

sarva-dharmān—all kinds of occupational duties; *parityajya*—giving up; *mām ekam*—unto Me only; *śaraṇam*—as shelter; *vraja*—go; *aham*—I; *tvām*—unto you; *sarva-pāpebhyaḥ*—from all the reactions of sinful life; *mokṣayiṣyāmi*—will give liberation; *mā*—do not; *śucaḥ*—worry.

TRANSLATION

" 'Abandon all varieties of religion and just surrender unto Me. I shall deliver you from all sinful reaction. Do not fear.'

TEXT 266

তাবৎ কর্মাণি কুর্বীত ন নির্বিদ্যেত যাবতা ।
মৎকথা-শ্রবণাদৌ বা শ্রদ্ধা যাবন্ন জায়তে ॥ ২৬৬ ॥

tāvat karmāṇi kurvīta
na nirvidyeta yāvatā
mat-kathā-śravaṇādau vā
śraddhā yāvan na jāyate

SYNONYMS

tāvat—up to that time; *karmāṇi*—fruitive activities; *kurvīta*—one should execute; *na nirvidyeta*—is not satiated; *yāvatā*—as long as; *mat-kathā*—of discourses about Me; *śravaṇa-ādau*—in the matter of *śravaṇam, kīrtanam,* and so on; *vā*—or; *śraddhā*—faith; *yāvat*—as long as; *na*—not; *jāyate*—is awakened.

TRANSLATION

" 'As long as one is not satiated by fruitive activity and has not awakened his taste for devotional service by śravaṇaṁ kīrtanaṁ viṣṇoḥ, one has to act according to the regulative principles of the Vedic injunctions.'

PURPORT

This is a quotation from *Śrīmad-Bhāgavatam* (11.20.9).

TEXT 267

পঞ্চবিধ মুক্তি ত্যাগ করে ভক্তগণ ।
ফল্গু করি' 'মুক্তি' দেখে নরকের সম ॥ ২৬৭ ॥

pañca-vidha mukti tyāga kare bhakta-gaṇa
phalgu kari' 'mukti' dekhe narakera sama

SYNONYMS

pañca-vidha—five kinds of; *mukti*—liberation; *tyāga kare*—give up; *bhakta-gaṇa*—devotees; *phalgu*—insignificant; *kari'*—considering; *mukti*—liberation; *dekhe*—see; *narakera*—to hell; *sama*—equal.

TRANSLATION

"Pure devotees reject the five kinds of liberation; indeed, liberation for them is very insignificant because they see it as hellish.

TEXT 268

সালোক্য-সার্ষ্টি-সামীপ্য-সারূপ্যৈকত্বমপ্যুত ।
দীয়মানং ন গৃহ্ণন্তি বিনা মৎসেবনং জনাঃ ॥ ২৬৮ ॥

sālokya-sārṣṭi-sāmīpya-
sārūpyaikatvam apy uta
dīyamānaṁ na gṛhṇanti
vinā mat-sevanaṁ janāḥ

SYNONYMS

sālokya—to live on the same planet as the Supreme Personality of Godhead; *sārṣṭi*—to possess equal opulence; *sāmīpya*—always associating with the Supreme Personality of Godhead; *sārūpya*—possessing equal bodily features; *ekatvam*—merging into the body of the Supreme Personality of Godhead; *api*—even; *uta*—certainly; *dīyamānam*—being offered; *na*—never; *gṛhṇanti*—accept; *vinā*—without; *mat*—My; *sevanam*—devotional service; *janāḥ*—devotees.

TRANSLATION

" 'Pure devotees always reject the five kinds of liberation, which include living in the spiritual Vaikuṇṭha planets, possessing the same opulences

possessed by the Supreme Lord, having the same bodily features as the Lord, associating with the Lord and merging into the body of the Lord. The pure devotees do not accept these benedictions without the service of the Lord.'

PURPORT

This is a verse from *Śrīmad-Bhāgavatam* (3.29.13).

TEXT 269

যো দুস্ত্যজান্ ক্ষিতিসুতস্বজনার্থদারান্
প্রার্থ্যাং শ্রিয়ং সুরবরৈঃ সদয়াবলোকাম্ ।
নৈচ্ছন্নৃপস্তদুচিতং মহতাং মধুদ্বিট্-
সেবানুরক্তমনসামভবোঽপি ফল্গুঃ ॥ ২৬৯ ॥

yo dustyajān kṣiti-suta-svajanārtha-dārān
prārthyāṁ śriyaṁ sura-varaiḥ sadayāvalokām
naicchan nṛpas tad ucitaṁ mahatāṁ madhu-dviṭ-
sevānurakta-manasām abhavo 'pi phalguḥ

SYNONYMS

yaḥ—one who; *dustyajān*—very difficult to give up; *kṣiti*—land; *suta*—children; *svajana*—relatives; *artha*—riches; *dārān*—and wife; *prārthyām*—desirable; *śriyam*—fortune; *sura-varaiḥ*—by the best of the demigods; *sa-dayā*—merciful; *avalokām*—whose glance; *na aicchat*—did not desire; *nṛpaḥ*—the King (Mahārāja Bharata); *tat*—that; *ucitam*—is befitting; *mahatām*—of great personalities; *madhu-dviṭ*—of the killer of the demon Madhu; *sevā-anurakta*—engaged in the service; *manasām*—the minds of whom; *abhavaḥ*—cessation of the repetition of birth and death; *api*—even; *phalguḥ*—insignificant.

TRANSLATION

" 'It is very difficult to give up material opulence, land, children, society, friends, riches, wife, or the blessings of the goddess of fortune, which are desired even by great demigods. King Bharata did not desire such things, and this was quite befitting his position because for a pure devotee whose mind is always engaged in service of the Lord, even liberation or merging into the existence of the Lord is insignificant. And what to speak of material opportunity?'

PURPORT

This is a verse from *Śrīmad-Bhāgavatam* (5.14.44) concerning the glorification of King Bharata, whom Śukadeva Gosvāmī was describing to King Parīkṣit.

TEXT 270

নারায়ণপরাঃ সর্বে ন কুতশ্চন বিভ্যতি।
স্বর্গাপবর্গনরকেষ্বপি তুল্যার্থদর্শিনঃ ॥ ২৭০ ॥

nārāyaṇa-parāḥ sarve
na kutaścana bibhyati
svargāpavarga-narakeṣv
api tulyārtha-darśinaḥ

SYNONYMS

nārāyaṇa-parāḥ—persons who are devotees of the Supreme Personality of Godhead Nārāyaṇa; *sarve*—all; *na*—never; *kutaścana*—anywhere; *bibhyati*—are afraid; *svarga*—in the heavenly planetary system; *apavarga*—on the path of liberation; *narakeṣu*—or in a hellish condition of life; *api*—even; *tulya*—equal; *artha*—value; *darśinaḥ*—seers of.

TRANSLATION

" 'A person who is a devotee of Lord Nārāyaṇa is not afraid of a hellish condition because he considers it the same as elevation to heavenly planets or liberation. The devotees of Lord Nārāyaṇa are accustomed to seeing all these things on the same level.'

PURPORT

This is a verse from *Śrīmad-Bhāgavatam* (6.17.28) regarding the personality Citraketu. Once when Citraketu saw the goddess Pārvatī sitting on the lap of Lord Śambhu (Śiva), he became a little ashamed and criticized Lord Śiva, who was sitting just like an ordinary man with his wife on his lap. For this reason Citraketu was cursed by Pārvatī. Later he became a demon named Vṛtrāsura. Citraketu was a very powerful king and a devotee, and he could certainly retaliate even against Lord Śiva, but when Pārvatī cursed him, he immediately accepted the curse with a bowed head. When he agreed to accept this curse, Lord Śiva praised him and told Pārvatī that a devotee of Lord Nārāyaṇa is never afraid of accepting any position provided there is a chance to serve the Supreme Personality of Godhead. This is the purport of *nārāyaṇa-parāḥ sarve na kutaścana bibhyati.*

TEXT 271

মুক্তি, কর্ম—দুই বস্তু ত্যজে ভক্তগণ।
সেই দুই স্থাপ' তুমি 'সাধ্য', 'সাধন' ॥ ২৭১ ॥

mukti, karma——dui vastu tyaje bhakta-gaṇa
sei dui sthāpa' tumi 'sādhya', 'sādhana'

SYNONYMS

mukti—liberation; *karma*—fruitive activities; *dui*—two; *vastu*—things; *tyaje*—give up; *bhakta-gaṇa*—the devotees; *sei*—those; *dui*—two; *sthāpa'*—establish; *tumi*—you; *sādhya*—the goal of life; *sādhana*—the process of achievement.

TRANSLATION

"Both liberation and fruitive activity are rejected by devotees. You are trying to establish these things as life's goal and the process to attain it."

TEXT 272

সন্ন্যাসী দেখিয়া মোরে করহ বঞ্চন ।
না কহিলা তেঞি সাধ্য-সাধন-লক্ষণ ॥ ২৭২ ॥

sannyāsī dekhiyā more karaha vañcana
nā kahilā teñi sādhya-sādhana-lakṣaṇa

SYNONYMS

sannyāsī—a person in the renounced order of life; *dekhiyā*—seeing; *more*—unto Me; *karaha*—you do; *vañcana*—duplicity; *nā kahilā*—did not describe; *teñi*—therefore; *sādhya*—objective; *sādhana*—process of achievement; *lakṣaṇa*—symptoms.

TRANSLATION

Śrī Caitanya Mahāprabhu continued speaking to the Tattvavādī ācārya: "Seeing that I am a mendicant in the renounced order of life, you have been playing with Me in a duplicitous way. You have not actually described the process and ultimate objective."

TEXT 273

শুনি' তত্ত্বাচার্য হৈলা অন্তরে লজ্জিত ।
প্রভুর বৈষ্ণবতা দেখি, হইলা বিস্মিত ॥ ২৭৩ ॥

śuni' tattvācārya hailā antare lajjita
prabhura vaiṣṇavatā dekhi, ha-ilā vismita

SYNONYMS

śuni'—hearing; *tattva-ācārya*—the *ācārya* of the Tattvavāda *sampradāya*; *hailā*—became; *antare*—within the mind; *lajjita*—ashamed; *prabhura*—of Lord Śrī Caitanya Mahāprabhu; *vaiṣṇavatā*—devotion in Vaiṣṇavism; *dekhi*—seeing; *ha-ilā*—became; *vismita*—struck with wonder.

TRANSLATION

After hearing Śrī Caitanya Mahāprabhu, the ācārya of the Tattvavāda sampradāya became very ashamed. Upon observing Śrī Caitanya Mahāprabhu's rigid faith in Vaiṣṇavism, he was struck with wonder.

TEXT 274

আচার্য কহে,—তুমি যেই কহ, সেই সত্য হয় ।
সর্বশাস্ত্রে বৈষ্ণবের এই সুনিশ্চয় ॥ ২৭৪ ॥

ācārya kahe,——tumi yei kaha, sei satya haya
sarva-śāstre vaiṣṇavera ei suniścaya

SYNONYMS

ācārya kahe—the Tattvavādī *ācārya* said; *tumi*—You; *yei*—whatever; *kaha*—say; *sei*—that; *satya*—truth; *haya*—is; *sarva-śāstre*—in all revealed scriptures; *vaiṣṇavera*—of the devotees of Lord Viṣṇu; *ei*—this; *su-niścaya*—conclusion.

TRANSLATION

The Tattvavādī ācārya replied, "What You have said is certainly factual. It is the conclusion of all the revealed scriptures of the Vaiṣṇavas.

TEXT 275

তথাপি মধ্বাচার্য যে করিয়াছে নির্বন্ধ ।
সেই আচরিয়ে সবে সম্প্রদায়-সম্বন্ধ ॥ ২৭৫ ॥

tathāpi madhvācārya ye kariyāche nirbandha
sei ācariye sabe sampradāya-sambandha

SYNONYMS

tathāpi—still; *madhva-ācārya*—Madhvācārya; *ye*—whatever; *kariyāche*—formulated; *nirbandha*—rules and regulations; *sei*—that; *ācariye*—we practice; *sabe*—all; *sampradāya*—party; *sambandha*—relationship.

TRANSLATION

"Still, whatever Madhvācārya has ascertained to be the formula for our party, we practice as a party policy."

TEXT 276

প্রভু কহে,—কর্মী, জ্ঞানী,—দুই ভক্তিহীন।
তোমার সম্প্রদায়ে দেখি সেই দুই চিহ্ন ॥ ২৭৬ ॥

prabhu kahe, —karmī, jñānī, —dui bhakti-hīna
tomāra sampradāye dekhi sei dui cihna

SYNONYMS

prabhu kahe—Lord Śrī Caitanya Mahāprabhu said; *karmī*—fruitive worker; *jñānī*—mental speculator; *dui*—both of them; *bhakti-hīna*—nondevotees; *tomāra*—your; *sampradāye*—in the community; *dekhi*—I see; *sei*—those; *dui*—both; *cihna*—symptoms.

TRANSLATION

Śrī Caitanya Mahāprabhu said, "Both the fruitive worker and the speculative philosopher are considered nondevotees. We see both elements present in your sampradāya.

TEXT 277

সবে, এক গুণ দেখি তোমার সম্প্রদায়ে।
সত্যবিগ্রহ করি' ঈশ্বরে করহ নিশ্চয়ে ॥ ২৭৭ ॥

sabe, eka guṇa dekhi tomāra sampradāye
satya-vigraha kari' īśvare karaha niścaye

SYNONYMS

sabe—in all; *eka*—one; *guṇa*—quality; *dekhi*—I see; *tomāra*—your; *sampradāye*—in the party; *satya-vigraha*—the form of the Lord as truth; *kari'*—accepting; *īśvare*—the Supreme Personality of Godhead; *karaha*—you do; *niścaye*—ascertain.

TRANSLATION

"The only qualification that I see in your sampradāya is that you accept the form of the Lord as truth."

PURPORT

Śrī Caitanya Mahāprabhu wanted to point out to the Tattvavādī *ācārya,* who belonged to the Madhvācārya-sampradāya, that their general behavior did not favor pure devotional service, which must be devoid of the taints of fruitive activity and speculative knowledge. As far as fruitive activity is concerned, the contamination is elevation to a higher standard of life, and for speculative knowledge the contamination is merging into the existence of the Absolute Truth. The Tattvavāda *sampradāya* of the Madhvācārya school sticks to the principle of *varṇāśrama-dharma,* which involves fruitive activity. Their ultimate goal (*mukti*) is simply a form of desire. A pure devotee should be free from all kinds of desire. He simply engages in the service of the Lord. Nonetheless, Caitanya Mahāprabhu was pleased that the Madhvācārya-sampradāya, or the Tattvavāda *sampradāya,* accepted the transcendental form of the Lord. This is the great qualification of these Vaiṣṇava *sampradāyas.*

It is the Māyāvāda *sampradāya* that does not accept the transcendental form of the Lord. If a Vaiṣṇava *sampradāya* is also carried away by that impersonal attitude, that *sampradāya* has no position at all. It is a fact that there are many so-called Vaiṣṇavas whose ultimate aim is to merge into the existence of the Lord. The *sahajiyās'* Vaiṣṇava philosophy is to become one with the Supreme. Śrī Caitanya Mahāprabhu points out that Śrī Mādhavendra Purī accepted Madhvācārya only because his *sampradāya* accepted the transcendental form of the Lord.

TEXT 278

এইমত তাঁর ঘরে গর্ব চূর্ণ করি'।
ফল্গুতীর্থে তবে চলি আইলা গৌরহরি ॥ ২৭৮ ॥

ei-mata tāṅra ghare garva cūrṇa kari'
phalgu-tīrthe tabe cali āilā gaurahari

SYNONYMS

ei-mata—in this way; *tāṅra ghare*—at his place; *garva*—pride; *cūrṇa*—broken; *kari'*—making; *phalgu-tīrthe*—to the holy place named Phalgu-tīrtha; *tabe*—then; *cali*—walking; *āilā*—came; *gaura-hari*—Lord Śrī Caitanya Mahāprabhu.

TRANSLATION

Thus Śrī Caitanya Mahāprabhu broke the pride of the Tattvavādīs to pieces. He then went to the holy place known as Phalgu-tīrtha.

TEXT 279

ত্রিতকূপে বিশালার করি' দরশন।
পঞ্চাপ্সরা-তীর্থে আইলা শচীর নন্দন ॥ ২৭৯ ॥

tritakūpe viśālāra kari' daraśana
pañcāpsarā-tīrthe āilā śacīra nandana

SYNONYMS

tritakūpe—to Tritakūpa; *viśālāra*—of the Deity named Viśālā; *kari'*—doing; *daraśana*—visiting; *pañca-apsarā-tīrthe*—to Pañcāpsarā-tīrtha; *āilā*—came; *śacīra nandana*—the son of mother Śacī.

TRANSLATION

Śrī Caitanya Mahāprabhu, the son of mother Śacī, went to Tritakūpa, and after seeing the Viśālā Deity there, He went to the holy place known as Pañcāpsarā-tīrtha.

PURPORT

The Apsarās, denizens of the heavenly planets, are generally known as dancing girls. The girls in the heavenly planets are exquisitely beautiful, and if a woman on earth is found to be very beautiful, she is compared to the Apsarās. There were five Apsarās named Latā, Budbudā, Samīcī, Saurabheyī and Varṇā. It is said that these five beautiful dancing girls were sent by Indra to break the severe austerity of a saintly person called Acyuta Ṛṣi. This action was typical of Indra, the King of heaven. Whenever Indra discovered someone undergoing severe austerities, he would begin to fear for his post. Indra is always anxious about his position, fearing that if someone becomes more powerful than him, he would lose his elevated position. As soon as he would see a saint undergoing severe austerities, he would send dancing girls to distract him. Even the great saint Viśvāmitra Muni fell victim to his plan.

When the five Apsarās went to break Acyuta Ṛṣi's meditation, they were all chastised and cursed by the saint. As a result, the girls turned into crocodiles in a lake that came to be known as Pañcāpsarā. Lord Rāmacandra also visited this place. From Śrī Nārada Muni's narration, it is understood that when Arjuna went to visit the holy places, he learned about the condemnation of the five Apsarās. He delivered them from their abominable condition, and from that day the lake came to be known as Pañcāpsarā, and it became a place of pilgrimage.

TEXT 280

গোকর্ণে শিব দেখি' আইলা দ্বৈপায়নি।
সূর্পারক-তীর্থে আইলা ন্যাসিশিরোমণি ॥ ২৮০ ॥

gokarṇe śiva dekhi' āilā dvaipāyani
sūrpāraka-tīrthe āilā nyāsi-śiromaṇi

SYNONYMS

gokarṇe—in the place named Gokarṇa; *śiva*—the temple of Lord Śiva; *dekhi'*—seeing; *āilā*—came; *dvaipāyani*—to Dvaipāyani; *sūrpāraka-tīrthe*—to the holy place named Sūrpāraka; *āilā*—came; *nyāsi-śiromaṇi*—the best of the *sannyāsīs,* Śrī Caitanya Mahāprabhu.

TRANSLATION

After seeing Pañcāpsarā, Śrī Caitanya Mahāprabhu went to Gokarṇa. While there, He visited the temple of Lord Śiva, and then He went to Dvaipāyani. Śrī Caitanya Mahāprabhu, the crown jewel of all sannyāsīs, then went to Sūrpāraka-tīrtha.

PURPORT

Gokarṇa is situated in North Kānāḍā in the Mahārāṣṭra province. It is about twenty miles southeast of Kāraoyāra. This place is very famous for the temple of Lord Śiva known as Mahā-baleśvara. Hundreds and thousands of pilgrims come to see this temple. Sūrpāraka is about twenty-six miles north of Bombay. In the Mahārāṣṭra province near Bombay is a district known as Thānā and a place known as Sopārā. Sūrpāraka is mentioned in the *Mahābhārata* (*Śānti-parva,* Chapter 41, verses 66-67).

TEXT 281

কোলাপুরে লক্ষ্মী দেখি' দেখেন ক্ষীর-ভগবতী ।
লাঙ্গ-গণেশ দেখি' দেখেন চোর-পার্বতী ॥ ২৮১ ॥

kolāpure lakṣmī dekhi' dekhena kṣīra-bhagavatī
lāṅga-gaṇeśa dekhi' dekhena cora-pārvatī

SYNONYMS

kolāpure—at Kolāpura; *lakṣmī*—the goddess of fortune; *dekhi'*—seeing; *dekhena*—he visited; *kṣīra-bhagavatī*—the temple of Kṣīra-bhagavatī; *lāṅga-gaṇeśa*—the deity Lāṅga-gaṇeśa; *dekhi'*—seeing; *dekhena*—He sees; *cora-pārvatī*—the goddess Pārvatī, who is known as a thief.

TRANSLATION

Śrī Caitanya Mahāprabhu then visited the town of Kolāpura, where He saw the goddess of fortune in the temple of Kṣīra-bhagavatī and Lāṅga-gaṇeśa in another temple, known as Cora-pārvatī.

PURPORT

Kolāpura is a town in the Mahārāṣṭra province formerly known as Bombay Pradesh. Formerly it was a native state, and it is bordered on the north by the district of Sāṅtārā, on the east and south by the district of Belagāma, and on the west by the district of Ratnagiri. In this place there is a river named Urṇā. From the *Bombay Gazette* it is understood that there were about 250 temples there, out of which six are very famous. These are (1) Ambābāi, or Mahālakṣmī Mandira, (2) Viṭhobā Mandira, (3) Ṭemblāi Mandira, (4) Mahākālī Mandira, (5) Phirāṅga-i, or Pratyaṅgirā Mandira, and (6) Yyāllāmmā Mandira.

TEXT 282

তথা হৈতে পাণ্ডরপুরে আইলা গৌরচন্দ্র ।
বিঠ্ঠল-ঠাকুর দেখি' পাইলা আনন্দ ॥ ২৮২ ॥

tathā haite pāṇḍarapure āilā gauracandra
viṭhṭhala-ṭhākura dekhi' pāilā ānanda

SYNONYMS

tathā haite—from there; *pāṇḍara-pure*—to Pāṇḍarapura; *āilā*—came; *gauracandra*—Lord Śrī Caitanya Mahāprabhu; *viṭhṭhala-ṭhākura*—the Deity known as Viṭhṭhala; *dekhi'*—seeing; *pāilā*—got; *ānanda*—great happiness.

TRANSLATION

From there Śrī Caitanya Mahāprabhu went to Pāṇḍarapura, where He happily saw the temple of Viṭhṭhala Ṭhākura.

PURPORT

This city of Pāṇḍarapura is situated on the River Bhīmā. It is said that Śrī Caitanya Mahāprabhu initiated Tukārāma when He visited Pāṇḍarapura. This Tukārāma Ācārya became very famous in the Mahārāṣṭra province, and he spread the *saṅkīrtana* movement all over the province. The *saṅkīrtana* party belonging to Tukārāma is still very popular in Bombay in the province of Mahārāṣṭra. Tukārāma was a disciple of Śrī Caitanya Mahāprabhu, and his book is known as *Abhaṅga*. His *saṅkīrtana* party exactly resembles the Gauḍīya-Vaiṣṇava *saṅkīrtana* parties, for they chant the holy name of the Lord with *mṛdaṅga* and *karatālas*.

The Lord Viṭhṭhaladeva mentioned in this verse is a form of Lord Viṣṇu with four hands. He is Nārāyaṇa.

TEXT 283

প্রেমাবেশে কৈল বহুত কীর্তন-নর্তন ।
তাহাঁ এক বিপ্র তাঁরে কৈল নিমন্ত্রণ ॥ ২৮৩ ॥

premāveśe kaila bahuta kīrtana-nartana
tāhāṅ eka vipra tāṅre kaila nimantraṇa

SYNONYMS

prema-āveśe—in the great ecstasy of love; *kaila*—performed; *bahuta*—much; *kīrtana-nartana*—chanting and dancing; *tāhāṅ*—there; *eka*—one; *vipra*—*brāhmaṇa*; *tāṅre*—unto Him; *kaila*—did; *nimantraṇa*—invitation.

TRANSLATION

Śrī Caitanya Mahāprabhu chanted and danced in various ways as usual, and one brāhmaṇa, seeing Him in ecstatic love, was very pleased. He even invited the Lord to his home for lunch.

TEXT 284

বহুত আদরে প্রভুকে ভিক্ষা করাইল ।
ভিক্ষা করি' তথা এক শুভবার্তা পাইল ॥ ২৮৪ ॥

bahuta ādare prabhuke bhikṣā karāila
bhikṣā kari' tathā eka śubha-vārtā pāila

SYNONYMS

bahuta ādare—with great love; *prabhuke*—unto Lord Śrī Caitanya Mahāprabhu; *bhikṣā karāila*—offered lunch; *bhikṣā kari'*—after finishing His lunch; *tathā*—there; *eka*—one; *śubha-vārtā*—auspicious news; *pāila*—got.

TRANSLATION

This brāhmaṇa offered Śrī Caitanya Mahāprabhu food with great respect and love. After finishing His lunch, the Lord received auspicious news.

TEXT 285

মাধব-পুরীর শিষ্য 'শ্রীরঙ্গ-পুরী' নাম ।
সেই গ্রামে বিপ্রগৃহে করেন বিশ্রাম ॥ ২৮৫ ॥

mādhava-purīra śiṣya 'śrī-raṅga-purī' nāma
sei grāme vipra-gṛhe karena viśrāma

SYNONYMS

mādhava-purīra śiṣya—one disciple of Mādhavendra Purī; *śrī-raṅga-purī*—Śrī Raṅga Purī; *nāma*—named; *sei grāme*—in that village; *vipra-gṛhe*—in the house of a *brāhmaṇa; karena viśrāma*—rests.

TRANSLATION

Śrī Caitanya Mahāprabhu received word that Śrī Raṅga Purī, one of the disciples of Śrī Mādhavendra Purī, was present in that village at the home of a brāhmaṇa.

TEXT 286

শুনিয়া চলিলা প্রভু তাঁরে দেখিবারে ।
বিপ্রগৃহে বসি' আছেন, দেখিলা তাঁহারে ॥ ২৮৬ ॥

śuniyā calilā prabhu tāṅre dekhibāre
vipra-gṛhe vasi' āchena, dekhilā tāṅhāre

SYNONYMS

śuniyā—hearing; *calilā*—went; *prabhu*—Śrī Caitanya Mahāprabhu; *tāṅre*—him; *dekhibāre*—to see; *vipra-gṛhe*—at the house of the *brāhmaṇa; vasi'*—sitting; *āchena*—was; *dekhilā*—saw; *tāṅhāre*—him.

TRANSLATION

Hearing this news, Śrī Caitanya Mahāprabhu immediately went to see Śrī Raṅga Purī at the brāhmaṇas home. Upon entering, the Lord saw him sitting there.

TEXT 287

প্রেমাবেশে করে তাঁরে দণ্ড-পরণাম ।
অশ্রু, পুলক, কম্প, সর্বাঙ্গে পড়ে ঘাম ॥ ২৮৭ ॥

premāveśe kare tāṅre daṇḍa-paraṇāma
aśru, pulaka, kampa, sarvāṅge paḍe ghāma

SYNONYMS

prema-āveśe—in ecstatic love; *kare*—does; *tāṅre*—unto him; *daṇḍa-paraṇāma*—obeisances, falling flat; *aśru*—tears; *pulaka*—jubilation; *kampa*—

trembling; *sarva-aṅge*—all over the body; *paḍe*—there was; *ghāma*—perspiration.

TRANSLATION

As soon as Śrī Caitanya Mahāprabhu saw the brāhmaṇa, He immediately began to offer him obeisances in ecstatic love, falling flat to the ground. The symptoms of transcendental transformation were visible—namely, tears, jubilation, trembling and perspiration.

TEXT 288

দেখিয়া বিস্মিত হৈল শ্রীরঙ্গ-পুরীর মন।
'উঠহ শ্রীপাদ' বলি' বলিলা বচন ॥ ২৮৮ ॥

dekhiyā vismita haila śrī-raṅga-purīra mana
'uṭhaha śrīpāda' bali' balilā vacana

SYNONYMS

dekhiyā—seeing; *vismita*—astonished; *haila*—became; *śrī-raṅga-purīra*—of Śrī Raṅga Purī; *mana*—the mind; *uṭhaha*—get up; *śrī-pāda*—Your Holiness; *bali'*—saying; *balilā vacana*—began to speak.

TRANSLATION

Upon seeing Śrī Caitanya Mahāprabhu in such an ecstatic mood, Śrī Raṅga Purī said, "Your Holiness, please get up.

TEXT 289

শ্রীপাদ, ধর মোর গোসাঞির সম্বন্ধ।
তাহা বিনা অন্যত্র নাহি এই প্রেমার গন্ধ ॥ ২৮৯ ॥

śrīpāda, dhara mora gosāñira sambandha
tāhā vinā anyatra nāhi ei premāra gandha

SYNONYMS

śrī-pāda—O Your Holiness; *dhara*—You hold; *mora*—my; *gosāñira*—with Śrī Mādhavendra Purī; *sambandha*—relationship; *tāhā vinā*—without him; *anyatra*—elsewhere; *nāhi*—there is not; *ei*—this; *premāra*—of ecstasy; *gandha*—flavor.

TRANSLATION

"Your Holiness is certainly related to Śrī Mādhavendra Purī, without whom there is no flavor of ecstatic love."

PURPORT

Śrīla Bhaktisiddhānta Sarasvatī Ṭhākura remarks that in the disciplic succession of Madhvācārya —up to the advent of His Holiness Śrīpāda Lakṣmīpati Tīrtha—only Lord Kṛṣṇa was worshiped. After Śrīla Mādhavendra Purī, worship of both Rādhā and Kṛṣṇa was established. For this reason Śrī Mādhavendra Purī is accepted as the root of worship in ecstatic love. Unless one is connected to the disciplic succession of Mādhavendra Purī, there is no possibility of awakening the symptoms of ecstatic love. The word *gosāñi* is significant in this connection. The spiritual master who is fully surrendered unto the Supreme Personality of Godhead and has no business other than the Lord's service is called the best of the *paramahaṁsas.* A *paramahaṁsa* has no program for sense gratification; he is interested only in satisfying the senses of the Lord. One who has control of the senses in this way is called a *gosāñi* or a *gosvāmī,* master of the senses. The senses cannot be controlled unless one is engaged in the service of the Lord; therefore the bona fide spiritual master, who has full control over his senses, engages twenty-four hours a day in the Lord's service. He can therefore be addressed as *gosāñi* or *gosvāmī.* The title *gosvāmī* cannot be inherited but can be given only to a bona fide spiritual master.

There were six great Gosvāmīs of Vṛndāvana—Śrīla Rūpa, Sanātana, Bhaṭṭa Raghunātha, Śrī Jīva, Gopāla Bhaṭṭa and Dāsa Raghunātha—and none of them inherited the title of *gosvāmī.* All the Gosvāmīs of Vṛndāvana were bona fide spiritual masters situated on the highest platform of devotional service, and for that reason they were called *gosvāmīs.* All the temples of Vṛndāvana were certainly started by the six Gosvāmīs. Later the worship in the temples was entrusted to some householder disciples of the Gosvāmīs, and since then the hereditary title of *gosvāmī* has been used. However, only one who is a bona fide spiritual master expanding the cult of Śrī Caitanya Mahāprabhu, the Kṛṣṇa consciousness movement, and who is in full control of his senses can be addressed as a *gosvāmī.* Unfortunately, the hereditary process is going on; therefore at the present moment, in most cases the title is being misused due to ignorance of the word's etymology.

TEXT 290

এত বলি' প্রভুকে উঠাঞা কৈল আলিঙ্গন ।
গলাগলি করি' দুঁহে করেন ক্রন্দন ॥ ২৯০ ॥

eta bali' prabhuke uṭhāñā kaila āliṅgana
galāgali kari' duṅhe karena krandana

SYNONYMS

eta bali'—saying this; *prabhuke*—Lord Śrī Caitanya Mahāprabhu; *uṭhāñā*—getting up; *kaila*—did; *āliṅgana*—embracing; *galāgali*—shoulder to shoulder; *kari'*—doing; *duṅhe*—both of them; *karena*—do; *krandana*—crying.

TRANSLATION

After saying this, Śrī Raṅga Purī lifted Śrī Caitanya Mahāprabhu and embraced Him. When they both embraced, they began to cry in ecstasy.

TEXT 291

ক্ষণেকে আবেশ ছাড়ি' দুঁহার ধৈর্য হৈল ।
ঈশ্বর-পুরীর সম্বন্ধ গোসাঞি জানাইল ॥ ২৯১ ॥

kṣaṇeke āveśa chāḍi' duṅhāra dhairya haila
īśvara-purīra sambandha gosāñi jānāila

SYNONYMS

kṣaṇeke—after just a few moments; *āveśa*—ecstasy; *chāḍi'*—giving up; *duṅhāra*—of both of them; *dhairya*—patience; *haila*—there was; *īśvara-purīra*—of Īśvara Purī; *sambandha*—relationship; *gosāñi*—Śrī Caitanya Mahāprabhu; *jānāila*—disclosed.

TRANSLATION

After some moments, they came to their senses and became patient. Śrī Caitanya Mahāprabhu then informed Śrī Raṅga Purī about His relationship with Īśvara Purī.

TEXT 292

অদ্ভুত প্রেমের বন্যা দুঁহার উথলিল ।
দুঁহে মান্য করি' দুঁহে আনন্দে বসিল ॥ ২৯২ ॥

adbhuta premera vanyā duṅhāra uthalila
duṅhe mānya kari' duṅhe ānande vasila

SYNONYMS

adbhuta—wonderful; *premera*—of love of Godhead; *vanyā*—inundation; *duṅhāra*—of both of them; *uthalila*—arose; *duṅhe*—both of them; *mānya kari'*—offering respect; *duṅhe*—both of them; *ānande*—with great happiness; *vasila*—sat down.

TRANSLATION

They were both inundated by the wonderful ecstasy of love, which was aroused in both of them. They finally sat down and respectfully began to converse.

TEXT 293

দুই জনে কৃষ্ণকথা কহে রাত্রি-দিনে।
এইমতে গোঙাইল পাঁচ-সাত দিনে ॥ ২৯৩ ॥

dui jane kṛṣṇa-kathā kahe rātri-dine
ei-mate goṅāila pāṅca-sāta dine

SYNONYMS

dui jane—both the persons; *kṛṣṇa-kathā*—topics of Kṛṣṇa; *kahe*—speak; *rātri-dine*—day and night; *ei-mate*—in this way; *goṅāila*—passed; *pāṅca-sāta*—five to seven; *dine*—days.

TRANSLATION

In this way they discussed topics about Lord Kṛṣṇa continuously for five to seven days.

TEXT 294

কৌতুকে পুরী তাঁরে পুছিল জন্মস্থান।
গোসাঞি কৌতুকে কহেন 'নবদ্বীপ' নাম ॥ ২৯৪ ॥

kautuke purī tāṅre puchila janma-sthāna
gosāñi kautuke kahena 'navadvīpa' nāma

SYNONYMS

kautuke—out of curiosity; *purī*—Śrī Raṅga Purī; *tāṅre*—Him; *puchila*—asked; *janma-sthāna*—the place of birth; *gosāñi*—Śrī Caitanya Mahāprabhu; *kautuke*—as a matter of course; *kahena*—said; *nava-dvīpa*—Navadvīpa; *nāma*—name.

TRANSLATION

Out of curiosity, Śrī Raṅga Purī asked Śrī Caitanya Mahāprabhu about His birthplace, and the Lord informed him that it was Navadvīpa-dhāma.

TEXT 295

শ্রীমাধব-পুরীর সঙ্গে শ্রীরঙ্গ-পুরী।
পূর্বে আসিয়াছিলা তেঁহো নদীয়া-নগরী ॥ ২৯৫ ॥

śrī-mādhava-purīra saṅge śrī-raṅga-purī
pūrve āsiyāchilā teṅho nadīyā-nagarī

SYNONYMS

śrī-mādhava-purīra saṅge—with Śrī Mādhavendra Purī; *śrī-raṅga-purī*—Śrī Raṅga Purī; *pūrve*—formerly; *āsiyāchilā*—came; *teṅho*—he; *nadīyā-nagarī*—to the city of Nadia.

TRANSLATION

Śrī Raṅga Purī had formerly gone to Navadvīpa with Śrī Mādhavendra Purī, and he therefore remembered the incidents that took place there.

TEXT 296

জগন্নাথমিশ্র-ঘরে ভিক্ষা যে করিল ।
অপূর্ব মোচার ঘণ্ট তাহাঁ যে খাইল ॥ ২৯৬ ॥

jagannātha-miśra-ghare bhikṣā ye karila
apūrva mocāra ghaṇṭa tāhāṅ ye khāila

SYNONYMS

jagannātha-miśra-ghare—in the house of Śrī Jagannātha Miśra; *bhikṣā*—lunch; *ye*—that; *karila*—took; *apūrva*—unprecedented; *mocāra ghaṇṭa*—curry made of plantain flowers; *tāhāṅ*—there; *ye*—that; *khāila*—ate.

TRANSLATION

As soon as Śrī Raṅga Purī recalled Navadvīpa, he also recalled accompanying Śrī Mādhavendra Purī to the house of Jagannātha Miśra, where he took lunch. He even remembered the taste of an unprecedented curry made of banana flowers.

TEXT 297

জগন্নাথের ব্রাহ্মণী, তেঁহ—মহা-পতিব্রতা ।
বাৎসল্যে হয়েন তেঁহ যেন জগন্মাতা ॥ ২৯৭ ॥

jagannāthera brāhmaṇī, teṅha——mahā-pativratā
vātsalye hayena teṅha yena jagan-mātā

SYNONYMS

jagannāthera—of Jagannātha Miśra; *brāhmaṇī*—wife; *teṅha*—she; *mahā*—great; *pati-vratā*—devoted to her husband; *vātsalye*—in affection; *hayena*—was; *teṅha*—she; *yena*—as if; *jagat-mātā*—the mother of the whole universe.

TRANSLATION

Śrī Raṅga Purī also remembered the wife of Jagannātha Miśra. She was very devoted and chaste. As for her affection, she was exactly like the mother of the universe.

TEXT 298

রন্ধনে নিপুণা তাঁ-সম নাহি ত্রিভুবনে ।
পুত্রসম স্নেহ করেন সন্ন্যাসি-ভোজনে ॥ ২৯৮ ॥

randhane nipuṇā tāṅ-sama nāhi tribhuvane
putra-sama sneha karena sannyāsi-bhojane

SYNONYMS

randhane—in cooking; *nipuṇā*—very expert; *tāṅ-sama*—like her; *nāhi*—there is none; *tri-bhuvane*—in the three worlds; *putra-sama*—like to her own sons; *sneha karena*—she was affectionate; *sannyāsi-bhojane*—in feeding the *sannyāsīs.*

TRANSLATION

He also remembered how Śrī Jagannātha Miśra's wife, Śacīmātā, was expert in cooking. He recalled that she was very affectionate toward the sannyāsīs and fed them exactly like her own sons.

TEXT 299

তাঁর এক যোগ্য পুত্র করিয়াছে সন্ন্যাস ।
'শঙ্করারণ্য' নাম তাঁর অল্প বয়স ॥ ২৯৯ ॥

tāṅra eka yogya putra kariyāche sannyāsa
'śaṅkarāraṇya' nāma tāṅra alpa vayasa

SYNONYMS

tāṅra—her; *eka*—one; *yogya*—deserving; *putra*—son; *kariyāche*—has accepted; *sannyāsa*—the renounced order of life; *śaṅkara-araṇya*—Śaṅkarāraṇya; *nāma*—named; *tāṅra*—his; *alpa*—little; *vayasa*—age.

TRANSLATION

Śrī Raṅga Purī also understood that one of her deserving sons accepted the renounced order at a very young age. His name was Śaṅkarāraṇya.

TEXT 300

এই তীর্থে শঙ্করারণ্যের সিদ্ধিপ্রাপ্তি হৈল ।
প্রস্তাবে শ্রীরঙ্গ-পুরী এতেক কহিল ॥ ৩০০ ॥

ei tīrthe śaṅkarāraṇyera siddhi-prāpti haila
prastāve śrī-raṅga-purī eteka kahila

SYNONYMS

ei tīrthe—in this holy place; *śaṅkarāraṇyera*—of Śaṅkarāraṇya; *siddhi-prāpti*—attainment of perfection; *haila*—became fulfilled; *prastāve*—in the course of conversation; *śrī-raṅga-purī*—Śrī Raṅga Purī; *eteka*—thus; *kahila*—spoke.

TRANSLATION

Śrī Raṅga Purī informed Śrī Caitanya Mahāprabhu that in this holy place, Pāṇḍarapura, the sannyāsī named Śaṅkarāraṇya attained perfection.

PURPORT

Śrī Caitanya Mahāprabhu's elder brother was named Viśvarūpa. He left home before Śrī Caitanya Mahāprabhu and accepted the *sannyāsī* order under the name of Śaṅkarāraṇya Svāmī. He traveled all over the country and finally went to Pāṇḍarapura, where he passed away after attaining perfection. In other words, he entered the spiritual world after giving up his mortal body at Pāṇḍarapura.

TEXT 301

প্রভু কহে,—পূর্বাশ্রমে তেঁহ মোর ভ্রাতা ।
জগন্নাথ মিশ্র—পূর্বাশ্রমে মোর পিতা ॥ ৩০১ ॥

prabhu kahe,——pūrvāśrame teṅha mora bhrātā
jagannātha miśra——pūrvāśrame mora pitā

SYNONYMS

prabhu kahe—the Lord replied; *pūrva-āśrame*—in My previous *āśrama; teṅha*—He; *mora bhrātā*—My brother; *jagannātha miśra*—Jagannātha Miśra; *pūrva-āśrame*—in My previous *āśrama; mora pitā*—My father.

TRANSLATION

Śrī Caitanya Mahāprabhu said, "In My previous āśrama, Śaṅkarāraṇya was My brother, and Jagannātha Miśra was My father."

TEXT 302

এইমত দুইজনে ইষ্টগোষ্ঠী করি'।
দ্বারকা দেখিতে চলিলা শ্রীরঙ্গপুরী ॥ ৩০২ ॥

ei-mata dui-jane iṣṭa-goṣṭhī kari'
dvārakā dekhite calilā śrī-raṅga-purī

SYNONYMS

ei-mata—in this way; *dui-jane*—both of them; *iṣṭa-goṣṭhī kari'*—discussing many topics; *dvārakā dekhite*—to see Dvārakā; *calilā*—started; *śrī-raṅga-purī*—Śrī Raṅga Purī.

TRANSLATION

After finishing his talks with Śrī Caitanya Mahāprabhu, Śrī Raṅga Purī started for Dvārakā-dhāma.

TEXT 303

দিন চারি তথা প্রভুকে রাখিল ব্রাহ্মণ।
ভীমানদী স্নান করি' করেন বিঠ্ঠল দর্শন ॥ ৩০৩ ॥

dina cāri tathā prabhuke rākhila brāhmaṇa
bhīmā-nadī snāna kari' karena viṭhṭhala darśana

SYNONYMS

dina—days; *cāri*—four; *tathā*—there; *prabhuke*—Lord Caitanya Mahāprabhu; *rākhila*—kept; *brāhmaṇa*—the *brāhmaṇa*; *bhīmā-nadī*—in the River Bhīmā; *snāna kari'*—bathing; *karena*—does; *viṭhṭhala darśana*—visit the temple of Viṭhṭhala.

TRANSLATION

After Śrī Raṅga Purī departed for Dvārakā, Śrī Caitanya Mahāprabhu remained with the brāhmaṇa at Pāṇḍarapura for four more days. He took His bath in the Bhīmā River and visited the temple of Viṭhṭhala.

TEXT 304

তবে মহাপ্রভু আইলা কৃষ্ণবেণ্বা-তীরে।
নানা তীর্থ দেখি' তাহাঁ দেবতা-মন্দিরে ॥ ৩০৪ ॥

tabe mahāprabhu āilā kṛṣṇa-veṇvā-tīre
nānā tīrtha dekhi' tāhāṅ devatā-mandire

SYNONYMS

tabe—thereafter; *mahāprabhu*—Śrī Caitanya Mahāprabhu; *āilā*—came; *kṛṣṇa-veṇvā-tīre*—to the bank of the River Kṛṣṇa-veṇvā; *nānā*—various; *tīrtha*—holy places; *dekhi'*—seeing; *tāhāṅ*—there; *devatā-mandire*—in the temples of some gods.

TRANSLATION

Śrī Caitanya Mahāprabhu next went to the bank of the Kṛṣṇa-veṇvā River, where He visited many holy places and the temples of various gods.

PURPORT

This river is another branch of the River Kṛṣṇā. It is said that Ṭhākura Bilvamaṅgala resided on the banks of this river. This river is sometimes called the Vīṇā, the Veṇī, the Sinā and the Bhīmā.

TEXT 305

ব্রাহ্মণ-সমাজ সব—বৈষ্ণব-চরিত ।
বৈষ্ণব সকল পড়ে 'কৃষ্ণকর্ণামৃত' ॥ ৩০৫ ॥

brāhmaṇa-samāja saba——vaiṣṇava-carita
vaiṣṇava sakala paḍe 'kṛṣṇa-karṇāmṛta'

SYNONYMS

brāhmaṇa-samāja—the community of *brāhmaṇas*; *saba*—all; *vaiṣṇava-carita*—pure devotees; *vaiṣṇava sakala*—all the Vaiṣṇavas; *paḍe*—study; *kṛṣṇa-karṇāmṛta*—the *Kṛṣṇa-karṇāmṛta* of Bilvamaṅgala Ṭhākura.

TRANSLATION

The brāhmaṇa community there was composed of pure devotees, who regularly studied a book entitled Kṛṣṇa-karṇāmṛta, which was composed by Bilvamaṅgala Ṭhākura.

PURPORT

This book was composed by Bilvamaṅgala Ṭhākura in 112 verses. There are two or three other books bearing the same name, and there are also two commentaries on Bilvamaṅgala's book. One commentary was written by Kṛṣṇadāsa Kavirāja Gosvāmī and the other by Caitanya dāsa Gosvāmī.

TEXT 306

কৃষ্ণকর্ণামৃত শুনি' প্রভুর আনন্দ হৈল ।
আগ্রহ করিয়া পুঁথি লেখাঞা লৈল ॥ ৩০৬ ॥

kṛṣṇa-karṇāmṛta suni' prabhura ānanda haila
āgraha kariyā puṅthi lekhāñā laila

SYNONYMS

kṛṣṇa-karṇāmṛta śuni'—after hearing *Kṛṣṇa-karṇāmṛta; prabhura*—of Lord Śrī Caitanya Mahāprabhu; *ānanda haila*—there was great happiness; *āgraha kariyā*—with great eagerness; *puṅthi*—the book; *lekhāñā*—getting copied; *laila*—took.

TRANSLATION

Śrī Caitanya Mahāprabhu was very pleased to hear the book Kṛṣṇa-karṇāmṛta, and with great eagerness He had it copied and took it with Him.

TEXT 307

'কর্ণামৃত'-সম বস্তু নাহি ত্রিভুবনে ।
যাহা হৈতে হয় কৃষ্ণে শুদ্ধপ্রেমজ্ঞানে ॥ ৩০৭ ॥

'karṇāmṛta'-sama vastu nāhi tribhuvane
yāhā haite haya kṛṣṇe śuddha-prema-jñāne

SYNONYMS

karṇāmṛta—*Kṛṣṇa-karṇāmṛta; sama*—like; *vastu nāhi*—there is nothing; *tribhuvane*—in the three worlds; *yāhā haite*—from which; *haya*—there is; *kṛṣṇe*—unto Lord Kṛṣṇa; *śuddha-prema-jñāne*—knowledge of pure devotional service.

TRANSLATION

There is no comparison to Kṛṣṇa-karṇāmṛta within the three worlds. By studying this book, one is elevated to the knowledge of pure devotional service to Kṛṣṇa.

TEXT 308

সৌন্দর্য-মাধুর্য-কৃষ্ণলীলার অবধি ।
সেই জানে, যে 'কর্ণামৃত' পড়ে নিরবধি ॥ ॥ ৩০৮ ॥

saundarya-mādhurya-kṛṣṇa-līlāra avadhi
sei jāne, ye 'karṇāmṛta' paḍe niravadhi

SYNONYMS

saundarya—beauty; *mādhurya*—sweetness; *kṛṣṇa-līlāra*—of the pastimes of Lord Kṛṣṇa; *avadhi*—limit; *sei jāne*—he knows; *ye*—one who; *karṇāmṛta*—the book *Kṛṣṇa-karṇāmṛta*; *paḍe*—studies; *niravadhi*—constantly.

TRANSLATION

One who constantly reads Kṛṣṇa-karṇāmṛta can fully understand the beauty and melodious taste of the pastimes of Lord Kṛṣṇa.

TEXT 309

'ব্রহ্মসংহিতা', 'কর্ণামৃত' দুই পুঁথি পাঞা ।
মহারত্নপ্রায় পাই আইলা সঙ্গে লঞা ॥ ৩০৯ ॥

'brahma-saṁhitā', 'karṇāmṛta' dui puṅthi pāñā
mahā-ratna-prāya pāi āilā saṅge lañā

SYNONYMS

brahma-saṁhitā—the book *Brahma-saṁhitā*; *karṇāmṛta*—the book *Kṛṣṇa-karṇāmṛta*; *dui*—two; *puṅthi*—books; *pāñā*—getting; *mahā-ratna-prāya*—like the most valuable jewels; *pāi*—getting; *āilā*—came back; *saṅge*—with Him; *lañā*—taking.

TRANSLATION

The Brahma-saṁhitā and Kṛṣṇa-karṇāmṛta were two books that Śrī Caitanya Mahāprabhu considered to be most valuable jewels. Therefore He took them with Him on His return trip.

TEXT 310

তাপী স্নান করি' আইলা মাহিষ্মতীপুরে ।
নানা তীর্থ দেখি তাহাঁ নর্মদার তীরে ॥ ৩১০ ॥

tāpī snāna kari' āilā māhiṣmatī-pure
nānā tīrtha dekhi tāhāṅ narmadāra tīre

SYNONYMS

tāpī—in the Tāpī River; *snāna kari'*—taking a bath; *āilā*—arrived; *māhiṣmatī-pure*—at Māhiṣmatī-pura; *nānā tīrtha*—many holy places; *dekhi*—seeing; *tāhāṅ*—there; *narmadāra tīre*—on the bank of the River Narmadā.

TRANSLATION

Śrī Caitanya Mahāprabhu next arrived at the banks of the River Tāpī. After bathing there, He went to Māhiṣmatī-pura. While there, He saw many holy places on the banks of the River Narmadā.

PURPORT

The River Tāpī is presently known as Tāpti. The river's source is a mountain called Multāi, and the river flows through the state of Saurāṣṭra and into the western Arabian Sea. Māhiṣmatī-pura is mentioned in *Mahābhārata* in connection with Sahadeva's victory. Sahadeva, the youngest brother of the Pāṇḍavas, conquered that part of the country. As stated in *Mahābhārata:*

tato ratnāny upādāya
purīṁ māhiṣmatīṁ yayau
tatra nīlena rājñā sa
cakre yuddhaṁ nararṣabhaḥ

"After acquiring jewels, Sahadeva went to the city of Māhiṣmatī, where he fought with a king called Nīla."

TEXT 311

ধনুস্তীর্থ দেখি' করিলা নির্বিন্ধ্যাতে স্নানে ।
ঋষ্যমূক-গিরি আইলা দণ্ডকারণ্যে ॥ ৩১১ ॥

dhanus-tīrtha dekhi' karilā nirvindhyāte snāne
ṛṣyamūka-giri āilā daṇḍakāraṇye

SYNONYMS

dhanuḥ-tīrtha—Dhanus-tīrtha; *dekhi'*—seeing; *karilā*—did; *nirvindhyāte*—in the River Nirvindhyā; *snāne*—bathing; *ṛṣyamūka-giri*—at the Ṛṣyamūka Mountain; *āilā*—arrived; *daṇḍaka-araṇye*—in the forest known as Daṇḍakāraṇya.

TRANSLATION

The Lord next arrived at Dhanus-tīrtha, where He took His bath in the River Nirvindhyā. He then arrived at Ṛṣyamūka Mountain and then went to Daṇḍakāraṇya.

PURPORT

According to some opinions, Ṛṣyamūka is a chain of mountains beginning at the village of Hāmpi-grāma in the district of Belāri. The mountain chain begins along the bank of the River Tuṅgabhadrā, which gradually reaches the state of Hyderabad. According to other opinions, this hill is situated in Madhya Pradesh and bears the present name of Rāmpa. Daṇḍakāraṇya is a spacious tract of land which begins north of Khāndeśa and extends up to the southern Āhammada-nagara through Nāsika and Āuraṅgābāda. The Godāvarī River flows through this tract of land, and there is a great forest there where Lord Rāmacandra lived.

TEXT 312

'সপ্ততাল-বৃক্ষ' দেখে কানন-ভিতর ।
অতি বৃদ্ধ, অতি স্থূল, অতি উচ্চতর ॥ ৩১২ ॥

'saptatāla-vṛkṣa' dekhe kānana-bhitara
ati vṛddha, ati sthūla, ati uccatara

SYNONYMS

sapta-tāla-vṛkṣa—seven palm trees; *dekhe*—sees; *kānana bhitara*—within the forest; *ati vṛddha*—very old; *ati sthūla*—very bulky; *ati uccatara*—very high.

TRANSLATION

Śrī Caitanya Mahāprabhu then visited a place within the forest called Saptatāla. All the trees there were very old, very bulky and very high.

PURPORT

The name Saptatāla is mentioned in the *Kiṣkindhyā-kāṇḍa* Chapter of the *Rāmāyaṇa* and is described in the eleventh and twelfth sections of this chapter.

TEXT 313

সপ্ততাল দেখি' প্রভু আলিঙ্গন কৈল ।
সশরীরে সপ্ততাল বৈকুণ্ঠে চলিল ॥ ৩১৩ ॥

saptatāla dekhi' prabhu āliṅgana kaila
saśarīre saptatāla vaikuṇṭhe calila

SYNONYMS

sapta-tāla dekhi'—after seeing the seven palm trees; *prabhu*—Lord Caitanya Mahāprabhu; *āliṅgana kaila*—embraced; *sa-śarīre*—with their bodies; *sapta-tāla*—the seven palm trees; *vaikuṇṭhe calila*—returned to Vaikuṇṭhaloka.

TRANSLATION

After seeing the seven palm trees, Śrī Caitanya Mahāprabhu embraced them. As a result, they all returned to Vaikuṇṭhaloka, the spiritual world.

TEXT 314

শূন্যস্থল দেখি' লোকের হৈল চমৎকার ।
লোকে কহে, এ সন্ন্যাসী—রাম-অবতার ॥ ৩১৪ ॥

śūnya-sthala dekhi' lokera haila camatkāra
loke kahe, e sannyāsī——rāma-avatāra

SYNONYMS

śūnya-sthala—the vacant place; *dekhi'*—seeing; *lokera*—of the people in general; *haila*—there was; *camatkāra*—astonishment; *loke kahe*—all people began to say; *e sannyāsī*—this *sannyāsī*; *rāma-avatāra*—incarnation of Lord Rāmacandra.

TRANSLATION

After the seven palm trees departed for the Vaikuṇṭhas, everyone was astonished to see them gone. The people then began to say, "This sannyāsī called Śrī Caitanya Mahāprabhu must be an incarnation of Lord Rāmacandra.

TEXT 315

সশরীরে তাল গেল শ্রীবৈকুণ্ঠ-ধাম ।
ঐছে শক্তি কার হয়, বিনা এক রাম ॥ ৩১৫ ॥

saśarīre tāla gela śrī-vaikuṇṭha-dhāma
aiche śakti kāra haya, vinā eka rāma

SYNONYMS

sa-śarīre—with the material body; *tāla*—the palm trees; *gela*—went; *śrī-vaikuṇṭha-dhāma*—to the spiritual kingdom, known as Vaikuṇṭha; *aiche*—such; *śakti*—power; *kāra*—whose; *haya*—is; *vinā*—without; *eka*—one; *rāma*—Lord Rāmacandra.

TRANSLATION

"Only Lord Rāmacandra has the power to send seven palm trees to the spiritual Vaikuṇṭha planets."

TEXT 316

প্রভু আসি' কৈল পম্পা-সরোবরে স্নান।
পঞ্চবটী আসি, তাহাঁ করিল বিশ্রাম ॥ ৩১৬ ॥

prabhu āsi' kaila pampā-sarovare snāna
pañcavaṭī āsi, tāhāṅ karila viśrāma

SYNONYMS

prabhu—Śrī Caitanya Mahāprabhu; *āsi'*—coming; *kaila*—did; *pampā-sarovare*—in the lake known as Pampā; *snāna*—bathing; *pañcavaṭī āsi*—then coming to Pañcavaṭī; *tāhāṅ*—there; *karila*—took; *viśrāma*—rest.

TRANSLATION

Eventually Śrī Caitanya Mahāprabhu arrived at a lake known as Pampā, where He took His bath. He then went to a place called Pañcavaṭī, where He rested.

PURPORT

According to some, the old name of the Tuṅgabhadrā River was Pambā. According to others, Vijaya-nagara, the capital of the state, was known as Pampā-tīrtha. Yet according to others, there is a lake near Anāguṇḍi in the direction of Hyderabad. The River Tuṅgabhadrā also flows through there. There are many different opinions about the lake called Pampā-sarovara.

TEXT 317

নাসিকে ত্র্যম্বক দেখি' গেলা ব্রহ্মগিরি।
কুশাবর্ত্তে আইলা যাহাঁ জন্মিলা গোদাবরী ॥ ৩১৭ ॥

nāsike tryambaka dekhi' gelā brahmagiri
kuśāvarte āilā yāhāṅ janmilā godāvarī

SYNONYMS

nāsike—at the holy place Nāsika; *tryambaka*—a deity of Lord Śiva; *dekhi'*—after seeing; *gelā*—went; *brahmagiri*—to the place known as Brahmagiri; *kuśāvarte āilā*—then He came to the holy place known as Kuśāvarta; *yāhāṅ*—where; *janmilā*—took birth; *godāvarī*—the River Godāvarī.

TRANSLATION

Śrī Caitanya Mahāprabhu then visited Nāsika, where He saw the deity Tryambaka. He then went to Brahma-giri and then to Kuśāvarta, the source of the River Godāvarī.

PURPORT

Kuśāvarta is located in the western *ghāṭa,* at Sahyādri. It is near Nāsika, a holy place, but according to some it was situated in the valley of Vindhya.

TEXT 318

সপ্ত গোদাবরী আইলা করি' তীর্থ বহুতর ।
পুনরপি আইলা প্রভু বিদ্যানগর ॥ ৩১৮ ॥

sapta godāvarī āilā kari' tīrtha bahutara
punarapi āilā prabhu vidyānagara

SYNONYMS

sapta godāvarī—to the place known as Sapta-godāvarī; *āilā*—came; *kari' tīrtha bahutara*—visiting various holy places; *punarapi*—again; *āilā*—came back; *prabhu*—Śrī Caitanya Mahāprabhu; *vidyā-nagara*—to the place where He met Rāmānanda Rāya.

TRANSLATION

After visiting many other holy places, the Lord went to Sapta-godāvarī. At last he returned to Vidyānagara.

PURPORT

In this way Śrī Caitanya Mahāprabhu traveled from the source of the Godāvarī River and eventually visited the northern side of Hyderabad state. He finally arrived at the state of Kaliṅga.

TEXT 319

রামানন্দ রায় শুনি' প্রভুর আগমন ।
আনন্দে আসিয়া কৈল প্রভুসহ মিলন ॥ ৩১৯ ॥

rāmānanda rāya suni' prabhura āgamana
ānande āsiyā kaila prabhu-saha milana

SYNONYMS

rāmānanda rāya—Rāmānanda Rāya; *śuni'*—hearing; *prabhura*—of Lord Caitanya Mahāprabhu; *āgamana*—return; *ānande*—in great happiness; *āsiyā*—coming; *kaila*—did; *prabhu-saha*—with Lord Caitanya Mahāprabhu; *milana*—meeting.

TRANSLATION

When Rāmānanda Rāya heard of Śrī Caitanya Mahāprabhu's arrival, he was very pleased, and he immediately went to see Him.

TEXT 320

দণ্ডবৎ হঞা পড়ে চরণে ধরিয়া।
আলিঙ্গন কৈল প্রভু তাঁরে উঠাঞা ॥ ৩২০ ॥

daṇḍavat hañā paḍe caraṇe dhariyā
āliṅgana kaila prabhu tāṅre uṭhāñā

SYNONYMS

daṇḍavat hañā—like a stick; *paḍe*—fell; *caraṇe*—the lotus feet; *dhariyā*—catching; *āliṅgana*—embracing; *kaila*—did; *prabhu*—Śrī Caitanya Mahāprabhu; *tāṅre*—him; *uṭhāñā*—getting up.

TRANSLATION

When Rāmānanda Rāya fell flat, touching the lotus feet of Śrī Caitanya Mahāprabhu, the Lord immediately raised him to his feet and embraced him.

TEXT 321

দুই জনে প্রেমাবেশে করেন ক্রন্দন।
প্রেমানন্দে শিথিল হৈল দুঁহাকার মন ॥ ৩২১ ॥

dui jane premāveśe karena krandana
premānande śithila haila duṅhākāra mana

SYNONYMS

dui jane—both of them; *prema-āveśe*—in ecstatic love; *karena*—do; *krandana*—crying; *prema-ānande*—in ecstatic love; *śithila haila*—became slackened; *duṅhākāra*—of both of them; *mana*—minds.

TRANSLATION

In great ecstatic love they both began to cry, and thus their minds were slackened.

TEXT 322

কতক্ষণে দুই জনা সুস্থির হঞা।
নানা ইষ্টগোষ্ঠী করে একত্র বসিয়া ॥ ৩২২ ॥

kata-kṣaṇe dui janā susthira hañā
nānā iṣṭa-goṣṭhī kare ekatra vasiyā

SYNONYMS

kata-kṣaṇe—after some time; *dui*—two; *janā*—people; *su-sthira hañā*—coming to their senses; *nānā*—various; *iṣṭa-goṣṭhī*—discussions; *kare*—do; *ekatra*—together; *vasiyā*—sitting.

TRANSLATION

After some time, they both regained their senses and sat together to discuss various subjects.

TEXT 323

তীর্থযাত্রা-কথা প্রভু সকল কহিলা ।
কর্ণামৃত, ব্রহ্মসংহিতা,—দুই পুঁথি দিলা ॥ ৩২৩ ॥

tīrtha-yātrā-kathā prabhu sakala kahilā
karṇāmṛta, brahma-saṁhitā, —dui puṅthi dilā

SYNONYMS

tīrtha-yātrā-kathā—topics of His pilgrimage; *prabhu*—Lord Śrī Caitanya Mahāprabhu; *sakala kahilā*—described everything; *karṇāmṛta*—the book named *Kṛṣṇa-karṇāmṛta*; *brahma-saṁhitā*—the book named *Brahma-saṁhitā*; *dui*—two; *puṅthi*—scriptures; *dilā*—delivered.

TRANSLATION

Śrī Caitanya Mahāprabhu gave Rāmānanda Rāya a vivid description of His travels to the holy places and told him how He had acquired the two books named Kṛṣṇa-karṇāmṛta and Brahma-saṁhitā. The Lord delivered the books to Rāmānanda Rāya.

TEXT 324

প্রভু কহে,—তুমি যেই সিদ্ধান্ত কহিলে ।
এই দুই পুঁথি সেই সব সাক্ষী দিলে ॥ ৩২৪ ॥

prabhu kahe, —tumi yei siddhānta kahile
ei dui puṅthi sei saba sākṣī dile

SYNONYMS

prabhu kahe—the Lord said; *tumi*—you; *yei*—whatever; *siddhānta*—conclusion; *kahile*—informed; *ei dui*—these two; *puṅthi*—books; *sei*—that; *saba*—everything; *sākṣī*—evidence; *dile*—gave.

TRANSLATION

The Lord said, "Whatever you have told Me about devotional service is all supported by these two books."

TEXT 325

রায়ের আনন্দ হৈল পুস্তক পাইয়া ।
প্রভু-সহ আস্বাদিল, রাখিল লিখিয়া ॥ ৩২৫ ॥

rāyera ānanda haila pustaka pāiyā
prabhu-saha āsvādila, rākhila likhiyā

SYNONYMS

rāyera—of Rāya Rāmānanda; *ānanda*—happiness; *haila*—there was; *pustaka pāiyā*—getting those two books; *prabhu-saha*—with the Lord; *āsvādila*—tasted; *rākhila*—kept; *likhiyā*—writing.

TRANSLATION

Rāmānanda Rāya was very happy to receive these books. He tasted their contents along with the Lord and made a copy of each.

TEXT 326

'গোসাঞি' আইলা' গ্রামে হৈল কোলাহল ।
প্রভুকে দেখিতে লোক আইল সকল ॥ ৩২৬ ॥

'gosāñi' āilā' grāme haila kolāhala
prabhuke dekhite loka āila sakala

SYNONYMS

gosāñi—Śrī Caitanya Mahāprabhu; *āilā'*—has returned; *grāme*—in the village; *haila*—there was; *kolāhala*—commotion; *prabhuke*—Lord Śrī Caitanya Mahāprabhu; *dekhite*—to see; *loka*—people; *āila*—came there; *sakala*—all.

TRANSLATION

News spread in the village of Vidyānagara about Śrī Caitanya Mahāprabhu's arrival, and everyone came to see Him once again.

TEXT 327

লোক দেখি' রামানন্দ গেলা নিজ-ঘরে ।
মধ্যাহ্নে উঠিলা প্রভু ভিক্ষা করিবারে ॥ ৩২৭ ॥

loka dehki' rāmānanda gelā nija-ghare
madhyāhne uṭhilā prabhu bhikṣā karibāre

SYNONYMS

loka dekhi'—seeing the people; *rāmānanda*—Rāya Rāmānanda; *gelā*—departed; *nija-ghare*—to his own home; *madhyāhne*—at noon; *uṭhilā prabhu*—Śrī Caitanya Mahāprabhu got up; *bhikṣā karibāre*—to take His lunch.

TRANSLATION

After seeing the people who gathered there, Śrī Rāmānanda Rāya returned to his own home. At noon, Śrī Caitanya Mahāprabhu got up to take His lunch.

TEXT 328

রাত্রিকালে রায় পুনঃ কৈল আগমন ।
দুই জনে কৃষ্ণকথায় কৈল জাগরণ ॥ ৩২৮ ॥

rātri-kāle rāya punaḥ kaila āgamana
dui jane kṛṣṇa-kathāya kaila jāgaraṇa

SYNONYMS

rātri-kāle—at night; *rāya*—Rāmānanda Rāya; *punaḥ*—again; *kaila*—did; *āgamana*—coming; *dui jane*—the two of them; *kṛṣṇa-kathāya*—in discourses on topics of Kṛṣṇa; *kaila*—did; *jāgaraṇa*—keeping the night.

TRANSLATION

Śrī Rāmānanda Rāya returned at night, and both he and the Lord discussed topics concerning Kṛṣṇa. Thus they passed the night.

TEXT 329

দুই জনে কৃষ্ণকথা কহে রাত্রি-দিনে ।
পরম-আনন্দে গেল পাঁচ-সাত দিনে ॥ ৩২৯ ॥

dui jane kṛṣṇa-kathā kahe rātri-dine
parama-ānande gela pāṅca-sāta dine

SYNONYMS

dui jane—both of them; *kṛṣṇa-kathā*—topics of Kṛṣṇa; *kahe*—speak; *rātri-dine*—day and night; *parama-ānande*—in great happiness; *gela*—passed; *pāṅca-sāta dine*—five to seven days.

TRANSLATION

Rāmānanda Rāya and Śrī Caitanya Mahāprabhu discussed Kṛṣṇa day and night, and thus they passed from five to seven days in great happiness.

TEXT 330

রামানন্দ কহে,—প্রভু, তোমার আজ্ঞা পাঞা ।
রাজাকে লিখিলুঁ আমি বিনয় করিয়া ॥ ৩৩০ ॥

rāmānanda kahe, ——prabhu, tomāra ājñā pāñā
rājāke likhiluṅ āmi vinaya kariyā

SYNONYMS

rāmānanda kahe—Rāmānanda Rāya said; *prabhu*—my dear Lord; *tomāra ājñā*—Your permission; *pāñā*—getting; *rājāke likhiluṅ*—have written a letter to the king; *āmi*—I; *vinaya kariyā*—with great humility.

TRANSLATION

Rāmānanda Rāya said, "My dear Lord, with Your permission I have already written a letter to the king with great humility.

TEXT 331

রাজা মোরে আজ্ঞা দিল নীলাচলে যাইতে ।
চলিবার উদ্‌যোগ আমি লাগিয়াছি করিতে ॥ ৩৩১ ॥

rājā more ājñā dila nīlācale yāite
calibāra udyoga āmi lāgiyāchi karite

SYNONYMS

rājā—the king; *more*—unto me; *ājñā dila*—has given an order; *nīlācale yāite*—to go to Jagannātha Purī; *calibāra*—to go; *udyoga*—arrangement; *āmi*—I; *lāgiyāchi*—began; *karite*—to do.

TRANSLATION

"The king has already given me an order to return to Jagannātha Purī, and I am making arrangements to do this."

TEXT 332

প্রভু কহে,—এথা মোর এ-নিমিত্তে আগমন।
তোমা লঞা নীলাচলে করিব গমন ॥ ৩৩২ ॥

prabhu kahe, ——ethā mora e-nimitte āgamana
tomā lañā nīlācale kariba gamana

SYNONYMS

prabhu kahe—Lord Śrī Caitanya Mahāprabhu said; *ethā*—here; *mora*—My; *e-nimitte*—for this reason; *āgamana*—coming back; *tomā lañā*—taking you; *nīlācale*—to Jagannātha Purī; *kariba*—I shall do; *gamana*—going.

TRANSLATION

Śrī Caitanya Mahāprabhu then said, "It is for this purpose alone that I have returned. I want to take you with Me to Jagannātha Purī."

TEXT 333

রায় কহে,—প্রভু, আগে চল নীলাচলে।
মোর সঙ্গে হাতী-ঘোড়া, সৈন্য-কোলাহলে ॥ ৩৩৩॥

rāya kahe, ——prabhu, āge cala nīlācale
mora saṅge hātī-ghoḍā, sainya-kolāhale

SYNONYMS

rāya kahe—Rāmānanda Rāya replied; *prabhu*—Lord; *āge cala*—You go ahead; *nīlācale*—to Jagannātha Purī; *mora saṅge*—with me; *hātī-ghoḍā*—elephants and horses; *sainya*—soldiers; *kolāhale*—tumultuous roaring.

TRANSLATION

Rāmānanda Rāya said, "My dear Lord, it is better that You proceed to Jagannātha Purī alone because with me there will be many horses, elephants and soldiers, all roaring tumultuously.

TEXT 334

দিন-দশে ইহা-সবার করি' সমাধান।
তোমার পাছে পাছে আমি করিব প্রয়াণ ॥ ৩৩৪ ॥

dina-daśe ihā-sabāra kari' samādhāna
tomāra pāche pāche āmi kariba prayāṇa

SYNONYMS

dina-daśe—within ten days; *ihā-sabāra*—of all of this; *kari' samādhāna*—making adjustment; *tomāra*—You; *pāche pāche*—following; *āmi*—I; *kariba*—shall do; *prayāṇa*—going.

TRANSLATION

"I shall make arrangements within ten days. Following You, I shall go to Nīlācala without delay."

TEXT 335

তবে মহাপ্রভু তাঁরে আসিতে আজ্ঞা দিয়া ।
নীলাচলে চলিলা প্রভু আনন্দিত হঞা ॥ ৩৩৫ ॥

tabe mahāprabhu tāṅre āsite ājñā diyā
nīlācale calilā prabhu ānandita hañā

SYNONYMS

tabe—then; *mahāprabhu*—Śrī Caitanya Mahāprabhu; *tāṅre*—unto him; *āsite*—to come; *ājñā diyā*—giving an order; *nīlācale*—to Jagannātha Purī; *calilā*—departed; *prabhu*—Lord Śrī Caitanya Mahāprabhu; *ānandita hañā*—with great pleasure.

TRANSLATION

Giving orders to Rāmānanda Rāya to come to Nīlācala, Śrī Caitanya Mahāprabhu departed for Jagannātha Purī with great pleasure.

TEXT 336

যেই পথে পূর্বে প্রভু কৈলা আগমন ।
সেই পথে চলিলা দেখি, সর্ব বৈষ্ণবগণ ॥ ৩৩৬ ॥

yei pathe pūrve prabhu kailā āgamana
sei pathe calilā dekhi, sarva vaiṣṇava-gaṇa

SYNONYMS

yei pathe—the path by which; *pūrve*—formerly; *prabhu*—Lord Śrī Caitanya Mahāprabhu; *kailā āgamana*—came; *sei pathe*—by that way; *calilā*—departed; *dekhi*—seeing; *sarva*—all; *vaiṣṇava-gaṇa*—Vaiṣṇavas.

TRANSLATION

Śrī Caitanya Mahāprabhu returned by the same road He formerly took to Vidyānagara, and all the Vaiṣṇavas along the way saw Him again.

TEXT 337

যাহাঁ যায়, লোক উঠে হরিধ্বনি করি'।
দেখি' আনন্দিত-মন হৈলা গৌরহরি ॥ ৩৩৭ ॥

yāhāṅ yāya, loka uṭhe hari-dhvani kari'
dekhi' ānandita-mana hailā gaurahari

SYNONYMS

yāhāṅ yāya—wherever He goes; *loka uṭhe*—people stand up; *hari-dhvani kari'*—vibrating the holy name of Hare Kṛṣṇa *mantra; dekhi'*—by seeing; *ānandita*—happy; *mana*—in mind; *hailā*—became; *gaura-hari*—Lord Śrī Caitanya Mahāprabhu.

TRANSLATION

Wherever Śrī Caitanya Mahāprabhu went, the holy name of Śrī Hari was vibrated. Seeing this, the Lord became very happy.

TEXT 338

আলালনাথে আসি' কৃষ্ণদাসে পাঠাইল।
নিত্যানন্দ-আদি নিজগণে বোলাইল ॥ ৩৩৮ ॥

ālālanāthe āsi' kṛṣṇadāse pāṭhāila
nityānanda-ādi nija-gaṇe bolāila

SYNONYMS

ālālanāthe—to the place known as Ālālanātha; *āsi'*—coming; *kṛṣṇa-dāse*—Kṛṣṇadāsa, His assistant; *pāṭhāila*—sent ahead; *nityānanda*—Lord Nityānanda; *ādi*—and others; *nija-gaṇe*—personal associates; *bolāila*—called for.

TRANSLATION

When the Lord reached Ālālanātha, He sent His assistant Kṛṣṇadāsa ahead to call for Nityānanda and other personal associates.

TEXT 339

প্রভুর আগমন শুনি' নিত্যানন্দ রায়।
উঠিয়া চলিলা, প্রেমে থেহ নাহি পায় ॥ ৩৩৯ ॥

prabhura āgamana śuni' nityānanda rāya
uṭhiyā calilā, preme theha nāhi pāya

SYNONYMS

prabhura—of Lord Śrī Caitanya Mahāprabhu; *āgamana*—arrival; *śuni'*—hearing; *nityānanda rāya*—Lord Nityānanda; *uṭhiyā calilā*—got up and started; *preme*—in great ecstasy; *theha*—patience; *nāhi pāya*—does not get.

TRANSLATION

As soon as Nityānanda received news of Śrī Caitanya Mahāprabhu's arrival, He immediately got up and started out to see Him. Indeed, He was very impatient in His great ecstasy.

TEXT 340

জগদানন্দ, দামোদর-পণ্ডিত, মুকুন্দ ।
নাচিয়া চলিলা, দেহে না ধরে আনন্দ ॥ ৩৪০ ॥

jagadānanda, dāmodara-paṇḍita, mukunda
nāciyā calilā, dehe nā dhare ānanda

SYNONYMS

jagadānanda—Jagadānanda; *dāmodara-paṇḍita*—Dāmodara Paṇḍita; *mukunda*—Mukunda; *nāciyā*—dancing; *calilā*—departed; *dehe*—the body; *nā dhare*—does not hold; *ānanda*—happiness.

TRANSLATION

Śrī Nityānanda Rāya, Jagadānanda, Dāmodara Paṇḍita and Mukunda all became ecstatic in their happiness, and dancing along the way, they went to meet the Lord.

TEXT 341

গোপীনাথাচার্য চলিলা আনন্দিত হঞা ।
প্রভুরে মিলিলা সবে পথে লাগ্ পাঞা ॥ ৩৪১ ॥

gopīnāthācārya calilā ānandita hañā
prabhure mililā sabe pathe lāg pāñā

SYNONYMS

gopīnātha-ācārya—Gopīnātha Ācārya; *calilā*—departed; *ānandita*—in happiness; *hañā*—being; *prabhure*—Lord Śrī Caitanya Mahāprabhu; *mililā*—met; *sabe*—all; *pathe*—along the way; *lāg*—contact; *pāñā*—getting.

TRANSLATION

Gopīnātha Ācārya also went in a very happy mood. They all went to meet the Lord, and they finally contacted Him on the way.

TEXT 342

প্রভু প্রেমাবেশে সবায় কৈল আলিঙ্গন।
প্রেমাবেশে সবে করে আনন্দ-ক্রন্দন ॥ ৩৪২ ॥

prabhu premāveśe sabāya kaila āliṅgana
premāveśe sabe kare ānanda-krandana

SYNONYMS

prabhu—Lord Śrī Caitanya Mahāprabhu; *prema-āveśe*—in ecstatic love; *sabāya*—all of them; *kaila āliṅgana*—embraced; *prema-āveśe*—in ecstatic love; *sabe kare*—all of them did; *ānanda-krandana*—crying in pleasure.

TRANSLATION

The Lord was also filled with ecstatic love, and He embraced them all. Out of their love, they began to cry with pleasure.

TEXT 343

সার্বভৌম ভট্টাচার্য আনন্দে চলিলা।
সমুদ্রের তীরে আসি' প্রভুরে মিলিলা ॥ ৩৪৩ ॥

sārvabhauma bhaṭṭācārya ānande calilā
samudrera tīre āsi' prabhure mililā

SYNONYMS

sārvabhauma bhaṭṭācārya—Sārvabhauma Bhaṭṭācārya; *ānande*—in pleasure; *calilā*—went; *samudrera tīre*—on the beach by the ocean; *āsi'*—coming; *prabhure mililā*—met the Lord.

TRANSLATION

Sārvabhauma Bhaṭṭācārya also went to see the Lord with great pleasure, and he met Him on the beach by the sea.

TEXT 344

সার্বভৌম মহাপ্রভুর পড়িলা চরণে।
প্রভু তাঁরে উঠাঞা কৈল আলিঙ্গনে ॥ ৩৪৪ ॥

sārvabhauma mahāprabhura paḍilā caraṇe
prabhu tāṅre uṭhāñā kaila āliṅgane

SYNONYMS

sārvabhauma—Sārvabhauma Bhaṭṭācārya; *mahāprabhura*—of Lord Śrī Caitanya Mahāprabhu; *paḍilā*—fell down; *caraṇe*—at the feet; *prabhu*—Śrī Caitanya Mahāprabhu; *tāṅre*—him; *uṭhāñā*—getting up; *kaila āliṅgane*—embraced.

TRANSLATION

Sārvabhauma Bhaṭṭācārya fell down at the lotus feet of the Lord, and the Lord pulled him up and embraced him.

TEXT 345

প্রেমাবেশে সার্বভৌম করিলা রোদনে ।
সবা-সঙ্গে আইলা প্রভু ঈশ্বর-দরশনে ॥ ৩৪৫ ॥

premāveśe sārvabhauma karilā rodane
sabā-saṅge āilā prabhu īśvara-daraśane

SYNONYMS

prema-āveśe—in ecstatic love; *sārvabhauma*—Sārvabhauma; *karilā rodane*—cried; *sabā-saṅge*—with all of them; *āilā*—came; *prabhu*—Śrī Caitanya Mahāprabhu; *īśvara-daraśane*—to see the Jagannātha temple.

TRANSLATION

Sārvabhauma Bhaṭṭācārya cried in great ecstatic love. Then, accompanied by them all, the Lord went to the temple of Jagannātha.

TEXT 346

জগন্নাথ-দরশন প্রেমাবেশে কৈল ।
কম্প-স্বেদ-পুলকাশ্রুতে শরীর ভাসিল ॥ ৩৪৬ ॥

jagannātha-daraśana premāveśe kaila
kampa-sveda-pulakāśrute śarīra bhāsila

SYNONYMS

jagannātha-daraśana—visiting Lord Jagannātha; *prema-āveśe*—in ecstatic love; *kaila*—made; *kampa*—trembling; *sveda*—perspiration; *pulaka*—jubilation; *aśrute*—with tears; *śarīra*—the whole body; *bhāsila*—was inundated.

TRANSLATION

Due to ecstatic love experienced upon visiting Lord Jagannātha, inundations of trembling, perspiration, tears and jubilation swept the body of Śrī Caitanya Mahāprabhu.

TEXT 347

বহু নৃত্যগীত কৈল প্রেমাবিষ্ট হঞা ।
পাণ্ডাপাল আইল সবে মালা-প্রসাদ লঞা ॥ ৩৪৭ ॥

bahu nṛtya-gīta kaila premāviṣṭa hañā
pāṇḍā-pāla āila sabe mālā-prasāda lañā

SYNONYMS

bahu—much; *nṛtya-gīta*—dancing and chanting; *kaila*—performed; *prema-āviṣṭa*—in ecstatic love; *hañā*—being; *pāṇḍā-pāla*—the priests and attendants; *āila*—came; *sabe*—all; *mālā-prasāda*—a garland and remnants of the food of Jagannātha; *lañā*—offering.

TRANSLATION

In ecstatic love Śrī Caitanya Mahāprabhu danced and chanted. At that time all the attendants and priests came to offer Him a garland and the remnants of Lord Jagannātha's food.

PURPORT

Those who are priests engaged in Lord Jagannātha's service are called *pāṇḍās* or *paṇḍitas,* and they are *brāhmaṇas.* The attendants who look after the temple's external affairs are called *pālas.* Both priests and attendants went together to see Śrī Caitanya Mahāprabhu.

TEXT 348

মালা-প্রসাদ পাঞা প্রভু সুস্থির হইলা ।
জগন্নাথের সেবক সব আনন্দে মিলিলা ॥ ৩৪৮ ॥

mālā-prasāda pāñā prabhu susthira ha-ilā
jagannāthera sevaka saba ānande mililā

SYNONYMS

mālā-prasāda—the garland and *prasāda; pāñā*—getting; *prabhu*—Śrī Caitanya Mahāprabhu; *su-sthira ha-ilā*—became patient; *jagannāthera*—of Lord Jagannātha; *sevaka*—servants; *saba*—all; *ānande mililā*—met Him in great pleasure.

TRANSLATION

Śrī Caitanya Mahāprabhu became patient after receiving the garland and prasāda of Lord Jagannātha. All the servants of Lord Jagannātha met Śrī Caitanya Mahāprabhu with great pleasure.

TEXT 349

কাশীমিশ্র আসি' প্রভুর পড়িলা চরণে ।
মান্য করি' প্রভু তাঁরে কৈল আলিঙ্গনে ॥ ৩৪৯ ॥

kāśī-miśra āsi' prabhura paḍilā caraṇe
mānya kari' prabhu tāṅre kaila āliṅgane

SYNONYMS

kāśī-miśra—Kāśī Miśra; *āsi'*—coming; *prabhura*—of the Lord; *paḍilā*—fell down; *caraṇe*—at the feet; *mānya kari'*—with great respect; *prabhu*—Lord Śrī Caitanya Mahāprabhu; *tāṅre*—unto him; *kaila*—did; *āliṅgane*—embracing.

TRANSLATION

Afterward, Kāśī Miśra came and fell down at the lotus feet of the Lord, and the Lord respectfully embraced him.

TEXT 350

প্রভু লঞা সার্বভৌম নিজ-ঘরে গেলা ।
মোর ঘরে ভিক্ষা বলি' নিমন্ত্রণ কৈলা ॥ ৩৫০ ॥

prabhu lañā sārvabhauma nija-ghare gelā
mora ghare bhikṣā bali' nimantraṇa kailā

SYNONYMS

prabhu lañā—taking Lord Śrī Caitanya Mahāprabhu; *sārvabhauma*—Sārvabhauma Bhaṭṭācārya; *nija-ghare*—to his own home; *gelā*—went; *mora*—my; *ghare*—at home; *bhikṣā*—luncheon; *bali'*—saying; *nimantraṇa kailā*—invited.

TRANSLATION

Sārvabhauma Bhaṭṭācārya then took the Lord with him to his home, saying, "Today's luncheon will be at my home." In this way he invited the Lord.

TEXT 351

দিব্য মহাপ্রসাদ অনেক আনাইল ।
পীঠা-পানা আদি জগন্নাথ যে খাইল ॥ ৩৫১ ॥

divya mahā-prasāda aneka ānāila
pīṭhā-pānā ādi jagannātha ye khāila

SYNONYMS

divya—very nice; *mahā-prasāda*—remnants of food from Jagannātha; *aneka*—various; *ānāila*—brought; *pīṭhā-pānā ādi*—such as cakes and condensed milk; *jagannātha*—Lord Jagannātha; *ye*—which; *khāila*—ate.

TRANSLATION

Sārvabhauma Bhaṭṭācārya brought various types of food remnants that had been left by Lord Jagannātha. He brought all kinds of cakes and condensed milk preparations.

TEXT 352

মধ্যাহ্ন করিলা প্রভু নিজগণ লঞা ।
সার্বভৌম-ঘরে ভিক্ষা করিলা আসিয়া ॥ ৩৫২ ॥

madhyāhna karilā prabhu nija-gaṇa lañā
sārvabhauma-ghare bhikṣā karilā āsiyā

SYNONYMS

madhyāhna—noon lunch; *karilā*—performed; *prabhu*—Śrī Caitanya Mahāprabhu; *nija-gaṇa lañā*—accompanied by associates; *sārvabhauma-ghare*—at the home of Sārvabhauma Bhaṭṭācārya; *bhikṣā*—lunch; *karilā*—performed; *āsiyā*—coming.

TRANSLATION

Accompanied by all His associates, Śrī Caitanya Mahāprabhu went to Sārvabhauma Bhaṭṭācārya's house and took His noon lunch there.

TEXT 353

ভিক্ষা করাঞা তাঁরে করাইল শয়ন ।
আপনে সার্বভৌম করে পাদসম্বাহন ॥ ৩৫৩ ॥

bhikṣā karāñā tāṅre karāila śayana
āpane sārvabhauma kare pāda-saṁvāhana

SYNONYMS

bhikṣā karāñā—after giving lunch; *tāṅre*—Him; *karāila*—made; *śayana*—lie down to rest; *āpane*—personally; *sārvabhauma*—Sārvabhauma Bhaṭṭācārya; *kare*—does; *pāda-saṁvāhana*—massaging the legs.

TRANSLATION

After offering food to Śrī Caitanya Mahāprabhu, Sārvabhauma Bhaṭṭācārya made Him lie down to rest, and he personally began to massage the legs of the Lord.

TEXT 354

প্রভু তাঁরে পাঠাইল ভোজন করিতে ।
সেই রাত্রি তাঁর ঘরে রহিলা তাঁর প্রীতে ॥ ৩৫৪ ॥

prabhu tāṅre pāṭhāila bhojana karite
sei rātri tāṅra ghare rahilā tāṅra prīte

SYNONYMS

prabhu—Śrī Caitanya Mahāprabhu; *tāṅre*—him; *pāṭhāila*—sent; *bhojana karite*—to take lunch; *sei rātri*—that night; *tāṅra ghare*—at his home; *rahilā*—remained; *tāṅra prīte*—just to satisfy him.

TRANSLATION

Śrī Caitanya Mahāprabhu then sent Sārvabhauma Bhaṭṭācārya to take his lunch, and the Lord remained that night in his home just to please him.

TEXT 355

সার্বভৌম-সঙ্গে আর লঞা নিজগণ ।
তীর্থযাত্রা-কথা কহি' কৈল জাগরণ ॥ ৩৫৫ ॥

sārvabhauma-saṅge āra lañā nija-gaṇa
tīrtha-yātrā-kathā kahi' kaila jāgaraṇa

SYNONYMS

sārvabhauma-saṅge—with Sārvabhauma Bhaṭṭācārya; *āra*—and; *lañā nija-gaṇa*—taking His own associates; *tīrtha-yātrā-kathā*—topics of the pilgrimage; *kahi'*—telling; *kaila*—did; *jāgaraṇa*—keeping the night.

TRANSLATION

Śrī Caitanya Mahāprabhu and His personal associates remained with Sārvabhauma Bhaṭṭācārya. They stayed awake the entire night hearing the narration of the Lord's pilgrimage.

TEXT 356

প্রভু কহে,—এত তীর্থ কৈলুঁ পর্যটন।
তোমা-সম বৈষ্ণব না দেখিলুঁ একজন ॥ ৩৫৬ ॥

prabhu kahe, ——eta tīrtha kailuṅ paryaṭana
tomā-sama vaiṣṇava nā dekhiluṅ eka-jana

SYNONYMS

prabhu kahe—the Lord said; *eta tīrtha*—to so many holy places; *kailuṅ paryaṭana*—I have traveled; *tomā-sama*—like you; *vaiṣṇava*—devotee; *nā*—not; *dekhiluṅ*—I could see; *eka-jana*—one man.

TRANSLATION

The Lord told Sārvabhauma Bhaṭṭācārya, "I have traveled to many holy places, but I could not find a Vaiṣṇava as good as you anywhere."

TEXT 357

এক রামানন্দ রায় বহু সুখ দিল।
ভট্ট কহে,—এই লাগি' মিলিতে কহিল ॥ ৩৫৭ ॥

eka rāmānanda rāya bahu sukha dila
bhaṭṭa kahe, ——ei lāgi' milite kahila

SYNONYMS

eka—one; *rāmānanda rāya*—Rāmānanda Rāya; *bahu sukha*—much pleasure; *dila*—gave; *bhaṭṭa kahe*—Sārvabhauma Bhaṭṭācārya replied; *ei lāgi'*—for this reason; *milite*—to meet; *kahila*—I requested.

TRANSLATION

Śrī Caitanya Mahāprabhu continued, "I received much pleasure from the talks of Rāmānanda Rāya." Bhaṭṭācārya replied, "For this reason I requested that You meet him."

PURPORT

In the *Śrī Caitanya-candrodaya* (eighth part) Śrī Caitanya Mahāprabhu said, "Sārvabhauma, I have traveled to many holy places, but I cannot find a Vaiṣṇava as good as you anywhere. However, I must admit that Rāmānanda Rāya is wonderful."

Sārvabhauma Bhaṭṭācārya replied, "Therefore, my Lord,I requested that You see him."

Śrī Caitanya Mahāprabhu then said, "There are, of course, many Vaiṣṇavas in these holy places, and most of them worship Lord Nārāyaṇa. Others, who are called Tattvavādīs, are also Lakṣmī-Nārāyaṇa worshipers, but they do not belong to the pure Vaiṣṇava cult. There are many worshipers of Lord Śiva, and there are also many atheists. Regardless, My dear Bhaṭṭācārya, I very much like Rāmānanda Rāya and his opinions."

TEXT 358

তীর্থযাত্রা-কথা এই কৈলুঁ সমাপন ।
সংক্ষেপে কহিলুঁ, বিস্তার না যায় বর্ণন ॥ ৩৫৮ ॥

tīrtha-yātrā-kathā ei kailuṅ samāpana
saṅkṣepe kahiluṅ, vistāra nā yāya varṇana

SYNONYMS

tīrtha-yātrā-kathā—topics of the pilgrimage; *ei*—these; *kailuṅ samāpana*—I have finished; *saṅkṣepe kahiluṅ*—I have described in brief; *vistāra*—expansively; *nā yāya varṇana*—it is not possible to describe.

TRANSLATION

Thus I have ended my narration about Śrī Caitanya Mahāprabhu's pilgrimage, describing it in brief. It cannot be described very broadly.

PURPORT

Śrīla Bhaktisiddhānta Sarasvatī Ṭhākura points out that in the seventy-fourth verse of this chapter it is stated that Śrī Caitanya Mahāprabhu visited the temple of Śiyālī-bhairavī, but actually at Śiyālī, Śrī Caitanya Mahāprabhu visited the temple of Śrī Bhū-varāha. Near Śiyālī and Cidambaram there is a temple known as Śrī Muṣṇam. In this temple there is a Deity of Śrī Bhū-varāha. In the jurisdiction of Cidambaram there is a district known as southern Ārkaṭa. The town of Śiyālī is in that district. There is a temple of Śrī Bhū-varāhadeva nearby, not Bhairavī-devī. This is Śrīla Bhaktisiddhānta Sarasvatī Ṭhākura's conclusion.

TEXT 359

অনন্ত চৈতন্যলীলা কহিতে না জানি ।
লোভে লজ্জা খাঞা তার করি টানাটানি ॥ ৩৫৯ ॥

ananta caitanya-līlā kahite nā jāni
lobhe lajjā khāñā tāra kari ṭānāṭāni

SYNONYMS

ananta—unlimited; *caitanya-līlā*—pastimes of Lord Caitanya; *kahite*—to speak; *nā jāni*—I do not know; *lobhe*—out of greed; *lajjā khāñā*—becoming shameless; *tāra*—of them; *kari*—I do; *ṭānāṭāni*—some attempt only.

TRANSLATION

The pastimes of Lord Caitanya are unlimited. No one can properly describe His activities, yet I make the attempt out of greed. This but reveals my shamelessness.

TEXT 360

প্রভুর তীর্থযাত্রা-কথা শুনে যেই জন ।
চৈতন্যচরণে পায় গাঢ় প্রেমধন ॥ ৩৬০ ॥

prabhura tīrtha-yātrā-kathā śune yei jana
caitanya-caraṇe pāya gāḍha prema-dhana

SYNONYMS

prabhura—of Lord Śrī Caitanya Mahāprabhu; *tīrtha-yātrā*—touring of sacred pilgrimages; *kathā*—topics about; *śune*—hears; *yei*—who; *jana*—person; *caitanya-caraṇe*—at the lotus feet of Śrī Caitanya Mahāprabhu; *pāya*—gets; *gāḍha*—deep; *prema-dhana*—riches of ecstatic love.

TRANSLATION

Whoever hears of Śrī Caitanya Mahāprabhu's pilgrimage to various holy places attains the riches of very deep ecstatic love.

PURPORT

Śrīla Bhaktisiddhānta Sarasvatī Ṭhākura remarks, "The impersonalists imagine some forms of the Absolute Truth through the direct perception of their senses. The impersonalists worship such imaginary forms, but neither *Śrīmad-Bhāgavatam* nor Śrī Caitanya Mahāprabhu accepts this sense gratificatory worship to be of any spiritual significance." The Māyāvādīs imagine themselves to be the Supreme. They imagine that the Supreme has no personal form and that all His forms are imaginary like the will-o'-the-wisp or a flower in the sky. Both Māyāvādīs and those who imagine forms of God are misguided. According to them, worship of the Deity or any form of the Lord is a result of the conditioned soul's illusion. However, Śrī Caitanya Mahāprabhu confirms the conclusion of *Śrīmad-Bhāgavatam* on the strength of His philosophy of *acintya-bhedābheda-tattva*. That philosophy holds that the Supreme Lord is simultaneously one with and different from His creation. That is to say, there is unity in diversity. In this way Śrī Caitanya Mahāprabhu proved the impotence of fruitive workers, speculative empiric philosophers and mystic *yogīs*. The realization of such men is simply a waste of time and energy.

To set the example, Śrī Caitanya Mahāprabhu personally visited temples in various holy places. Wherever He visited, He immediately exhibited His ecstatic love for the Supreme Personality of Godhead. When a Vaiṣṇava visits the temple of a demigod, his vision of that demigod is different from the vision of the impersonalists and Māyāvādīs. *Brahma-saṁhitā* supports this. A Vaiṣṇava's visit to the temple of Lord Śiva is different from a nondevotee's visit. The nondevotee considers the deity of Lord Śiva an imaginary form because he ultimately thinks that the Supreme Absolute Truth is void. However, a Vaiṣṇava sees Lord Śiva as being simultaneously one with and different from the Supreme Lord. In this regard, the example of milk and yogurt is given. Yogurt is actually nothing but milk, but at the same time it is not milk. It is simultaneously one with milk yet different from it. This is the philosophy of Śrī Caitanya Mahāprabhu, and it is confirmed by *Bhagavad-gītā:*

mayā tatam idaṁ sarvaṁ
jagad avyakta-mūrtinā
mat-sthāni sarva-bhūtāni
na cāhaṁ teṣv avasthitaḥ

"By Me, in My unmanifested form, this entire universe is pervaded. All beings are in Me, but I am not in them." (Bg. 9.4)

The Absolute Truth, God, is everything, but this does not mean that everything is God. For this reason Śrī Caitanya Mahāprabhu and His followers visited the temples of all the demigods, but they did not see them in the same way an impersonalist sees them. Everyone should follow in the footsteps of Śrī Caitanya Mahāprabhu and visit all temples. Sometimes mundane *sahajiyās* suppose that the *gopīs* visited the temple of Kātyāyanī in the same way mundane people visit the temple of Devī. However, the *gopīs* prayed to Kātyāyanī to grant them Kṛṣṇa as their husband. Mundaners visit the temple of Kātyāyanī to receive some material profit. That is the difference between a Vaiṣṇava's visit and a nondevotee's visit.

Not understanding the process of the disciplic succession, so-called logicians put forward the theory of henotheism (*pañcopāsanā*); that is, they believe that the worship of one god does not deny the existence of other gods. Such philosophical speculation is not accepted by Śrī Caitanya Mahāprabhu or by Vaiṣṇavas. Impersonalists may accept any number of deities, but Vaiṣṇavas only accept Kṛṣṇa as the Supreme and reject all others. Māyāvāda deity worship is certainly idolatry, and their imaginary deity worship has recently been transformed into Māyāvāda impersonalism. For want of Kṛṣṇa consciousness, people are victimized by the Māyāvāda philosophy, and consequently they sometimes become staunch atheists. However, Śrī Caitanya Mahāprabhu established the process of self-realization by His own personal behavior. As stated in *Caitanya-caritāmṛta:*

sthāvara-jaṅgama dekhe, nā dekhe tāra mūrti
sarvatra haya nija iṣṭa-deva-sphūrti

"The *mahā-bhāgavata,* the advanced devotee, certainly sees everything mobile and immobile, but he does not exactly see their forms. Rather, everywhere he sees the form of the Supreme Lord immediately manifest. Seeing the energy of the Supreme Personality of Godhead, the Vaiṣṇava immediately remembers the transcendental form of the Lord." (Cc. *Madhya* 8.274)

TEXT 361

চৈতন্যচরিত শুন শ্রদ্ধা-ভক্তি করি' ।
মাৎসর্য ছাড়িয়া মুখে বল 'হরি' 'হরি' ॥ ৩৬১ ॥

caitanya-carita śuna śraddhā-bhakti kari'
mātsarya chāḍiyā mukhe bala 'hari' 'hari'

SYNONYMS

caitanya-carita—the activities of Lord Śrī Caitanya Mahāprabhu; *śuna*—hear; *śraddhā*—faith; *bhakti*—devotion; *kari'*—accepting; *mātsarya*—envy; *chāḍiyā*—giving up; *mukhe*—by the mouth; *bala*—say; *hari hari*—the holy name of the Lord (Hari, Hari).

TRANSLATION

Please hear the transcendental pastimes of Lord Śrī Caitanya Mahāprabhu with faith and devotion. Giving up envy of the Lord, everyone chant the Lord's holy name, Hari.

TEXT 362

এই কলিকালে আর নাহি কোন ধর্ম।
বৈষ্ণব, বৈষ্ণবশাস্ত্র, এই কহে মর্ম ॥ ৩৬২ ॥

ei kali-kāle āra nāhi kona dharma
vaiṣṇava, vaiṣṇava-śāstra, ei kahe marma

SYNONYMS

ei kali-kāle—in this age of Kali; *āra*—other; *nāhi kona*—there is not any; *dharma*—religious principle; *vaiṣṇava*—devotee; *vaiṣṇava-śāstra*—devotional literature; *ei kahe marma*—this is the purport.

TRANSLATION

In this age of Kali, there are no genuine religious principles. There are only the Vaiṣṇava devotees and the Vaiṣṇava devotional scriptures. This is the sum and substance of everything.

PURPORT

One must have firm faith in the process of devotional service and the scriptures that support it. If one hears the activities of Śrī Caitanya Mahāprabhu with faith, he can be freed from his envious position. *Śrīmad-Bhāgavatam* is meant for such nonenvious persons (*nirmatsarāṇāṁ satām*). In this age a person should not envy Śrī Caitanya Mahāprabhu's movement but should chant the holy names of Hari and Kṛṣṇa, the *mahā-mantra*. That is the sum and substance of eternal religion, known as *sanātana-dharma*. The real Vaiṣṇava is a pure devotee and fully realized soul, and a Vaiṣṇava *śāstra* refers to *śruti*, or the *Vedas*, which are called *śabda-pramāṇa*, the evidence of transcendental sound. If one strictly follows the Vedic literature and chants the holy name of the Supreme Personality of Godhead, he will actually be situated in the transcendental disciplic succession. Those who want to attain life's ultimate goal must follow this principle. In *Śrīmad-Bhāgavatam* (11.19.17), it is said:

śrutiḥ pratyakṣam aitihyam
anumānaṁ catuṣṭayam
pramāṇeṣv anavasthānād
vikalpāt sa virajyate

"Vedic literature, direct perception, history and hypothesis are the four kinds of evidential proofs. Everyone should stick to these principles for the realization of the Absolute Truth."

TEXT 363

চৈতন্যচন্দ্রের লীলা—অগাধ, গম্ভীর ।
প্রবেশ করিতে নারি,- স্পর্শি রহি' তীর ॥ ৩৬৩ ॥

caitanya-candrera līlā——agādha, gambhīra
praveśa karite nāri, ——sparśi rahi' tīra

SYNONYMS

caitanya-candrera līlā—the pastimes of Lord Śrī Caitanya Mahāprabhu; *agādha*—unfathomable; *gambhīra*—deep; *praveśa karite*—to enter into; *nāri*—I am unable; *sparśi*—I touch; *rahi' tīra*—standing on the bank.

TRANSLATION

The pastimes of Śrī Caitanya Mahāprabhu are just like an unfathomable ocean. It is not possible for me to enter into them. Simply standing on the shore, I am but touching the water.

TEXT 364

চৈতন্যচরিত শ্রদ্ধায় শুনে যেই জন ।
যতেক বিচারে, তত পায় প্রেমধন ॥ ৩৬৪ ॥

caitanya-caritra śraddhāya śune yei jana
yateka vicāre, tata pāya prema-dhana

SYNONYMS

caitanya-carita—the pastimes of Śrī Caitanya Mahāprabhu; *śraddhāya*—with faith; *śune*—hears; *yei jana*—which person; *yateka vicāre*—as far as he analytically studies; *tata*—so far; *pāya*—he gets; *prema-dhana*—the riches of ecstatic love.

TRANSLATION

Whoever hears the pastimes of Śrī Caitanya Mahāprabhu with faith, analytically studying them, attains the ecstatic riches of love of Godhead.

TEXT 365

শ্রীরূপ-রঘুনাথ-পদে যার আশ ।
চৈতন্যচরিতামৃত কহে কৃষ্ণদাস ॥ ৩৬৫ ॥

śrī-rūpa-raghunātha pade yāra āśa
caitanya-caritāmṛta kahe kṛṣṇadāsa

SYNONYMS

śrī-rūpa—Śrīla Rūpa Gosvāmī; *raghunātha*—Śrīla Raghunātha dāsa Gosvāmī; *pade*—at the lotus feet; *yāra*—whose; *āśa*—expectation; *caitanya-caritāmṛta*—the book named *Caitanya-caritāmṛta*; *kahe*—describes; *kṛṣṇa-dāsa*—Śrīla Kṛṣṇadāsa Kavirāja Gosvāmī.

TRANSLATION

Praying at the lotus feet of Śrī Rūpa and Śrī Raghunātha and always desiring their mercy, I, Kṛṣṇadāsa, narrate Śrī Caitanya-caritāmṛta, following in their footsteps.

PURPORT

As usual the author concludes the chapter by reciting the names of Śrī Rūpa and Raghunātha and reinstating himself at their lotus feet.

Thus end the Bhaktivedanta purports to the Śrī Caitanya-caritāmṛta, Madhya-līlā, *Ninth Chapter, describing Śrī Caitanya Mahāprabhu's travels to many holy places in South India.*

CHAPTER 10

The Lord's Return to Jagannātha Purī

While Śrī Caitanya Mahāprabhu was traveling in South India, Sārvabhauma Bhaṭṭācārya had many talks with King Pratāparudra. When Mahārāja Pratāparudra requested the Bhaṭṭācārya to arrange an interview with the Lord, Bhaṭṭācārya assured him that he would try to do so as soon as Caitanya Mahāprabhu returned from South India. When the Lord returned to Jagannātha Purī from His South Indian tour, He lived at the home of Kāśī Miśra. Sārvabhauma Bhaṭṭācārya introduced many Vaiṣṇavas to Śrī Caitanya Mahāprabhu after His return. The father of Rāmānanda Rāya, Bhavānanda Rāya, offered another son named Vāṇīnātha Paṭṭanāyaka for the Lord's service. Śrī Caitanya Mahāprabhu informed His associates about the pollution of Kṛṣṇadāsa brought about by his association with the Bhaṭṭathāris, and thus the Lord proposed to give him leave. Nityānanda Prabhu sent Kṛṣṇadāsa to Bengal to inform the Navadvīpa devotees about the Lord's return to Jagannātha Purī. All the devotees of Navadvīpa thus began arranging to come to Jagannātha Purī. At this time Paramānanda Purī was at Navadvīpa, and immediately upon hearing news of the Lord's return, he started for Jagannātha Purī accompanied by a *brāhmaṇa* named Kamalākānta. Puruṣottama Bhaṭṭācārya, a resident of Navadvīpa, was educated at Vārāṇasī. He accepted the renounced order from Caitanyānanda, but he himself took the name of Svarūpa. Thus he arrived at the lotus feet of Śrī Caitanya Mahāprabhu. After the demise of Śrī Īśvara Purī, his disciple Govinda, following his instructions, went to see Caitanya Mahāprabhu. Due to his relationship with Keśava Bhāratī, Brahmānanda Bhāratī was also respectfully received by Śrī Caitanya Mahāprabhu. When he arrived at Jagannātha Purī, he was advised to give up the deerskin clothing he wore. When Brahmānanda understood Śrī Caitanya Mahāprabhu correctly, he accepted Him as Kṛṣṇa himself. However, when Sārvabhauma Bhaṭṭācārya addressed Śrī Caitanya Mahāprabhu as Kṛṣṇa, the Lord immediately protested. In the meantime, Kāśīśvara Gosvāmī also came to see Caitanya Mahāprabhu. In this chapter, devotees from many different areas come to see Caitanya Mahāprabhu, and they are exactly like many rivers that come from many places to finally flow into the sea.

TEXT 1

তং বন্দে গৌরজলদং স্বস্য যো দর্শনামৃতৈঃ।
বিচ্ছেদাবগ্রহম্লান-ভক্তশস্যান্যজীবয়ৎ ॥ ১ ॥

taṁ vande gaura-jaladaṁ
svasya yo darśanāmṛtaiḥ
vicchedāvagraha-mlāna-
bhakta-śasyāny ajīvayat

SYNONYMS

tam—unto Him; *vande*—I offer my respectful obeisances; *gaura*—Śrī Caitanya Mahāprabhu; *jala-dam*—rain cloud; *svasya*—of Himself; *yaḥ*—He who; *darśana-amṛtaiḥ*—by the nectar of the audience; *viccheda*—because of separation; *avagraha*—scarcity of rain; *mlāna*—morose, dried up; *bhakta*—devotees; *śasyāni*—food grains; *ajīvayat*—saved.

TRANSLATION

I offer my respectful obeisances unto Lord Śrī Caitanya Mahāprabhu, who is compared to a cloud that pours water on fields of grain, which are like devotees suffering due to a shortage of rain. Separation from Śrī Caitanya Mahāprabhu is like a drought, but when the Lord returns, His presence is like a nectarean rain that falls on all the grains and saves them from perishing.

TEXT 2

জয় জয় শ্রীচৈতন্য জয় নিত্যানন্দ ।
জয়াদ্বৈতচন্দ্র জয় গৌরভক্তবৃন্দ ॥ ২ ॥

jaya jaya śrī-caitanya jaya nityānanda
jayādvaita-candra jaya gaura-bhakta-vṛnda

SYNONYMS

jaya jaya—all glories; *śrī-caitanya*—to Lord Śrī Caitanya Mahāprabhu; *jaya*—all glories; *nityānanda*—to Nityānanda Prabhu; *jaya*—all glories; *advaita-candra*—to Advaita Ācārya; *jaya*—all glories; *gaura-bhakta-vṛndra*—to all the devotees of Śrī Caitanya Mahāprabhu.

TRANSLATION

All glories to Lord Caitanya. All glories to Nityānanda. All glories to Advaitacandra. And all glories to all the devotees of Lord Caitanya.

TEXT 3

পূর্বে যবে মহাপ্রভু চলিলা দক্ষিণে ।
প্রতাপরুদ্র রাজা তবে বোলাইল সার্বভৌমে ॥ ৩ ॥

pūrve yabe mahāprabhu calilā dakṣiṇe
pratāparudra rājā tabe bolāila sārvabhaume

SYNONYMS

pūrve—formerly; *yabe*—when; *mahāprabhu*—Śrī Caitanya Mahāprabhu; *calilā*—departed; *dakṣiṇe*—for His South Indian tour; *pratāparudra*—Pratāparudra; *rājā*—the King; *tabe*—at that time; *bolāila*—called for; *sārvabhaume*—Sārvabhauma Bhaṭṭācārya.

TRANSLATION

When Śrī Caitanya Mahāprabhu departed for South India, King Pratāparudra called Sārvabhauma Bhaṭṭācārya to his palace.

TEXT 4

বসিতে আসন দিল করি' নমস্কারে ।
মহাপ্রভুর বার্তা তবে পুছিল তাঁহারে ॥ ৪ ॥

vasite āsana dila kari' namaskāre
mahāprabhura vārtā tabe puchila tāṅhāre

SYNONYMS

vasite—to sit; *āsana*—sitting place; *dila*—offered; *kari'*—doing; *namaskāre*—obeisances; *mahāprabhura*—of Śrī Caitanya Mahāprabhu; *vārtā*—news; *tabe*—at that time; *puchila*—inquired; *tāṅhāre*—from him.

TRANSLATION

When Sārvabhauma Bhaṭṭācārya met with the King, the King offered him a seat with all respects and inquired about news of Śrī Caitanya Mahāprabhu.

TEXT 5

শুনিলাঙ তোমার ঘরে এক মহাশয় ।
গৌড় হইতে আইলা, তেঁহো মহা-কৃপাময় ॥ ৫ ॥

śunilāṅa tomāra ghare eka mahāśaya
gauḍa ha-ite āilā, teṅho mahā-kṛpāmaya

SYNONYMS

śunilāṅa—I have heard; *tomāra*—your; *ghare*—at home; *eka*—one; *mahāśaya*—great personality; *gauḍa ha-ite*—from Bengal; *āilā*—has come; *teṅho*—He; *mahā-kṛpā-maya*—very merciful.

TRANSLATION

The King said to the Bhaṭṭācārya, "I have heard that one great personality has come from Bengal and is staying at your home. I have also heard that He is very, very merciful.

TEXT 6

তোমারে বহু কৃপা কৈলা, কহে সর্বজন।
কৃপা করি' করাহ মোরে তাঁহার দর্শন ॥ ৬ ॥

tomāre bahu kṛpā kailā, kahe sarva-jana
kṛpā kari' karāha more tāṅhāra darśana

SYNONYMS

tomāre—unto you; *bahu kṛpā*—great mercy; *kailā*—showed; *kahe*—says; *sarva-jana*—everyone; *kṛpā kari'*—being merciful; *karāha*—arrange; *more*—for me; *tāṅhāra*—His; *darśana*—interview.

TRANSLATION

"I have also heard that this great personality has shown you great favor. At any rate, this is what I hear from many different people. Now, being merciful upon me, you should do me the favor of arranging an interview."

TEXT 7

ভট্ট কহে,—যে শুনিলা সব সত্য হয়।
তাঁর দর্শন তোমার ঘটন না হয় ॥ ৭ ॥

bhaṭṭa kahe,——ye śunilā saba satya haya
tāṅra darśana tomāra ghaṭana nā haya

SYNONYMS

bhaṭṭa kahe—Bhaṭṭācārya replied; *ye*—what; *śunilā*—you have heard; *saba*—all; *satya*—true; *haya*—is; *tāṅra darśana*—His interview; *tomāra*—of you; *ghaṭana*—happening; *nā haya*—is not.

TRANSLATION

The Bhaṭṭācārya replied, "All that you have heard is true, but as far as an interview is concerned, it is very difficult to arrange.

TEXT 8

বিরক্ত সন্ন্যাসী তেঁহো রহেন নির্জনে ।
স্বপ্নেহ না করেন তেঁহো রাজদরশনে ॥ ৮ ॥

virakta sannyāsī teṅho rahena nirjane
svapneha nā karena teṅho rāja-daraśane

SYNONYMS

virakta—detached; *sannyāsī*—in the renounced order; *teṅho*—He; *rahena*—keeps Himself; *nirjane*—in a solitary place; *svapneha*—even in dreams; *nā*—does not; *karena*—do; *teṅho*—he; *rāja-daraśane*—interview with a king.

TRANSLATION

"Śrī Caitanya Mahāprabhu is in the renounced order and is very much detached from worldly affairs. He stays in solitary places, and even in dreams He does not grant interviews to a king.

TEXT 9

তথাপি প্রকারে তোমা করাইতাম দরশন ।
সম্প্রতি করিলা তেঁহো দক্ষিণ গমন ॥ ৯ ॥

tathāpi prakāre tomā karāitāma daraśana
samprati karilā teṅho dakṣiṇa gamana

SYNONYMS

tathāpi—yet; *prakāre*—somehow or other; *tomā*—you; *karāitāma*—I would have arranged; *daraśana*—interview; *samprati*—recently; *karilā*—has done; *teṅho*—He; *dakṣiṇa*—to the southern part of India; *gamana*—departure.

TRANSLATION

"Still, I would have tried to arrange your interview, but He has recently left to tour South India."

TEXT 10

রাজা কহে,—জগন্নাথ ছাড়ি' কেনে গেলা ।
ভট্ট কহে,—মহান্তের এই এক লীলা ॥ ১০ ॥

rājā kahe, ——jagannātha chāḍi' kene gelā
bhaṭṭa kahe, ——mahāntera ei eka līlā

SYNONYMS

rājā kahe—the King said; *jagannātha chāḍi'*—leaving the palace of Lord Jagannātha; *kene gelā*—why did He leave; *bhaṭṭa kahe*—Sārvabhauma Bhaṭṭācārya replied; *mahāntera*—of a great person; *ei*—this; *eka*—one; *līlā*—pastime.

TRANSLATION

The King asked, "Why has He left Jagannātha Purī?" Bhaṭṭācārya replied, "Such are the pastimes of a great personality.

TEXT 11

তীর্থ পবিত্র করিতে করে তীর্থভ্রমণ ।
সেই ছলে নিস্তারয়ে সাংসারিক জন ॥ ১১ ॥

tīrtha pavitra karite kare tīrtha-bhramaṇa
sei chale nistāraye sāṁsārika jana

SYNONYMS

tīrtha—holy places; *pavitra karite*—to purify; *kare*—does; *tīrtha-bhramaṇa*—touring in places of pilgrimage; *sei chale*—on that plea; *nistāraye*—delivers; *sāṁsārika*—conditioned; *jana*—souls.

TRANSLATION

"Great saints go to holy places of pilgrimage in order to purify them. For that reason Caitanya Mahāprabhu is visiting many tīrthas and delivering many, many conditioned souls.

TEXT 12

ভবদ্বিধা ভাগবতাস্তীর্থীভূতাঃ স্বয়ং বিভো ।
তীর্থীকুর্বন্তি তীর্থানি স্বান্তঃস্থেন গদাভৃতা ॥ ১২ ॥

bhavad-vidhā bhāgavatās
tīrthī-bhūtāḥ svayaṁ vibho
tīrthī-kurvanti tīrthāni
svāntaḥ-sthena gadābhṛtā

SYNONYMS

bhavat—your good self; *vidhāḥ*—like; *bhāgavatāḥ*—devotees; *tīrthī*—as holy places of pilgrimage; *bhūtāḥ*—existing; *svayam*—themselves; *vibho*—O almighty one; *tīrthī-kurvanti*—make into holy places of pilgrimage; *tīrthāni*—the holy places; *sva-antaḥ-sthena*—being situated in their hearts; *gadā-bhṛtā*—by the Personality of Godhead.

TRANSLATION

" 'Saints of your caliber are themselves places of pilgrimage. Because of their purity, they are constant companions of the Lord, and therefore they can purify even the places of pilgrimage.'

PURPORT

This verse spoken by Mahārāja Yudhiṣṭhira to Vidura in the *Śrīmad-Bhāgavatam* (1.13.10) is also quoted in the *Ādi-līlā* (1.63).

TEXT 13

বৈষ্ণবের এই হয় এক স্বভাব নিশ্চল ।
তেঁহো জীব নহেন, হন স্বতন্ত্র ঈশ্বর ॥ ১৩ ॥

vaiṣṇavera ei haya eka svabhāva niścala
teṅho jīva nahena, hana svatantra īśvara

SYNONYMS

vaiṣṇavera—of great devotees; *ei*—this; *haya*—is; *eka*—one; *sva-bhāva*—nature; *niścala*—unflinching; *teṅho*—he; *jīva*—conditioned soul; *nahena*—is not; *hana*—is; *svatantra*—independent; *īśvara*—controller.

TRANSLATION

"A Vaiṣṇava travels to places of pilgrimage to purify them and reclaim fallen conditioned souls. This is one of the duties of a Vaiṣṇava. Actually, Śrī Caitanya Mahāprabhu is not a living entity but the Supreme Personality of Godhead Himself. Consequently, He is a fully independent controller, yet in His position as a devotee, He carries out the activities of a devotee."

PURPORT

Śrīla Bhaktisiddhānta Sarasvatī Ṭhākura points out that because there are many permanent residents in holy places who do not precisely follow the rules and regulations governing living in a sacred place, exalted devotees have to go to these places to reclaim them. This is the business of a Vaiṣṇava. A Vaiṣṇava is unhappy to see others materially enmeshed. Although Śrī Caitanya Mahāprabhu is the worshipable Deity of all Vaiṣṇavas, the activities of a Vaiṣṇava were taught by Him. Nonetheless, He is the complete and independent Supreme Personality of

Godhead. He is *pūrṇaḥ śuddho nitya-muktaḥ*. He is complete, completely uncontaminated and eternal. He is *sanātana*, for He has no beginning or end.

TEXT 14

রাজা কহে,—তাঁরে তুমি যাইতে কেনে দিলে।
পায় পড়ি' যত্ন করি' কেনে না রাখিলে ॥ ১৪ ॥

rājā kahe, —tāṅre tumi yāite kene dile
pāya paḍi' yatna kari' kene nā rākhile

SYNONYMS

rājā kahe—the King said; *tāṅre*—Him; *tumi*—you; *yāite*—to go; *kene*—why; *dile*—allowed; *pāya*—at His lotus feet; *paḍi'*—falling; *yatna kari'*—endeavoring very much; *kene*—why; *nā*—not; *rākhile*—kept.

TRANSLATION

Upon hearing this, the King replied, "Why did you allow Him to leave? Why didn't you fall at His lotus feet and keep Him here?"

TEXT 15

ভট্টাচার্য কহে,—তেঁহো স্বয়ং ঈশ্বর স্বতন্ত্র।
সাক্ষাৎ শ্রীকৃষ্ণ, তেঁহো নহে পরতন্ত্র ॥ ১৫ ॥

bhaṭṭācārya kahe, —teṅho svayaṁ īśvara svatantra
sākṣāt śrī-kṛṣṇa, teṅho nahe para-tantra

SYNONYMS

bhaṭṭācārya kahe—Sārvabhauma replied; *teṅho*—He; *svayam*—personally; *īśvara*—the Supreme Personality of Godhead; *svatantra*—independent; *sākṣāt*—directly; *śrī-kṛṣṇa*—Lord Kṛṣṇa; *teṅho*—He; *nahe*—is not; *para-tantra*—dependent on anyone.

TRANSLATION

Sārvabhauma Bhaṭṭācārya replied, "Śrī Caitanya Mahāprabhu is the Supreme Personality of Godhead Himself and is completely independent. Being Lord Kṛṣṇa Himself, He is not dependent on anyone.

TEXT 16

তথাপি রাখিতে তাঁরে বহু যত্ন কৈলুঁ।
ঈশ্বরের স্বতন্ত্র ইচ্ছা, রাখিতে নারিলুঁ ॥ ১৬ ॥

tathāpi rākhite tāṅre bahu yatna kailuṅ
īśvarera svatantra icchā, rākhite nāriluṅ

SYNONYMS

tathāpi—still; *rākhite*—to keep; *tāṅre*—Him; *bahu*—various; *yatna*—endeavors; *kailuṅ*—I made; *īśvarera*—of the Supreme Personality of Godhead; *svatantra*—independent; *icchā*—desire; *rākhite*—to keep; *nāriluṅ*—I was unable.

TRANSLATION

"Still, I endeavored very hard to keep Him here, but because He is the Supreme Personality of Godhead and completely independent, I was not successful."

TEXT 17

রাজা কহে,—ভট্ট তুমি বিজ্ঞশিরোমণি ।
তুমি তাঁরে 'কৃষ্ণ' কহ, তাতে সত্য মানি ॥ ১৭ ॥

rājā kahe, ——bhaṭṭa tumi vijña-śiromaṇi
tumi tāṅre 'kṛṣṇa' kaha, tāte satya māni

SYNONYMS

rājā kahe—the King said; *bhaṭṭa*—Sārvabhauma Bhaṭṭācārya; *tumi*—you; *vijña-śiromaṇi*—the most experienced learned scholar; *tumi*—you; *tāṅre*—Him; *kṛṣṇa kaha*—address as Lord Kṛṣṇa; *tāte*—your statement; *satya māni*—I accept as true.

TRANSLATION

The King said, "Bhaṭṭācārya, you are the most learned and experienced person I know. Therefore when you address Śrī Caitanya Mahāprabhu as Lord Kṛṣṇa, I accept this as the truth.

PURPORT

This is the way to advance in spiritual science. One must accept the words of an *ācārya,* a bona fide spiritual master, to clear the path for spiritual advancement. This is the secret of success. However, one's guide must be a spiritual master who is actually an unalloyed devotee strictly following the instructions of the previous *ācārya* without deviation. Whatever the spiritual master says must be accepted by the disciple. Only then is success certain. This is the Vedic system.

Sārvabhauma Bhaṭṭācārya was a *brāhmaṇa* and a realized soul, whereas Pratāparudra was a *kṣatriya. Kṣatriya* kings used to obey very faithfully the orders of learned *brāhmaṇas* and saintly persons, and in this way they would rule their country. Similarly, *vaiśyas* used to follow the king's orders, and the *śūdras* used to serve the three higher castes. In this way the *brāhmaṇas, kṣatriyas, vaiśyas* and *śūdras* used to live cooperatively performing their respective duties. Consequently society was peaceful, and people were able to discharge the duties of Kṛṣṇa consciousness. Thus they were happy in this life and able to return home, back to Godhead.

TEXT 18

পুনরপি ইহাঁ তাঁর হৈলে আগমন ।
একবার দেখি' করি সফল নয়ন ॥ ১৮ ॥

punarapi ihāṅ tāṅra haile āgamana
eka-bāra dekhi' kari saphala nayana

SYNONYMS

punarapi—again; *ihāṅ*—here; *tāṅra*—His; *haile*—when there is; *āgamana*—arrival; *eka-bāra*—once; *dekhi'*—seeing; *kari*—I make; *sa-phala*—fruitful; *nayana*—my eyes.

TRANSLATION

"When Śrī Caitanya Mahāprabhu returns again, I wish to see Him just once in order to make my eyes perfect."

TEXT 19

ভট্টাচার্য কহে,—তেঁহো আসিবে অল্পকালে ।
রহিতে তাঁরে এক স্থান চাহিয়ে বিরলে ॥ ১৯ ॥

bhaṭṭācārya kahe, —teṅho āsibe alpa-kāle
rahite tāṅre eka sthāna cāhiye virale

SYNONYMS

bhaṭṭācārya kahe—Sārvabhauma Bhaṭṭācārya replied; *teṅho*—He; *āsibe*—will come; *alpa-kāle*—very soon; *rahite*—to keep; *tāṅre*—Him; *eka*—one; *sthāna*—place; *cāhiye*—I want; *virale*—secluded.

TRANSLATION

Sārvabhauma Bhaṭṭācārya replied, "His Holiness Lord Śrī Caitanya Mahāprabhu will return very soon. I wish to have a nice place ready for Him, a place solitary and peaceful.

TEXT 20

ঠাকুরের নিকট, আর হইবে নির্জনে ।
এমত নির্ণয় করি' দেহ' এক স্থানে ॥ ২০ ॥

ṭhākurera nikaṭa, āra ha-ibe nirjane
e-mata nirṇaya kari' deha' eka sthāne

SYNONYMS

ṭhākurera nikaṭa—near the place of Lord Jagannātha; *āra*—also; *ha-ibe*—must be; *nirjane*—secluded; *e-mata*—in this way; *nirṇaya kari'*—considering carefully; *deha'*—please give; *eka sthāne*—one place.

TRANSLATION

"Lord Caitanya's residence should be very secluded and also near the temple of Jagannātha. Please consider this proposal and give me a nice place for Him."

TEXT 21

রাজা কহে,—ঐছে কাশীমিশ্রের ভবন ।
ঠাকুরের নিকট, হয় পরম নির্জন ॥ ২১ ॥

rājā kahe, —aiche kāśī-miśrera bhavana
ṭhākurera nikaṭa, haya parama nirjana

SYNONYMS

rājā kahe—the King replied; *aiche*—exactly like that; *kāśī-miśrera bhavana*—the house of Kāśī Miśra; *ṭhākurera nikaṭa*—near Lord Jagannātha; *haya*—is; *parama*—very; *nirjana*—secluded.

TRANSLATION

The King replied, "Kāśī Miśra's house is exactly what you require. It is near the temple and is very secluded, calm and quiet."

TEXT 22

এত কহি' রাজা রহে উৎকণ্ঠিত হঞা ।
ভট্টাচার্য কাশীমিশ্রে কহিল আসিয়া ॥ ২২ ॥

eta kahi' rājā rahe utkaṇṭhita hañā
bhaṭṭācārya kāśī-miśre kahila āsiyā

SYNONYMS

eta kahi'—saying this; *rājā*—the King; *rahe*—remained; *utkaṇṭhita*—very anxious; *hañā*—being; *bhaṭṭācārya*—Sārvabhauma Bhaṭṭācārya; *kāśī-miśre*—unto Kāśī Miśra; *kahila*—said; *āsiyā*—coming.

TRANSLATION

After saying this, the King became very anxious for the Lord to return. Sārvabhauma Bhaṭṭācārya then went to Kāśī Miśra to convey the King's desire.

TEXT 23

কাশীমিশ্র কহে,—আমি বড় ভাগ্যবান্।
মোর গৃহে 'প্রভুপাদের' হবে অবস্থান ॥ ২৩ ॥

kāśī-miśra kahe, —āmi baḍa bhāgyavān
mora gṛhe 'prabhu-pādera' habe avasthāna

SYNONYMS

kāśī-miśra kahe—Kāśī Miśra said; *āmi*—I; *baḍa*—very much; *bhāgyavān*—fortunate; *mora gṛhe*—in my home; *prabhu-pādera*—of the Lord of the *prabhus*; *habe*—there will be; *avasthāna*—staying.

TRANSLATION

When Kāśī Miśra heard the proposal, he said, "I am very fortunate that Śrī Caitanya Mahāprabhu, the Lord of all prabhus, will stay at my home."

PURPORT

In this verse the word Prabhupāda, referring to Śrī Caitanya Mahāprabhu, is significant. Regarding this, Śrīla Bhaktisiddhānta Sarasvatī Gosvāmī Prabhupāda comments, "Śrī Caitanya Mahāprabhu is the Supreme Personality of Godhead Himself, Śrī Kṛṣṇa, and all His servants address Him as Prabhupāda. This means that there are many *prabhus* taking shelter under His lotus feet." The pure Vaiṣṇava is addressed as *prabhu,* and this address is an etiquette observed between Vaiṣṇavas. When many *prabhus* remain under the shelter of the lotus feet of another *prabhu,* the address Prabhupāda is given. Śrī Nityānanda Prabhu and Śrī Advaita Prabhu are also addressed as Prabhupāda. Śrī Caitanya Mahāprabhu, Śrī Advaita Prabhu and Śrī Nityānanda Prabhu are all *viṣṇu-tattva,* the Supreme Personality of Godhead, Lord Viṣṇu. Therefore all living entities are under Their lotus feet. Lord Viṣṇu is the eternal Lord of everyone, and the representative of Lord Viṣṇu is the Lord's confidential servant. Such a person acts as the spiritual master for neophyte Vaiṣṇavas;

therefore the spiritual master is as respectable as Śrī Kṛṣṇa Caitanya or Lord Viṣṇu Himself. For this reason the spiritual master is addressed as Oṁ Viṣṇupāda or Prabhupāda. The *ācārya,* the spiritual master, is generally respected by others as Śrīpāda, and the initiated Vaiṣṇavas are addressed as Prabhu. Prabhu, Prabhupāda and Viṣṇupāda are described in revealed scriptures like *Śrīmad-Bhāgavatam, Caitanya-caritāmṛta* and *Caitanya-bhāgavata.* In this regard, these scriptures present evidence accepted by unalloyed devotees.

The *prākṛta-sahajiyās* are not even worthy of being called Vaiṣṇavas. They think that only caste *gosvāmīs* should be called Prabhupāda. Such ignorant *sahajiyās* call themselves *vaiṣṇava-dāsa-anudāsa,* which means the servant of the servant of the Vaiṣṇavas. However, they are opposed to addressing a pure Vaiṣṇava as Prabhupāda. In other words, they are envious of a bona fide spiritual master who is addressed as Prabhupāda, and they commit offenses by considering a bona fide spiritual master an ordinary human being or a member of a certain caste. Śrīla Bhaktisiddhānta Sarasvatī Ṭhākura describes such *sahajiyās* as most unfortunate. Because of their misconceptions, they fall into a hellish condition.

TEXT 24

এইমত পুরুষোত্তমবাসী যত জন ।
প্রভুকে মিলিতে সবার উৎকণ্ঠিত মন ॥ ২৪ ॥

ei-mata puruṣottama-vāsī yata jana
prabhuke milite sabāra utkaṇṭhita mana

SYNONYMS

ei-mata—in this way; *puruṣottama-vāsī*—the residents of Jagannātha Purī; *yata*—all; *jana*—persons; *prabhuke*—Lord Śrī Caitanya Mahāprabhu; *milite*—to meet; *sabāra*—of everyone; *utkaṇṭhita*—anxious; *mana*—mind.

TRANSLATION

Thus all the residents of Jagannātha Purī, which is also known as Puruṣottama, were very anxious to meet Śrī Caitanya Mahāprabhu again.

TEXT 25

সর্বলোকের উৎকণ্ঠা যবে অত্যন্ত বাড়িল ।
মহাপ্রভু দক্ষিণ হৈতে তবহি আইল ॥ ২৫ ॥

sarva-lokera utkaṇṭhā yabe atyanta bāḍila
mahāprabhu dakṣiṇa haite tabahi āila

SYNONYMS

sarva-lokera—of all people; *utkaṇṭhā*—anxieties; *yabe*—when; *atyanta*—very much; *bāḍila*—increased; *mahāprabhu*—Śrī Caitanya Mahāprabhu; *dakṣiṇa haite*—from South India; *tabahi*—at that very time; *āila*—returned.

TRANSLATION

While all the residents of Jagannātha Purī were thus anxious, the Lord returned from South India.

TEXT 26

শুনি' আনন্দিত হৈল সবাকার মন ।
সবে আসি' সার্ব্বভৌমে কৈল নিবেদন ॥ ২৬ ॥

śuni' ānandita haila sabākāra mana
sabe āsi' sārvabhaume kaila nivedana

SYNONYMS

śuni'—hearing; *ānandita*—happy; *haila*—were; *sabākāra*—of everyone; *mana*—the minds; *sabe āsi'*—everyone coming; *sārvabhaume*—unto Sārvabhauma Bhaṭṭācārya; *kaila*—did; *nivedana*—submission.

TRANSLATION

Hearing of the Lord's return, everyone became very happy, and they all went to Sārvabhauma Bhaṭṭācārya and spoke to him as follows.

TEXT 27

প্রভুর সহিত আমা-সবার করাহ মিলন ।
তোমার প্রসাদে পাই প্রভুর চরণ ॥ ২৭ ॥

prabhura sahita āmā-sabāra karāha milana
tomāra prasāde pāi prabhura caraṇa

SYNONYMS

prabhura sahita—with Śrī Caitanya Mahāprabhu; *āmā-sabāra*—of all of us; *karāha*—arrange; *milana*—meeting; *tomāra*—your; *prasāde*—by mercy; *pāi*—we get; *prabhura caraṇa*—the lotus feet of the Lord.

TRANSLATION

"Please arrange our meeting with Śrī Caitanya Mahāprabhu. It is only by your mercy that we can attain the shelter of the lotus feet of the Lord."

TEXT 28

ভট্টাচার্য কহে,—কালি কাশীমিশ্রের ঘরে ।
প্রভু যাইবেন, তাহাঁ মিলাব সবারে ॥ ২৮ ॥

bhaṭṭācārya kahe, —kāli kāśī-miśrera ghare
prabhu yāibena, tāhāṅ milāba sabāre

SYNONYMS

bhaṭṭācārya kahe—Bhaṭṭācārya replied; *kāli*—tomorrow; *kāśī-miśrera ghare*—in the house of Kāśī Miśra; *prabhu*—the Lord; *yāibena*—will go; *tāhāṅ*—there; *milāba sabāre*—I shall arrange for a meeting with all of you.

TRANSLATION

The Bhaṭṭācārya replied to the people, "Tomorrow the Lord will be at the house of Kāśī Miśra. I shall arrange for you all to meet Him."

TEXT 29

আর দিন মহাপ্রভু ভট্টাচার্যের সঙ্গে ।
জগন্নাথ দরশন কৈল মহারঙ্গে ॥ ২৯ ॥

āra dina mahāprabhu bhaṭṭācāryera saṅge
jagannātha daraśana kaila mahā-raṅge

SYNONYMS

āra dina—the next day; *mahāprabhu*—Śrī Caitanya Mahāprabhu; *bhaṭṭācāryera saṅge*—with Sārvabhauma Bhaṭṭācārya; *jagannātha*—of Lord Jagannātha; *daraśana*—visiting the temple; *kaila*—did; *mahā-raṅge*—with great enthusiasm.

TRANSLATION

The next day Śrī Caitanya Mahāprabhu arrived and went with Sārvabhauma Bhaṭṭācārya, with great enthusiasm, to see the temple of Lord Jagannātha.

TEXT 30

মহাপ্রসাদ দিয়া তাহাঁ মিলিলা সেবকগণ ।
মহাপ্রভু সবাকারে কৈল আলিঙ্গন ॥ ৩০ ॥

mahā-prasāda diyā tāhāṅ mililā sevaka-gaṇa
mahāprabhu sabākāre kaila āliṅgana

SYNONYMS

mahā-prasāda—remnants of the food of Lord Jagannātha; *diyā*—delivering; *tāhāṅ*—there; *mililā*—met; *sevaka-gaṇa*—the servants of Lord Jagannātha; *mahāprabhu*—Śrī Caitanya Mahāprabhu; *sabākāre*—unto all of them; *kaila*—did; *āliṅgana*—embracing.

TRANSLATION

All the servants of Lord Jagannātha delivered remnants of the Lord's food to Śrī Caitanya Mahāprabhu. In return, Caitanya Mahāprabhu embraced them all.

TEXT 31

দর্শন করি' মহাপ্রভু চলিলা বাহিরে ।
ভট্টাচার্য আনিল তাঁরে কাশীমিশ্র-ঘরে ॥ ৩১ ॥

darśana kari' mahāprabhu calilā bāhire
bhaṭṭācārya ānila tāṅre kāśī-miśra-ghare

SYNONYMS

darśana kari'—seeing Lord Jagannātha; *mahāprabhu*—Śrī Caitanya Mahāprabhu; *calilā*—departed; *bāhire*—outside; *bhaṭṭācārya*—Sārvabhauma Bhaṭṭācārya; *ānila*—brought; *tāṅre*—Him; *kāśī-miśra-ghare*—to the house of Kāśī Miśra.

TRANSLATION

After seeing Lord Jagannātha, Śrī Caitanya Mahāprabhu left the temple. Bhaṭṭācārya then took Him to the house of Kāśī Miśra.

TEXT 32

কাশীমিশ্র আসি' পড়িল প্রভুর চরণে ।
গৃহ-সহিত আত্মা তাঁরে কৈল নিবেদনে ॥ ৩২ ॥

kāśī-miśra āsi' paḍila prabhura caraṇe
gṛha-sahita ātmā tāṅre kaila nivedane

SYNONYMS

kāśī-miśra—Kāśī Miśra; *āsi'*—coming; *paḍila*—fell down; *prabhura*—of Lord Śrī Caitanya Mahāprabhu; *caraṇe*—at the lotus feet; *gṛha-sahita*—with his house; *ātmā*—his personal self; *tāṅre*—unto Him; *kaila*—did; *nivedane*—submit.

TRANSLATION

When Śrī Caitanya Mahāprabhu arrived at his house, Kāśī Miśra immediately fell down at His lotus feet and surrendered himself and all his possessions.

TEXT 33

প্রভু চতুর্ভুজ-মূর্তি তাঁরে দেখাইল ।
আত্মসাৎ করি' তারে আলিঙ্গন কৈল ॥ ৩৩ ॥

prabhu catur-bhuja-mūrti tāṅre dekhāila
ātmasāt kari' tāre āliṅgana kaila

SYNONYMS

prabhu—Śrī Caitanya Mahāprabhu; *catuḥ-bhuja-mūrti*—four-armed form; *tāṅre*—unto him; *dekhāila*—showed; *ātmasāt kari'*—accepting; *tāre*—him; *āliṅgana kaila*—embraced.

TRANSLATION

Śrī Caitanya Mahāprabhu then showed Kāśī Miśra His four-armed form. Then, accepting him for His service, the Lord embraced him.

TEXT 34

তবে মহাপ্রভু তাহাঁ বসিলা আসনে ।
চৌদিকে বসিলা নিত্যানন্দাদি ভক্তগণে ॥ ৩৪ ॥

tabe mahāprabhu tāhāṅ vasilā āsane
caudike vasilā nityānandādi bhakta-gaṇe

SYNONYMS

tabe—at that time; *mahāprabhu*—Śrī Caitanya Mahāprabhu; *tāhāṅ*—there; *vasilā*—sat down; *āsane*—on His seat; *cau-dike*—on four sides; *vasilā*—sat down; *nityānanda-ādi*—headed by Lord Nityānanda; *bhakta-gaṇe*—all the devotees.

TRANSLATION

Śrī Caitanya Mahāprabhu next sat down at the place prepared for Him, and all the devotees, headed by Lord Nityānanda Prabhu, surrounded Him.

TEXT 35

সুখী হৈলা দেখি' প্রভু বাসার সংস্থান।
যেই বাসায় হয় প্রভুর সর্ব-সমাধান ॥ ৩৫ ॥

sukhī hailā dekhi' prabhu vāsāra saṁsthāna
yei vāsāya haya prabhura sarva-samādhāna

SYNONYMS

sukhī hailā—became very happy; *dekhi'*—by seeing; *prabhu*—Śrī Caitanya Mahāprabhu; *vāsāra*—of the residential quarters; *saṁsthāna*—situation; *yei vāsāya*—at which place; *haya*—there is; *prabhura*—of Śrī Caitanya Mahāprabhu; *sarva-samādhāna*—fulfillment of all necessities.

TRANSLATION

Śrī Caitanya Mahāprabhu was very happy to see His residential quarters, in which all His necessities were taken care of.

TEXT 36

সার্বভৌম কহে,—প্রভু, যোগ্য তোমার বাসা।
তুমি অঙ্গীকার কর,—কাশীমিশ্রের আশা ॥ ৩৬ ॥

sārvabhauma kahe, —prabhu, yogya tomāra vāsā
tumi aṅgīkāra kara, —kāśī-miśrera āśā

SYNONYMS

sārvabhauma—Sārvabhauma Bhaṭṭācārya; *kahe*—said; *prabhu*—my dear Lord; *yogya*—just befitting; *tomāra*—Your; *vāsā*—residential quarters; *tumi*—You; *aṅgīkāra kara*—accept; *kāśī-miśrera āśā*—the hope of Kāśī Miśra.

TRANSLATION

Sārvabhauma Bhaṭṭācārya said, "This place is just befitting You. Please accept it. It is the hope of Kāśī Miśra that You do."

TEXT 37

প্রভু কহে,—এই দেহ তোমা-সবাকার।
যেই তুমি কহ, সেই সম্মত আমার ॥ ৩৭ ॥

prabhu kahe, —ei deha tomā-sabākāra
yei tumi kaha, sei sammata āmāra

SYNONYMS

prabhu kahe—Śrī Caitanya Mahāprabhu said; *ei deha*—this body; *tomā-sabākāra*—of all of you; *yei*—whatever; *tumi*—you; *kaha*—say; *sei*—that; *sammata āmāra*—accepted by Me.

TRANSLATION

Śrī Caitanya Mahāprabhu said, "My body belongs to all of you. Therefore I agree to whatever you say."

TEXT 38

তবে সার্বভৌম প্রভুর দক্ষিণ-পার্শ্বে বসি' ।
মিলাইতে লাগিলা সব পুরুষোত্তমবাসী ॥ ৩৮ ॥

tabe sārvabhauma prabhura dakṣiṇa-pārśve vasi'
milāite lāgilā saba puruṣottama-vāsī

SYNONYMS

tabe—thereafter; *sārvabhauma*—Sārvabhauma; *prabhura*—of Śrī Caitanya Mahāprabhu; *dakṣiṇa-pārśve*—by the right side; *vasi'*—sitting; *milāite*—to introduce; *lāgilā*—began; *saba*—all; *puruṣottama-vāsī*—residents of Puruṣottama (Jagannātha Purī).

TRANSLATION

After this, Sārvabhauma Bhaṭṭācārya, sitting at the right hand of the Lord, began to introduce all the inhabitants of Puruṣottama, Jagannātha Purī.

TEXT 39

এই সব লোক, প্রভু, বৈসে নীলাচলে ।
উৎকণ্ঠিত হঞাছে সবে তোমা মিলিবারে ॥ ৩৯ ॥

ei saba loka, prabhu, vaise nīlācale
utkaṇṭhita hañāche sabe tomā milibāre

SYNONYMS

ei saba loka—all these people; *prabhu*—my Lord; *vaise*—reside; *nīlācale*—at Jagannātha Purī; *utkaṇṭhita hañāche*—they have become very anxious; *sabe*—all; *tomā*—You; *milibāre*—to meet.

TRANSLATION

The Bhaṭṭācārya said, "My dear Lord, all these people who are residents of Nīlācala, Jagannātha Purī, have been very anxious to meet You.

TEXT 40

তৃষিত চাতক যৈছে করে হাহাকার ।
তৈছে এই সব,—সবে কর অঙ্গীকার ॥ ৪০ ॥

tṛṣita cātaka yaiche kare hāhākāra
taiche ei saba, ——sabe kara aṅgīkāra

SYNONYMS

tṛṣita—thirsty; *cātaka*—the *cātaka* bird; *yaiche*—just as; *kare*—does; *hāhā-kāra*—vibration of disappointment; *taiche*—similarly; *ei saba*—all of these; *sabe*—all of them; *kara aṅgīkāra*—kindly accept.

TRANSLATION

"In Your absence all these people have been exactly like thirsty cātaka birds crying in disappointment. Kindly accept them."

TEXT 41

জগন্নাথ-সেবক এই, নাম - জনার্দন ।
অনবসরে করে প্রভুর শ্রীঅঙ্গ-সেবন ॥ ৪১ ॥

jagannātha-sevaka ei, nāma——janārdana
anavasare kare prabhura śrī-aṅga-sevana

SYNONYMS

jagannātha-sevaka—servitor of Lord Jagannātha; *ei*—this; *nāma*—named; *janārdana*—Janārdana; *anavasare*—during the time of renovation; *kare*—does; *prabhura*—of the Lord; *śrī-aṅga*—of the transcendental body; *sevana*—service.

TRANSLATION

Sārvabhauma Bhaṭṭācārya first introduced Janārdana, saying, "Here is Janārdana, servant of Lord Jagannātha. He renders service to the Lord when it is time to renovate His transcendental body."

PURPORT

During Anavasara, after the Snāna-yātrā ceremony, Lord Jagannātha is absent from the temple for fifteen days so He can be renovated. This occurs annually. Janārdana, who is here being introduced to Śrī Caitanya Mahāprabhu, was rendering this service at the time. The renovation of Lord Jagannātha is also known as Nava-yauvana, which indicates that the Jagannātha Deity is being fully restored to youth.

TEXT 42

কৃষ্ণদাস-নাম এই সুবর্ণ-বেত্রধারী ।
শিখি মাহাতি-নাম এই লিখনাধিকারী ॥ ৪২ ॥

kṛṣṇadāsa-nāma ei suvarṇa-vetra-dhārī
śikhi māhāti-nāma ei likhanādhikārī

SYNONYMS

kṛṣṇa-dāsa—Kṛṣṇadāsa; *nāma*—named; *ei*—this; *suvarṇa*—golden; *vetra-dhārī*—carrier of the cane; *śikhi māhāti*—Śikhi Māhiti; *nāma*—named; *ei*—this; *likhana-adhikārī*—entrusted with writing.

TRANSLATION

Sārvabhauma Bhaṭṭācārya continued, "This is Kṛṣṇadāsa, who carries a golden cane, and here is Śikhi Māhiti, who is in charge of writing.

PURPORT

The person in charge of writing is also called *deulakaraṇa-padaprāpta karmacārī.* He is employed especially to write a calendar called *Mātalā-pāṅji.*

TEXT 43

প্রদ্যুম্নমিশ্র ইঁহ বৈষ্ণব প্রধান ।
জগন্নাথের মহা-সোয়ার ইঁহ 'দাস' নাম ॥ ৪৩ ॥

pradyumna-miśra iṅha vaiṣṇava pradhāna
jagannāthera mahā-soyāra iṅha 'dāsa' nāma

SYNONYMS

pradyumna-miśra—Pradyumna Miśra; *iṅha*—this person; *vaiṣṇava pradhāna*—chief of all the Vaiṣṇavas; *jagannāthera*—of Lord Jagannātha; *mahā-soyāra*—great servitor; *iṅha*—this; *dāsa nāma*—designated as *dāsa.*

TRANSLATION

"This is Pradyumna Miśra, who is chief of all Vaiṣṇavas. He is a great servitor of Jagannātha, and his name is dāsa.

PURPORT

In Orissa most of the *brāhmaṇas* have the title *dāsa.* Generally it is understood that the word *dāsa* refers to those other than the *brāhmaṇas,* but in Orissa the *brāhmaṇas* use the *dāsa* title. This is confirmed by Culli Bhaṭṭa. Actually, everyone is *dāsa* because everyone is a servant of the Supreme Personality of Godhead. In that sense, the bona fide *brāhmaṇa* has first claim to the appellation *dāsa*. Therefore in this case the designation *dāsa* is not incompatible.

TEXT 44

মুরারি মাহাতি ইঁহ—শিখিমাহাতির ভাই ।
তোমার চরণ বিনু আর গতি নাই ॥ ৪৪ ॥

murāri māhāti iṅha——śikhi-māhātira bhāi
tomāra caraṇa vinu āra gati nāi

SYNONYMS

murāri māhāti—Murāri Māhiti; *iṅha*—this; *śikhi-māhātira*—of Śikhi Māhiti; *bhāi*—younger brother; *tomāra*—Your; *caraṇa*—lotus feet; *vinu*—without; *āra*—any other; *gati*—destination; *nāi*—he does not have.

TRANSLATION

"This is Murāri Māhiti, the brother of Śikhi Māhiti. He has nothing other than Your lotus feet.

TEXT 45

চন্দনেশ্বর, সিংহেশ্বর, মুরারি ব্রাহ্মণ ।
বিষ্ণুদাস,—ইঁহ ধ্যায়ে তোমার চরণ ॥ ৪৫ ॥

candaneśvara, siṁheśvara, murāri brāhmaṇa
viṣṇu-dāsa, ——iṅha dhyāye tomāra caraṇa

SYNONYMS

candaneśvara—Candaneśvara; *siṁheśvara*—Siṁheśvara; *murāri brāhmaṇa*—the *brāhmaṇa* named Murāri; *viṣṇu-dāsa*—Viṣṇudāsa; *iṅha*—all of them; *dhyāye*—meditate; *tomāra*—Your; *caraṇa*—on the lotus feet.

TRANSLATION

"Here are Candaneśvara, Siṁheśvara, Murāri Brāhmaṇa and Viṣṇudāsa. They are all constantly engaged in meditating on Your lotus feet.

TEXT 46

প্রহররাজ মহাপাত্র ইঁহ মহামতি।
পরমানন্দ মহাপাত্র ইঁহার সংহতি ॥ ৪৬ ॥

prahara-rāja mahā-pātra iṅha mahā-mati
paramānanda mahā-pātra iṅhāra saṁhati

SYNONYMS

prahara-rāja—Prahararāja; *mahā-pātra*—Mahāpātra; *iṅha*—this; *mahā-mati*—very intelligent; *paramānanda mahā-pātra*—Paramānanda Mahāpātra; *iṅhāra*—of him; *saṁhati*—combination.

TRANSLATION

"This is Paramānanda Prahararāja, who is also known as Mahāpātra. He is very, very intelligent.

PURPORT

Prahararāja is a designation given to *brāhmaṇas* who represent the king when the throne is vacant. In Orissa, between the time of a king's death and the enthronement of another king, a representative must sit on the throne. This representative is called Prahararāja. The Prahararāja is generally selected from a family of priests close to the king. During the time of Śrī Caitanya Mahāprabhu, the Prahararāja was Paramānanda Prahararāja.

TEXT 47

এ-সব বৈষ্ণব—এই ক্ষেত্রের ভূষণ।
একান্তভাবে চিন্তে সবে তোমার চরণ ॥ ৪৭ ॥

e-saba vaiṣṇava——ei kṣetrera bhūṣaṇa
ekānta-bhāve cinte sabe tomāra caraṇa

SYNONYMS

e-saba vaiṣṇava—all these pure devotees; *ei kṣetrera*—of this holy place; *bhūṣaṇa*—ornaments; *ekānta-bhāve*—without deviation; *cinte*—meditate; *sabe*—all; *tomāra caraṇa*—on Your lotus feet.

TRANSLATION

"All these pure devotees serve as ornaments to Jagannātha Purī. They are always undeviatingly meditating upon Your lotus feet."

TEXT 48

তবে সবে ভূমে পড়ে দণ্ডবৎ হঞা ।
সবা আলিঙ্গিলা প্রভু প্রসাদ করিয়া ॥ ৪৮ ॥

tabe sabe bhūme paḍe daṇḍavat hañā
sabā āliṅgilā prabhu prasāda kariyā

SYNONYMS

tabe—thereafter; *sabe*—all of them; *bhūme*—on the ground; *paḍe*—fell down; *daṇḍa-vat*—flat like rods; *hañā*—becoming; *sabā*—all of them; *āliṅgilā*—embraced; *prabhu*—Śrī Caitanya Mahāprabhu; *prasāda kariyā*—being very merciful.

TRANSLATION

After this introduction, everyone fell to the ground like rods. Being very merciful upon them all, Śrī Caitanya Mahāprabhu embraced each and every one of them.

TEXT 49

হেনকালে আইলা তথা ভবানন্দ রায় ।
চারিপুত্র-সঙ্গে পড়ে মহাপ্রভুর পায় ॥ ৪৯ ॥

hena-kāle āilā tathā bhavānanda rāya
cāri-putra-saṅge paḍe mahāprabhura pāya

SYNONYMS

hena-kāle—at this time; *āilā*—came; *tathā*—there; *bhavānanda rāya*—Bhavānanda Rāya; *cāri-putra-saṅge*—with his four sons; *paḍe*—fell down; *mahāprabhura pāya*—at the lotus feet of Śrī Caitanya Mahāprabhu.

TRANSLATION

At this time Bhavānanda Rāya appeared with his four sons, and all of them fell down at the lotus feet of Śrī Caitanya Mahāprabhu.

PURPORT

Bhavānanda Rāya had five sons, one of whom was the exalted personality known as Rāmānanda Rāya. Bhavānanda Rāya first met Śrī Caitanya Mahāprabhu after His return from South India. At that time Rāmānanda Rāya was still serving at his government post; therefore when Bhavānanda Rāya went to see Śrī Caitanya Mahāprabhu, he went with his other four sons. They were named Vāṇīnātha, Gopīnātha, Kalānidhi and Sudhānidhi. A description of Bhavānanda Rāya and his five sons is given in the *Ādi-līlā* (10.133).

TEXT 50

সার্ব্বভৌম কহে,—এই রায় ভবানন্দ।
ইঁহার প্রথম পুত্র—রায় রামানন্দ ॥ ৫০ ॥

sārvabhauma kahe, ——ei rāya bhavānanda
iṅhāra prathama putra——rāya rāmānanda

SYNONYMS

sārvabhauma kahe—Sārvabhauma Bhaṭṭācārya continued to speak; *ei*—this person; *rāya bhavānanda*—Bhavānanda Rāya; *iṅhāra*—his; *prathama putra*—first son; *rāya rāmānanda*—Rāmānanda Rāya.

TRANSLATION

Sārvabhauma Bhaṭṭācārya continued, "This is Bhavānanda Rāya, the father of Śrī Rāmānanda Rāya, who is his first son."

TEXT 51

তবে মহাপ্রভু তাঁরে কৈল আলিঙ্গন।
স্তুতি করি' কহে রামানন্দ-বিবরণ ॥ ৫১ ॥

tabe mahāprabhu tāṅre kaila āliṅgana
stuti kari' kahe rāmānanda-vivaraṇa

SYNONYMS

tabe—thereupon; *mahāprabhu*—Śrī Caitanya Mahāprabhu; *tāṅre*—unto him; *kaila*—did; *āliṅgana*—embracing; *stuti kari'*—praising very highly; *kahe*—said; *rāmānanda*—of Rāmānanda Rāya; *vivaraṇa*—description.

TRANSLATION

Śrī Caitanya Mahāprabhu embraced Bhavānanda Rāya and with great respect spoke of his son Rāmānanda Rāya.

TEXT 52

রামানন্দ-হেন রত্ন যাঁহার তনয় ।
তাঁহার মহিমা লোকে কহন না যায় ॥ ৫২ ॥

rāmānanda-hena ratna yāṅhāra tanaya
tāṅhāra mahimā loke kahana nā yāya

SYNONYMS

rāmānanda-hena—like Rāmānanda Rāya; *ratna*—jewel; *yāṅhāra*—whose; *tanaya*—son; *tāṅhāra*—his; *mahimā*—glorification; *loke*—within this world; *kahana*—to describe; *nā*—not; *yāya*—is possible.

TRANSLATION

Śrī Caitanya Mahāprabhu honored Bhavānanda Rāya by saying, "The glories of a person who has a jewel of a son like Rāmānanda Rāya cannot be described within this mortal world.

TEXT 53

সাক্ষাৎ পাণ্ডু তুমি, তোমার পত্নী কুন্তী ।
পঞ্চপাণ্ডব তোমার পঞ্চপুত্র মহামতি ॥ ৫৩ ॥

sākṣāt pāṇḍu tumi, tomāra patnī kuntī
pañca-pāṇḍava tomāra pañca-putra mahā-mati

SYNONYMS

sākṣāt pāṇḍu—directly Mahārāja Pāṇḍu; *tumi*—you; *tomāra*—your; *patnī*—wife; *kuntī*—like Kuntīdevī; *pañca-pāṇḍava*—five Pāṇḍavas; *tomāra*—your; *pañca-putra*—five sons; *mahā-mati*—all highly intellectual.

TRANSLATION

"You are Mahārāja Pāṇḍu himself, and your wife is Kuntīdevī herself. All your highly intellectual sons are representatives of the five Pāṇḍavas."

TEXT 54

রায় কহে,—আমি শূদ্র, বিষয়ী,অধম ।
তবু তুমি স্পর্শ,—এই ঈশ্বর-লক্ষণ ॥ ৫৪ ॥

rāya kahe, —āmi śūdra, viṣayī, adhama
tabu tumi sparśa, —ei īśvara-lakṣaṇa

SYNONYMS

rāya kahe—Bhavānanda Rāya replied; *āmi śūdra*—I belong to the fourth class of the social divisions; *viṣayī*—engaged in mundane affairs; *adhama*—very fallen; *tabu*—still; *tumi*—You; *sparśa*—touch; *ei*—this; *īśvara-lakṣaṇa*—sign of the Supreme Personality of Godhead.

TRANSLATION

After hearing Śrī Caitanya Mahāprabhu's praise, Bhavānanda Rāya submitted, "I am in the fourth class of the social order, and I engage in mundane affairs. Although I am very fallen, You have still touched us. This is proof that You are the Supreme Personality of Godhead."

PURPORT

As stated in *Bhagavad-gītā* (5.18):

vidyā-vinaya-sampanne
brāhmaṇe gavi hastini
śuni caiva śvapāke ca
paṇḍitāḥ sama-darśinaḥ

"The humble sage, by virtue of true knowledge, sees with equal vision a learned and gentle *brāhmaṇa,* a cow, an elephant, a dog and a dog-eater [outcaste]."

Those who are highly advanced in spiritual understanding do not care about a person's material condition. A spiritually advanced person sees the spiritual identity of every living being, and consequently he makes no distinction between a learned *brāhmaṇa,* a dog, a *caṇḍāla* or anyone else. He is not influenced by the material body but sees a person's spiritual identity. Consequently Bhavānanda Rāya appreciated Śrī Caitanya Mahāprabhu's statement, which showed that the Lord did not consider the social position of Bhavānanda Rāya, who belonged to the *śūdra* caste engaged in mundane activities. Rather, the Lord considered the spiritual position of Bhavānanda Rāya, Rāmānanda Rāya and his brothers. The servant of the Lord is also similarly inclined. He gives shelter to any person—any living entity— regardless of whether one belongs to a *brāhmaṇa* family or is a *caṇḍāla.* The spiritual master reclaims all people and encourages everyone in spiritual life. By taking shelter of such a devotee, one can make his life successful. As confirmed in *Śrīmad-Bhāgavatam* (2.4.18):

kirāta-hūṇāndhra-pulinda-pulkaśā
ābhīra-śumbhā yavanāḥ khasādayaḥ
ye 'nye ca pāpā yad-apāśrayāśrayāḥ
śudhyanti tasmai prabhaviṣṇave namaḥ

"Kirāta, Hūṇa, Āndhra, Pulinda, Pulkaśa, Ābhīra, Śumbha, Yavana and the Khasa races, and even others who are addicted to sinful acts, can be purified by taking shelter of the devotees of the Lord due to His being the supreme power. I beg to offer my respectful obeisances unto Him."

Whoever takes shelter of the Supreme Personality of Godhead or His pure devotee is elevated to the spiritual order and purified from material contamination. This is also confirmed in *Bhagavad-gītā* (9.32):

māṁ hi pārtha vyapāśritya
ye 'pi syuḥ pāpa-yonayaḥ
striyo vaiśyās tathā śūdrās
te 'pi yānti parāṁ gatim

"O son of Pṛthā, those who take shelter in Me, though they be of lower birth—women, *vaiśyas* [merchants], as well as *śūdras* [workers]—can approach the supreme destination."

TEXT 55

নিজ-গৃহ-বিত্ত-ভৃত্য-পঞ্চপুত্র-সনে ।
আত্মা সমর্পিলুঁ আমি তোমার চরণে ॥ ৫৫ ॥

nija-gṛha-vitta-bhṛtya-pañca-putra-sane
ātmā samarpiluṅ āmi tomāra caraṇe

SYNONYMS

nija—own; *gṛha*—house; *vitta*—wealth; *bhṛtya*—servants; *pañca-putra*—five sons; *sane*—with; *ātmā*—self; *samarpiluṅ*—surrender; *āmi*—I; *tomāra*—Your; *caraṇe*—at the lotus feet.

TRANSLATION

Appreciating Śrī Caitanya Mahāprabhu's favor, Bhavānanda Rāya also said, "Along with my home, riches, servants and five sons, I surrender myself at Your lotus feet.

PURPORT

This is the process of surrender. As Śrīla Bhaktivinoda Ṭhākura sings:

mānasa, deha, geha, yo kichu mora
arpiluṅ tuyā pade nanda-kiśora!
(*Śaraṇāgati*)

When one surrenders unto the lotus feet of the Lord, he does so with everything in his possession—his house, his body, his mind and whatever else he possesses. If there is any obstruction to this surrendering process, one should immediately give it up without attachment. If one can surrender with all his family members, there is no need to take *sannyāsa*. However, if the surrendering process is hampered by so-called family members, one should immediately give them up to complete the surrendering process.

TEXT 56

এই বাণীনাথ রহিবে তোমার চরণে ।
যবে যেই আজ্ঞা, তাহা করিবে সেবনে ॥ ৫৬ ॥

ei vāṇīnātha rahibe tomāra caraṇe
yabe yei ājñā, tāhā karibe sevane

SYNONYMS

ei vāṇīnātha—this Vāṇīnātha; *rahibe*—will remain; *tomāra caraṇe*—at Your lotus feet; *yabe*—when; *yei*—whatever; *ājñā*—order; *tāhā*—that; *karibe*—will execute; *sevane*—service.

TRANSLATION

"This son Vāṇīnātha will remain at Your lotus feet to always immediately attend to Your orders and serve You.

TEXT 57

আত্মীয়-জ্ঞানে মোরে সঙ্কোচ না করিবে ।
যেই যবে ইচ্ছা, তবে সেই আজ্ঞা দিবে ॥ ৫৭ ॥

ātmīya-jñāne more saṅkoca nā karibe
yei yabe icchā, tabe sei ājñā dibe

SYNONYMS

ātmīya-jñāne—by considering as a relative; *more*—me; *saṅkoca*—hesitation; *nā*—do not; *karibe*—do; *yei*—whatever; *yabe*—whenever; *icchā*—Your desire; *tabe*—then; *sei*—that; *ājñā*—order; *dibe*—kindly give.

TRANSLATION

"My dear Lord, please consider me Your relative. Do not hesitate to order whatever You desire at any time You desire it."

TEXT 58

প্রভু কহে,—কি সঙ্কোচ, তুমি নহ পর।
জন্মে জন্মে তুমি আমার সবংশে কিঙ্কর ॥ ৫৮ ॥

prabhu kahe,——ki saṅkoca, tumi naha para
janme janme tumi āmāra savaṁśe kiṅkara

SYNONYMS

prabhu kahe—the Lord replied; *ki saṅkoca*—what hesitation; *tumi*—you; *naha*—are not; *para*—outsider; *janme janme*—birth after birth; *tumi*—you; *āmāra*—My; *sa-vaṁśe*—with family members; *kiṅkara*—servant.

TRANSLATION

Śrī Caitanya Mahāprabhu accepted Bhavānanda Rāya's offer, saying, "I accept without hesitation because you are not an outsider. Birth after birth you have been my servant along with your family members.

TEXT 59

দিন-পাঁচ-সাত ভিতরে আসিবে রামানন্দ।
তাঁর সঙ্গে পূর্ণ হবে আমার আনন্দ ॥ ৫৯ ॥

dina-pāñca-sāta bhitare āsibe rāmānanda
tāṅra saṅge pūrṇa habe āmāra ānanda

SYNONYMS

dina-pāñca-sāta—five or seven days; *bhitare*—within; *āsibe*—will come; *rāmānanda*—Rāmānanda; *tāṅra saṅge*—with him; *pūrṇa habe*—will be full; *āmāra*—my; *ānanda*—pleasure.

TRANSLATION

"Śrī Rāmānanda Rāya is coming within five to seven days. As soon as he arrives, my desires will be fulfilled. I take great pleasure in his company."

TEXT 60

এত বলি' প্রভু তাঁরে কৈল আলিঙ্গন।
তাঁর পুত্র সব শিরে ধরিল চরণ ॥ ৬০ ॥

eta bali' prabhu tāṅre kaila āliṅgana
tāṅra putra saba śire dharila caraṇa

SYNONYMS

eta bali'—saying this; *prabhu*—Śrī Caitanya Mahāprabhu; *tāṅre*—unto him; *kaila*—did; *āliṅgana*—embracing; *tāṅra putra*—his sons; *saba*—all; *śire*—on the head; *dharila*—kept; *caraṇa*—His feet.

TRANSLATION

Saying this, Śrī Caitanya Mahāprabhu embraced Bhavānanda Rāya. The Lord then touched the heads of his sons with His lotus feet.

TEXT 61

তবে মহাপ্রভু তাঁরে ঘরে পাঠাইল ।
বাণীনাথ-পট্টনায়কে নিকটে রাখিল ॥ ৬১ ॥

tabe mahāprabhu tāṅre ghare pāṭhāila
vāṇīnātha-paṭṭanāyake nikaṭe rākhila

SYNONYMS

tabe—thereafter; *mahāprabhu*—Śrī Caitanya Mahāprabhu; *tāṅre*—him (Bhavānanda Rāya); *ghare*—to his home; *pāṭhāila*—sent back; *vāṇīnātha-paṭṭanāyake*—Vāṇīnātha Paṭṭanāyaka; *nikaṭe*—near; *rākhila*—kept.

TRANSLATION

Śrī Caitanya Mahāprabhu then sent Bhavānanda Rāya back to his home, and He kept only Vāṇīnātha Paṭṭanāyaka in His personal service.

TEXT 62

ভট্টাচার্য সব লোকে বিদায় করাইল ।
তবে প্রভু কালা-কৃষ্ণদাসে বোলাইল ॥ ৬২ ॥

bhaṭṭācārya saba loke vidāya karāila
tabe prabhu kālā-kṛṣṇadāse bolāila

SYNONYMS

bhaṭṭācārya—Sārvabhauma Bhaṭṭācārya; *saba loke*—all persons; *vidāya karāila*—asked to leave; *tabe*—at that time; *prabhu*—Śrī Caitanya Mahāprabhu; *kālā-kṛṣṇadāse*—Kālā Kṛṣṇadāsa; *bolāila*—called for.

TRANSLATION

Sārvabhauma Bhaṭṭācārya then asked all the people to leave. Afterward, Śrī Caitanya Mahāprabhu called for Kālā Kṛṣṇadāsa, who accompanied the Lord during His South Indian tour.

TEXT 63

প্রভু কহে,—ভট্টাচার্য, শুনহ ইঁহার চরিত।
দক্ষিণ গিয়াছিল ইঁহ আমার সহিত ॥ ৬৩ ॥

prabhu kahe,——bhaṭṭācārya, śunaha iṅhāra carita
dakṣiṇa giyāchila iṅha āmāra sahita

SYNONYMS

prabhu kahe—Śrī Caitanya Mahāprabhu said; *bhaṭṭācārya*—My dear Bhaṭṭācārya; *śunaha*—just hear; *iṅhāra carita*—his character; *dakṣiṇa giyāchila*—went to South India; *iṅha*—this man; *āmāra sahita*—with Me.

TRANSLATION

Śrī Caitanya Mahāprabhu said, "My dear Bhaṭṭācārya, just consider this man's character. He went with Me to South India.

TEXT 64

ভট্টথারি-কাছে গেলা আমারে ছাড়িয়া।
ভট্টথারি হৈতে ইঁহারে আনিলুঁ উদ্ধারিয়া ॥ ৬৪ ॥

bhaṭṭathāri-kāche gelā āmāre chāḍiyā
bhaṭṭathāri haite iṅhāre āniluṅ uddhāriyā

SYNONYMS

bhaṭṭathāri-kāche—in the associaton of the Bhaṭṭathāris; *gelā*—he went; *āmāre chāḍiyā*—giving up My company; *bhaṭṭathāri haite*—from the Bhaṭṭathāris; *iṅhāre*—him; *āniluṅ*—I brought; *uddhāriyā*—after rescuing.

TRANSLATION

"He left My company to associate with the Bhaṭṭathāris, but I rescued him from their company and brought him here.

TEXT 65

এবে আমি ইহাঁ আনি' করিলাঙ বিদায়।
যাহাঁ ইচ্ছা, যাহ, আমা-সনে নাহি আর দায় ॥ ৬৫ ॥

ebe āmi ihāṅ āni' karilāṅa vidāya
yāhāṅ icchā, yāha, āmā-sane nāhi āra dāya

SYNONYMS

ebe—now; *āmi*—I; *ihāṅ*—here; *āni'*—bringing; *karilāṅa vidāya*—have asked to go away; *yāhāṅ icchā*—wherever he likes; *yāha*—go; *āmā-sane*—with Me; *nāhi āra*—there is no more; *dāya*—responsibility.

TRANSLATION

"Now that I have brought him here, I am asking him to leave. Now he can go wherever he likes, for I am no longer responsible for him."

PURPORT

Kālā Kṛṣṇadāsa was influenced and allured by nomads or gypsies, who enticed him with women. *Māyā* is so strong that Kālā Kṛṣṇadāsa left Śrī Caitanya Mahāprabhu's company to join gypsy women. Even though a person may associate with Śrī Caitanya Mahāprabhu, he can be allured by *māyā* and leave the Lord's company due to his slight independence. Only one who is overwhelmed by *māyā* can be so unfortunate as to leave Śrī Caitanya Mahāprabhu's company, yet unless one is very conscientious, the influence of *māyā* can drag one away, even though he be the personal assistant of Śrī Caitanya Mahāprabhu. And what to speak of others? The Bhaṭṭathāris used to increase their numbers by using women to allure outsiders. This is factual evidence showing that it is possible at any time to fall down from the Lord's association. One need only misuse his little independence. Once fallen and separated from the Supreme Personality of Godhead's association, one becomes a candidate for suffering in the material world. Although rejected by Śrī Caitanya Mahāprabhu, Kālā Kṛṣṇadāsa was given another chance, as the following verses relate.

TEXT 66

এত শুনি' কৃষ্ণদাস কান্দিতে লাগিল।
মধ্যাহ্ন করিতে মহাপ্রভু চলি' গেল ॥ ৬৬ ॥

eta śuni' kṛṣṇadāsa kāndite lāgila
madhyāhna karite mahāprabhu cali' gela

SYNONYMS

eta śuni'—hearing this; *kṛṣṇadāsa*—Kālā Kṛṣṇadāsa; *kāndite lāgila*—began to cry; *madhyāhna*—noon lunch; *karite*—to execute; *mahāprabhu*—Śrī Caitanya Mahāprabhu; *cali' gela*—left.

TRANSLATION

Hearing the Lord reject him, Kālā Kṛṣṇadāsa began to cry. However, Śrī Caitanya Mahāprabhu, not caring for him, immediately left to take His noon lunch.

TEXT 67

নিত্যানন্দ, জগদানন্দ, মুকুন্দ, দামোদর ।
চারিজনে যুক্তি তবে করিলা অন্তর ॥ ৬৭ ॥

nityānanda, jagadānanda, mukunda, dāmodara
cāri-jane yukti tabe karilā antara

SYNONYMS

nityānanda—Lord Nityānanda Prabhu; *jagadānanda*—Jagadānanda; *mukunda*—Mukunda; *dāmodara*—Dāmodara; *cāri-jane*—four persons; *yukti*—plan; *tabe*—thereupon; *karilā*—did; *antara*—within the mind.

TRANSLATION

After this, the other devotees—headed by Nityānanda Prabhu, Jagadānanda, Mukunda and Dāmodara—began to consider a certain plan.

PURPORT

Even though a person is rejected by the Supreme Personality of Godhead, the devotees of the Lord do not reject him; therefore the Lord's devotees are more merciful than the Lord Himself. Śrīla Narottama dāsa Ṭhākura thus sings, *chāḍiyā vaiṣṇava-sevā nistāra pāyeche kebā:* one cannot be relieved from material clutches without engaging in the service of pure devotees. The Lord Himself may sometimes be very hard, but the devotees are always kind. Thus Kālā Kṛṣṇadāsa received the mercy of the four devotees mentioned above.

TEXT 68

গৌড়দেশে পাঠাইতে চাহি একজন ।
'আই'কে কহিবে যাই, প্রভুর আগমন ॥ ৬৮ ॥

gauḍa-deśe pāṭhāite cāhi eka-jana
'āi'ke kahibe yāi, prabhura āgamana

SYNONYMS

gauḍa-deśe—to Bengal; *pāṭhāite*—to send; *cāhi*—we want; *eka-jana*—one person; *āike*—mother Śacīdevī; *kahibe*—will inform; *yāi*—going; *prabhura*—of Śrī Caitanya Mahāprabhu; *āgamana*—arrival.

TRANSLATION

The Lord's four devotees considered, "We want a person to go to Bengal just to inform Śacīmātā about Śrī Caitanya Mahāprabhu's arrival at Jagannātha Purī.

TEXT 69

অদ্বৈত-শ্রীবাসাদি যত ভক্তগণ ।
সবেই আসিবে শুনি' প্রভুর আগমন ॥ ৬৯ ॥

advaita-śrīvāsādi yata bhakta-gaṇa
sabei āsibe śuni' prabhura āgamana

SYNONYMS

advaita—Advaita Prabhu; *śrīvāsa-ādi*—and all the devotees like Śrīvāsa; *yata*—all; *bhakta-gaṇa*—devotees; *sabei*—all; *āsibe*—will come; *śuni'*—hearing; *prabhura*—of Śrī Caitanya Mahāprabhu; *āgamana*—arrival.

TRANSLATION

"After hearing news of Śrī Caitanya Mahāprabhu's arrival, devotees like Advaita and Śrīvāsa will certainly come to see Him.

TEXT 70

এই কৃষ্ণদাসে দিব গৌড়ে পাঠাঞা ।
এত কহি' তারে রাখিলেন আশ্বাসিয়া ॥ ৭০ ॥

ei kṛṣṇadāse diba gauḍe pāṭhāñā
eta kahi' tāre rākhilena āśvāsiyā

SYNONYMS

ei—this; *kṛṣṇadāse*—Kālā Kṛṣṇadāsa; *diba*—away; *gauḍe*—to Bengal; *pāṭhāñā*—let us send; *eta kahi'*—saying this; *tāre*—him; *rākhilena*—they kept; *āśvāsiyā*—giving assurance.

TRANSLATION

"Let us therefore send Kṛṣṇadāsa to Bengal." Saying this, they kept Kṛṣṇadāsa engaged in the service of the Lord and gave him assurance.

PURPORT

Because Śrī Caitanya Mahāprabhu rejected him, Kālā Kṛṣṇadāsa became very, very sorry and began to cry. Therefore the Lord's devotees took compassion upon him, gave him assurance and encouraged him to continue to engage in the Lord's service.

TEXT 71

আর দিনে প্রভুস্থানে কৈল নিবেদন।
আজ্ঞা দেহ' গৌড়-দেশে পাঠাই একজন ॥ ৭১ ॥

āra dine prabhu-sthāne kaila nivedana
ājñā deha' gauḍa-deśe pāṭhāi eka-jana

SYNONYMS

āra dine—next day; *prabhu-sthāne*—before Lord Śrī Caitanya Mahāprabhu; *kaila*—did; *nivedana*—submission; *ājñā deha'*—please give permission; *gauḍa-deśe*—to Bengal; *pāṭhāi*—we may send; *eka-jana*—one person.

TRANSLATION

The next day, all the devotees asked Śrī Caitanya Mahāprabhu, "Please give permission for a person to go to Bengal.

TEXT 72

তোমার দক্ষিণ-গমন শুনি' শচী 'আই'।
অদ্বৈতাদি ভক্ত সব আছে দুঃখ পাই' ॥ ৭২ ॥

tomāra dakṣiṇa-gamana śuni' śacī 'āi'
advaitādi bhakta saba āche duḥkha pāi'

SYNONYMS

tomāra—Your; *dakṣiṇa-gamana*—South Indian tour; *śuni'*—hearing; *śacī āi*—mother Śacī; *advaita-ādi*—Śrī Advaita Prabhu and others; *bhakta*—devotees; *saba*—all; *āche*—remain; *duḥkha pāi'*—in great unhappiness.

TRANSLATION

"Mother Śacī and all the devotees headed by Advaita Prabhu are all very unhappy due to not receiving news about Your return from Your South Indian tour.

TEXT 73

একজন যাই' কহুক্ শুভ সমাচার।
প্রভু কহে,—সেই কর, যে ইচ্ছা তোমার ॥ ৭৩ ॥

eka-jana yāi' kahuk śubha samācāra
prabhu kahe, —sei kara, ye icchā tomāra

SYNONYMS

eka-jana—one person; *yāi'*—going; *kahuk*—may inform; *śubha samācāra*—this auspicious news; *prabhu kahe*—the Lord replied; *sei kara*—do that; *ye*—whatever; *icchā*—desire; *tomāra*—your.

TRANSLATION

"One person should go to Bengal and inform them about the auspicious news of Your return to Jagannātha Purī." Upon hearing this, Śrī Caitanya Mahāprabhu replied, "Do whatever you decide."

TEXT 74

তবে সেই কৃষ্ণদাসে গৌড়ে পাঠাইল।
বৈষ্ণব-সবাকে দিতে মহাপ্রসাদ দিল ॥ ৭৪ ॥

tabe sei kṛṣṇadāse gauḍe pāṭhāila
vaiṣṇava-sabāke dite mahā-prasāda dila

SYNONYMS

tabe—thereafter; *sei*—that; *kṛṣṇadāse*—Kṛṣṇadāsa; *gauḍe*—to Bengal; *pāṭhāila*—sent; *vaiṣṇava-sabāke*—to all the Vaiṣṇavas; *dite*—to deliver; *mahā-prasāda*—the remnants of Jagannātha's food; *dila*—they gave.

TRANSLATION

In this way Kālā Kṛṣṇadāsa was sent to Bengal, and he was given sufficient quantities of Lord Jagannātha's food remnants to distribute there.

TEXT 75

তবে গৌড়দেশে আইলা কালা-কৃষ্ণদাস।
নবদ্বীপে গেল তেঁহ শচী-আই-পাশ ॥ ৭৫ ॥

tabe gauḍa-deśe āilā kālā-kṛṣṇadāsa
navadvīpe gela teṅha śacī-āi-pāśa

SYNONYMS

tabe—then; *gauḍa-deśe*—to Bengal; *āilā*—came; *kālā-kṛṣṇadāsa*—Kālā Kṛṣṇadāsa; *navadvīpe*—to Navadvīpa; *gela*—went; *teṅha*—he; *śacī-aī-pāśa*—before mother Śacī.

TRANSLATION

Thus Kālā Kṛṣṇadāsa went to Bengal, and he first went to Navadvīpa to see mother Śacī.

TEXT 76

মহাপ্রসাদ দিয়া তাঁরে কৈল নমস্কার।
দক্ষিণ হৈতে আইলা প্রভু,—কহে সমাচার ॥ ৭৬ ॥

mahā-prasāda diyā tāṅre kaila namaskāra
dakṣiṇa haite āilā prabhu, ——kahe samācāra

SYNONYMS

mahā-prasāda diyā—delivering the *mahā-prasāda*; *tāṅre*—unto Śacīmātā; *kaila namaskāra*—he offered respects by bowing down; *dakṣiṇa haite*—from the South India tour; *āilā*—came back; *prabhu*—Lord Śrī Caitanya Mahāprabhu; *kahe samācāra*—he delivered this news.

TRANSLATION

Upon reaching mother Śacī, Kālā Kṛṣṇadāsa first offered his obeisances and delivered the food remnants [mahā-prasāda]. He then informed her of the good news that Śrī Caitanya Mahāprabhu had returned from His South Indian tour.

TEXT 77

শুনিয়া আনন্দিত হৈল শচীমাতার মন।
শ্রীবাসাদি আর যত যত ভক্তগণ ॥ ৭৭ ॥

śuniyā ānandita haila śacīmātāra mana
śrīvāsādi āra yata yata bhakta-gaṇa

SYNONYMS

śuniyā—hearing; *ānandita*—very happy; *haila*—became; *śacī-mātāra*—of mother Śacī; *mana*—mind; *śrīvāsa-ādi*—headed by Śrīvāsa; *āra*—and others; *yata yata*—all; *bhakta-gaṇa*—devotees.

TRANSLATION

This good news gave much pleasure to mother Śacī, as well as to all the devotees of Navadvīpa, headed by Śrīvāsa Ṭhākura.

TEXT 78

শুনিয়া সবার হৈল পরম উল্লাস ।
অদ্বৈত-আচার্য-গৃহে গেলা কৃষ্ণদাস ॥ ৭৮ ॥

śuniyā sabāra haila parama ullāsa
advaita-ācārya-gṛhe gelā kṛṣṇadāsa

SYNONYMS

śuniyā—hearing; *sabāra*—of all; *haila*—there was; *parama*—supreme; *ullāsa*—happiness; *advaita-ācārya*—of Advaita Ācārya Prabhu; *gṛhe*—to the home; *gelā*—went; *kṛṣṇadāsa*—Kṛṣṇadāsa.

TRANSLATION

Hearing of Lord Caitanya's return to Purī, everyone became very glad. Kṛṣṇadāsa next went to the house of Advaita Ācārya.

TEXT 79

আচার্যেরে প্রসাদ দিয়া করি' নমস্কার ।
সম্যক্ কহিল মহাপ্রভুর সমাচার ॥ ৭৯ ॥

ācāryere prasāda diyā kari' namaskāra
samyak kahila mahāprabhura samācāra

SYNONYMS

ācāryere—unto Śrī Advaita Ācārya; *prasāda*—the remnants of Jagannātha's food; *diyā*—delivering; *kari'*—making; *namaskāra*—obeisances; *samyak*—completely; *kahila*—informed; *mahāprabhura*—of Śrī Caitanya Mahāprabhu; *samācāra*—news.

TRANSLATION

After paying Him respectful obeisances, Kṛṣṇadāsa offered mahā-prasāda to Advaita Ācārya. He then informed Him of the news of Lord Caitanya in complete detail.

TEXT 80

শুনি' আচার্য-গোসাঞির আনন্দ হইল ।
প্রেমাবেশে হুঙ্কার বহু নৃত্য-গীত কৈল ॥ ৮০ ॥

śuni' ācārya-gosāñira ānanda ha-ila
premāveśe huṅkāra bahu nṛtya-gīta kaila

SYNONYMS

śuni'—hearing; *ācārya*—Advaita Ācārya; *gosāñira*—of the spiritual master; *ānanda ha-ila*—there was much jubilation; *prema-āveśe*—in great ecstasy; *huṅkāra*—rumbling sound; *bahu*—various; *nṛtya-gīta*—chanting and dancing; *kaila*—performed.

TRANSLATION

When Advaita Ācārya Gosvāmī heard of Śrī Caitanya Mahāprabhu's return, He became very pleased. In His great ecstasy of love, He made a rumbling sound and danced and chanted for a long time.

TEXT 81

হরিদাস ঠাকুরের হৈল পরম আনন্দ ।
বাসুদেব দত্ত, গুপ্ত মুরারি, সেন শিবানন্দ ॥ ৮১ ॥

haridāsa ṭhākurera haila parama ānanda
vāsudeva datta, gupta murāri, sena śivānanda

SYNONYMS

haridāsa ṭhākurera—of Haridāsa Ṭhākura; *haila*—was; *parama*—topmost; *ānanda*—ecstasy; *vāsudeva datta*—Vāsudeva Datta; *gupta murāri*—Murāri Gupta; *sena śivānanda*—Śivānanda Sena.

TRANSLATION

Also hearing this auspicious news, Haridāsa Ṭhākura became very pleased. So also did Vāsudeva Datta, Murāri Gupta and Śivānanda Sena.

TEXT 82

আচার্যরত্ন, আর পণ্ডিত বক্রেশ্বর ।
আচার্যনিধি, আর পণ্ডিত গদাধর ॥ ৮২ ॥

ācāryaratna, āra paṇḍita vakreśvara
ācāryanidhi, āra paṇḍita gadādhara

SYNONYMS

ācāryaratna—Ācāryaratna; *āra*—and; *paṇḍita vakreśvara*—Vakreśvara Paṇḍita; *ācāryanidhi*—Ācāryanidhi; *āra*—also; *paṇḍita gadādhara*—Gadādhara Paṇḍita.

TRANSLATION

Ācāryaratna, Vakreśvara Paṇḍita, Ācāryanidhi and Gadādhara Paṇḍita were all very pleased to hear this news.

TEXT 83

শ্রীরাম পণ্ডিত আর পণ্ডিত দামোদর ।
শ্রীমান্ পণ্ডিত, আর বিজয়, শ্রীধর ॥ ৮৩ ॥

śrīrāma paṇḍita āra paṇḍita dāmodara
śrīmān paṇḍita, āra vijaya, śrīdhara

SYNONYMS

śrī-rāma paṇḍita—Śrīrāma Paṇḍita; *āra*—and; *paṇḍita dāmodara*—Dāmodara Paṇḍita; *śrīmān paṇḍita*—Śrīmān Paṇḍita; *āra*—and; *vijaya*—Vijaya; *śrīdhara*—Śrīdhara.

TRANSLATION

Śrīrāma Paṇḍita, Dāmodara Paṇḍita, Śrīmān Paṇḍita, Vijaya and Śrīdhara were also very pleased to hear it.

TEXT 84

রাঘবপণ্ডিত, আর আচার্য নন্দন ।
কতেক কহিব আর যত প্রভুর গণ ॥ ৮৪ ॥

rāghava-paṇḍita, āra ācārya nandana
kateka kahiba āra yata prabhura gaṇa

SYNONYMS

rāghava-paṇḍita—Rāghava Paṇḍita; *āra*—and; *ācārya nandana*—the son of Advaita Ācārya; *kateka*—how many; *kahiba*—shall I describe; *āra*—other; *yata*—all; *prabhura gaṇa*—associates of Śrī Caitanya Mahāprabhu.

TRANSLATION

Rāghava Paṇḍita, the son of Advaita Ācārya and all the devotees became very satisfied.

TEXT 85

শুনিয়া সবার হৈল পরম উল্লাস ।
সবে মেলি' গেলা শ্রীঅদ্বৈতের পাশ ॥ ৮৫ ॥

śuniyā sabāra haila parama ullāsa
sabe meli' gelā śrī-advaitera pāśa

SYNONYMS

śuniyā—hearing; *sabāra*—of everyone; *haila*—there was; *parama ullāsa*—great ecstasy; *sabe meli'*—all together; *gelā*—went; *śrī-advaitera pāśa*—to the house of Śrī Advaita Ācārya.

TRANSLATION

Everyone was very much pleased, and together they arrived at the house of Advaita Ācārya.

TEXT 86

আচার্যের সবে কৈল চরণ বন্দন ।
আচার্য-গোসাঁই সবারে কৈল আলিঙ্গন ॥ ৮৬ ॥

ācāryera sabe kaila caraṇa vandana
ācārya-gosāñi sabāre kaila āliṅgana

SYNONYMS

ācāryera—of Advaita Ācārya; *sabe*—all; *kaila*—did; *caraṇa vandana*—offering obeisances at the lotus feet; *ācārya-gosāñi*—Advaita Ācārya; *sabāre*—to all; *kaila*—did; *āliṅgana*—embracing.

TRANSLATION

All the devotees offered respectful obeisances at the lotus feet of Advaita Ācārya, and in return Advaita Ācārya embraced them all.

TEXT 87

দিন দুই-তিন আচার্য মহোৎসব কৈল ।
নীলাচল যাইতে আচার্য যুক্তি দৃঢ় কৈল ॥ ৮৭ ॥

dina dui-tina ācārya mahotsava kaila
nīlācala yāite ācārya yukti dṛḍha kaila

SYNONYMS

dina dui-tina—for two or three days; *ācārya*—Advaita Ācārya; *mahotsava*—festival; *kaila*—performed; *nīlācala*—to Jagannātha Purī; *yāite*—to go; *ācārya*—Advaita Ācārya; *yukti*—consideration; *dṛḍha*—firm; *kaila*—made.

TRANSLATION

Advaita Ācārya then held a festival that lasted two or three days. Thereafter, they all made a firm decision to go to Jagannātha Purī.

TEXT 88

সবে মেলি' নবদ্বীপে একত্র হঞা ।
নীলাদ্রি চলিল শচীমাতার আজ্ঞা লঞা ॥ ৮৮ ॥

sabe meli' navadvīpe ekatra hañā
nīlādri calila śacīmātāra ājñā lañā

SYNONYMS

sabe—all; *meli'*—meeting; *navadvīpe*—at Navadvīpa; *ekatra hañā*—being together; *nīlādri*—to Jagannātha Purī; *calila*—departed; *śacī-mātāra*—of mother Śacī; *ājñā*—permission; *lañā*—taking.

TRANSLATION

All the devotees met together at Navadvīpa and, with mother Śacī's permission, departed for Nīlādri, Jagannātha Purī.

TEXT 89

প্রভুর সমাচার শুনি' কুলীনগ্রামবাসী ।
সত্যরাজ-রামানন্দ মিলিলা সবে আসি' ॥ ৮৯ ॥

prabhura samācāra śuni' kulīna-grāma-vāsī
satyarāja-rāmānanda mililā sabe āsi'

SYNONYMS

prabhura—of Śrī Caitanya Mahāprabhu; *samācāra*—news; *śuni'*—hearing; *kulīna-grāma-vāsī*—the inhabitants of Kulīna-grāma; *satyarāja*—Satyarāja; *rāmānanda*—Rāmānanda; *mililā*—met; *sabe*—all; *āsi'*—coming.

TRANSLATION

The inhabitants of Kulīna-grāma—Satyarāja, Rāmānanda and all the other devotees there—came and joined Advaita Ācārya.

TEXT 90

মুকুন্দ, নরহরি, রঘুনন্দন খণ্ড হৈতে।
আচার্যের ঠাঞি আইলা নীলাচল যাইতে॥ ৯০॥

mukunda, narahari, raghunandana khaṇḍa haite
ācāryera ṭhāñi āilā nīlācala yāite

SYNONYMS

mukunda—Mukunda; *narahari*—Narahari; *raghunandana*—Raghunandana; *khaṇḍa haite*—from the place known as Khaṇḍa; *ācāryera ṭhāñi*—to Advaita Ācārya; *āilā*—came; *nīlācala yāite*—to go to Nīlācala (Jagannātha Purī).

TRANSLATION

Mukunda, Narahari, Raghunandana and all the others came from Khaṇḍa to Advaita Ācārya's home to accompany Him to Jagannātha Purī.

TEXT 91

সেকালে দক্ষিণ হৈতে পরমানন্দপুরী।
গঙ্গাতীরে-তীরে আইলা নদীয়া নগরী॥ ৯১॥

se-kāle dakṣiṇa haite paramānanda-purī
gaṅgā-tīre-tīre āilā nadīyā nagarī

SYNONYMS

se-kāle—at that time; *dakṣiṇa haite*—from the South; *paramānanda-purī*—Paramānanda Purī; *gaṅgā-tīre-tīre*—along the bank of the Ganges; *āilā*—came; *nadīyā nagarī*—to the town of Nadia.

TRANSLATION

At that time Paramānanda Purī also came from South India. Traveling along the banks of the Ganges, he ultimately reached the town of Nadia.

TEXT 92

আইর মন্দিরে সুখে করিলা বিশ্রাম ।
আই তাঁরে ভিক্ষা দিলা করিয়া সম্মান ॥ ৯২ ॥

āira mandire sukhe karilā viśrāma
āi tāṅre bhikṣā dilā kariyā sammāna

SYNONYMS

āira mandire—at the house of Śacīmātā; *sukhe*—in happiness; *karilā*—took; *viśrāma*—lodging; *āi*—mother Śacī; *tāṅre*—unto him; *bhikṣā dilā*—gave boarding; *kariyā sammāna*—with great respect.

TRANSLATION

At Navadvīpa, Paramānanda Purī took his board and lodging at the house of Śacīmātā. She provided him with everything very respectfully.

TEXT 93

প্রভুর আগমন তেঁহ তাহাঁঞি শুনিল ।
শীঘ্র নীলাচল যাইতে তাঁর ইচ্ছা হৈল ॥ ৯৩ ॥

prabhura āgamana teṅha tāhāññi śunila
śīghra nīlācala yāite tāṅra icchā haila

SYNONYMS

prabhura āgamana—Śrī Caitanya Mahāprabhu's return; *teṅha*—he; *tāhāññi*—there; *śunila*—heard; *śīghra*—very soon; *nīlācala*—to Jagannātha Purī; *yāite*—to go; *tāṅra*—his; *icchā*—desire; *haila*—became.

TRANSLATION

While residing at the house of Śacīmātā, Paramānanda Purī heard the news of Śrī Caitanya Mahāprabhu's return to Jagannātha Purī. He therefore decided to go there as soon as possible.

TEXT 94

প্রভুর এক ভক্ত – 'দ্বিজ কমলাকান্ত' নাম ।
তাঁরে লঞা নীলাচলে করিলা প্রয়াণ ॥ ৯৪ ॥

prabhura eka bhakta——'dvija kamalākānta' nāma
tāṅre lañā nīlācale karilā prayāṇa

SYNONYMS

prabhura—of Śrī Caitanya Mahāprabhu; *eka bhakta*—one devotee; *dvija kamalākānta*—Dvija Kamalākānta; *nāma*—named; *tāṅre*—him; *lañā*—accepting as his companion; *nīlācale*—to Jagannātha Purī; *karilā*—did; *prayāṇa*—departure.

TRANSLATION

There was a devotee of Śrī Caitanya Mahāprabhu named Dvija Kamalākānta, whom Paramānanda Purī took with him to Jagannātha Purī.

TEXT 95

সত্বরে আসিয়া তেঁহ মিলিলা প্রভুরে ।
প্রভুর আনন্দ হৈল পাঞা তাঁহারে ॥ ৯৫ ॥

satvare āsiyā teṅha mililā prabhure
prabhura ānanda haila pāñā tāṅhāre

SYNONYMS

satvare—very soon; *āsiyā*—coming; *teṅha*—he; *mililā*—met; *prabhure*—Śrī Caitanya Mahāprabhu; *prabhura*—of Śrī Caitanya Mahāprabhu; *ānanda*—happiness; *haila*—was; *pāñā*—getting; *tāṅhāre*—him.

TRANSLATION

Paramānanda Purī very soon arrived at Śrī Caitanya Mahāprabhu's place. The Lord was very happy to see him.

TEXT 96

প্রেমাবেশে কৈল তাঁর চরণ বন্দন ।
তেঁহ প্রেমাবেশে কৈল প্রভুরে আলিঙ্গন ॥ ৯৬ ॥

premāveśe kaila tāṅra caraṇa vandana
teṅha premāveśe kaila prabhure āliṅgana

SYNONYMS

prema-āveśe—in great ecstasy; *kaila*—did; *tāṅra*—his; *caraṇa vandana*—worshiping the feet; *teṅha*—Paramānanda Purī; *prema-āveśe*—in great ecstasy; *kaila*—did; *prabhure*—unto Śrī Caitanya Mahāprabhu; *āliṅgana*—embracing.

TRANSLATION

In a great ecstasy of love, the Lord worshiped the lotus feet of Paramānanda Purī, and in turn Paramānanda Purī embraced the Lord in great ecstasy.

TEXT 97

প্রভু কহে,—তোমা-সঙ্গে রহিতে বাঞ্ছা হয়।
মোরে কৃপা করি' কর নীলাদ্রি আশ্রয়॥ ৯৭॥

prabhu kahe, ——tomā-saṅge rahite vāñchā haya
more kṛpā kari' kara nīlādri āśraya

SYNONYMS

prabhu kahe—Śrī Caitanya Mahāprabhu said; *tomā-saṅge*—with you; *rahite*—to stay; *vāñchā haya*—I desire; *more*—unto Me; *kṛpā kari'*—doing a favor; *kara*—accept; *nīlādri*—at Jagannātha Purī; *āśraya*—shelter.

TRANSLATION

Śrī Caitanya Mahāprabhu said, "Please stay with Me and thus show Me favor, accepting the shelter of Jagannātha Purī."

TEXT 98

পুরী কহে,—তোমা-সঙ্গে রহিতে বাঞ্ছা করি'।
গৌড় হৈতে চলি' আইলাঙ নীলাচল-পুরী॥ ৯৮॥

purī kahe, ——tomā-saṅge rahite vāñchā kari'
gauḍa haite cali' āilāṅa nīlācala-purī

SYNONYMS

purī kahe—Paramānanda Purī replied; *tomā-saṅge*—with You; *rahite*—to stay; *vāñchā kari'*—desiring; *gauḍa haite*—from Bengal; *cali'*—traveling; *āilāṅa*—I have come; *nīlācala-purī*—to Jagannātha Purī.

TRANSLATION

Paramānanda Purī replied, "I also wish to stay with You. Therefore I have come from Bengal, Gauḍa, to Jagannātha Purī.

TEXT 99

দক্ষিণ হৈতে শুনি' তোমার আগমন।
শচী আনন্দিত, আর যত ভক্তগণ ॥ ৯৯ ॥

dakṣiṇa haite śuni' tomāra āgamana
śacī ānandita, āra yata bhakta-gaṇa

SYNONYMS

dakṣiṇa haite—from South India; *śuni'*—hearing; *tomāra āgamana*—Your return; *śacī*—mother Śacī; *ānandita*—very happy; *āra*—and; *yata*—all; *bhakta-gaṇa*—devotees.

TRANSLATION

"At Navadvīpa, mother Śacī and all the other devotees were very glad to hear about Your return from South India.

TEXT 100

সবে আসিতেছেন তোমারে দেখিতে।
তাঁ-সবার বিলম্ব দেখি' আইলাঙ ত্বরিতে ॥ ১০০

sabe āsitechena tomāre dekhite
tāṅ-sabāra vilamba dekhi' āilāṅa tvarite

SYNONYMS

sabe—all; *āsitechena*—are coming; *tomāre*—You; *dekhite*—to see; *tāṅ-sabāra*—of all of them; *vilamba*—delay; *dekhi'*—seeing; *āilāṅa*—I have come; *tvarite*—very quickly.

TRANSLATION

They are all coming here to see You, but seeing that they were delayed, I came alone very quickly."

TEXT 101

কাশীমিশ্রের আবাসে নিভৃতে এক ঘর।
প্রভু তাঁরে দিল, আর সেবার কিঙ্কর ॥ ১০১ ॥

kāśī-miśrera āvāse nibhṛte eka ghara
prabhu tāṅre dila, āra sevāra kiṅkara

SYNONYMS

kāśī-miśrera—of Kāśī Miśra; *āvāse*—at the house; *nibhṛte*—solitary; *eka*—one; *ghara*—room; *prabhu*—Śrī Caitanya Mahāprabhu; *tāṅre*—unto Paramānanda Purī; *dila*—gave; *āra*—and; *sevāra*—to serve him; *kiṅkara*—one servant.

TRANSLATION

There was a solitary room at Kāśī Miśra's house, and Śrī Caitanya Mahāprabhu gave it to Paramānanda Purī. He also gave him one servant.

TEXT 102

আর দিনে আইলা স্বরূপ দামোদর ।
প্রভুর অত্যন্ত মর্মী, রসের সাগর ॥ ১০২ ॥

āra dine āilā svarūpa dāmodara
prabhura atyanta marmī, rasera sāgara

SYNONYMS

āra dine—next day; *āilā*—came; *svarūpa dāmodara*—Svarūpa Dāmodara; *prabhura*—of Śrī Caitanya Mahāprabhu; *atyanta*—very; *marmī*—intimate friend; *rasera*—of transcendental mellows; *sāgara*—ocean.

TRANSLATION

Svarūpa Dāmodara also arrived the next day. He was a very intimate friend of Śrī Caitanya Mahāprabhu, and he was an ocean of transcendental mellows.

PURPORT

Svarūpa is the name of a *brahmacārī* in Śaṅkarācārya's disciplic succession. In the Vedic discipline there are ten names for *sannyāsīs,* and it is customary for a *brahmacārī* assisting a *sannyāsī* of the designation Tīrtha or Āśrama to receive the title Svarūpa. Dāmodara Svarūpa was formerly a resident of Navadvīpa, and his name was Puruṣottama Ācārya. When he went to Vārāṇasī, he took *sannyāsa* from a *sannyāsī* designated Tīrtha. Although he received the title Svarūpa in his *brahmacārī* stage, he did not change his name when he took *sannyāsa.* Actually as a *sannyāsī* he should have been called Tīrtha, but he chose to retain his original *brahmacārī* title as Svarūpa.

TEXT 103

'পুরুষোত্তম আচার্য' তাঁর নাম পূর্বাশ্রমে ।
নবদ্বীপে ছিলা তেঁহ প্রভুর চরণে ॥ ১০৩ ॥

'puruṣottama ācārya' tāṅra nāma pūrvāśrame
navadvīpe chilā teṅha prabhura caraṇe

SYNONYMS

puruṣottama ācārya—Puruṣottama Ācārya; *tāṅra*—his; *nāma*—name; *pūrva-āśrame*—in the previous *āśrama*; *navadvīpe*—at Navadvīpa; *chilā*—was; *teṅha*—he; *prabhura*—of Śrī Caitanya Mahāprabhu; *caraṇe*—at the feet.

TRANSLATION

When Svarūpa Dāmodara was residing at Navadvīpa under the shelter of Śrī Caitanya Mahāprabhu, his name was Puruṣottama Ācārya.

TEXT 104

প্রভুর সন্ন্যাস দেখি' উন্মত্ত হঞা ।
সন্ন্যাস গ্রহণ কৈল বারাণসী গিয়া ॥ ১০৪ ॥

prabhura sannyāsa dekhi' unmatta hañā
sannyāsa grahaṇa kaila vārāṇasī giyā

SYNONYMS

prabhura—of Lord Śrī Caitanya Mahāprabhu; *sannyāsa dekhi'*—when he saw the *sannyāsa* order; *unmatta hañā*—he became just like a madman; *sannyāsa grahaṇa kaila*—he also accepted the renounced order of life; *vārāṇasī*—to Vārāṇasī; *giyā*—going.

TRANSLATION

After seeing that Śrī Caitanya Mahāprabhu accepted the renounced order, Puruṣottama Ācārya became like a madman and immediately went to Vārāṇasī to take sannyāsa.

TEXT 105

'চৈতন্যানন্দ' গুরু তাঁর আজ্ঞা দিলেন তাঁরে ।
বেদান্ত পড়িয়া পড়াও সমস্ত লোকেরে ॥ ১০৫ ॥

'caitanyānanda' guru tāṅra ājñā dilena tāṅre
vedānta paḍiyā paḍāo samasta lokere

SYNONYMS

caitanya-ānanda—of the name Caitanyānanda Bhāratī; *guru*—spiritual master; *tāṅra*—his; *ājñā*—order; *dilena*—gave; *tāṅre*—to him; *vedānta paḍiyā*—reading the *Vedanta-sūtra*; *paḍāo*—teach; *samasta*—all; *lokere*—people.

TRANSLATION

At the conclusion of his sannyāsa, his spiritual master, Caitanyānanda Bhāratī, ordered him, "Read Vedanta-sūtra and teach it to all others."

TEXT 106

পরম বিরক্ত তেঁহ পরম পণ্ডিত ।
কায়মনে আশ্রিয়াছে শ্রীকৃষ্ণ-চরিত ॥ ১০৬ ॥

parama virakta teṅha parama paṇḍita
kāya-mane āśriyāche śrī-kṛṣṇa-carita

SYNONYMS

parama—very; *virakta*—renounced; *teṅha*—he; *parama*—great; *paṇḍita*—learned scholar; *kāya-mane*—with body and mind; *āśriyāche*—took shelter of; *śrī-kṛṣṇa-carita*—the Personality of Godhead Śrī Kṛṣṇa.

TRANSLATION

Svarūpa Dāmodara was a great renunciate as well as a great learned scholar. With heart and soul he took shelter of the Supreme Personality of Godhead, Śrī Kṛṣṇa.

TEXT 107

'নিশ্চিন্তে কৃষ্ণ ভজিব' এই ত' কারণে ।
উন্মাদে করিল তেঁহ সন্ন্যাস গ্রহণে ॥ ১০৭ ॥

'niścinte kṛṣṇa bhajiba' ei ta' kāraṇe
unmāde karila teṅha sannyāsa grahaṇe

SYNONYMS

niścinte—without disturbance; *kṛṣṇa*—Lord Kṛṣṇa; *bhajiba*—I shall worship; *ei*—for this; *ta'*—certainly; *kāraṇe*—reason; *unmāde*—ecstatic; *karila*—did; *teṅha*—he; *sannyāsa*—the renounced order of life; *grahaṇe*—taking.

TRANSLATION

He was very enthusiastic to worship Śrī Kṛṣṇa without disturbance; therefore it was almost in madness that he accepted the sannyāsa order.

TEXT 108

সন্ন্যাস করিলা শিখা-সূত্রত্যাগ-রূপ ।
যোগপট্ট না নিল, নাম হৈল 'স্বরূপ' ॥ ১০৮ ॥

sannyāsa karilā śikhā-sūtra-tyāga-rūpa
yoga-paṭṭa nā nila, nāma haila 'svarūpa'

SYNONYMS

sannyāsa karilā—accepted the *sannyāsa* order; *śikhā*—tuft of hair; *sūtra*—sacred thread; *tyāga*—giving up; *rūpa*—in the form of; *yoga-paṭṭa*—saffron colored dress; *nā nila*—did not accept; *nāma*—name; *haila*—was; *svarūpa*—Svarūpa.

TRANSLATION

Upon accepting sannyāsa, Puruṣottama Ācārya followed the regulative principles by giving up his tuft of hair and sacred thread, but he did not accept the saffron colored dress. Also, he did not accept a sannyāsī title but remained as a naiṣṭhika-brahmacārī.

PURPORT

There are regulative principles governing the renounced order. One has to perform eight kinds of *śrāddha.* One must offer oblations to one's forefathers and perform the sacrifice of *virajā-homa.* Then one must cut off the tuft of hair called a *śikhā* and also give up the sacred thread. These are preliminary processes in the acceptance of *sannyāsa,* and Svarūpa Dāmodara accepted all these. However, Puruṣottama Ācārya did not accept the saffron color, a *sannyāsī* name or a *daṇḍa.* He retained his *brahmacārī* name. Actually Puruṣottama Ācārya did not accept the *sannyāsa* order formally, but he renounced worldly life. He did not want to be disturbed by the formality of the *sannyāsa* order. He simply wanted to worship Lord Śrī Kṛṣṇa without disturbance; therefore with heart and soul he took up the renounced order but not the formalities accompanying it. Renunciation means not doing anything but serving the Supreme Personality of Godhead, Śrī Kṛṣṇa. When one acts on this platform, trying to please the Supreme Personality of Godhead, one is both a *sannyāsī* and a *yogī.* This is confirmed in *Bhagavad-gītā* (6.1):

śrī bhagavān uvāca
anāśritaḥ karma-phalaṁ
kāryaṁ karma karoti yaḥ
sa sannyāsī ca yogī ca
na niragnir na cākriyaḥ

"The Blessed Lord said: One who is unattached to the fruits of his work and who works as he is obligated is in the renounced order of life, and he is the true mystic, not he who lights no fire and performs no work."

TEXT 109

গুরু-ঠাঞি আজ্ঞা মাগি' আইলা নীলাচলে।
রাত্রিদিনে কৃষ্ণপ্রেম-আনন্দ-বিহ্বলে ॥ ১০৯ ॥

guru-ṭhāñi ājñā māgi' āilā nīlācale
rātri-dine kṛṣṇa-prema-ānanda-vihvale

SYNONYMS

guru-ṭhāñi—from his spiritual master; *ājñā māgi'*—asking permission; *āilā*—came; *nīlācale*—to Jagannātha Purī; *rātri-dine*—day and night; *kṛṣṇa-prema-ānanda*—by ecstatic love of Kṛṣṇa; *vihvale*—overwhelmed.

TRANSLATION

After taking permission from his sannyāsa-guru, Svarūpa Dāmodara went to Nīlācala and accepted the shelter of Śrī Caitanya Mahāprabhu. Then all day and night, in ecstatic love of Kṛṣṇa, he enjoyed transcendental mellows in the loving service of the Lord.

TEXT 110

পাণ্ডিত্যের অবধি, বাক্য নাহি কারো সনে।
নির্জনে রহয়ে, লোক সব নাহি জানে ॥ ১১০ ॥

pāṇḍityera avadhi, vākya nāhi kāro sane
nirjane rahaye, loka saba nāhi jāne

SYNONYMS

pāṇḍityera avadhi—the limit of learned scholarship; *vākya nāhi*—no word; *kāro sane*—with anyone; *nirjane*—in a solitary place; *rahaye*—stays; *loka*—people in general; *saba*—all; *nāhi jāne*—do not know.

TRANSLATION

Svarūpa Dāmodara was the limit of all learned scholarship, but he did not exchange words with anyone. He simply remained in a solitary place, and no one could understand where he was.

TEXT 111

কৃষ্ণরস-তত্ত্ব-বেত্তা, দেহ—প্রেমরূপ।
সাক্ষাৎ মহাপ্রভুর দ্বিতীয় স্বরূপ ॥ ১১১ ॥

kṛṣṇa-rasa-tattva-vettā, deha——prema-rūpa
sākṣāt mahāprabhura dvitīya svarūpa

SYNONYMS

kṛṣṇa-rasa—of transcendental mellows in relationship with Kṛṣṇa; *tattva*—of the truth; *vettā*—cognizant; *deha*—body; *prema-rūpa*—personified *prema*; *sākṣāt*—directly; *mahāprabhura*—of Śrī Caitanya Mahāprabhu; *dvitīya*—second; *svarūpa*—representation.

TRANSLATION

Śrī Svarūpa Dāmodara was the personification of ecstatic love, fully cognizant of the transcendental mellows in relationship with Kṛṣṇa. He directly represented Śrī Caitanya Mahāprabhu as His second expansion.

TEXT 112

গ্রন্থ, শ্লোক, গীত কেহ প্রভু-পাশে আনে।
স্বরূপ পরীক্ষা কৈলে, পাছে প্রভু শুনে ॥ ১১২ ॥

grantha, śloka, gīta keha prabhu-pāśe āne
svarūpa parīkṣā kaile, pāche prabhu śune

SYNONYMS

grantha—scriptures; *śloka*—verses; *gīta*—songs; *keha*—anyone; *prabhu-pāśe*—to Śrī Caitanya Mahāprabhu; *āne*—brings; *svarūpa*—Svarūpa Dāmodara; *parīkṣā kaile*—after he examined; *pāche*—later; *prabhu*—Śrī Caitanya Mahāprabhu; *śune*—hears.

TRANSLATION

If someone wrote a book or composed verses and songs and wanted to recite them before Śrī Caitanya Mahāprabhu, Svarūpa Dāmodara would first

examine them and then correctly present them. Only then would Śrī Caitanya Mahāprabhu agree to listen.

TEXT 113

ভক্তিসিদ্ধান্ত-বিরুদ্ধ, আর রসাভাস।
শুনিতে না হয় প্রভুর চিত্তের উল্লাস ॥ ১১৩ ॥

bhakti-siddhānta-viruddha, āra rasābhāsa
śunite nā haya prabhura cittera ullāsa

SYNONYMS

bhakti-siddhānta—conclusive statements about the science of devotional service; *viruddha*—opposing; *āra*—and; *rasa-ābhāsa*—overlapping of transcendental mellows; *śunite*—to hear; *nā*—not; *haya*—becomes; *prabhura*—of Śrī Caitanya Mahāprabhu; *cittera*—of the heart; *ullāsa*—jubilation.

TRANSLATION

Śrī Caitanya Mahāprabhu was never pleased to hear books or verses opposed to the conclusive statements of devotional service. The Lord did not like hearing rasābhāsa, the overlapping of transcendental mellows.

PURPORT

Bhakti-siddhānta-viruddha refers to that which is against the principle of unity in diversity, philosophically known as *acintya-bhedābheda*—simultaneously oneness and difference. *Rasābhāsa* may appear to be a transcendental mellow, but actually it is not. Those who are pure Vaiṣṇavas should avoid these things opposed to devotional service. These misconceptions practically parallel the Māyāvāda philosophy. If one indulges in Māyāvāda philosophy, he gradually falls down from the platform of devotional service. By overlapping mellows (*rasābhāsa*) one eventually becomes a *prākṛta-sahajiyā* and takes everything to be very easy. One may also become a member of the *bāula* community and gradually become attracted to material activities. Śrī Caitanya Mahāprabhu has therefore advised us to avoid *bhakti-siddhānta-viruddha* and *rasābhāsa*. In this way the devotee can remain pure and free from falldowns. Everyone should try to remain aloof from *bhakti-siddhānta-viruddha* and *rasābhāsa*.

TEXT 114

অতএব স্বরূপ আগে করে পরীক্ষণ।
শুদ্ধ হয় যদি, প্রভুরে করা'ন শ্রবণ ॥ ১১৪ ॥

ataeva svarūpa āge kare parīkṣaṇa
śuddha haya yadi, prabhure karā'na śravaṇa

SYNONYMS

ataeva—therefore; *svarūpa*—Svarūpa Dāmodara; *āge*—at first; *kare*—does; *parīkṣaṇa*—examination; *śuddha*—pure; *haya*—is; *yadi*—if; *prabhure*—unto Lord Śrī Caitanya Mahāprabhu; *karā'na*—causes; *śravaṇa*—hearing.

TRANSLATION

It was the practice for Svarūpa Dāmodara Gosvāmī to examine all literatures to find out whether their conclusions were correct. Only then would he allow them to be heard by Śrī Caitanya Mahāprabhu.

PURPORT

Śrīla Bhaktisiddhānta Sarasvatī Ṭhākura says that if something impedes the execution of devotional service, it should be understood to be impure. Pure devotees of the Lord do not accept impure principles. Impure devotees accept *rasābhāsa,* or overlapping, contradictory mellows, and other principles opposed to the *bhakti* path. The followers of such impure principles are never accepted as pure devotees. There are many parties following the path of *rasābhāsa,* and the followers are sometimes adored by ordinary men. Those who adopt the conclusions of *rasābhāsa* and *bhakti-siddhānta-viruddha* are never accepted as devotees of Śrī Caitanya Mahāprabhu. Svarūpa Dāmodara Gosvāmī never approved such followers as Gauḍīya Vaiṣṇavas, nor did he allow them even to meet the Supreme Lord Śrī Caitanya Mahāprabhu.

TEXT 115

বিদ্যাপতি, চণ্ডীদাস, শ্রীগীতগোবিন্দ ।
এই তিন গীতে করা'ন প্রভুর আনন্দ ॥ ১১৫ ॥

vidyāpati, caṇḍīdāsa, śrī-gīta-govinda
ei tina gīte karā'na prabhura ānanda

SYNONYMS

vidyā-pati—an old Vaiṣṇava poet from the province of Mithilā; *caṇḍī-dāsa*—a Bengali Vaiṣṇava poet born in the village of Nānnura in the Birbhum district; *śrī-gīta-govinda*—a celebrated poem by Jayadeva Gosvāmī; *ei*—these; *tina*—three; *gīte*—songs; *karā'na*—cause; *prabhura*—of Śrī Caitanya Mahāprabhu; *ānanda*—happiness.

TRANSLATION

Śrī Svarūpa Dāmodara used to read the poems of Vidyāpati and Caṇḍīdāsa and Jayadeva Gosvāmī's Śrī Gīta-govinda. He used to make Śrī Caitanya Mahāprabhu very happy by singing these songs.

TEXT 116

সঙ্গীতে—গন্ধর্ব-সম, শাস্ত্রে বৃহস্পতি ।
দামোদর-সম আর নাহি মহামতি ॥ ১১৬ ॥

saṅgīte——gandharva-sama, śāstre bṛhaspati
dāmodara-sama āra nāhi mahā-mati

SYNONYMS

saṅgīte—in music; *gandharva-sama*—just like the Gandharvas; *śāstre*—in discussions of revealed scriptures; *bṛhaspati*—like Bṛhaspati, the priest of the heavenly demigods; *dāmodara-sama*—equal to Svarūpa Dāmodara; *āra*—anyone else; *nāhi*—there is not; *mahā-mati*—great personality.

TRANSLATION

Svarūpa Dāmodara was as expert a musician as the Gandharvas, and in scriptural discussion he was just like Bṛhaspati, the priest of the heavenly gods. Therefore it is to be concluded that there was no great personality quite like Svarūpa Dāmodara.

PURPORT

Svarūpa Dāmodara Gosvāmī was very expert in music as well as Vedic scriptures. Śrī Caitanya Mahāprabhu used to call him Dāmodara because of his expert singing and musical skills. The name Dāmodara was given by Śrī Caitanya Mahāprabhu and added to the name given by his *sannyāsa-guru.* He was therefore known as Svarūpa Dāmodara, or Dāmodara Svarūpa. He compiled a book of music named *Saṅgīta-dāmodara.*

TEXT 117

অদ্বৈত-নিত্যানন্দের পরম প্রিয়তম ।
শ্রীবাসাদি ভক্তগণের হয় প্রাণ-সম ॥ ১১৭ ॥

advaita-nityānandera parama priyatama
śrīvāsādi bhakta-gaṇera haya prāṇa-sama

SYNONYMS

advaita—of Advaita Ācārya; *nityānandera*—of Lord Nityānanda Prabhu; *parama*—very much; *priya-tama*—dear; *śrīvāsa-ādi*—beginning with Śrīvāsa; *bhakta-gaṇera*—of the devotees; *haya*—is; *prāṇa-sama*—exactly like the life and soul.

TRANSLATION

Śrī Svarūpa Dāmodara was very dear to Advaita Ācārya and Nityānanda Prabhu, and he was the life and soul of all the devotees, headed by Śrīvāsa Ṭhākura.

TEXT 118

সেই দামোদর আসি' দণ্ডবৎ হৈলা ।
চরণে পড়িয়া শ্লোক পড়িতে লাগিলা ॥ ১১৮ ॥

sei dāmodara āsi' daṇḍavat hailā
caraṇe paḍiyā śloka paḍite lāgilā

SYNONYMS

sei dāmodara—that Svarūpa Dāmodara; *āsi'*—coming; *daṇḍa-vat hailā*—fell flat to offer obeisances; *caraṇe paḍiyā*—falling down at the lotus feet; *śloka*—a verse; *paḍite lāgilā*—began to recite.

TRANSLATION

It was Svarūpa Dāmodara who came to Jagannātha Purī and fell flat before the lotus feet of Śrī Caitanya Mahāprabhu, offering Him obeisances and reciting a verse.

TEXT 119

হেলোদ্ধূনিত-খেদয়া বিশদয়া প্রোন্মীলদামোদয়া
শাম্যচ্ছাস্ত্রবিবাদয়া রসদয়া চিত্তার্পিতোন্মাদয়া ।
শশ্বদ্ভক্তিবিনোদয়া স-মদয়া মাধুর্যমর্যাদয়া
শ্রীচৈতন্য দয়ানিধে তব দয়া ভূয়াদমন্দোদয়া ॥ ১১৯ ॥

heloddhūnita-khedayā viśadayā pronmīlad-āmodayā
śāmyac-chāstra-vivādayā rasadayā cittārpitonmādayā
śaśvad-bhakti-vinodayā sa-madayā mādhurya-maryādayā
śrī-caitanya dayā-nidhe tava dayā bhūyād amandodayā

SYNONYMS

helā—very easily; *uddhūnita*—driven away; *khedayā*—lamentation; *viśadayā*—which purifies everything; *pronmīlat*—awakening; *āmodayā*—transcendental bliss; *śāmyat*—mitigating; *śāstra*—of revealed scriptures; *vivādayā*—disagreements; *rasa-dayā*—distributing all transcendental mellows; *citta*—in the heart; *arpita*—fixed; *unmādayā*—jubilation; *śaśvat*—always; *bhakti*—devotional service; *vinodayā*—stimulating; *sa-madayā*—full of ecstasy; *mādhurya*—of conjugal love; *maryādayā*—the limit; *śrī-caitanya*—O Lord Śrī Caitanya Mahāprabhu; *dayā-nidhe*—ocean of mercy; *tava*—Your; *dayā*—mercy; *bhūyāt*—let it be; *amanda*—of good fortune; *udayā*—in which there is awakening.

TRANSLATION

"O ocean of mercy, Śrī Caitanya Mahāprabhu! Let there be an awakening of Your auspicious mercy, which easily drives away all kinds of material lamentation. By Your mercy, everything is made pure and blissful. It awakens transcendental bliss and covers all gross material pleasures. By Your auspicious mercy, quarrels and disagreements arising among different scriptures are vanquished. Your auspicious mercy causes the heart to jubilate by pouring forth transcendental mellows. Your mercy always stimulates devotional service, which is full of joy. You are always glorifying the conjugal love of God. May transcendental bliss be awakened within my heart by Your causeless mercy."

PURPORT

This important verse quoted from *Śrī Caitanya-candrodaya-nāṭaka* (8.10) specifically describes the Lord's causeless mercy. Śrīla Bhaktisiddhānta Sarasvatī Ṭhākura explains that Śrī Caitanya Mahāprabhu, who is the most magnanimous Personality of Godhead, distributes His causeless mercy in three ways to the conditioned soul. Every living entity is morose in the material world because he is always in want. He undergoes a great struggle for existence and tries to minimize his miserable condition by squeezing the utmost pleasure out of this world. However, the living entity is never successful in this endeavor. While in a miserable condition, a person sometimes seeks the favor of the Supreme Personality of Godhead, but this is very difficult for materialistic people to obtain. However, when one becomes Kṛṣṇa conscious by the grace of the Lord, the flavor of the lotus feet of the Lord expands, and in this way a materialist may gain freedom from his miseries. Actually his mind is cleansed by his transcendental connection with the lotus feet of the Lord. At such a time one is enlightened by the loving service of the Lord.

There are many different kinds of scripture, and by reading them one often becomes puzzled. However, when one receives the mercy of the Lord, his confusion is mitigated. Not only are scriptural disparities resolved, but a kind of transcendental bliss is awakened, and in this way one is fully satisfied. The transcendental loving service of the Lord constantly engages the conditioned soul in serving the Lord's lotus feet. Through such fortunate engagement, one's transcendental love for Kṛṣṇa is increased. One's position is thus completely purified, and one is filled with transcendental bliss accompanied by the spirit soul's jubilation.

Thus the transcendental causeless mercy of Lord Kṛṣṇa is manifest in the heart of the devotee. At such a time, material needs no longer exist. The lamentation that invariably accompanies material desires also vanishes. By the grace of the Lord one is elevated to the transcendental position, and then the transcendental mellows of the spiritual world are manifest in him. One's devotional service then becomes firm, and one engages in the Lord's transcendental loving service with great determination. All these combine to fully awaken the devotee's heart with love of Kṛṣṇa.

In the beginning, a conditioned soul is bereft of Kṛṣṇa consciousness and is always morose in his material activities. Later, by associating with a pure devotee, one becomes inquisitive to know the Absolute Truth. In this way one begins to engage in the transcendental service of the Lord.

It is by the Lord's grace that all misconceptions are vanquished and the heart cleansed of all material dirt. It is only then that the pleasure of transcendental bliss is awakened. By the Lord's mercy one is finally convinced of the value of devotional service. When one can see the pastimes of the Lord everywhere, he is firmly situated in transcendental bliss. Such a devotee is relieved of all kinds of material desires, and he preaches the glories of the Lord all over the world. Kṛṣṇa conscious activities separate one from material activities and the desire for liberation. At every step the devotee feels himself connected with the Supreme Personality of Godhead. Although such a devotee may sometimes be involved in household life, he is untouched by material existence due to his constant engagement in devotional service. Thus everyone is advised to take shelter of devotional service to become happy and liberated.

TEXT 120

উঠাঞা মহাপ্রভু কৈল আলিঙ্গন ।
দুইজনে প্রেমাবেশে হৈল অচেতন ॥ ১২০ ॥

uṭhāñā mahāprabhu kaila āliṅgana
dui-jane premāveśe haila acetana

SYNONYMS

uṭhāñā—after raising him; *mahāprabhu*—Lord Śrī Caitanya Mahāprabhu; *kaila*—made; *āliṅgana*—embracing; *dui-jane*—two persons; *prema-āveśe*—in the ecstasy of love; *haila*—became; *acetana*—unconscious.

TRANSLATION

Śrī Caitanya Mahāprabhu raised Svarūpa Dāmodara to his feet and embraced him. They both became ecstatic in love and fell unconscious.

TEXT 121

কতক্ষণে দুই জনে স্থির যবে হৈলা ।
তবে মহাপ্রভু তাঁরে কহিতে লাগিলা ॥ ১২১ ॥

kata-kṣaṇe dui jane sthira yabe hailā
tabe mahāprabhu tāṅre kahite lāgilā

SYNONYMS

kata-kṣaṇe—after some time; *dui jane*—both persons; *sthira*—patient; *yabe*—when; *hailā*—became; *tabe*—at that time; *mahāprabhu*—Śrī Caitanya Mahāprabhu; *tāṅre*—unto him; *kahite*—to speak; *lāgilā*—began.

TRANSLATION

After they had both regained their patience, Śrī Caitanya Mahāprabhu began to speak.

TEXT 122

তুমি যে আসিবে, আজি স্বপ্নেতে দেখিল ।
ভাল হৈল, অন্ধ যেন দুই নেত্র পাইল ॥ ১২২ ॥

tumi ye āsibe, āji svapnete dekhila
bhāla haila, andha yena dui netra pāila

SYNONYMS

tumi—you; *ye*—that; *āsibe*—will come; *āji*—today; *svapnete*—in dream; *dekhila*—I saw; *bhāla haila*—it is very good; *andha*—a blind man; *yena*—as if; *dui*—two; *netra*—eyes; *pāila*—got back.

TRANSLATION

Śrī Caitanya Mahāprabhu said, "I saw in a dream that you were coming, and so this is very auspicious. I have been like a blind man, but your coming here restores My vision."

TEXT 123

স্বরূপ কহে,—প্রভু, মোর ক্ষম' অপরাধ ।
তোমা ছাড়ি' অন্যত্র গেনু, করিনু প্রমাদ ॥ ১২৩ ॥

svarūpa kahe,——prabhu, mora kṣama' aparādha
tomā chāḍi' anyatra genu, karinu pramāda

SYNONYMS

svarūpa kahe—Svarūpa Dāmodara said; *prabhu*—my Lord; *mora*—my; *kṣama'*—please excuse; *aparādha*—offense; *tomā*—You; *chāḍi'*—giving up; *anyatra*—elsewhere; *genu*—I went; *karinu*—I have done; *pramāda*—great mistake.

TRANSLATION

Svarūpa said, "My dear Lord, please excuse my offense. I gave up Your company to go elsewhere, and that was my great mistake.

TEXT 124

তোমার চরণে মোর নাহি প্রেম-লেশ ।
তোমা ছাড়ি' পাপী মুঞি গেনু অন্য দেশ ॥ ১২৪ ॥

tomāra caraṇe mora nāhi prema-leśa
tomā chāḍi' pāpī muñi genu anya deśa

SYNONYMS

tomāra caraṇe—at Your lotus feet; *mora*—my; *nāhi*—there is not; *prema-leśa*—a trace of love; *tomā*—You; *chāḍi'*—giving up; *pāpī*—sinful; *muñi*—I; *genu*—went; *anya deśa*—to another country.

TRANSLATION

"My dear Lord, I do not even possess a trace of love at Your lotus feet. If I did, how could I go to another country? I am therefore a most sinful man.

TEXT 125

মুঞি তোমা ছাড়িল, তুমি মোরে না ছাড়িলা ।
কৃপা-পাশ গলে বান্ধি' চরণে আনিলা ॥ ১২৫ ॥

muñi tomā chāḍila, tumi more nā chāḍilā
kṛpā-pāśa gale bāndhi' caraṇe ānilā

SYNONYMS

muñi—I; *tomā*—You; *chāḍila*—gave up; *tumi*—You; *more*—me; *nā*—did not; *chāḍilā*—give up; *kṛpā*—of mercy; *pāśa*—by the rope; *gale*—by the neck; *bāndhi'*—binding; *caraṇe*—at Your lotus feet; *ānilā*—You brought back.

TRANSLATION

"I gave up your company, but You did not give me up. By Your merciful rope You have bound me by the neck and brought me back again to Your lotus feet."

TEXT 126

তবে স্বরূপ কৈল নিতাইর চরণ বন্দন ।
নিত্যানন্দপ্রভু কৈল প্রেম-আলিঙ্গন ॥ ১২৬ ॥

tabe svarūpa kaila nitāira caraṇa vandana
nityānanda-prabhu kaila prema-āliṅgana

SYNONYMS

tabe—thereafter; *svarūpa*—Svarūpa Dāmodara; *kaila*—did; *nitāira*—of Nityānanda Prabhu; *caraṇa*—of the lotus feet; *vandana*—worship; *nityānanda-prabhu*—Lord Nityānanda; *kaila*—did; *prema-āliṅgana*—embracing in love.

TRANSLATION

Svarūpa Dāmodara then worshiped the lotus feet of Nityānanda Prabhu, and Nityānanda in turn embraced him in the ecstasy of love.

TEXT 127

জগদানন্দ, মুকুন্দ, শঙ্কর, সার্বভৌম ।
সবা-সঙ্গে যথাযোগ্য করিল মিলন ॥ ১২৭ ॥

jagadānanda, mukunda, śaṅkara, sārvabhauma
sabā-saṅge yathā-yogya karila milana

SYNONYMS

jagadānanda—Jagadānanda; *mukunda*—Mukunda; *śaṅkara*—Śaṅkara; *sārvabhauma*—Sārvabhauma; *sabā-saṅge*—with all; *yathā-yogya*—as is befitting; *karila*—did; *milana*—meeting.

TRANSLATION

After worshiping Nityānanda Prabhu, Svarūpa Dāmodara met Jagadānanda, Mukunda, Śaṅkara and Sārvabhauma, as was befitting.

TEXT 128

পরমানন্দ পুরীর কৈল চরণ বন্দন ।
পুরী-গোসাঞি তাঁরে কৈল প্রেম-আলিঙ্গন ॥ ১২৮ ॥

paramānanda purīra kaila caraṇa vandana
purī-gosāñi tāṅre kaila prema-āliṅgana

SYNONYMS

paramānanda purīra—of Paramānanda Purī; *kaila*—he did; *caraṇa vandana*—worshiping the lotus feet; *purī-gosāñi*—Paramānanda Purī; *tāṅre*—unto him; *kaila*—did; *prema-āliṅgana*—embracing in love.

TRANSLATION

Svarūpa Dāmodara also offered his worshipful prayers at the lotus feet of Paramānanda Purī, who, in return, embraced him in ecstatic love.

TEXT 129

মহাপ্রভু দিল তাঁরে নিভৃতে বাসাঘর ।
জলাদি-পরিচর্যা লাগি' দিল এক কিঙ্কর ॥ ১২৯ ॥

mahāprabhu dila tāṅre nibhṛte vāsā-ghara
jalādi-paricaryā lāgi' dila eka kiṅkara

SYNONYMS

mahāprabhu—Śrī Caitanya Mahāprabhu; *dila*—gave; *tāṅre*—unto him; *nibhṛte*—in a solitary place; *vāsā-ghara*—residential quarters; *jala-ādi*—supplying water, etc.; *paricaryā*—service; *lāgi'*—for the purpose of; *dila*—gave; *eka*—one; *kiṅkara*—servant.

TRANSLATION

Śrī Caitanya Mahāprabhu then gave Svarūpa Dāmodara residence in a solitary place and ordered one servant to serve him with a supply of water and other necessities.

TEXT 130

আর দিন সার্বভৌম-আদি ভক্ত-সঙ্গে ।
বসিয়া আছেন মহাপ্রভু কৃষ্ণকথা-রঙ্গে ॥ ১৩০ ॥

āra dina sārvabhauma-ādi bhakta-saṅge
vasiyā āchena mahāprabhu kṛṣṇa-kathā-raṅge

SYNONYMS

āra dina—the next day; *sārvabhauma-ādi*—headed by Sārvabhauma Bhaṭṭācārya; *bhakta-saṅge*—with the devotees; *vasiyā āchena*—was sitting;

mahāprabhu—Śrī Caitanya Mahāprabhu; *kṛṣṇa-kathā-raṅge*—engaged in discussions of topics concerning Kṛṣṇa.

TRANSLATION

The next day Śrī Caitanya Mahāprabhu sat with all the devotees, headed by Sārvabhauma Bhaṭṭācārya, and they discussed the pastimes of Kṛṣṇa.

TEXT 131

হেনকালে গোবিন্দের হৈল আগমন ।
দণ্ডবৎ করি' কহে বিনয়-বচন ॥ ১৩১ ॥

hena-kāle govindera haila āgamana
daṇḍavat kari' kahe vinaya-vacana

SYNONYMS

hena-kāle—at that time; *govindera*—of Govinda; *haila*—there was; *āgamana*—arrival; *daṇḍavat kari'*—offering obeisances; *kahe*—says; *vinaya-vacana*—submissive words.

TRANSLATION

At that time Govinda appeared on the scene, offered his respectful obeisances and spoke submissively.

TEXT 132

ঈশ্বর-পুরীর ভৃত্য,—'গোবিন্দ' মোর নাম ।
পুরী-গোসাঞির আজ্ঞায় আইনু তোমার স্থান॥১৩২॥

īśvara-purīra bhṛtya,——'govinda' mora nāma
purī-gosāñira ājñāya āinu tomāra sthāna

SYNONYMS

īśvara-purīra bhṛtya—servant of Īśvara Purī; *govinda mora nāma*—my name is Govinda; *purī-gosāñira*—of Īśvara Purī; *ājñāya*—on the order; *āinu*—I have come; *tomāra*—to your; *sthāna*—place.

TRANSLATION

"I am the servant of Īśvara Purī. My name is Govinda, and, following the orders of my spiritual master, I have come here.

TEXT 133

সিদ্ধিপ্রাপ্তিকালে গোসাঞি আজ্ঞা কৈল মোরে।
কৃষ্ণচৈতন্য-নিকটে রহি সেবিহ তাঁহারে ॥ ১৩৩ ॥

siddha-prāpti-kāle gosāñi ājñā kaila more
kṛṣṇa-caitanya-nikaṭe rahi seviha tāṅhāre

SYNONYMS

siddhi-prāpti-kāle—at the time of his departure from this mortal world to achieve the highest perfection of life; *gosāñi*—my spiritual master; *ājñā*—order; *kaila*—made; *more*—unto me; *kṛṣṇa-caitanya-nikaṭe*—at the place of Śrī Kṛṣṇa Caitanya; *rahi*—remaining; *seviha*—render service; *tāṅhāre*—unto Him.

TRANSLATION

"Just before his departure from this mortal world to attain the highest perfection, Īśvara Purī told me that I should go to Śrī Caitanya Mahāprabhu and render service unto Him.

TEXT 134

কাশীশ্বর আসিবেন সব তীর্থ দেখিয়া।
প্রভু-আজ্ঞায় মুঞি আইনু তোমা-পদে ধাঞা॥১৩৪॥

kāśīśvara āsibena saba tīrtha dekhiyā
prabhu-ājñāya muñi āinu tomā-pade dhāñā

SYNONYMS

kāśīśvara—Kāśīśvara; *āsibena*—will come; *saba*—all; *tīrtha*—holy places; *dekhiyā*—visiting; *prabhu-ājñāya*—under the order of my spiritual master; *muñi*—I; *āinu*—have come; *tomā*—to your; *pade*—lotus feet; *dhāñā*—running.

TRANSLATION

"Kāśīśvara will also come here after visiting all the holy places. However, following the orders of my spiritual master, I have hastily come to be present at Your lotus feet."

TEXT 135

গোসাঞি কহিল, 'পুরীশ্বর' বাৎসল্য করে মোরে।
কৃপা করি' মোর ঠাঞি পাঠাইলা তোমারে ॥১৩৫॥

gosāñi kahila, 'purīśvara' vātsalya kare more
kṛpā kari' mora ṭhāñi pāṭhāilā tomāre

SYNONYMS

gosāñi kahila—Śrī Caitanya Mahāprabhu replied; *purīśvara*—Īśvara Purī; *vātsalya*—paternal affection; *kare*—does; *more*—unto Me; *kṛpā kari'*—being merciful; *mora ṭhāñi*—to My place; *pāṭhāilā*—sent; *tomāre*—you.

TRANSLATION

Śrī Caitanya Mahāprabhu replied, "My spiritual master, Īśvara Purī, always favors me with paternal affection. Therefore, out of his causeless mercy, he has sent you here."

TEXT 136

এত শুনি' সার্বভৌম প্রভুরে পুছিল।
পুরী-গোসাঞি শূদ্র-সেবক কাঁহে ত' রাখিল ॥১৩৬॥

eta śuni' sārvabhauma prabhure puchila
purī-gosāñi śūdra-sevaka kāṅhe ta' rākhila

SYNONYMS

eta śuni'—hearing this; *sārvabhauma*—Sārvabhauma Bhaṭṭācārya; *prabhure*—unto the Lord; *puchila*—inquired; *purī-gosāñi*—Īśvara Purī; *śūdra-sevaka*—a servant who is a *śūdra*; *kāṅhe ta'*—why; *rākhila*—kept.

TRANSLATION

After hearing this, Sārvabhauma Bhaṭṭācārya asked Śrī Caitanya Mahāprabhu, "Why did Īśvara Purī keep a servant who comes from a śūdra family?"

PURPORT

Both Kāśīśvara and Govinda were personal servants of Īśvara Purī. After Īśvara Purī's demise, Kāśīśvara went to visit all the holy places of India. Following the orders of his spiritual master, Govinda immediately went to Śrī Caitanya Mahāprabhu for shelter. Govinda came from a *śūdra* family, but because he was initiated by Īśvara Purī, he was certainly a *brāhmaṇa*. Sārvabhauma Bhaṭṭācārya here asked Śrī Caitanya Mahāprabhu why Īśvara Purī accepted a disciple from a *śūdra* family. According to the *smṛti-śāstra*, which gives directions for the management of the *varṇāśrama* institution, a *brāhmaṇa* cannot accept a disciple from the lower castes. In other words, a *kṣatriya, vaiśya* or *śūdra* cannot be accepted as a servant. If a spiritual master accepts such a person, he is contaminated. Sārvabhauma Bhaṭṭācārya therefore asked why Īśvara Purī accepted a servant or disciple born of a *śūdra* family.

In answer to this, Śrī Caitanya Mahāprabhu replied that his spiritual master, Īśvara Purī, was so empowered that he was as good as the Supreme Personality of Godhead. As such, Īśvara Purī was the spiritual master of the whole world. He was not a servant to any mundane rule or regulation. An empowered spiritual master like Īśvara Purī can bestow his mercy upon anyone, irrespective of caste or creed. The conclusion is that an empowered spiritual master is authorized by Kṛṣṇa and should be considered to be as good as the Supreme Personality of Godhead Himself. That is the verdict of Viśvanātha Cakravartī: *sākṣād-dharitvena samasta-śāstraiḥ*. An authorized spiritual master is as good as Hari, the Supreme Personality of Godhead. If Hari is free to act as He likes, the empowered spiritual master is also free. As Hari is not subject to the criticism of mundane rules and regulations, the spiritual master empowered by Him is also not subjected. According to *Caitanya-caritāmṛta* (*Antya-līlā* 7.11): *kṛṣṇa-śakti vinā nahe tāra pravartana*. An authorized spiritual master empowered by Kṛṣṇa can spread the glories of the holy name of the Lord, for he has power of attorney from the Supreme Personality of Godhead. In the mundane world, anyone possessing his master's power of attorney can act on behalf of his master. Similarly, a spiritual master empowered by Kṛṣṇa through his bona fide spiritual master should be considered as good as the Supreme Personality of Godhead Himself. That is the meaning of *sākṣād-dharitvena*. Śrī Caitanya Mahāprabhu therefore describes the activities of the Supreme Personality of Godhead and the bona fide spiritual master as follows.

TEXT 137

প্রভু কহে,—ঈশ্বর হয় পরম স্বতন্ত্র ।
ঈশ্বরের কৃপা নহে বেদ-পরতন্ত্র ॥ ১৩৭ ॥

prabhu kahe,——īśvara haya parama svatantra
īśvarera kṛpā nahe veda-paratantra

SYNONYMS

prabhu kahe—Śrī Caitanya Mahāprabhu said; *īśvara*—the Supreme Personality of Godhead or Īśvara Purī; *haya*—is; *parama*—supremely; *svatantra*—independent; *īśvarera*—of the Supreme Personality of Godhead or of Īśvara Purī; *kṛpā*—the mercy; *nahe*—is not; *veda-paratantra*—subjected to the Vedic rules.

TRANSLATION

Śrī Caitanya Mahāprabhu said, "Both the Supreme Personality of Godhead and the spiritual master, Īśvara Purī, are completely independent. Therefore

the mercy of the Supreme Personality of Godhead and Īśvara Purī is not subjected to any Vedic rules and regulations.

TEXT 138

ঈশ্বরের কৃপা জাতি-কুলাদি না মানে ।
বিদুরের ঘরে কৃষ্ণ করিলা ভোজনে ॥ ১৩৮ ॥

īśvarera kṛpā jāti-kulādi nā māne
vidurera ghare kṛṣṇa karilā bhojane

SYNONYMS

īśvarera kṛpā—the mercy of the Lord; *jāti*—caste; *kula-ādi*—family, etc.; *nā māne*—does not obey; *vidurera*—of Vidura; *ghare*—at the home; *kṛṣṇa*—Lord Kṛṣṇa; *karilā*—did; *bhojane*—eating.

TRANSLATION

"The mercy of the Supreme Personality of Godhead is not restricted to the jurisdiction of caste and creed. Vidura was a śūdra, yet Kṛṣṇa accepted lunch at his home.

TEXT 139

স্নেহ-লেশাপেক্ষা মাত্র শ্রীকৃষ্ণ-কৃপার ।
স্নেহবশ হঞা করে স্বতন্ত্র আচার ॥ ১৩৯ ॥

sneha-leśāpekṣā mātra śrī-kṛṣṇa-kṛpāra
sneha-vaśa hañā kare svatantra ācāra

SYNONYMS

sneha—of affection; *leśa*—on a trace; *apekṣā*—reliance; *mātra*—only; *śrī-kṛṣṇa*—of Lord Śrī Kṛṣṇa; *kṛpāra*—of the mercy; *sneha-vaśa*—obliged by affection; *hañā*—being; *kare*—does; *svatantra*—independent; *ācāra*—behavior.

TRANSLATION

"Lord Kṛṣṇa's mercy is dependent only on affection. Being obliged only by affection, Lord Kṛṣṇa acts very independently.

PURPORT

Lord Śrī Kṛṣṇa, the Supreme Personality of Godhead, is merciful, but His mercy does not depend on mundane rules and regulations. He is dependent only on affection and nothing else. Service to Lord Kṛṣṇa can be rendered in two ways. One can serve the Lord in affection or in veneration. When service is rendered in affection, it is the Lord's special mercy. When service is rendered in veneration, it is doubtful whether Kṛṣṇa's mercy is actually involved. If Kṛṣṇa's mercy is there, it is not dependent on any prescribed caste or creed. Śrī Caitanya Mahāprabhu wanted to inform Sārvabhauma Bhaṭṭācārya that Lord Kṛṣṇa is the spiritual master of everyone, and He does not care for mundane caste or creed. Therefore Śrī Caitanya Mahāprabhu cited the example of Lord Kṛṣṇa's accepting food at the house of Vidura, who was a *śūdra* by birth. By the same token, Īśvara Purī, an empowered spiritual master, could show mercy to anyone. As such, he accepted Govinda, although the boy was born in a *śūdra* family. When Govinda was initiated, he became a *brāhmaṇa* and was accepted as Īśvara Purī's personal servant. In the *Hari-bhakti-vilāsa,* Śrī Sanātana Gosvāmī states that if one is initiated by a bona fide spiritual master, he immediately becomes a *brāhmaṇa.* A pseudo spiritual master cannot transform a person into a *brāhmaṇa,* but an authorized spiritual master can do so. This is the verdict of *śāstra,* Śrī Caitanya Mahāprabhu and all the Gosvāmīs.

TEXT 140

মর্যাদা হৈতে কোটি সুখ স্নেহ-আচরণে ।
পরমানন্দ হয় যার নাম-শ্রবণে ॥ ১৪০ ॥

maryādā haite koṭi sukha sneha-ācaraṇe
paramānanda haya yāra nāma-śravaṇe

SYNONYMS

maryādā haite—greater than veneration and awe; *koṭi*—millions of times; *sukha*—happiness; *sneha*—with affection; *ācaraṇe*—in dealings; *parama-ānanda*—transcendental bliss; *haya*—there is; *yāra*—whose; *nāma*—holy name; *śravaṇe*—by hearing.

TRANSLATION

"In conclusion, dealings in affection with the Supreme Personality of Godhead bring happiness many millions of times greater than dealings with Him in awe and veneration. Simply by hearing the holy name of the Lord, the devotee is merged in transcendental bliss."

TEXT 141

এত বলি' গোবিন্দেরে কৈল আলিঙ্গন ।
গোবিন্দ করিল প্রভুর চরণ বন্দন ॥ ১৪১ ॥

eta bali' govindere kaila āliṅgana
govinda karila prabhura caraṇa vandana

SYNONYMS

eta bali'—saying this; *govindere*—unto Govinda; *kaila*—did; *āliṅgana*—embracing; *govinda*—Govinda; *karila*—did; *prabhura*—of Lord Śrī Caitanya Mahāprabhu; *caraṇa vandana*—worshiping the lotus feet.

TRANSLATION

After saying this, Śrī Caitanya Mahāprabhu embraced Govinda, and Govinda in turn offered his respectful obeisances unto Śrī Caitanya Mahāprabhu's lotus feet.

TEXT 142

প্রভু কহে,—ভট্টাচার্য, করহ বিচার।
গুরুর কিঙ্কর হয় মান্য সে আমার ॥ ১৪২ ॥

prabhu kahe,—bhaṭṭācārya, karaha vicāra
gurura kiṅkara haya mānya se āmāra

SYNONYMS

prabhu kahe—Śrī Caitanya Mahāprabhu said; *bhaṭṭācārya*—My dear Bhaṭṭācārya; *karaha vicāra*—just consider; *gurura kiṅkara*—the servant of the spiritual master; *haya*—is; *mānya*—respectable; *se*—he; *āmāra*—to Me.

TRANSLATION

Śrī Caitanya Mahāprabhu then continued speaking to Sārvabhauma Bhaṭṭācārya. "Consider this point. The servant of the spiritual master is always respectable for Me.

TEXT 143

তাঁহারে আপন-সেবা করাইতে না যুয়ায়।
গুরু আজ্ঞা দিয়াছেন, কি করি উপায় ॥ ১৪৩ ॥

tāṅhāre āpana-sevā karāite nā yuyāya
guru ājñā diyāchena, ki kari upāya

SYNONYMS

tāṅhāre—him; *āpana-sevā*—personal service; *karāite*—to engage to do; *nā yuyāya*—is not befitting; *guru*—the spiritual master; *ājñā*—order; *diyāchena*—has given; *ki*—what; *kari*—can I do; *upāya*—remedy.

TRANSLATION

"As such, it is not befitting that the guru's servant should engage in My personal service. Yet My spiritual master has given this order. What shall I do?"

PURPORT

If a *guru's* servant or disciple becomes Godbrother to another disciple, they respect one another as *prabhu,* or master. No one should disrespect his Godbrother. For this reason Śrī Caitanya Mahāprabhu asked Sārvabhauma Bhaṭṭācārya what to do about Govinda. Govinda was the personal servant of Īśvara Purī, Śrī Caitanya Mahāprabhu's spiritual master. Īśvara Purī ordered Govinda to become Śrī Caitanya Mahāprabhu's personal servant, so what was to be done? Śrī Caitanya Mahāprabhu was therefore inquiring from Bhaṭṭācārya, an experienced friend.

TEXT 144

ভট্ট কহে,—গুরুর আজ্ঞা হয় বলবান্ ।
গুরু-আজ্ঞা না লঙ্ঘিয়ে, শাস্ত্র—প্রমাণ ॥ ১৪৪ ॥

bhaṭṭa kahe,——gurura ājñā haya balavān
guru-ājñā nā laṅghiye, śāstra——pramāṇa

SYNONYMS

bhaṭṭa kahe—Sārvabhauma Bhaṭṭācārya said; *gurura ājñā*—the order of the spiritual master; *haya*—is; *balavān*—strong; *guru-ājñā*—the order of the spiritual master; *nā*—not; *laṅghiye*—we can disobey; *śāstra*—scriptural; *pramāṇa*—injunction.

TRANSLATION

Sārvabhauma Bhaṭṭācārya said, "The order of the spiritual master is very strong and cannot be disobeyed. That is the injunction of the śāstras, the revealed scriptures.

TEXT 145

স শুশ্রুবান্মাতরি ভার্গবেণ পিতুর্নিয়োগাৎ প্রহৃতং দ্বিষদ্বৎ ।
প্রত্যগৃহীদগ্রজশাসনং তদাজ্ঞা গুরূণাং হ্যবিচারণীয়া ॥১৪৫॥

sa śuśruvān mātari bhārgaveṇa
pitur niyogāt prahṛtaṁ dviṣadvat
pratyagṛhīd agraja-śāsanaṁ tad
ājñā gurūṇāṁ hy avicāraṇīyā

SYNONYMS

saḥ—He; *śuśruvān*—the brother of Lord Rāmacandra; *mātari*—unto the mother; *bhārgaveṇa*—by Paraśurāma; *pituḥ*—of the father; *niyogāt*—by the order; *prahṛtam*—killing; *dviṣat-vat*—like an enemy; *pratyagṛhīt*—accepted; *agra-ja-śāsanam*—the order of the elder brother; *tat*—that; *ājñā*—order; *gurūṇām*—of superior persons, such as the spiritual master or father; *hi*—because; *avicāraṇīyā*—to be obeyed without consideration.

TRANSLATION

" 'Being ordered by his father, Paraśurāma killed his mother, Reṇukā, just as if she were an enemy. Lakṣmaṇa, the younger brother of Lord Rāmacandra, immediately engaged Himself in the service of His elder brother and accepted His orders. The order of the spiritual master must be obeyed without consideration.'

PURPORT

This is a quotation from the *Purāṇas* (*Raghu-vaṁśa* 14.46). Lord Rāmacandra's statement to Sītā given below is from the *Rāmāyaṇa* (*Ayodhyā-kāṇḍa* 22.9).

TEXT 146

নির্বিচারং গুরোরাজ্ঞা ময়া কার্যা মহাত্মনঃ ।
শ্রেয়ো হ্যেবং ভবত্যাশ্চ মম চৈব বিশেষতঃ ॥ ১৪৬ ॥

nirvicāraṁ guror ājñā
mayā kāryā mahātmanaḥ
śreyo hy evaṁ bhavatyāś ca
mama caiva viśeṣataḥ

SYNONYMS

nirvicāram—to be obeyed without consideration; *guroḥ*—of the spiritual master; *ājñā*—the order; *mayā*—by Me; *kāryā*—must be done; *mahā-ātmanaḥ*—of the great soul; *śreyaḥ*—good fortune; *hi*—indeed; *evam*—thus; *bhavatyāḥ*—for you; *ca*—and; *mama*—for Me; *ca*—also; *eva*—certainly; *viśeṣataḥ*—specifically.

TRANSLATION

" 'The order of a great personality like a father must be executed without consideration because there is good fortune in such an order for both of us. In particular, there is good fortune for Me.' "

TEXT 147

তবে মহাপ্রভু তাঁরে কৈল অঙ্গীকার ।
আপন-শ্রীঅঙ্গ-সেবায় দিল অধিকার ॥ ১৪৭ ॥

tabe mahāprabhu tāṅre kaila aṅgīkāra
āpana-śrī-aṅga-sevāya dila adhikāra

SYNONYMS

tabe—after that; *mahāprabhu*—Śrī Caitanya Mahāprabhu; *tāṅre*—unto Govinda; *kaila*—did; *aṅgīkāra*—acceptance; *āpana*—personal; *śrī-aṅga*—of the transcendental body; *sevāya*—in the service; *dila*—gave; *adhikāra*—responsibility.

TRANSLATION

After Sārvabhauma Bhaṭṭācārya said this, Śrī Caitanya Mahāprabhu embraced Govinda and engaged him in the service of His personal body.

TEXT 148

প্রভুর প্রিয় ভৃত্য করি' সবে করে মান ।
সকল বৈষ্ণবের গোবিন্দ করে সমাধান ॥ ১৪৮ ॥

prabhura priya bhṛtya kari' sabe kare māna
sakala vaiṣṇavera govinda kare samādhāna

SYNONYMS

prabhura—of Lord Śrī Caitanya Mahāprabhu; *priya*—dear; *bhṛtya*—servant; *kari'*—understanding; *sabe*—all; *kare*—do; *māna*—respect; *sakala*—all; *vaiṣṇavera*—of devotees; *govinda*—Govinda; *kare*—does; *samādhāna*—service.

TRANSLATION

Everyone respected Govinda as the dearest servant of Śrī Caitanya Mahāprabhu, and Govinda served all the Vaiṣṇavas and saw to their needs.

TEXT 149

ছোট-বড়-কীর্তনীয়া—দুই হরিদাস ।
রামাই, নন্দাই রহে গোবিন্দের পাশ ॥ ১৪৯ ॥

choṭa-baḍa-kīrtanīyā—dui haridāsa
rāmāi, nandāi rahe govindera pāśa

SYNONYMS

choṭa-baḍa—junior and senior; *kīrtanīyā*—musicians; *dui*—two; *hari-dāsa*—Haridāsa; *rāmāi*—Rāmāi; *nandāi*—Nandāi; *rahe*—stay; *govindera pāśa*—with Govinda.

TRANSLATION

Both Haridāsa senior and Haridāsa junior, who were musicians, as well as Rāmāi and Nandāi, used to stay with Govinda.

TEXT 150

গোবিন্দের সঙ্গে করে প্রভুর সেবন।
গোবিন্দের ভাগ্যসীমা না যায় বর্ণন ॥ ১৫০ ॥

govindera saṅge kare prabhura sevana
govindera bhāgya-sīmā nā yāya varṇana

SYNONYMS

govindera saṅge—with Govinda; *kare*—do; *prabhura*—of Śrī Caitanya Mahāprabhu; *sevana*—service; *govindera*—of Govinda; *bhāgya-sīmā*—the limit of fortune; *nā*—not; *yāya varṇana*—can be described.

TRANSLATION

They all remained with Govinda to serve Śrī Caitanya Mahāprabhu; therefore no one could estimate the good fortune of Govinda.

TEXT 151

আর দিনে মুকুন্দদত্ত কহে প্রভুর স্থানে।
ব্রহ্মানন্দ-ভারতী আইলা তোমার দরশনে ॥ ১৫১ ॥

āra dine mukunda-datta kahe prabhura sthāne
brahmānanda-bhāratī āilā tomāra daraśane

SYNONYMS

āra dine—the next day; *mukunda-datta*—Mukunda Datta; *kahe*—said; *prabhura*—of Śrī Caitanya Mahāprabhu; *sthāne*—at the place; *brahmānanda-bhāratī*—Brahmānanda Bhāratī; *āilā*—has come; *tomāra daraśane*—to see You.

TRANSLATION

The next day Mukunda Datta informed Śrī Caitanya Mahāprabhu, "Brahmānanda Bhāratī has come to see You."

TEXT 152

আজ্ঞা দেহ' যদি তাঁরে আনিয়ে এথাই ।
প্রভু কহে,—গুরু তেঁহ, যাব তাঁর ঠাঞি ॥ ১৫২ ॥

ājñā deha' yadi tāṅre āniye ethāi
prabhu kahe,——guru teṅha, yāba tāṅra ṭhāñi

SYNONYMS

ājñā deha'—order; *yadi*—if; *tāṅre*—him; *āniye*—I can bring; *ethāi*—here; *prabhu kahe*—Śrī Caitanya Mahāprabhu said; *guru teṅha*—he is My spiritual master; *yāba*—I shall go; *tāṅra ṭhāñi*—to his place.

TRANSLATION

Mukunda Datta then asked the Lord, "Shall I bring him here?" Śrī Caitanya Mahāprabhu said, "Brahmānanda Bhāratī is like My spiritual master. It is better that I go to him."

TEXT 153

এত বলি' মহাপ্রভু ভক্তগণ-সঙ্গে ।
চলি' আইলা ব্রহ্মানন্দ-ভারতীর আগে ॥ ১৫৩ ॥

eta bali' mahāprabhu bhakta-gaṇa-saṅge
cali' āilā brahmānanda-bhāratīra āge

SYNONYMS

eta bali'—saying this; *mahāprabhu*—Śrī Caitanya Mahāprabhu; *bhakta-gaṇa-saṅge*—with the devotees; *cali'*—walking; *āilā*—came; *brahmānanda-bhāratīra*—of Brahmānanda Bhāratī; *āge*—in the presence.

TRANSLATION

After saying this, Śrī Caitanya Mahāprabhu and His devotees came before the presence of Brahmānanda Bhāratī.

TEXT 154

ব্রহ্মানন্দ পরিয়াছে মৃগচর্মাম্বর ।
তাহা দেখি' প্রভু দুঃখ পাইলা অন্তর ॥ ১৫৪ ॥

brahmānanda pariyāche mṛga-carmāmbara
tāhā dekhi' prabhu duḥkha pāilā antara

SYNONYMS

brahmānanda—Brahmānanda; *pariyāche*—did wear; *mṛga-carma-ambara*—a garment made of deerskin; *tāhā dekhi'*—seeing that; *prabhu*—Śrī Caitanya Mahāprabhu; *duḥkha*—unhappiness; *pāilā*—got; *antara*—within Himself.

TRANSLATION

When Śrī Caitanya Mahāprabhu and His devotees approached him, they saw that he was covered with a deerskin. Seeing this, Śrī Caitanya Mahāprabhu became very unhappy.

PURPORT

Brahmānanda Bhāratī belonged to the Śaṅkara-sampradāya. The title *bhāratī* indicates one of the ten *sannyāsīs* in the Śaṅkara-sampradāya. It is customary for a person who has renounced the world to cover his body with a deerskin or the bark of a tree. This is enjoined by *Manu-saṁhitā*. However, if a *sannyāsī* who has renounced the world simply wears a deerskin and does not spiritually advance, he is simply puffed up and conceited. Śrī Caitanya Mahāprabhu did not like to see Brahmānanda Bhāratī wearing a deerskin.

TEXT 155

দেখিয়া ত' ছদ্ম কৈল যেন দেখে নাঞি ।
মুকুন্দেরে পুছে,—কাহাঁ ভারতী-গোসাঞি ॥ ১৫৫ ॥

dekhiyā ta' chadma kaila yena dekhe nāñi
mukundere puche,——kāhāṅ bhāratī-gosāñi

SYNONYMS

dekhiyā—seeing; *ta'*—certainly; *chadma kaila*—pretended; *yena*—as if; *dekhe*—sees; *nāñi*—not; *mukundere puche*—inquired from Mukunda; *kāhāṅ*—where; *bhāratī-gosāñi*—Brahmānanda Bhāratī, my spiritual master.

TRANSLATION

Seeing Brahmānanda Bhāratī thus attired, Caitanya Mahāprabhu pretended not to see him. Instead, He asked Mukunda Datta, "Where is Brahmānanda Bhāratī, My spiritual master?"

TEXT 156

মুকুন্দ কহে,—এই আগে দেখ বিভ্তমান ।
প্রভু কহে,—তেঁহ নহেন, তুমি অগেয়ান ॥ ১৫৬॥

mukunda kahe,——ei āge dekha vidyamāna
prabhu kahe,——teṅha nahena, tumi ageyāna

SYNONYMS

mukunda kahe—Mukunda said; *ei āge*—here in front; *dekha*—see; *vidyamāna*—present; *prabhu kahe*—Śrī Caitanya Mahāprabhu replied; *teṅha nahena*—he is not; *tumi ageyāna*—you are incorrect.

TRANSLATION

Mukunda Datta replied, "Here is Brahmānanda Bhāratī, in Your presence." The Lord replied, "You are incorrect. This is not Brahmānanda Bhāratī.

TEXT 157

অন্যেরে অন্য কহ, নাহি তোমার জ্ঞান ।
ভারতী-গোসাঞি কেনে পরিবেন চাম ॥ ১৫৭ ॥

anyere anya kaha, nāhi tomāra jñāna
bhāratī-gosāñi kene paribena cāma

SYNONYMS

anyere—another; *anya kaha*—you talk of someone else; *nāhi*—there is not; *tomāra*—your; *jñāna*—knowledge; *bhāratī*—Brahmānanda Bhāratī; *gosāñi*—My spiritual master; *kene*—why; *paribena*—should wear; *cāma*—skin.

TRANSLATION

"You must be talking of someone else, for this is surely not Brahmānanda Bhāratī. You simply have no knowledge. Why should Brahmānanda Bhāratī wear a deerskin?"

TEXT 158

শুনি' ব্রহ্মানন্দ করে হৃদয়ে বিচারে ।
মোর চর্মাম্বর এই না ভায় ইঁহারে ॥ ১৫৮ ॥

śuni' brahmānanda kare hṛdaye vicāre
mora carmāmbara ei nā bhāya iṅhāre

SYNONYMS

śuni'—hearing; *brahmānanda*—Brahmānanda; *kare*—does; *hṛdaye*—within himself; *vicāre*—consideration; *mora*—my; *carma-ambara*—deerskin garment; *ei*—this; *nā*—not; *bhāya*—is approved; *iṅhāre*—by Śrī Caitanya Mahāprabhu.

TRANSLATION

When Brahmānanda Bhāratī heard this, he thought, "My deerskin is not approved by Śrī Caitanya Mahāprabhu."

TEXT 159

ভাল কহেন,—চর্মাম্বর দম্ভ লাগি' পরি ।
চর্মাম্বর-পরিধানে সংসার না তরি ॥ ১৫৯ ॥

bhāla kahena,——carmāmbara dambha lāgi' pari
carmāmbara-paridhāne saṁsāra nā tari

SYNONYMS

bhāla—well; *kahena*—He said; *carma-ambara*—the garment of deerskin; *dambha*—prestige; *lāgi'*—for the matter of; *pari*—I put on; *carma-ambara-paridhāne*—by putting on a garment of skin; *saṁsāra*—the material world; *nā tari*—I cannot cross.

TRANSLATION

Thus admitting his mistake, Brahmānanda Bhāratī thought, "He spoke well. I put on this deerskin only for prestige. I cannot cross over the ocean of nescience simply by wearing a deerskin.

TEXT 160

আজি হৈতে না পরিব এই চর্মাম্বর ।
প্রভু বহির্বাস আনাইলা জানিয়া অন্তর ॥ ১৬০ ॥

āji haite nā pariba ei carmāmbara
prabhu bahirvāsa ānāilā jāniyā antara

SYNONYMS

āji haite—from today; *nā pariba*—I shall not put on; *ei*—this; *carma-ambara*—deerskin garment; *prabhu*—Śrī Caitanya Mahāprabhu; *bahiḥ-vāsa*—the cloth of a *sannyāsī*; *ānāilā*—had someone bring; *jāniyā*—knowing; *antara*—his contemplation.

TRANSLATION

"From today on I shall not wear this deerskin." As soon as Brahmānanda Bhāratī decided this, Śrī Caitanya Mahāprabhu, understanding his mind, immediately sent for the robes of a sannyāsī.

TEXT 161

চর্মাম্বর ছাড়ি' ব্রহ্মানন্দ পরিল বসন ।
প্রভু আসি' কৈল তাঁর চরণ বন্দন ॥ ১৬১ ॥

carmāmbara chāḍi' brahmānanda parila vasana
prabhu āsi' kaila tāṅra caraṇa vandana

SYNONYMS

carma-ambara chāḍi'—giving up the deerskin garment; *brahmānanda*—Brahmānanda Bhāratī; *parila*—put on; *vasana*—cloth garment; *prabhu*—Śrī Caitanya Mahāprabhu; *āsi'*—coming; *kaila*—did; *tāṅra*—his; *caraṇa vandana*—worshiping the feet.

TRANSLATION

As soon as Brahmānanda Bhāratī gave up his deerskin and covered himself with sannyāsī robes, Śrī Caitanya Mahāprabhu came and offered His respects at his lotus feet.

TEXT 162

ভারতী কহে,—তোমার আচার লোক শিখাইতে ।
পুনঃ না করিবে নতি, ভয় পাঙ চিত্তে ॥ ১৬২ ॥

bhāratī kahe,——tomāra ācāra loka śikhāite
punaḥ nā karibe nati, bhaya pāṅa citte

SYNONYMS

bhāratī kahe—Brahmānanda Bhāratī said; *tomāra*—Your; *ācāra*—behavior; *loka*—people in general; *śikhāite*—to teach; *punaḥ*—again; *nā*—not; *karibe*—will do; *nati*—obeisances; *bhaya*—fear; *pāṅa*—I get; *citte*—within the mind.

TRANSLATION

Brahmānanda Bhāratī said, "You instruct the general populace by Your behavior. I will not do anything against Your wishes; otherwise You will not offer me respects but will neglect me. I am afraid of this.

TEXT 163

সাম্প্রতিক 'দুই ব্রহ্ম' ইহাঁ 'চলাচল' ।
জগন্নাথ—অচল ব্রহ্ম, তুমি ত' সচল ॥ ১৬৩ ॥

sāmpratika 'dui brahma' ihāṅ 'calācala'
jagannātha——acala brahma, tumi ta' sacala

SYNONYMS

sāmpratika—at the present moment; *dui brahma*—two Brahmans, or spiritual identities; *ihāṅ*—here; *cala-acala*—moving and not moving; *jagannātha*—Lord Jagannātha; *acala brahma*—not moving Brahman; *tumi*—You; *ta'*—but; *sa-cala*—moving Brahman.

TRANSLATION

"At the present moment I see two Brahmans. One Brahman is Lord Jagannātha, who does not move and the other Brahman, who is moving, is You. Lord Jagannātha is arcā-vigraha, the worshipable Deity, and it is He who is the non-moving Brahman. However, You are Lord Śrī Caitanya Mahāprabhu, and You are moving here and there. Both of You are the same Brahman, master of material nature, but You are playing two parts—one moving and one not moving. In this way two Brahmans are now residing at Jagannātha Purī, Puruṣottama.

TEXT 164

তুমি—গৌরবর্ণ, তেঁহ—শ্যামলবরণ ।
দুই ব্রহ্মে কৈল সব জগৎ-তারণ ॥ ১৬৪ ॥

tumi——gaura-varṇa, teṅha——śyāmala-varṇa
dui brahme kaila saba jagat-tāraṇa

SYNONYMS

tumi—You; *gaura-varṇa*—having a golden or fair complexion; *teṅha*—He; *śyāmala-varṇa*—having a blackish complexion; *dui brahme*—both Brahmans; *kaila*—performed; *saba jagat*—of the whole world; *tāraṇa*—deliverance.

TRANSLATION

"Of the two Brahmans, You are fair complexioned, and the other, Lord Jagannātha, is blackish. However, both of You are delivering the whole world."

TEXT 165

প্রভু কহে,—সত্য কহি, তোমার আগমনে ।
দুই ব্রহ্ম প্রকটিল শ্রীপুরুষোত্তমে ॥ ১৬৫ ॥

prabhu kahe,——satya kahi, tomara āgamane
dui brahma prakaṭila śrī-puruṣottame

SYNONYMS

prabhu kahe—Lord Śrī Caitanya Mahāprabhu said; *satya kahi*—I speak the truth; *tomāra āgamane*—by your presence; *dui brahma*—two Brahmans; *prakaṭila*—appeared; *śrī-puruṣottame*—at Jagannātha Purī.

TRANSLATION

Lord Śrī Caitanya Mahāprabhu replied, "Actually, to tell you the truth, due to your presence there are now two Brahmans at Jagannātha Purī.

TEXT 166

'ব্রহ্মানন্দ' নাম তুমি—গৌর-ব্রহ্ম 'চল' ।
শ্যামবর্ণ জগন্নাথ বসিয়াছেন 'অচল' ॥ ১৬৬ ॥

'brahmānanda' nāma tumi——gaura-brahma 'cala'
śyāma-varṇa jagannātha vasiyāchena 'acala'

SYNONYMS

brahmānanda—Brahmānanda; *nāma tumi*—your name; *gaura-brahma*—the Brahman of the name Gaura; *cala*—both of them are moving; *śyāma-varṇa*—of blackish hue; *jagannātha*—Lord Jagannātha; *vasiyāchena*—is sitting; *acala*—without movement.

TRANSLATION

"Both Brahmānanda and Gaurahari are moving, whereas the blackish Lord Jagannātha is sitting tight and immobile."

PURPORT

Brahmānanda Bhāratī wanted to prove that there is no difference between the Supreme Lord and the *jīva,* and Caitanya Mahāprabhu wanted to prove that He and Brahmānanda Bhāratī were *jīvas.* Although the *jīvas* are Brahman, they are many, but the Supreme Lord, the Supreme Brahman, is one. On the other hand, Brahmānanda Bhāratī wanted to prove that Jagannātha and Śrī Caitanya Mahāprabhu are one, the Supreme Personality of Godhead, but to fulfill His mission, Śrī Caitanya Mahāprabhu appeared to be moving, whereas Lord Jagannātha appeared to be inert. However, both of them are one and the same. Thus this jolly argument was going on. Finally, Brahmānanda Bhāratī referred the whole matter to Sārvabhauma Bhaṭṭācārya for a final decision.

TEXT 167

ভারতী কহে,—সার্বভৌম, মধ্যস্থ হঞা ।
ইঁহার সনে আমার 'ন্যায়' বুঝ' মন দিয়া ॥ ১৬৭ ॥

bhāratī kahe,——sārvabhauma, madhyastha hañā
iṅhāra sane āmāra 'nyāya' bujha' mana diyā

SYNONYMS

bhāratī kahe—Brahmānanda Bhāratī said; *sārvabhauma*—O Sārvabhauma Bhaṭṭācārya; *madhya-stha hañā*—becoming a mediator; *iṅhāra sane*—with Lord Śrī Caitanya Mahāprabhu; *āmāra*—my; *nyāya*—logic; *bujha'*—try to understand; *mana diyā*—with attention.

TRANSLATION

Brahmānanda Bhāratī said, "My dear Sārvabhauma Bhaṭṭācārya, please become the mediator in this logical argument between Śrī Caitanya Mahāprabhu and me."

TEXT 168

'ব্যাপ্য' 'ব্যাপক'-ভাবে 'জীব'-'ব্রহ্মে' জানি ।
জীব—ব্যাপ্য, ব্রহ্ম—ব্যাপক, শাস্ত্রেতে বাখানি ॥ ১৬৮ ॥

'vyāpya' 'vyāpaka'-bhāve 'jīva'-'brahme' jāni
jīva——vyāpya, brahma——vyāpaka, śāstrete vākhāni

SYNONYMS

vyāpya—localized; *vyāpaka*—all-pervading; *bhāve*—in this way; *jīva*—living entity; *brahme*—the Supreme Lord; *jāni*—I know; *jīva*—the living entity; *vyāpya*—localized; *brahma*—the Supreme Lord; *vyāpaka*—all-pervading; *śāstrete*—in the revealed scripture; *vākhāni*—description.

TRANSLATION

Brahmānanda Bhāratī continued, "The living entity is localized, whereas the Supreme Brahman is all-pervading. That is the verdict of the revealed scriptures.

PURPORT

Brahmānanda Bhāratī drew Sārvabhauma Bhaṭṭācārya's attention because he wanted him to judge the argument. He then stated that Brahman, the Supreme Lord, is all-pervading. This is confirmed by *Bhagavad-gītā*:

kṣetrajñaṁ cāpi māṁ viddhi
sarva-kṣetreṣu bhārata
kṣetra-kṣetrajñayor jñānaṁ
yat taj jñānaṁ mataṁ mama

"O scion of Bharata, you should understand that I am also the knower in all bodies, and to understand this body and its owner is called knowledge. That is My opinion." (Bg. 13.3)

The Supreme Personality of Godhead in His Paramātmā feature is expanded everywhere. The *Brahma-saṁhitā* says, *aṇḍāntara-stha-paramāṇu-cayāntara-stham:* by virtue of His all-pervasive nature, the Supreme Lord is within the universe as well as within all elements of the universe. He is even within the atom. In this way the Supreme Lord Govinda is all-pervasive. On the other hand, the living entities are very, very small. It is said that the living entity is one ten-thousandth of the tip of a hair. Therefore the living entity is localized. Living entities rest on the Brahman effulgence, the bodily rays of the Supreme Personality of Godhead.

TEXT 169

চর্ম ঘুচাঞা কৈল আমারে শোধন ।
দোঁহার ব্যাপ্য-ব্যাপকত্বে এই ত' কারণ ॥ ১৬৯ ॥

carma ghucāñā kaila āmāre śodhana
doṅhāra vyāpya-vyāpakatve ei ta' kāraṇa

SYNONYMS

carma—deerskin; *ghucāñā*—taking away; *kaila*—did; *āmāre*—unto me; *śodhana*—purification; *doṅhāra*—of both of us; *vyāpya*—being localized; *vyāpakatve*—being all-pervasive; *ei*—this; *ta'*—indeed; *kāraṇa*—the cause.

TRANSLATION

"Śrī Caitanya Mahāprabhu purified me by taking away my deerskin. This is proof that He is all-pervasive and all-powerful and that I am subordinate to Him.

PURPORT

Brahmānanda Bhāratī herein asserts that Śrī Caitanya Mahāprabhu is the Supreme Brahman and that he is the subordinate Brahman. This is confirmed in the *Vedas: nityo nityānāṁ cetanaś cetanānām.* The Supreme Personality of Godhead is Brahman or Paraṁ Brahman, the chief of all living entities. Both the Supreme Brahman, or the Personality of Godhead, and the living entities are persons, but the Supreme Brahman is the predominator, whereas the living entities are predominated.

TEXT 170

স্বর্ণবর্ণো হেমাঙ্গো বরাঙ্গশ্চন্দনাঙ্গদী ।
সন্ন্যাসকৃচ্ছমঃ শান্তো নিষ্ঠা-শান্তি-পরায়ণঃ ॥ ১৭০ ॥

suvarṇa-varṇo hemāṅgo
varāṅgaś candanāṅgadī
sannyāsa-kṛc chamaḥ śānto
niṣṭhā-śānti-parāyaṇaḥ

SYNONYMS

suvarṇa—of gold; *varṇaḥ*—having the color; *hema-aṅgaḥ*—whose body was like molten gold; *vara-aṅgaḥ*—having a most beautiful body; *candana-aṅgadī*—whose body was smeared with sandalwood; *sannyāsa-kṛt*—practicing the renounced order of life; *śamaḥ*—equipoised; *śāntaḥ*—peaceful; *niṣṭhā*—of devotion; *śānti*—and of peace; *parāyaṇaḥ*—the highest resort.

TRANSLATION

" 'His bodily hue is golden, and His whole body is like molten gold. Every part of His body is very beautifully constructed and smeared with sandalwood pulp. Accepting the renounced order, the Lord is always equipoised. He is firmly fixed in His mission of chanting the Hare Kṛṣṇa mantra, and He is firmly situated in His dualistic conclusion and in His peace.'

PURPORT

This is a quote from the *Mahābhārata, Viṣṇu-sahasra-nāma-stotra* (127.92.75).

TEXT 171

এই সব নামের ইঁহ হয় নিজাস্পদ ।
চন্দনাক্ত প্রসাদ-ডোর—শ্রীভুজে অঙ্গদ ॥ ১৭১ ॥

ei saba nāmera iṅha haya nijāspada
candanākta prasāda-ḍora——śrī-bhuje aṅgada

SYNONYMS

ei saba—all these; *nāmera*—of names; *iṅha*—Śrī Caitanya Mahāprabhu; *haya*—is; *nija-āspada*—the reservoir; *candana-akta*—smeared with the pulp of sandalwood; *prasāda-ḍora*—the thread received from Jagannātha temple; *śrī-bhuje*—on His arms; *aṅgada*—ornaments.

TRANSLATION

"All the symptoms mentioned in the verse from Viṣṇu-sahasra-nāma-stotra are visible in the body of Śrī Caitanya Mahāprabhu. His arms are decorated with ornamental bangles made of sandalwood pulp and with the thread received from the Śrī Jagannātha Deity."

TEXT 172

ভট্টাচার্য কহে,—ভারতী, দেখি তোমার জয়।
প্রভু কহে,—যেই কহ, সেই সত্য হয়॥ ১৭২॥

bhaṭṭācārya kahe,——bhāratī, dekhi tomāra jaya
prabhu kahe,——yei kaha, sei satya haya

SYNONYMS

bhaṭṭācārya kahe—Bhaṭṭācārya said; *bhāratī*—O Brahmānanda Bhāratī; *dekhi*—I see; *tomāra jaya*—your victory; *prabhu kahe*—Lord Caitanya Mahāprabhu said; *yei kaha*—whatever you say; *sei*—that; *satya*—true; *haya*—is.

TRANSLATION

After hearing this, Sārvabhauma Bhaṭṭācārya rendered his judgment, saying, "Brahmānanda Bhāratī, I see that you are victorious." Śrī Caitanya Mahāprabhu immediately said, "I accept whatever Brahmānanda Bhāratī has said. It is quite all right with Me."

TEXT 173

গুরু-শিষ্য-ন্যায়ে সত্য শিষ্যের পরাজয়।
ভারতী কহে,—এহো নহে, অন্য হেতু হয়॥ ১৭৩॥

guru-śiṣya-nyāye satya śiṣyera parājaya
bhāratī kahe,——eho nahe, anya hetu haya

SYNONYMS

guru-śiṣya-nyāye—when there is a logical argument between the spiritual master and the disciple; *satya*—certainly; *śiṣyera*—of the disciple; *parājaya*—defeat; *bhāratī kahe*—Brahmānanda Bhāratī said; *eho nahe*—in this case it is not the fact; *anya hetu*—another cause; *haya*—there is.

TRANSLATION

Śrī Caitanya Mahāprabhu thus posed Himself as a disciple and accepted Brahmānanda Bhāratī as His spiritual master. He then said, "The disciple is

certainly defeated in an argument with the spiritual master." Brahmānanda Bhāratī immediately countered these words, saying, "This is not the cause of Your defeat. There is another cause.

TEXT 174

ভক্ত ঠাঞি হার' তুমি,—এ তোমার স্বভাব।
আর এক শুন তুমি আপন প্রভাব॥ ১৭৪॥

bhakta ṭhāñi hāra' tumi,——e tomāra svabhāva
āra eka śuna tumi āpana prabhāva

SYNONYMS

bhakta ṭhāñi—in the presence of a devotee; *hāra'*—become defeated; *tumi*—You; *e*—this; *tomāra*—Your; *sva-bhāva*—nature; *āra*—another; *eka*—one; *śuna*—hear; *tumi*—You; *āpana prabhāva*—Your own influence.

TRANSLATION

"This is Your natural characteristic. You accept defeat at the hands of Your devotee. There is is also another glory of Yours, which I ask You to hear attentively.

TEXT 175

আজন্ম করিনু মুঞি 'নিরাকার'-ধ্যান।
তোমা দেখি' 'কৃষ্ণ' হৈল মোর বিদ্যমান॥ ১৭৫॥

ājanma karinu muñi 'nirākāra'-dhyāna
tomā dekhi' 'kṛṣṇa' haila mora vidyamāna

SYNONYMS

ā-janma—since my birth; *karinu*—have done; *muñi*—I; *nirākāra-dhyāna*—meditation on impersonal Brahman; *tomā dekhi'*—by seeing You; *kṛṣṇa*—Lord Kṛṣṇa; *haila*—became; *mora*—my; *vidyamāna*—experience.

TRANSLATION

"I have been meditating on the impersonal Brahman since my birth, but since I have seen You, I have fully experienced Kṛṣṇa."

PURPORT

Brahmānanda Bhāratī admitted that when there is an argument between the spiritual master and the disciple, the spiritual master is naturally victorious, although the disciple may put forward a strong argument. In other words, it is customary that the words of the spiritual master are more worshipable than the words of a disciple. Under the circumstances, since Brahmānanda Bhāratī was in the position of a spiritual master, he emerged victorious over Śrī Caitanya Mahāprabhu, who considered Himself Brahmānanda Bhāratī's disciple. However, Brahmānanda Bhāratī reversed the argument and took the position of a devotee, admitting that Śrī Caitanya Mahāprabhu was the Supreme Personality of Godhead, Kṛṣṇa. This means that the Lord was voluntarily defeated out of affection for the devotee. He was defeated voluntarily because no one can defeat the Supreme Lord. Concerning this, the words of Bhīṣma in *Śrīmad-Bhāgavatam* are important:

sva-nigamam apahāya mat-pratijñām
ṛtam adhikartum avapluto ratha-sthaḥ
dhṛta-ratha-caraṇo 'bhyayāc caladgur
harir iva hantum ibhaṁ gatottarīyaḥ

"Fulfilling my desire and sacrificing His own promise, He got down from the chariot, took up its wheel, and ran toward me hurriedly, just as a lion goes to kill an elephant. He even dropped His outer garment on the way." (*Bhāg.* 1.9.37)

Kṛṣṇa promised not to fight in the Battle of Kurukṣetra, but in order to break Kṛṣṇa's promise, Bhīṣma attacked Arjuna in such a vigorous way that Kṛṣṇa was obliged to take up a chariot wheel and attack Bhīṣma. The Lord did this to show that His devotee was being maintained at the sacrifice of His own promise. Brahmānanda Bhāratī said, "Since the beginning of my life I was attached to impersonal Brahman realization, but as soon as I saw You, I became very much attached to the Personality of Godhead, Kṛṣṇa." Therefore Śrī Caitanya Mahāprabhu is Lord Kṛṣṇa Himself, and thus Brahmānanda Bhāratī became His devotee.

TEXT 176

কৃষ্ণনাম স্ফুরে মুখে, মনে নেত্রে কৃষ্ণ ।
তোমাকে তদ্রূপ দেখি' হৃদয়— সতৃষ্ণ ॥ ১৭৬ ॥

kṛṣṇa-nāma sphure mukhe, mane netre kṛṣṇa
tomāke tad-rūpa dekhi' hṛdaya——satṛṣṇa

SYNONYMS

kṛṣṇa-nāma—the holy name of Lord Kṛṣṇa; *sphure*—is manifest; *mukhe*—in the mouth; *mane*—in the mind; *netre*—before the eyes; *kṛṣṇa*—the presence of Lord Kṛṣṇa; *tomāke*—You; *tat-rūpa*—His form; *dekhi'*—I see; *hṛdaya*—my heart; *sa-tṛṣṇa*—very eager.

TRANSLATION

Brahmānanda Bhāratī continued, "Since I have seen You, I have been feeling Lord Kṛṣṇa's presence in my mind and have been seeing Him before my eyes. I now want to chant the holy name of Lord Kṛṣṇa. Over and above this, within my heart I consider You to be Kṛṣṇa, and I am therefore very eager to serve You.

TEXT 177

বিল্বমঙ্গল কৈল যৈছে দশা আপনার ।
ইহাঁ দেখি' সেই দশা হইল আমার ॥ ১৭৭ ॥

bilvamaṅgala kaila yaiche daśā āpanāra
ihāṅ dekhi' sei daśā ha-ila āmāra

SYNONYMS

bilva-maṅgala—Bilvamaṅgala; *kaila*—did; *yaiche*—as; *daśā*—condition; *āpanāra*—his own; *ihāṅ*—here; *dekhi'*—I see; *sei daśā*—that condition; *ha-ila*—became; *āmāra*—mine.

TRANSLATION

"Bilvamaṅgala Ṭhākura abandoned his impersonal realization for the realization of the Personality of Godhead. I now see that my condition is similar to his, for it has already changed."

PURPORT

In his early life, Bilvamaṅgala Ṭhākura was an impersonalist monist, and he used to meditate upon the impersonal Brahman effulgence. Later he became a devotee of Lord Kṛṣṇa, and his explanation for this change is given in a verse [text 178] that is quoted in *Bhakti-rasāmṛta-sindhu.* Gradually one comes to the stage of Bhagavān realization, realization of the Supreme Person, after having attained the lower stages of realization—impersonal Brahman realization and localized Paramātmā realization. This is described in *Caitanya-candrāmṛta* (5) by Prabodhānanda Sarasvatī:

kaivalyaṁ narakāyate tridaśa-pūr ākāśa-puṣpāyate
durdāntendriya-kāla-sarpa-paṭalī protkhāta-daṁṣṭrāyate
viśvaṁ pūrṇa-sukhāyate vidhi-mahendrādiś ca kīṭāyate
yat-kāruṇya-kaṭākṣa-vaibhava-vatāṁ taṁ gauram eva stamaḥ

Kaivalya, oneness in the effulgence of Brahman, appears hellish to the devotee. The heavenly planets, the abodes of the demigods, appear to a devotee like phantasmagoria. The *yogīs* meditate for sense control, but for the devotee the senses appear like serpents with broken teeth. The devotee doesn't have to control his senses, for his senses are already engaged in the Lord's service. Consequently there is no possibility that the senses will act like serpents. In the material condition, the senses are as strong as poisonous snakes. When the teeth are broken, the snake is no longer dangerous. The entire world is a replica of Vaikuṇṭha for the devotee because he has no anxiety. He sees that everything belongs to Kṛṣṇa, and he does not want to enjoy anything for himself. He does not even aspire for the position of Lord Brahmā or Indra. He simply wants to engage everything in the service of the Lord; therefore he has no problem. He stands in his original constitutional position. All this is possible when one receives Śrī Caitanya Mahāprabhu's merciful glance.

In the *Caitanya-candrāmṛta* there are many more verses illustrating this same principle.

dhik kurvati ca brahma-yoga-viduṣas taṁ gauracandraṁ numaḥ

tāvad brahma-kathā vimukta-padavī tāvan na tiktībhavet
tāvac cāpi viśṛṅkhalatvam ayate no loka-veda-sthitiḥ
tāvac chāstra-vidāṁ mithaḥ kalakalo nānā-bahir-vartmasu
śrī-caitanya-padāmbuja-priya-jano yāvan na dig-gocaraḥ

gauraś cauraḥ sakala-maharat ko 'pi me tīvra-vīryaḥ

A discussion of the impersonal Brahman is not very palatable to a devotee. The so-called regulations of the *śāstras* also appear null and void to him. There are many people who argue over the *śāstras,* but for a devotee such discussions are but tumultuous roaring. By the influence of Śrī Caitanya Mahāprabhu, all these problems disappear.

TEXT 178

অদ্বৈতবীথীপথিকৈরুপাস্যাঃ, স্বানন্দসিংহাসন-লব্ধদীক্ষাঃ ।
শঠেন কেনাপি বয়ং হঠেন, দাসীকৃতা গোপবধূবিটেন ॥১৭৮॥

advaita-vīthī-pathikair upāsyāḥ
svānanda-siṁhāsana-labdha-dīkṣāḥ
śaṭhena kenāpi vayaṁ haṭhena
dāsī-kṛtā gopa-vadhū-viṭena

SYNONYMS

advaita-vīthī—of the path of monism; *pathikaiḥ*—by the wanderers; *upāsyāḥ*—worshipable; *sva-ānanda*—of self-realization; *siṁhāsana*—on the throne; *labdha-dīkṣāḥ*—being initiated; *śaṭhena*—by a cheater; *kenāpi*—some; *vayam*—I; *haṭhena*—by force; *dāsī-kṛtā*—made into a maidservant; *gopa-vadhū-viṭena*—by a boy engaged in joking with the *gopīs.*

TRANSLATION

Brahmānanda Bhāratī concluded, " 'Although I was worshiped by those on the path of monism and initiated into self-realization through the yoga system, I am nonetheless forcibly turned into a maidservant by some cunning boy who is always joking with the gopīs.' "

PURPORT

This is a verse written by Bilvamaṅgala Ṭhākura. It is found in *Bhakti-rasāmṛta-sindhu* (3.1.44).

TEXT 179

প্রভু কহে,—কৃষ্ণে তোমার গাঢ় প্রেমা হয়।
যাহাঁ নেত্র পড়ে, তাহাঁ শ্রীকৃষ্ণ স্ফুরয় ॥ ১৭৯ ॥

prabhu kahe,——kṛṣṇe tomāra gāḍha premā haya
yāhāṅ netra paḍe, tāhāṅ śrī-kṛṣṇa sphuraya

SYNONYMS

prabhu kahe—Lord Śrī Caitanya Mahāprabhu replied; *kṛṣṇe*—unto Kṛṣṇa; *tomāra*—your; *gāḍha*—deep; *premā*—love; *haya*—there is; *yāhāṅ*—wherever; *netra*—eyes; *paḍe*—fall; *tāhāṅ*—there; *śrī-kṛṣṇa*—Lord Śrī Kṛṣṇa; *sphuraya*—becomes manifest.

TRANSLATION

Lord Śrī Caitanya Mahāprabhu replied, "You have a deep ecstatic love for Kṛṣṇa; therefore wherever your eyes turn, you simply heighten your Kṛṣṇa consciousness."

TEXT 180

ভট্টাচার্য কহে,—দোঁহার সুসত্য বচন।
আগে যদি কৃষ্ণ দেন সাক্ষাৎ দরশন ॥ ১৮০ ॥

bhaṭṭācārya kahe,——doṅhāra susatya vacana
āge yadi kṛṣṇa dena sākṣāt daraśana

SYNONYMS

bhaṭṭācārya kahe—Sārvabhauma Bhaṭṭācārya said; *doṅhāra*—of both; *su-satya*—correct; *vacana*—statements; *āge*—first; *yadi*—if; *kṛṣṇa*—Lord Kṛṣṇa; *dena*—gives; *sākṣāt*—direct; *daraśana*—audience.

TRANSLATION

Sārvabhauma Bhaṭṭācārya said, "Both Your statements are correct. Kṛṣṇa gives direct audience through His own mercy.

TEXT 181

প্রেম বিনা কভু নহে তাঁর সাক্ষাৎকার ।
ইঁহার কৃপাতে হয় দরশন ইঁহার ॥ ১৮১ ॥

prema vinā kabhu nahe tāṅra sākṣātkāra
iṅhāra kṛpāte haya daraśana iṅhāra

SYNONYMS

prema vinā—without ecstatic love; *kabhu nahe*—there is never; *tāṅra*—His; *sākṣātkāra*—direct meeting; *iṅhāra kṛpāte*—by the mercy of Śrī Caitanya Mahāprabhu; *haya*—becomes possible; *daraśana*—visit; *iṅhāra*—of Brahmānanda Bhāratī.

TRANSLATION

"Without having ecstatic love for Kṛṣṇa, one cannot see Him directly. Therefore through the mercy of Śrī Caitanya Mahāprabhu, Brahmānanda Bhāratī has acquired direct vision of the Lord."

PURPORT

Śrī Caitanya Mahāprabhu said, "You are Brahmānanda Bhāratī, an advanced devotee who ecstatically loves the Supreme Lord. Therefore you see Kṛṣṇa everywhere, and there is no doubt about it." Sārvabhauma Bhaṭṭācārya was a mediator between Śrī Caitanya Mahāprabhu and Brahmānanda Bhāratī, and his judgment was that an advanced devotee like Brahmānanda Bhāratī sees Kṛṣṇa by Kṛṣṇa's mercy. Kṛṣṇa directly presents Himself before the vision of an advanced devotee. Since Brahmānanda Bhāratī was an advanced devotee, he saw Kṛṣṇa in the person of Śrī Caitanya Mahāprabhu. In the words of *Brahma-saṁhitā* (5.38):

premāñjana-cchurita-bhakti-vilocanena
santaḥ sadaiva hṛdayeṣu vilokayanti
yaṁ śyāmasundaram acintya-guṇa-svarūpaṁ
govindam ādi-puruṣaṁ tam ahaṁ bhajāmi

"I worship the primeval Lord Govinda, who is always seen by the devotee whose eyes are anointed with the pulp of love. He is seen in His eternal form of Śyāmasundara situated within the heart of the devotee."

TEXT 182

প্রভু কহে,—'বিষ্ণু' 'বিষ্ণু', কি কহ সার্বভৌম।
'অতিস্তুতি' হয় এই নিন্দার লক্ষণ ॥ ১৮২ ॥

prabhu kahe,——'viṣṇu' 'viṣṇu', ki kaha sārvabhauma
'ati-stuti' haya ei nindāra lakṣaṇa

SYNONYMS

prabhu kahe—Śrī Caitanya Mahāprabhu said; *viṣṇu viṣṇu*—O Lord Viṣṇu, Lord Viṣṇu; *ki kaha*—what are you speaking; *sārvabhauma*—Sārvabhauma Bhaṭṭācārya; *ati-stuti*—overly glorifying; *haya*—is; *ei*—this; *nindāra lakṣaṇa*—symptom of blasphemy.

TRANSLATION

Śrī Caitanya Mahāprabhu said, "Sārvabhauma Bhaṭṭācārya, what are you saying? Lord Viṣṇu, save Me! Such glorification is simply another form of blasphemy."

PURPORT

Śrī Caitanya Mahāprabhu was a little embarrassed by Bhaṭṭācārya's statement; therefore He uttered the name Viṣṇu to save Himself. The Lord herein confirms that if one is overestimated, glorification is just another form of blasphemy. In this way He protests this so-called offensive statement.

TEXT 183

এত বলি' ভারতীরে লঞা নিজ-বাসা আইলা।
ভারতী-গোসাঞি প্রভুর নিকটে রহিলা ॥ ১৮৩ ॥

eta bali' bhāratīre lañā nija-vāsā āilā
bhāratī-gosāñi prabhura nikaṭe rahilā

SYNONYMS

eta bali'—saying this; *bhāratīre*—Brahmānanda Bhāratī; *lañā*—taking with Him; *nija-vāsā āilā*—returned to His own residence; *bhāratī-gosāñi*—Brahmānanda Bhāratī; *prabhura nikaṭe*—in the shelter of Śrī Caitanya Mahāprabhu; *rahilā*—remained.

TRANSLATION

After saying this, Śrī Caitanya Mahāprabhu took Brahmānanda Bhāratī with Him to His residence. From that time on, Brahmānanda Bhāratī remained with Śrī Caitanya Mahāprabhu.

TEXT 184

রামভদ্রাচার্য, আর ভগবান্ আচার্য।
প্রভু-পদে রহিলা দুঁহে ছাড়ি' সর্ব কার্য ॥ ১৮৪ ॥

rāmabhadrācārya, āra bhagavān ācārya
prabhu-pade rahilā duṅhe chāḍi' sarva kārya

SYNONYMS

rāmabhadra-ācārya—Rāmabhadra Ācārya; *āra*—and; *bhagavān-ācārya*—Bhagavān Ācārya; *prabhu-pade*—under the shelter of Śrī Caitanya Mahāprabhu; *rahilā*—remained; *duṅhe*—both of them; *chāḍi'*—giving up; *sarva kārya*—all other responsibilities.

TRANSLATION

Later, Rāmabhadra Ācārya and Bhagavān Ācārya also joined them, and, giving up all other responsibilities, remained under Śrī Caitanya Mahāprabhu's shelter.

TEXT 185

কাশীশ্বর গোসাঞি আইলা আর দিনে।
সম্মান করিয়া প্রভু রাখিলা নিজ স্থানে ॥ ১৮৫ ॥

kāśīśvara gosāñi āilā āra dine
sammāna kariyā prabhu rākhilā nija sthāne

SYNONYMS

kāśīśvara gosāñi—another devotee; *āilā*—came; *āra dine*—next day; *sammāna kariyā*—giving all respect; *prabhu*—Lord Śrī Caitanya Mahāprabhu; *rākhilā*—kept; *nija sthāne*—at His own place.

TRANSLATION

The next day, Kāśīśvara Gosāñi also came and remained with Śrī Caitanya Mahāprabhu, who received him with great respect.

TEXT 186

প্রভুকে লঞা করা'ন ঈশ্বর দরশন।
আগে লোক-ভিড় সব করি' নিবারণ ॥ ১৮৬ ॥

prabhuke lañā karā'na īśvara daraśana
āge loka-bhiḍa saba kari' nivāraṇa

SYNONYMS

prabhuke—Śrī Caitanya Mahāprabhu; *lañā*—taking; *karā'na*—helps in; *īśvara daraśana*—visiting Lord Jagannātha; *āge*—in front of; *loka-bhiḍa*—crowds of people; *saba*—all; *kari' nivāraṇa*—restraining.

TRANSLATION

Kāśīśvara used to usher Śrī Caitanya Mahāprabhu into the Jagannātha temple. He would precede the Lord into the crowd and keep the people from touching Him.

TEXT 187

যত নদ নদী যৈছে সমুদ্রে মিলয়।
ঐছে মহাপ্রভুর ভক্ত যাহাঁ তাহাঁ হয় ॥ ১৮৭ ॥

yata nada nadī yaiche samudre milaya
aiche mahāprabhura bhakta yāhāṅ tāhāṅ haya

SYNONYMS

yata—all; *nada nadī*—rivers; *yaiche*—as; *samudre*—in the sea; *milaya*—meet; *aiche*—similarly; *mahāprabhura*—of Śrī Caitanya Mahāprabhu; *bhakta*—devotees; *yāhāṅ tāhāṅ*—wherever; *haya*—they were.

TRANSLATION

As all the rivers flow into the sea, all the devotees throughout the country finally came to Śrī Caitanya Mahāprabhu's shelter.

TEXT 188

সবে আসি' মিলিলা প্রভুর শ্রীচরণে।
প্রভু কৃপা করি' সবায় রাখিল নিজ স্থানে ॥ ১৮৮ ॥

sabe āsi' mililā prabhura śrī-caraṇe
prabhu kṛpā kari' sabāya rākhila nija sthāne

SYNONYMS

sabe—all; *āsi'*—coming; *mililā*—met; *prabhura*—of Śrī Caitanya Mahāprabhu; *śrī-caraṇe*—under the shelter; *prabhu*—Śrī Caitanya Mahāprabhu; *kṛpā kari'*—showing mercy; *sabāya*—every one of them; *rākhila*—kept; *nija sthāne*—under His protection.

TRANSLATION

Since all the devotees came to Him for shelter, Lord Śrī Caitanya Mahāprabhu showed them all mercy and kept them under His protection.

TEXT 189

এই ত' কহিল প্রভুর বৈষ্ণব-মিলন ।
ইহা যেই শুনে, পায় চৈতন্য-চরণ ॥ ১৮৯ ॥

ei ta' kahila prabhura vaiṣṇava-milana
ihā yei śune, pāya caitanya-caraṇa

SYNONYMS

ei ta'—thus; *kahila*—I have described; *prabhura*—of Lord Caitanya Mahāprabhu; *vaiṣṇava-milana*—meeting with all the Vaiṣṇavas; *ihā*—this narration; *yei*—anyone who; *śune*—hears; *pāya*—gets; *caitanya-caraṇa*—the shelter of Śrī Caitanya Mahāprabhu.

TRANSLATION

Thus I have described the meeting of all the Vaiṣṇavas with Śrī Caitanya Mahāprabhu. Whoever hears this description ultimately attains His shelter.

TEXT 190

শ্রীরূপ-রঘুনাথ-পদে যার আশ ।
চৈতন্যচরিতামৃত কহে কৃষ্ণদাস ॥ ১৯০ ॥

śrī-rūpa-raghunātha-pade yāra āśa
caitanya-caritāmṛta kahe kṛṣṇadāsa

SYNONYMS

śrī-rūpa—Śrīla Rūpa Gosvāmī; *raghunātha*—Śrīla Raghunātha dāsa Gosvāmī; *pade*—at the lotus feet; *yāra*—whose; *āśa*—expectation; *caitanya-caritāmṛta*—

the book named *Caitanya-caritāmṛta; kahe*—describes; *kṛṣṇadāsa*—Śrīla Kṛṣṇadāsa Kavirāja Gosvāmī.

TRANSLATION

Praying at the lotus feet of Śrī Rūpa and Śrī Raghunātha, always desiring their mercy, I, Kṛṣṇadāsa, narrate Śrī Caitanya-caritāmṛta, following in their footsteps.

Thus end the Bhaktivedanta purports to the Śrī Caitanya-caritāmṛta, Madhya-līlā, *Tenth Chapter, describing the Lord's meeting the Vaiṣṇavas upon His return to Jagannātha Purī from South India.*

CHAPTER 11

The Beḍā-kīrtana Pastimes of Śrī Caitanya Mahāprabhu

Bhaktinivoda Ṭhākura summarizes the Eleventh Chapter in his *Amṛta-pravāha-bhāṣya.*

When Sārvabhauma Bhaṭṭācārya tried his best to arrange a meeting between Śrī Caitanya Mahāprabhu and King Pratāparudra, the Lord flatly denied his request. At this time Śrī Rāmānanda Rāya returned from his governmental post, and he praised King Pratāparudra highly in Lord Caitanya's presence. Because of this, the Lord became a little soft. The King also made promises to Sārvabhauma Bhaṭṭācārya, who hinted how the King might meet the Lord. During Anavasara, while Lord Jagannātha was resting for fifteen days, Śrī Caitanya Mahāprabhu, being unable to see Lord Jagannātha, went to Ālālanātha. Later, when the devotees from Bengal came to see Him, He returned to Jagannātha Purī. While Advaita Ācārya and the other devotees were coming to Jagannātha Purī, Svarūpa Dāmodara and Govinda, Śrī Caitanya Mahāprabhu's two personal assistants, went to receive all the devotees with garlands. From the roof of his palace, King Pratāparudra could see all the devotees arriving. Gopīnātha Ācārya stood on the roof with the King, and, following Sārvabhauma Bhaṭṭācārya's instructions, identified each and every devotee. The King discussed the devotees with Gopīnātha Ācārya, and he mentioned that the devotees were accepting *prasāda* without observing the regulative principles governing pilgrimages. They accepted *prasāda* without having shaved, and they neglected to fast in a holy place. Nonetheless, the King arranged residential quarters for all the devotees and saw to their *prasāda.* Śrī Caitanya Mahāprabhu talked very happily with Vāsudeva Datta and other devotees. Haridāsa Ṭhākura also came, and due to his humble and submissive attitude, Śrī Caitanya Mahāprabhu gave him a nice solitary place near the temple. After this, the Lord began performing *saṅkīrtana,* dividing all the devotees into four divisions. After *saṅkīrtana,* all the devotees left for their residential quarters.

TEXT 1

অত্যুদ্দণ্ডং তাণ্ডবং গৌরচন্দ্রঃ
কুর্বন্ ভক্তৈঃ শ্রীজগন্নাথগেহে ।

নানাভাবালঙ্কৃতাঙ্গঃ স্বধাম্না
চক্রে বিশ্বং প্রেমবন্যা-নিমগ্নম্ ॥ ১ ॥

atyuddaṇḍaṁ tāṇḍavaṁ gauracandraḥ
kurvan bhaktaiḥ śrī-jagannātha-gehe
nānā-bhāvālaṅkṛtāṅgaḥ sva-dhāmnā
cakre viśvaṁ prema-vanyā-nimagnam

SYNONYMS

ati—very much; *uddaṇḍam*—high jumping; *tāṇḍavam*—very graceful dancing; *gaura-candraḥ*—Lord Śrī Caitanya Mahāprabhu; *kurvan*—performing; *bhaktaiḥ*—with the devotees; *śrī-jagannātha-gehe*—in the temple of Lord Jagannātha; *nānā-bhāva-alaṅkṛta-aṅgaḥ*—having many ecstatic symptoms manifested in His transcendental body; *sva-dhāmnā*—by the influence of His ecstatic love; *cakre*—made; *viśvam*—the whole world; *prema-vanyā-nimagnam*—merged into the inundation of ecstatic love.

TRANSLATION

Śrī Caitanya Mahāprabhu merged the entire world into the ocean of ecstatic love by performing His beautiful dances within the temple of Jagannātha. He danced exquisitely and jumped high.

TEXT 2

জয় জয় শ্রীচৈতন্য জয় নিত্যানন্দ ।
জয়াদ্বৈতচন্দ্র জয় গৌরভক্তবৃন্দ ॥ ২ ॥

jaya jaya śrī-caitanya jaya nityānanda
jayādvaita-candra jaya gaura-bhakta-vṛnda

SYNONYMS

jaya jaya—all glories; *śrī-caitanya*—to Lord Caitanya; *jaya*—all glories; *nityānanda*—to Nityānanda Prabhu; *jaya*—all glories; *advaita-candra*—to Advaita Prabhu; *jaya*—all glories; *gaura-bhakta-vṛnda*—to the devotees of Lord Śrī Caitanya Mahāprabhu.

TRANSLATION

All glories to Lord Śrī Caitanya Mahāprabhu! All glories to Lord Nityānanda Prabhu! All glories to Śrī Advaita Prabhu! And all glories to the devotees of Śrī Caitanya Mahāprabhu!

TEXT 3

আর দিন সার্বভৌম কহে প্রভুস্থানে।
অভয়-দান দেহ' যদি, করি নিবেদনে ॥ ৩ ॥

āra dina sārvabhauma kahe prabhu-sthāne
abhaya-dāna deha' yadi, kari nivedane

SYNONYMS

āra dina—the next day; *sārvabhauma*—Sārvabhauma Bhaṭṭācārya; *kahe*—says; *prabhu-sthāne*—in the presence of Lord Caitanya Mahāprabhu; *abhaya-dāna*—the charity of fearlessness; *deha'*—You give; *yadi*—if; *kari*—I do; *nivedane*—submission.

TRANSLATION

The next day Sārvabhauma Bhaṭṭācārya requested Lord Śrī Caitanya Mahāprabhu to give him permission to submit a statement without fear.

TEXT 4

প্রভু কহে,— কহ তুমি, নাহি কিছু ভয়।
যোগ্য হৈলে করিব, অযোগ্য হৈলে নয় ॥ ৪ ॥

prabhu kahe,——kaha tumi, nāhi kichu bhaya
yogya haile kariba, ayogya haile naya

SYNONYMS

prabhu kahe—Lord Śrī Caitanya Mahāprabhu said; *kaha tumi*—yes, you can speak; *nāhi*—there is not; *kichu*—any; *bhaya*—fear; *yogya*—befitting; *haile*—if it is; *kariba*—I shall grant; *ayogya*—not befitting; *haile*—if it is; *naya*—then I shall not.

TRANSLATION

The Lord gave the Bhaṭṭācārya assurance that He could speak without fear, but added that if his statement were suitable He would accept it, and if it were not, He would reject it.

TEXT 5

সার্বভৌম কহে—এই প্রতাপরুদ্র রায়।
উৎকণ্ঠা হঞাছে, তোমা মিলিবারে চায় ॥ ৫ ॥

sārvabhauma kahe——ei pratāparudra rāya
utkaṇṭhā hañāche, tomā milibāre cāya

SYNONYMS

sārvabhauma kahe—Sārvabhauma Bhaṭṭācārya said; *ei*—this; *pratāparudra rāya*—King Pratāparudra of Jagannātha Purī; *utkaṇṭhā hañāche*—has been very anxious; *tomā*—You; *milibāre*—to meet; *cāya*—he wants.

TRANSLATION

Sārvabhauma Bhaṭṭācārya said, "There is a king named Pratāparudra Rāya. He is very anxious to meet You, and he wants Your permission."

TEXT 6

কর্ণে হস্ত দিয়া প্রভু স্মরে 'নারায়ণ' ।
সার্বভৌম, কহ কেন অযোগ্য বচন ॥ ৬ ॥

karṇe hasta diyā prabhu smare 'nārāyaṇa'
sārvabhauma, kaha kena ayogya vacana

SYNONYMS

karṇe—on the ears; *hasta*—hands; *diyā*—placing; *prabhu*—Śrī Caitanya Mahāprabhu; *smare*—remembers; *nārāyaṇa*—the holy name of Lord Nārāyaṇa; *sārvabhauma*—My dear Sārvabhauma; *kaha*—you say; *kena*—why; *ayogya vacana*—a request that is not suitable.

TRANSLATION

As soon as Śrī Caitanya Mahāprabhu heard this proposal, He immediately covered His ears with His hands and said, "My dear Sārvabhauma, why are you requesting such an undesirable thing from Me?

TEXT 7

বিরক্ত সন্ন্যাসী আমার রাজ-দরশন ।
স্ত্রী-দরশন-সম বিষের ভক্ষণ ॥ ৭ ॥

virakta sannyāsī āmāra rāja-daraśana
strī-daraśana-sama viṣera bhakṣaṇa

SYNONYMS

virakta—unattached; *sannyāsī*—person in the renounced order; *āmāra*—My; *rāja-daraśana*—meeting a king; *strī-daraśana*—meeting a woman; *sama*—like; *viṣera*—of poison; *bhakṣaṇa*—drinking.

TRANSLATION

"Since I am in the renounced order, it is as dangerous for Me to meet a king as to meet a woman. They are both just like drinking poison."

TEXT 8

নিষ্কিঞ্চনস্য ভগবদ্ভজনোন্মুখস্য
পারং পরং জিগমিষোর্ভবসাগরস্য ।
সন্দর্শনং বিষয়িণামথ যোষিতাঞ্চ
হা হন্ত হন্ত বিষভক্ষণতোঽপ্যসাধু ॥ ৮ ॥

niṣkiñcanasya bhagavad-bhajanonmukhasya
pāraṁ paraṁ jigamiṣor bhava-sāgarasya
sandarśanaṁ viṣayiṇām atha yoṣitāṁ ca
hā hanta hanta viṣa-bhakṣaṇato 'py asādhu

SYNONYMS

niṣkiñcanasya—of a person who has completely detached himself from material enjoyment; *bhagavat*—the Supreme Personality of Godhead; *bhajana*—in serving; *unmukhasya*—who is eager to be engaged; *pāram*—to the other side; *param*—distant; *jigamiṣoḥ*—who is desiring to go; *bhava-sāgarasya*—of the ocean of material existence; *sandarśanam*—the seeing (for some material purpose); *viṣayiṇām*—of persons engaged in material activities; *atha*—as well as; *yoṣitām*—of women; *ca*—also; *hā*—alas; *hanta hanta*—expression of great lamentation; *viṣa-bhakṣaṇataḥ*—than the act of drinking poison; *api*—even; *asādhu*—more abominable.

TRANSLATION

Greatly lamenting, the Lord then informed Sārvabhauma Bhaṭṭācārya, " 'Alas, for a person who is seriously desiring to cross the material ocean and engage in the transcendental loving service of the Lord without material motives, seeing a materialist engaged in sense gratification and seeing a woman who is similarly interested is more abominable than drinking poison willingly.' "

PURPORT

This is a quotation from *Śrī Caitanya-candrodaya-nāṭaka* (8.23). Thus Śrī Caitanya Mahāprabhu enunciates the principles for a *sannyāsī* renouncing the material world for spiritual advancement. Spiritual advancement is not meant for magic shows and jugglery but for crossing the material world and being transferred to the spiritual world. *Pāraṁ paraṁ jigamiṣoḥ* means desiring to go to the other side of the material world. There is a river called Vaitaraṇī, and on one side of this river is the material world, and on the other side is the spiritual world. Since the Vaitaraṇī River is compared to a great ocean, it is named *bhava-sāgara,* the ocean of repeated birth and death. Spiritual life aims at stopping this repetition of birth and death and entering into the spiritual world, where one can live eternally cognizant and blissful.

Unfortunately, the general populace does not know anything about spiritual life or the spiritual world. The spiritual world is mentioned in *Bhagavad-gītā* (8.20):

paras tasmāt tu bhāvo 'nyo
'vyakto 'vyaktāt sanātanaḥ
yaḥ sa sarveṣu bhūteṣu
naśyatsu na vinaśyati

"Yet there is another nature, which is eternal and is transcendental to this manifested and unmanifested matter. It is supreme and is never annihilated. When all in this world is annihilated, that part remains as it is."

Thus there is a spiritual nature beyond this material world, and that spiritual nature exists eternally. Spiritual advancement means stopping material activities and entering into spiritual activities. This is the process of *bhakti-yoga.* In the material world, the via media for sense gratification is mainly a woman. One who is seriously interested in spiritual life should strictly avoid women. A *sannyāsī* should never see a man or a woman for material benefit. In addition, talks with materialistic men and women are also dangerous, and they are compared to drinking poison. Śrī Caitanya Mahāprabhu was very strict on this point. He therefore refused to see King Pratāparudra, who was naturally always engaged in political and economic affairs. The Lord even refused to see the King despite the request of a personality like Sārvabhauma Bhaṭṭācārya, who was the Lord's intimate friend and devotee.

TEXT 9

সার্বভৌম কহে,—সত্য তোমার বচন ।
জগন্নাথ-সেবক রাজা কিন্তু ভক্তোত্তম ॥ ৯ ॥

sārvabhauma kahe,——satya tomāra vacana
jagannātha-sevaka rājā kintu bhaktottama

SYNONYMS

sārvabhauma kahe—Sārvabhauma Bhaṭṭācārya replied; *satya*—true; *tomāra*—Your; *vacana*—statement; *jagannātha-sevaka*—servant of Lord Jagannātha; *rājā*—the King; *kintu*—but; *bhakta-uttama*—a great devotee.

TRANSLATION

Sārvabhauma Bhaṭṭācārya replied, "My dear Lord, what You have said is correct, but this King is not an ordinary king. He is a great devotee and servant of Lord Jagannātha."

TEXT 10

প্রভু কহে,—তথাপি রাজা কালসর্পাকার ।
কাষ্ঠনারী-স্পর্শে যৈছে উপজে বিকার ॥ ১০ ॥

prabhu kahe,——tathāpi rājā kāla-sarpākāra
kāṣṭha-nārī-sparśe yaiche upaje vikāra

SYNONYMS

prabhu kahe—Lord Śrī Caitanya Mahāprabhu replied; *tathāpi*—still; *rājā*—the King; *kāla-sarpa-ākāra*—just like a venomous snake; *kāṣṭha-nārī*—a woman made of wood; *sparśe*—by touching; *yaiche*—as; *upaje*—arises; *vikāra*—agitation.

TRANSLATION

Śrī Caitanya Mahāprabhu said, "Although it is correct that the King is a great devotee, he is still to be considered a venomous snake. Similarly, even though a woman be made of wood, one becomes agitated simply by touching her form.

PURPORT

Śrī Cāṇakya Paṇḍita in his moral instructions has stated: *tyaja durjana-saṁsargaṁ bhaja sādhu-samāgamam.* This means that one has to abandon the association of materialistic people and associate with spiritually advanced people. However qualified a materialist may be, he is no better than a venomous serpent. Everyone knows that a snake is dangerous and poisonous, and when its hood is decorated with jewels, it is no less poisonous or dangerous. However qualified a materialist may be, he is no better than a snake decorated with jewels. One should therefore be careful in dealing with such materialists, just as one would be careful in dealing with a bejeweled serpent.

Even though a woman be made of wood or stone, she becomes attractive when decorated. One becomes sexually agitated even by touching the form. Therefore one should not trust his mind, which is so fickle that it can give way to enemies at any moment. The mind is always accompanied by six enemies—namely, *kāma, krodha, mada, moha, mātsarya* and *bhaya*—that is, lust, anger, intoxication, illusion, envy and fear. Although the mind may be merged in spiritual consciousness, one should always be very careful in dealing with it, just as one is careful in dealing with a snake. One should never think that his mind is trained and that he can do whatever he likes. One interested in spiritual life should always engage his mind in the service of the Lord so that the enemies of the mind, who always accompany the mind, will be subdued. If the mind is not engaged in Kṛṣṇa consciousness at every moment, there is a chance that it will give way to its enemies. In this way we become victims of the mind.

Chanting the Hare Kṛṣṇa *mantra* engages the mind at the lotus feet of Kṛṣṇa constantly; thus the mind's enemies do not have a chance to strike. Following Śrī Caitanya Mahāprabhu's example in these verses, we should be very careful in dealing with the mind, which should not be indulged in any circumstance. Once we indulge the mind, it can create havoc in this life, even though we may be spiritually advanced. The mind is specifically agitated through the association of materialistic men and women. Therefore Śrī Caitanya Mahāprabhu, through His personal behavior, warns everyone to avoid meeting a materialistic person or a woman.

TEXT 11

আকারাদপি ভেতব্যং স্ত্রীণাং বিষয়িণামপি ।
যথাহের্মনসঃ ক্ষোভস্তথা তস্যাকৃতেরপি ॥ ১১ ॥

ākārād api bhetavyaṁ
strīṇāṁ viṣayiṇām api
yathāher manasaḥ kṣobhas
tathā tasyākṛter api

SYNONYMS

ākārāt—from bodily features; *api*—even; *bhetavyam*—to be feared; *strīṇām*—of women; *viṣayiṇām*—of materialistic persons; *api*—even; *yathā*—as; *aheḥ*—from a serpent; *manasaḥ*—of the mind; *kṣobhaḥ*—agitation; *tathā*—so; *tasya*—of it; *ākṛteḥ*—from the appearance; *api*—even.

TRANSLATION

" 'Just as one is immediately frightened upon seeing a live serpent or even the form of a serpent, one endeavoring for self-realization should similarly

fear a materialistic person and a woman. Indeed, he should not even glance at their bodily features.'

PURPORT

This is a quotation from *Śrī Caitanya-candrodaya-nāṭaka* (8.24).

TEXT 12

ঐছে বাত পুনরপি মুখে না আনিবে ।
কহ যদি, তবে আমায় এথা না দেখিবে ॥ ১২ ॥

aiche vāta punarapi mukhe nā ānibe
kaha yadi, tabe āmāya ethā nā dekhibe

SYNONYMS

aiche vāta—such a request; *punarapi*—again; *mukhe*—in the mouth; *nā*—do not; *ānibe*—bring; *kaha yadi*—if you speak; *tabe*—then; *āmāya*—Me; *ethā*—here; *nā*—not; *dekhibe*—you will see.

TRANSLATION

"Bhaṭṭācārya, if you continue to speak like this, you will never see Me here again. Therefore you should never let such a request come from your mouth."

TEXT 13

ভয় পাঞা সার্বভৌম নিজ ঘরে গেলা ।
বাসায় গিয়া ভট্টাচার্য চিন্তিত হইলা ॥ ১৩ ॥

bhaya pāñā sārvabhauma nija ghare gelā
vāsāya giyā bhaṭṭācārya cintita ha-ilā

SYNONYMS

bhaya pāñā—being afraid; *sārvabhauma*—Sārvabhauma; *nija*—own; *ghare*—to home; *gelā*—returned; *vāsāya giyā*—reaching his residential place; *bhaṭṭācārya*—Bhaṭṭācārya; *cintita ha-ilā*—became meditative.

TRANSLATION

Being afraid, Sārvabhauma returned home and began to meditate on the matter.

TEXT 14

হেন কালে প্রতাপরুদ্র পুরুষোত্তমে আইলা ।
পাত্র-মিত্র-সঙ্গে রাজা দরশনে চলিলা ॥ ১৪ ॥

hena kāle pratāparudra puruṣottame āilā
pātra-mitra-saṅge rājā daraśane calilā

SYNONYMS

hena kāle—at this time; *pratāparudra*—King Pratāparudra; *puruṣottame*—at Jagannātha Purī; *āilā*—arrived; *pātra-mitra-saṅge*—accompanied by his secretaries, ministers, military officers and so on; *rājā*—the King; *daraśane*—to visit Lord Jagannātha; *calilā*—departed.

TRANSLATION

At this time, Mahārāja Pratāparudra arrived at Jagannātha Purī, Puruṣottama, and, accompanied by his secretaries, ministers and military officers, went to visit the temple of Lord Jagannātha.

PURPORT

It appears that Mahārāja Pratāparudra used to live at Kaṭaka, his capital. Later he shifted his capital to Khurdā, a few miles from Jagannātha Purī. Presently there is a railway station there called Khurdā Road.

TEXT 15

রামানন্দ রায় আইলা গজপতি-সঙ্গে ।
প্রথমেই প্রভুরে আসি' মিলিলা বহুরঙ্গে ॥ ১৫ ॥

rāmānanda rāya āilā gajapati-saṅge
prathamei prabhure āsi' mililā bahu-raṅge

SYNONYMS

rāmānanda rāya—Rāmānanda Rāya; *āilā*—came; *gaja-pati-saṅge*—with the King; *prathamei*—in the first instance; *prabhure*—unto Lord Caitanya Mahāprabhu; *āsi'*—coming; *mililā*—met; *bahu-raṅge*—with great pleasure.

TRANSLATION

When King Pratāparudra returned to Jagannātha Purī, Rāmānanda Rāya also came with him. Rāmānanda Rāya immediately went to meet Śrī Caitanya Mahāprabhu with great pleasure.

PURPORT

All Indian kings are given titles. Sometimes they are known as Chatrapati, sometimes Narapati and sometimes Aśvapati. The King of Orissa is addressed as Gajapati.

TEXT 16

রায় প্রণতি কৈল, প্রভু কৈল আলিঙ্গন।
দুই জনে প্রেমাবেশে করেন ক্রন্দন ॥ ১৬ ॥

rāya praṇati kaila, prabhu kaila āliṅgana
dui jane premāveśe karena krandana

SYNONYMS

rāya praṇati kaila—Rāmānanda Rāya offered his obeisances; *prabhu*—the Lord; *kaila*—did; *āliṅgana*—embracing; *dui jane*—both of them; *prema-āveśe*—in ecstatic love; *karena*—did; *krandana*—crying.

TRANSLATION

Upon meeting Śrī Caitanya Mahāprabhu, Rāmānanda Rāya offered his obeisances. The Lord embraced him, and both of them began to cry in the great ecstasy of love.

TEXT 17

রায়-সঙ্গে প্রভুর দেখি' স্নেহ-ব্যবহার।
সর্ব ভক্তগণের মনে হৈল চমৎকার ॥ ১৭ ॥

rāya-saṅge prabhura dekhi' sneha-vyavahāra
sarva bhakta-gaṇera mane haila camatkāra

SYNONYMS

rāya-saṅge—with Rāmānanda Rāya; *prabhura*—of Śrī Caitanya Mahāprabhu; *dekhi'*—seeing; *sneha-vyavahāra*—very intimate behavior; *sarva*—all; *bhakta-gaṇera*—of all the devotees; *mane*—in the mind; *haila*—there was; *camatkāra*—astonishment.

TRANSLATION

Seeing Lord Śrī Caitanya Mahāprabhu's intimate dealings with Śrī Rāmānanda Rāya, all the devotees there were astonished.

TEXT 18

রায় কহে,—তোমার আজ্ঞা রাজাকে কহিল।
তোমার ইচ্ছায় রাজা মোর বিষয় ছাড়াইল ॥ ১৮ ॥

rāya kahe,——tomāra ājñā rājāke kahila
tomāra icchāya rājā mora viṣaya chāḍāila

SYNONYMS

rāya kahe—Rāmānanda Rāya said; *tomāra ājñā*—Your order; *rājāke kahila*—I informed the King; *tomāra icchāya*—by Your grace; *rājā*—the King; *mora*—my; *viṣaya*—material activities; *chāḍāila*—gave me relief from.

TRANSLATION

Rāmānanda Rāya said, "I duly informed King Pratāparudra of Your order for me to retire from service. By Your grace, the King was pleased to relieve me of these material activites.

PURPORT

Śrī Caitanya Mahāprabhu requested Rāmānanda Rāya to retire from his governorship, and according to the Lord's desire, Rāmānanda Rāya petitioned the King. The King was very pleased to give him relief, and thus Rāmānanda Rāya retired from service and received a pension from the government.

TEXT 19

আমি কহি,— আমা হৈতে না হয় 'বিষয়'।
চৈতন্যচরণে রহোঁ, যদি আজ্ঞা হয় ॥ ১৯ ॥

āmi kahi,——āmā haite nā haya 'viṣaya'
caitanya-caraṇe rahoṅ, yadi ājñā haya

SYNONYMS

āmi kahi—I said; *āmā haite*—by me; *nā*—not; *haya*—is possible; *viṣaya*—government service; *caitanya-caraṇe*—at the lotus feet of Śrī Caitanya Mahāprabhu; *rahoṅ*—I may stay; *yadi ājñā haya*—if you kindly give me permission.

TRANSLATION

"I said, 'Your Majesty, I am now not willing to engage in political activities. I desire only to stay at the lotus feet of Śrī Caitanya Mahāprabhu. Kindly give me permission.'

TEXT 20

তোমার নাম শুনি' রাজা আনন্দিত হৈল।
আসন হৈতে উঠি' মোরে আলিঙ্গন কৈল ॥ ২০ ॥

tomāra nāma śuni' rājā ānandita haila
āsana haite uṭhi' more āliṅgana kaila

SYNONYMS

tomāra—Your; *nāma*—name; *śuni'*—hearing; *rājā*—the King; *ānandita*—very pleased; *haila*—became; *āsana haite*—from his throne; *uṭhi'*—standing; *more*—me; *āliṅgana kaila*—embraced.

TRANSLATION

"When I submitted this proposal, the King, immediately upon hearing Your name, was very pleased. Indeed, he instantly arose from his throne and embraced me.

TEXT 21

তোমার নাম শুনি' হৈল মহা-প্রেমাবেশ ।
মোর হাতে ধরি' করে পিরীতি বিশেষ ॥ ২১ ॥

tomāra nāma śuni' haila mahā-premāveśa
mora hāte dhari' kare pirīti viśeṣa

SYNONYMS

tomāra—Your; *nāma*—name; *śuni'*—hearing; *haila*—became; *mahā*—great; *prema-āveśa*—ecstasy of love; *mora hāte*—my hand; *dhari'*—catching; *kare*—does; *pirīti*—loving symptoms; *viśeṣa*—specific.

TRANSLATION

"My dear Lord, as soon as the King heard Your holy name, he was immediately overwhelmed by a great ecstatic love. Catching my hand, he displayed all the symptoms of love.

TEXT 22

তোমার যে বর্তন, তুমি খাও সেই বর্তন ।
নিশ্চিন্ত হঞা ভজ চৈতন্যের চরণ ॥ ২২ ॥

tomāra ye vartana, tumi khāo sei vartana
niścinta hañā bhaja caitanyera caraṇa

SYNONYMS

tomāra—Your; *ye*—whatever; *vartana*—remuneration; *tumi*—you; *khāo*—take; *sei*—that; *vartana*—pension; *niścinta hañā*—without anxiety; *bhaja*—just worship; *caitanyera*—of Lord Śrī Caitanya Mahāprabhu; *caraṇa*—the lotus feet.

TRANSLATION

"As soon as he heard my petition, he immediately granted me a pension without reductions. Thus the King granted me a full salary as a pension and requested me to engage without anxiety in the service of Your lotus feet.

TEXT 23

আমি–ছার, যোগ্য নহি তাঁর দরশনে ।
তাঁরে যেই ভজে তাঁর সফল জীবনে ॥ ২৩ ॥

āmi——chāra, yogya nahi tāṅra daraśane
tāṅre yei bhaje tāṅra saphala jīvane

SYNONYMS

āmi—I; *chāra*—very fallen; *yogya*—fit; *nahi*—not; *tāṅra*—His; *daraśane*—for interviewing; *tāṅre*—Him; *yei*—anyone who; *bhaje*—worships; *tāṅra*—his; *saphala*—successful; *jīvane*—life.

TRANSLATION

"Then Mahārāja Pratāparudra very humbly said, 'I am most fallen and abominable, and I am unfit to receive an interview with the Lord. One's life is successful if one engages in His service.'

TEXT 24

পরম কৃপালু তেঁহ ব্রজেন্দ্রনন্দন ।
কোন-জন্মে মোরে অবশ্য দিবেন দরশন ॥ ২৪ ॥

parama kṛpālu teṅha vrajendra-nandana
kona-janme more avaśya dibena daraśana

SYNONYMS

parama—very much; *kṛpālu*—merciful; *teṅha*—Lord Caitanya Mahāprabhu; *vrajendra-nandana*—the son of Mahārāja Nanda; *kona-janme*—in some future birth; *more*—unto me; *avaśya*—certainly; *dibena*—will give; *daraśana*—interview.

TRANSLATION

"The King then said, 'Śrī Caitanya Mahāprabhu is Kṛṣṇa, the son of Mahārāja Nanda. He is very merciful, and I hope that in a future birth He will allow me an interview.'

TEXT 25

যে তাঁহার প্রেম-আর্তি দেখিলুঁ তোমাতে ।
তার এক প্রেম-লেশ নাহিক আমাতে ॥ ২৫ ॥

ye tāṅhāra prema-ārti dekhiluṅ tomāte
tāra eka prema-leśa nāhika āmāte

SYNONYMS

ye—whatever; *tāṅhāra*—his; *prema-ārti*—painful feelings of love of Godhead; *dekhiluṅ*—I saw; *tomāte*—unto You; *tāra*—of that; *eka*—one; *prema-leśa*—fraction of love; *nāhika*—there is not; *āmāte*—in me.

TRANSLATION

"My Lord, I don't think that there is even a fraction of Mahārāja Pratāparudra's loving ecstasy in me."

TEXT 26

প্রভু কহে,—তুমি কৃষ্ণ-ভকতপ্রধান ।
তোমাকে যে প্রীতি করে, সেই ভাগ্যবান্ ॥ ২৬ ॥

prabhu kahe,——tumi kṛṣṇa-bhakata-pradhāna
tomāke ye prīti kare, sei bhāgyavān

SYNONYMS

prabhu kahe—Lord Śrī Caitanya Mahāprabhu said; *tumi*—you; *kṛṣṇa-bhakata-pradhāna*—the chief of the devotees of Lord Kṛṣṇa; *tomāke*—unto you; *ye*—anyone who; *prīti kare*—shows love; *sei*—such a person; *bhāgyavān*—most fortunate.

TRANSLATION

Śrī Caitanya Mahāprabhu then said, "My dear Rāmānanda Rāya, you are the foremost of all the devotees of Kṛṣṇa; therefore whoever loves you is certainly a very fortunate person.

TEXT 27

তোমাতে যে এত প্রীতি হইল রাজার।
এই গুণে কৃষ্ণ তাঁরে করিবে অঙ্গীকার ॥ ২৭ ॥

tomāte ye eta prīti ha-ila rājāra
ei guṇe kṛṣṇa tāṅre karibe aṅgīkāra

SYNONYMS

tomāte—unto you; *ye*—that; *eta*—so much; *prīti*—love; *ha-ila*—was; *rājāra*—of the King; *ei guṇe*—for this reason; *kṛṣṇa*—Lord Kṛṣṇa; *tāṅre*—him; *karibe aṅgīkāra*—will accept.

TRANSLATION

"Because the King has shown so much love for you, Lord Kṛṣṇa will certainly accept him.

PURPORT

King Pratāparudra requested an interview with Śrī Caitanya Mahāprabhu through the Bhaṭṭācārya, who duly submitted the request. The Lord, however, immediately refused this interview. Now when Rāmānanda Rāya informed the Lord how eager the King was to see Him, the Lord was immediately pleased. Śrī Caitanya Mahāprabhu requested Rāmānanda Rāya to retire from his government post and come to Śrī Puruṣottama-kṣetra (Jagannātha Purī) to live with Him. When this proposal was submitted to King Pratāparudra, he immediately accepted it and also encouraged Rāmānanda Rāya by allowing him a full pension. This was very much appreciated by the Lord, and this confirms the fact that the Lord is more pleased when one serves the servant of the Lord. In ordinary parlance it is said, "If you love me, love my dog." To approach the Supreme Personality of Godhead, one has to go through His confidential servant. This is the method. Śrī Caitanya Mahāprabhu clearly says, "Because the King loves you, Rāmānanda Rāya, he is very fortunate. Kṛṣṇa will certainly accept him due to his love for you."

TEXT 28

যে মে ভক্তজনাঃ পার্থ ন মে ভক্তাশ্চ তে জনাঃ।
মদ্ভক্তানাঞ্চ যে ভক্তাস্তে মে ভক্ততমা মতাঃ ॥ ২৮ ॥

ye me bhakta-janāḥ pārtha
na me bhaktāś ca te janāḥ
mad-bhaktānāṁ ca ye bhaktās
te me bhaktatamā matāḥ

SYNONYMS

ye—those who; *me*—My; *bhakta-janāḥ*—devotees; *pārtha*—O Pārtha; *na*—not; *me*—My; *bhaktāḥ*—devotees; *ca*—and; *te*—those; *janāḥ*—persons; *mat-bhaktānām*—of My devotees; *ca*—certainly; *ye*—those who; *bhaktāḥ*—devotees; *te*—such persons; *me*—My; *bhaktatamāḥ*—most advanced devotees; *matāḥ*—that is My opinion.

TRANSLATION

"Lord Kṛṣṇa told Arjuna, 'Those who are My direct devotees are actually not My devotees, but those who are the devotees of My servant are factually My devotees.'

PURPORT

Śrī Caitanya Mahāprabhu quotes this verse from the *Ādi Purāṇa*. The verse is also included in the *Laghu-bhāgavatāmṛta* (2.6).

TEXTS 29-30

আদরঃ পরিচর্যায়াং সর্বাঙ্গৈরভিবন্দনম্ ।
মদ্ভক্তপূজাভ্যধিকা সর্বভূতেষু মন্মতিঃ ॥ ২৯ ॥
মদর্থেষ্বঙ্গচেষ্টা চ বচসা মদ্গুণেরণম্ ।
ময্যর্পণঞ্চ মনসঃ সর্বকামবিবর্জনম্ ॥ ৩০ ॥

ādaraḥ paricaryāyāṁ
sarvāṅgair abhivandanam
mad-bhakta-pūjābhyadhikā
sarva-bhūteṣu man-matiḥ

mad-artheṣv aṅga-ceṣṭā ca
vacasā mad-guṇeraṇam
mayy arpaṇaṁ ca manasaḥ
sarva-kāma-vivarjanam

SYNONYMS

ādaraḥ—respect, care; *paricaryāyām*—in service; *sarva-aṅgaiḥ*—by all the parts of the body; *abhivandanam*—offering obeisances; *mat-bhakta*—of My devotees; *pūjā*—worshiping; *abhyadhikā*—very high; *sarva-bhūteṣu*—in all living entities; *mat-matiḥ*—realization of having a relationship with Me; *mat-artheṣu*—for the sake of My service; *aṅga-ceṣṭāḥ*—engaging the bodily energy; *ca*—and; *vacasā*—by words; *mat-guṇa-īraṇam*—describing My glories; *mayi*—unto Me; *arpaṇam*—dedicating; *ca*—and; *manasaḥ*—of the mind; *sarva-kāma*—all material desires; *vivarjanam*—giving up.

TRANSLATION

" 'My devotees take great care and respect in rendering Me service. They offer obeisances to Me with all their bodily limbs. They worship My devotees and find all living entities related to Me. For Me they engage the entire energy of their bodies. They engage the power of speech in the glorification of My qualities and form. They also dedicate their minds unto Me and try to give up all kinds of material desires. Thus My devotees are characterized.'

PURPORT

These two verses are quoted from *Śrīmad-Bhāgavatam* (11.19.21-22). They were spoken by the Supreme Personality of Godhead, Lord Kṛṣṇa, who was answering Uddhava's inquiry about devotional service.

TEXT 31

আরাধনানাং সর্বেষাং বিষ্ণোরারাধনং পরম্ ।
তস্মাৎ পরতরং দেবি তদীয়ানাং সমর্চনম্ ॥ ৩১ ॥

ārādhanānāṁ sarveṣāṁ
viṣṇor ārādhanaṁ param
tasmāt parataraṁ devi
tadīyānāṁ samarcanam

SYNONYMS

ārādhanānām—of varieties of worship; *sarveṣām*—all; *viṣṇoḥ*—of Lord Viṣṇu; *ārādhanam*—worship; *param*—the most exalted; *tasmāt*—and above such worship of Lord Viṣṇu; *parataram*—of greater value; *devi*—O goddess; *tadīyānām*—of persons in relationship with Lord Viṣṇu; *samarcanam*—rigid and firm worship.

TRANSLATION

"Lord Śiva told the goddess Durgā, 'My dear Devī, although the Vedas recommend worship of demigods, the worship of Lord Viṣṇu is topmost. However, above the worship of Lord Viṣṇu is the rendering of service to Vaiṣṇavas, who are related to Lord Viṣṇu.'

PURPORT

The *Vedas* are divided into three divisions—*karma-kāṇḍa, jñāna-kāṇḍa* and *upāsanā-kāṇḍa.* These are activities dealing with fruitive work, empiric philosophical speculation and worship. There are recommendations in the *Vedas* for the worship of various demigods as well as Lord Viṣṇu. Lord Śiva answers Durgā's question in this quotation from *Padma Purāṇa.* This verse is also included in *Laghu-*

bhāgavatāmṛta (2.4) by Śrīla Rūpa Gosvāmī. The words *viṣṇor ārādhanam* refer to the worship of Lord Viṣṇu, or Kṛṣṇa. Thus the supreme form of worship is the satisfaction of the Supreme Personality of Godhead Śrī Kṛṣṇa. It is further concluded that the worshiper of Lord Viṣṇu renders better service by worshiping the devotee of Lord Kṛṣṇa. There are different types of devotees—those in the *śānta-rasa, dāsya-rasa, sakhya-rasa, vātsalya-rasa* and *mādhurya-rasa.* Although all the *rasas* are on the transcendental platform, the *mādhurya-rasa* is the supreme transcendental mellow. Consequently it is concluded that the worship of devotees engaged in the Lord's service in the *mādhurya-rasa* is the supreme spiritual activity. Śrī Caitanya Mahāprabhu and His followers mainly worship Lord Kṛṣṇa in the *mādhurya-rasa.* Other Vaiṣṇava *ācāryas* recommended worship up to the *vātsalya-rasa.* Therefore Śrīla Rūpa Gosvāmī in his *Vidagdha-mādhava* (1.2) describes Śrī Caitanya Mahāprabhu's cult as supreme:

anarpita-carīṁ cirāt karuṇayāvatīrṇaḥ kalau
samarpayitum unnatojjvala-rasāṁ sva-bhakti-śriyam

Śrī Caitanya Mahāprabhu appeared in this age of Kali to exhibit the superexcellence of *mādhurya-rasa,* a gift never previously bestowed by any *ācārya* or incarnation. Consequently Śrī Caitanya Mahāprabhu is accepted as the most magnanimous incarnation. It is He only who distributed love of Kṛṣṇa while exhibiting the superexcellence of loving Kṛṣṇa in the conjugal *rasa.*

TEXT 32

দুরাপা হ্যল্পতপসঃ সেবা বৈকুণ্ঠবর্ত্মসু ॥
যত্রোপগীয়তে নিত্যং দেবদেবো জনার্দনঃ ॥ ৩২ ॥

durāpā hy alpa-tapasaḥ
sevā vaikuṇṭha-vartmasu
yatropagīyate nityaṁ
deva-devo janārdanaḥ

SYNONYMS

durāpā—very difficult to achieve; *hi*—certainly; *alpa-tapasaḥ*—by a person not advanced in spiritual life; *sevā*—service; *vaikuṇṭha-vartmasu*—unto persons on the path back home, back to Godhead; *yatra*—wherein; *upagīyate*—is worshiped and glorified; *nityam*—regularly; *deva-devaḥ*—the Supreme Personality of Godhead; *janārdanaḥ*—Lord Kṛṣṇa.

TRANSLATION

" 'Those whose austerity is meager can hardly obtain the service of the pure devotees progressing on the path back to the kingdom of Godhead, the

Vaikuṇṭhas. Pure devotees engage one hundred percent in glorifying the Supreme Lord, who is the Lord of the demigods and the controller of all living entities.' "

PURPORT

This is a quotation from *Śrīmad-Bhāgavatam* (3.7.20). This was spoken by Vidura in his conversation with Maitreya Ṛṣi, a great devotee of the Lord.

TEXT 33

পুরী, ভারতী-গোসাঞিঃ, স্বরূপ, নিত্যানন্দ ।
জগদানন্দ, মুকুন্দাদি যত ভক্তবৃন্দ ॥ ৩৩ ॥

purī, bhāratī-gosāñi, svarūpa, nityānanda
jagadānanda, mukundādi yata bhakta-vṛnda

SYNONYMS

purī—Paramānanda Purī; *bhāratī*—Brahmānanda Bhāratī; *gosāñi*—on the level of the spiritual master; *svarūpa*—Svarūpa Dāmodara Gosvāmī; *nityānanda*—Lord Nityānanda Prabhu; *jagadānanda*—Jagadānanda; *mukunda*—Mukunda; *ādi*—and others; *yata*—all; *bhakta-vṛnda*—devotees of Śrī Caitanya Mahāprabhu.

TRANSLATION

Paramānanda Purī, Brahmānanda Bhāratī Gosāñi, Svarūpa Dāmodara Gosāñi, Lord Nityānanda, Jagadānanda, Mukunda and others were present before the Lord at that time.

TEXT 34

চারি গোসাঞির কৈল রায় চরণ বন্দন ।
যথাযোগ্য সব ভক্তের করিল মিলন ॥ ৩৪ ॥

cāri gosāñira kaila rāya caraṇa vandana
yathā-yogya saba bhaktera karila milana

SYNONYMS

cāri gosāñira—of the four *gosāñis,* or spiritual masters; *kaila*—did; *rāya*—Rāmānanda Rāya; *caraṇa vandana*—worshiping the lotus feet; *yathā-yogya*—as it is befitting; *saba*—all; *bhaktera*—of the devotees; *karila*—did; *milana*—meeting.

TRANSLATION

Śrī Rāmānanda Rāya therefore offered his obeisances to all the Lord's devotees, in particular to the four spiritual masters. Thus Rāmānanda Rāya suitably met all the devotees.

PURPORT

The four spiritual masters referred to in this verse are Paramānanda Purī, Brahmānanda Bhāratī, Svarūpa Dāmodara and Lord Nityānanda.

TEXT 35

প্রভু কহে,—রায়, দেখিলে কমলনয়ন ?
রায় কহে—এবে যাই পাব দরশন ॥ ৩৫ ॥

prabhu kahe, ——rāya, dekhile kamala-nayana?
rāya kahe——ebe yāi pāba daraśana

SYNONYMS

prabhu kahe—the Lord said; *rāya*—My dear Rāmānanda Rāya; *dekhile*—have you seen; *kamala-nayana*—the lotus-eyed Lord Jagannātha; *rāya kahe*—Rāmānanda Rāya replied; *ebe yāi*—now I shall go; *pāba daraśana*—I shall visit the temple.

TRANSLATION

Śrī Caitanya Mahāprabhu next asked Rāmānanda Rāya, "Have you already visited the temple of the lotus-eyed Lord Jagannātha?" Rāmānanda Rāya replied, "I shall now go visit the temple."

TEXT 36

প্রভু কহে,—রায়, তুমি কি কার্য করিলে ?
ঈশ্বরে না দেখি' কেনে আগে এথা আইলে ? ৩৬ ॥

prabhu kahe, ——rāya, tumi ki kārya karile?
īśvare nā dekhi' kene āge ethā āile?

SYNONYMS

prabhu kahe—Śrī Caitanya Mahāprabhu said; *rāya*—My dear Rāmānanda Rāya; *tumi*—you; *ki kārya*—what; *karile*—have done; *īśvare*—the Supreme Personality of Godhead; *nā dekhi'*—without seeing; *kene*—why; *āge*—first; *ethā*—here; *āile*—you came.

TRANSLATION

Śrī Caitanya Mahāprabhu replied, "What have you done, My dear Rāya? Why did you not first see Lord Jagannātha and then come here? Why have you come here first?"

TEXT 37

রায় কহে, চরণ—রথ, হৃদয়—সারথি ।
যাহাঁ লঞা যায়, তাহাঁ যায় জীব-রথী ॥ ৩৭ ॥

rāya kahe, caraṇa——ratha, hṛdaya——sārathi
yāhāṅ lañā yāya, tāhāṅ yāya jīva-rathī

SYNONYMS

rāya kahe—Rāmānanda Rāya replied; *caraṇa*—the legs; *ratha*—chariot; *hṛdaya*—the heart; *sārathi*—chariot driver; *yāhāṅ*—wherever; *lañā*—taking; *yāya*—goes; *tāhāṅ*—there; *yāya*—goes; *jīva-rathī*—the living entity on the chariot.

TRANSLATION

Rāmānanda Rāya said, "The legs are like the chariot, and the heart is like the charioteer. Wherever the heart takes the living entity, the living entity is obliged to go."

PURPORT

In *Bhagavad-gītā* (18.61) Lord Kṛṣṇa explains:

īśvaraḥ sarva-bhūtānāṁ
hṛd-deśe 'rjuna tiṣṭhati
bhrāmayan sarva-bhūtāni
yantrārūḍhāni māyayā

"The Supreme Lord is situated in everyone's heart, O Arjuna, and is directing the wanderings of all living entities, who are seated as on a machine made of material energy."

Thus the living entity wanders within this universe riding upon a chariot (the body) bestowed by material nature. A similar explanation is given in the *Kaṭha Upaniṣad* (1.3.3,4):

ātmānaṁ rathinaṁ viddhi
śarīraṁ ratham eva tu
buddhiṁ tu sārathiṁ viddhi
manaḥ pragraham eva ca

indriyāṇi hayān āhur
viṣayāṁs teṣu gocarān
ātmendriya-mano-yuktaṁ
bhoktety āhur manīṣiṇaḥ

"The individual is the passenger in the car of the material body, and intelligence is the driver. Mind is the driving instrument, and the senses are the horses. The self is thus the enjoyer or sufferer in the association of the mind and senses. In this way it is understood by great thinkers."

Thus the living entity is the charioteer and the body the chariot offered by material nature. The mind is the reins controlling the horses, and the senses are the horses. Thus the living entity is the false enjoyer of the material world. One who is advanced in Kṛṣṇa consciousness can control the mind and intelligence. In other words, he can control the reins and the horses (the senses), even though the horses are very powerful. One who can control the senses by his mind and intelligence can very easily approach the Supreme Personality of Godhead, or Viṣṇu, who is the ultimate goal of life. *Tad viṣṇoḥ paramaṁ padaṁ sadā paśyanti sūrayaḥ.* Those who are actually advanced approach Lord Viṣṇu, their ultimate goal. Such people are never captivated by Lord Viṣṇu's external energy, the material world.

TEXT 38

আমি কি করিব, মন ইহাঁ লঞা আইল ।
জগন্নাথ-দরশনে বিচার না কৈল ॥ ৩৮ ॥

āmi ki kariba, mana ihāṅ lañā āila
jagannātha-daraśane vicāra nā kaila

SYNONYMS

āmi—I; *ki*—what; *kariba*—shall do; *mana*—my mind; *ihāṅ*—here; *lañā*—taking; *āila*—arrived; *jagannātha-daraśane*—to see Lord Jagannātha; *vicāra*—consideration; *nā*—did not; *kaila*—make.

TRANSLATION

Śrī Rāmānanda Rāya continued, "What shall I do? My mind has brought me here. I could not consider going first to Lord Jagannātha's temple."

TEXT 39

প্রভু কহে,—শীঘ্র গিয়া কর দরশন ।
ঐছে ঘর যাই' কর কুটুম্ব মিলন ॥ ৩৯ ॥

prabhu kahe, ——śīghra giyā kara daraśana
aiche ghara yāi' kara kuṭumba milana

SYNONYMS

prabhu kahe—Lord Śrī Caitanya Mahāprabhu said; *śīghra giyā*—going hastily; *kara daraśana*—see Lord Jagannātha; *aiche*—similarly; *ghara yāi'*—going home; *kara*—just do; *kuṭumba*—family; *milana*—meeting.

TRANSLATION

Śrī Caitanya Mahāprabhu advised, "Immediately go to Lord Jagannātha's temple to see the Lord. Then go home and meet your family members."

TEXT 40

প্রভু আজ্ঞা পাঞা রায় চলিলা দরশনে ।
রায়ের প্রেমভক্তি-রীতি বুঝে কোন্ জনে ॥ ৪০ ॥

prabhu ājñā pāñā rāya calilā daraśane
rāyera prema-bhakti-rīti bujhe kon jane

SYNONYMS

prabhu ājñā—the Lord's permission; *pāñā*—getting; *rāya*—Rāmānanda Rāya; *calilā*—departed; *daraśane*—to see Lord Jagannātha; *rāyera*—of Rāmānanda Rāya; *prema-bhakti*—of ecstatic love for Kṛṣṇa; *rīti*—process; *bujhe*—understands; *kon jane*—what person.

TRANSLATION

Having received Śrī Caitanya Mahāprabhu's permission, Rāmānanda Rāya hastily went to the temple of Lord Jagannātha. Who can understand the devotional service of Rāya Rāmānanda?

TEXT 41

ক্ষেত্রে আসি' রাজা সার্বভৌমে বোলাইলা ।
সার্বভৌমে নমস্করি' তাঁহারে পুছিলা ॥ ৪১ ॥

kṣetre āsi' rājā sārvabhaume bolāilā
sārvabhaume namaskari' tāṅhāre puchilā

SYNONYMS

kṣetre—to Jagannātha Purī; *āsi'*—coming; *rājā*—the King; *sārvabhaume*—for Sārvabhauma Bhaṭṭācārya; *bolāilā*—called; *sārvabhaume*—unto Sārvabhauma Bhaṭṭācārya; *namaskari'*—offering obeisances; *tāṅhāre puchilā*—he asked him.

TRANSLATION

When King Pratāparudra returned to Jagannātha Purī, he called for Sārvabhauma Bhaṭṭācārya. When Bhaṭṭācārya went to see the King, the King offered him respects and made the following inquiries.

TEXT 42

মোর লাগি' প্রভুপদে কৈলে নিবেদন ?
সার্বভৌম কহে,—কৈনু অনেক যতন ॥ ৪২ ॥

mora lāgi' prabhu-pade kaile nivedana?
sārvabhauma kahe, ——kainu aneka yatana

SYNONYMS

mora lāgi'—on my behalf; *prabhu-pade*—at the lotus feet of the Lord; *kaile nivedana*—did you submit my petition; *sārvabhauma kahe*—Sārvabhauma replied; *kainu*—I did; *aneka yatana*—much endeavor.

TRANSLATION

The King asked, "Have you submitted my petition to the Lord?" Sārvabhauma replied, "Yes, with much endeavor I have tried my best.

TEXT 43

তথাপি না করে তেঁহ রাজ-দরশন ।
ক্ষেত্র ছাড়ি' যাবেন পুনঃ যদি করি নিবেদন ॥ ৪৩ ॥

tathāpi nā kare teṅha rāja-daraśana
kṣetra chāḍi' yābena punaḥ yadi kari nivedana

SYNONYMS

tathāpi—yet; *nā kare*—does not do; *teṅha*—He; *rāja-daraśana*—visiting a king; *kṣetra chāḍi'*—leaving Jagannātha-kṣetra; *yābena*—He will go away; *punaḥ*—again; *yadi*—if; *kari nivedana*—I request.

TRANSLATION

"Yet despite my great endeavor, the Lord would not agree to see a king. Indeed, He said that if He were asked again, He would quit Jagannātha Purī and go elsewhere."

TEXT 44

শুনিয়া রাজার মনে দুঃখ উপজিল ।
বিষাদ করিয়া কিছু কহিতে লাগিল ॥ ৪৪ ॥

śuniyā rājāra mane duḥkha upajila
viṣāda kariyā kichu kahite lāgila

SYNONYMS

śuniyā—hearing; *rājāra*—of the King; *mane*—in the mind; *duḥkha*—unhappiness; *upajila*—arose; *viṣāda*—lamentation; *kariyā*—doing; *kichu*—something; *kahite*—to speak; *lāgila*—began.

TRANSLATION

Hearing this, the King became very unhappy and, greatly lamenting, began to speak as follows.

TEXT 45

পাপী নীচ উদ্ধারিতে তাঁর অবতার ।
জগাই মাধাই তেঁহ করিলা উদ্ধার ॥ ৪৫ ॥

pāpī nīca uddhārite tāṅra avatāra
jagāi mādhāi teṅha karilā uddhāra

SYNONYMS

pāpī—sinful; *nīca*—lowborn; *uddhārite*—to deliver; *tāṅra*—His; *avatāra*—incarnation; *jagāi*—Jagāi; *mādhāi*—Mādhāi; *teṅha*—he; *karilā uddhāra*—delivered.

TRANSLATION

The King said, "Śrī Caitanya Mahāprabhu has descended just to deliver all kinds of sinful, lowborn persons. Consequently He has delivered sinners like Jagāi and Mādhāi.

TEXT 46

প্রতাপরুদ্র ছাড়ি' করিবে জগৎ নিস্তার।
এই প্রতিজ্ঞা করি' করিয়াছেন অবতার? ৪৬॥

pratāparudra chāḍi' karibe jagat nistāra
ei pratijñā kari' kariyāchena avatāra?

SYNONYMS

pratāparudra chāḍi'—except for Pratāparudra; *karibe*—he will do; *jagat*—of the whole universe; *nistāra*—deliverance; *ei pratijñā*—this promise; *kari'*—making; *kariyāchena*—has made; *avatāra*—incarnation.

TRANSLATION

"Alas, has Śrī Caitanya Mahāprabhu incarnated to deliver all kinds of sinners with the exception of a king named Mahārāja Pratāparudra?

PURPORT

Śrī Caitanya Mahāprabhu's mission is thus described by Narottama dāsa Ṭhākura: *patita-pāvana-hetu tava avatāra/ mo-sama patita prabhu nā pāibe āra.* If Śrī Caitanya Mahāprabhu descended to reclaim sinners, then one who is the most sinful and lowborn is the first candidate for the Lord's consideration. Mahārāja Pratāparudra considered himself a most fallen soul because he had to deal with material things constantly and enjoy material profits. Śrī Caitanya Mahāprabhu's business was the deliverance of the most fallen. How, then, could He reject the King? The more fallen a person is, the more he has the right to be delivered by the Lord—provided, of course, he surrenders unto the Lord. Mahārāja Pratāparudra was a fully surrendered soul; therefore the Lord could not refuse him on the grounds that he was a worldly pounds-shillings man.

TEXT 47

অদর্শনীয়ানপি নীচজাতীন্
সংবীক্ষতে হন্ত তথাপি নো মাম্।
মদেকবর্জং কৃপয়িষ্যতীতি
নির্ণীয় কিং সোঽবততার দেবঃ॥ ৪৭॥

adarśanīyān api nīca-jātīn
saṁvīkṣate hanta tathāpi no mām

mad-eka-varjaṁ kṛpayiṣyatīti
nirṇīya kiṁ so 'vatatāra devaḥ

SYNONYMS

adarśanīyān—upon those who are unfit to be seen; *api*—although; *nīca-jātīn*—the lower class of men; *saṁvīkṣate*—puts His merciful glance; *hanta*—alas; *tathāpi*—still; *no*—not; *mām*—upon me; *mat*—myself; *eka*—alone; *varjam*—rejecting; *kṛpayiṣyati*—He will bestow His mercy; *iti*—thus; *nirṇīya*—deciding; *kim*—whether; *saḥ*—Lord Śrī Caitanya Mahāprabhu; *avatatāra*—has descended; *devaḥ*—the Supreme Personality of Godhead.

TRANSLATION

" 'Alas, has Śrī Caitanya Mahāprabhu made His advent deciding that He will deliver all others with the exception of me? He bestows His merciful glance upon many lower-class men who are usually not even to be seen.' "

PURPORT

This verse is found in the *Śrī Caitanya-candrodaya-nāṭaka* (8.28).

TEXT 48

তাঁর প্রতিজ্ঞা - মোরে না করিবে দরশন ।
মোর প্রতিজ্ঞা - তাঁহা বিনা ছাড়িব জীবন ॥ ৪৮ ॥

tāṅra pratijñā——more nā karibe daraśana
mora pratijñā——tāṅhā vinā chāḍiba jīvana

SYNONYMS

tāṅra pratijñā—His determination; *more*—unto me; *nā*—not; *karibe*—will do; *daraśana*—seeing; *mora pratijñā*—my promise; *tāṅhā vinā*—without Him; *chāḍiba*—I will give up; *jīvana*—life.

TRANSLATION

Mahārāja Pratāparudra continued, "If Śrī Caitanya Mahāprabhu is determined not to see me, then I am determined to give up my life if I do not see Him.

PURPORT

A devotee with Mahārāja Pratāparudra's determination will certainly be victorious in advancing in Kṛṣṇa consciousness. Śrī Kṛṣṇa confirms this in *Bhagavad-gītā* (9.14):

satataṁ kīrtayanto māṁ
yatantaś ca dṛḍha-vratāḥ
namasyantaś ca māṁ bhaktyā
nitya-yuktā upāsate

"Always chanting My glories, endeavoring with great determination, bowing down before Me, these great souls perpetually worship Me with devotion."

These are the symptoms of a *mahātmā* engaged in the Lord's service in full Kṛṣṇa consciousness. Thus Mahārāja Pratāparudra's determination is very exalted and is called *dṛḍha-vrata.* Because of this determination, he was finally able to receive Lord Caitanya's direct mercy.

TEXT 49

যদি সেই মহাপ্রভুর না পাই কৃপা-ধন।
কিবা রাজ্য, কিবা দেহ,—সব অকারণ ॥ ৪৯ ॥

yadi sei mahāprabhura nā pāi kṛpā-dhana
kibā rājya, kibā deha, ——saba akāraṇa

SYNONYMS

yadi—if; *sei*—that; *mahāprabhura*—of Lord Śrī Caitanya Mahāprabhu; *nā*—not; *pāi*—I get; *kṛpā-dhana*—the treasure of mercy; *kibā rājya*—what is the value of my kingdom; *kibā deha*—what is the value of this body; *saba akāraṇa*—everything useless.

TRANSLATION

"If I do not receive Śrī Caitanya Mahāprabhu's mercy, my body and my kingdom are certainly useless."

PURPORT

This is an excellent example of *dṛḍha-vrata,* determination. If one does not receive the Supreme Personality of Godhead's mercy, one's life is defeated. In *Śrīmad-Bhāgavatam* (5.5.5) it is said: *parābhavas tāvad abodha-jāto yāvan na jijñāsata ātma-tattvam.* Unless one inquires into spiritual life, everything is useless. Without spiritual inquiry, our labor and the object of our labor are simply a waste of time.

TEXT 50

এত শুনি' সার্বভৌম হইলা চিন্তিত।
রাজার অনুরাগ দেখি' হইলা বিস্মিত ॥ ৫০ ॥

eta śuni' sārvabhauma ha-ilā cintita
rājāra anurāga dekhi' ha-ilā vismita

SYNONYMS

eta śuni'—hearing this; *sārvabhauma*—Sārvabhauma; *ha-ilā*—became; *cintita*—very thoughtful; *rājāra*—of the King; *anurāga*—attachment; *dekhi'*—seeing; *ha-ilā*—became; *vismita*—astonished.

TRANSLATION

Hearing King Pratāparudra's determination, Sārvabhauma Bhaṭṭācārya became thoughtful. Indeed, he was very astonished to see the King's determination.

PURPORT

Sārvabhauma Bhaṭṭācārya was astonished because such determination is not possible for a worldly man attached to material enjoyment. The King certainly had ample opportunity for material enjoyment, but he was thinking that his kingdom and everything else was useless if he could not see Śrī Caitanya Mahāprabhu. This is certainly sufficient cause for astonishment. In *Śrīmad-Bhāgavatam* it is stated that *bhakti,* devotional service, must be unconditional. No material impediments can actually check the advancement of devotional service, be it executed by a common man or a king. In any case, devotional service rendered to the Lord is always complete, despite the devotee's material position. Devotional service is so exalted that it can be executed by anyone in any position. One simply must be *dṛḍha-vrata,* firmly determined.

TEXT 51

ভট্টাচার্য কহে,—দেব না কর বিষাদ ।
তোমারে প্রভুর অবশ্য হইবে প্রসাদ ॥ ৫১ ॥

bhaṭṭācārya kahe——deva nā kara viṣāda
tomāre prabhura avaśya ha-ibe prasāda

SYNONYMS

bhaṭṭācārya kahe—Bhaṭṭācārya said; *deva*—O King; *nā kara viṣāda*—do not be worried; *tomāre*—unto you; *prabhura*—of Lord Śrī Caitanya Mahāprabhu; *avaśya*—certainly; *ha-ibe*—there must be; *prasāda*—mercy.

TRANSLATION

Finally Sārvabhauma Bhaṭṭācārya said, "My dear King, do not worry. Because of your firm determination, I am sure that Śrī Caitanya Mahāprabhu's mercy will definitely be bestowed upon you."

PURPORT

Due to King Pratāparudra's firm determination, Bhaṭṭācārya predicted that Śrī Caitanya Mahāprabhu's mercy would be there without fail. As confirmed elsewhere in *Caitanya-caritāmṛta* (*Madhya,* 19.151), *guru-kṛṣṇa-prasāde pāya bhakti-latā-bīja:* "By the mercy of the spiritual master and Kṛṣṇa, one gets the seed of devotional service." Bhaṭṭācārya was supposed to be the spiritual master of King Pratāparudra, and he gave his blessings to the effect that the Lord would be merciful upon the King. The mercy of the spiritual master and Kṛṣṇa combine to grant success to a devotee engaged in Kṛṣṇa consciousness. This is confirmed by the *Vedas:*

yasya deve parā bhaktir
yathā deva tathā gurau
tasyaite kathitā hy arthāḥ
prakāśante mahātmanaḥ

"Only unto those great souls who have implicit faith in both the Lord and the spiritual master are all the imports of Vedic knowledge automatically revealed." (*Śvetāśvatara Upaniṣad* 6.23)

Mahārāja Pratāparudra had firm faith in Bhaṭṭācārya, who declared Śrī Caitanya Mahāprabhu to be the Supreme Personality of Godhead. Having firm faith in Bhaṭṭācārya as his spiritual master, King Pratāparudra immediately accepted Śrī Caitanya Mahāprabhu as the Supreme Lord. Thus he began worshiping Śrī Caitanya Mahāprabhu in his mind. This is the process of devotional service. According to *Bhagavad-gītā* (9.34):

man-manā bhava mad-bhakto
mad-yājī māṁ namaskuru
mām evaiṣyasi yuktvaivam
ātmānaṁ mat-parāyaṇaḥ

"Engage your mind always in thinking of Me, become My devotee, offer obeisances and worship Me. Being completely absorbed in Me, surely you will come to Me."

This process is very simple. One need only be firmly convinced by the spiritual master that Kṛṣṇa is the Supreme Personality of Godhead. If one decides this, he can make further progress by thinking of Kṛṣṇa, chanting of Kṛṣṇa and glorifying Him. There is then no doubt that such a fully surrendered devotee will receive the blessings of Lord Kṛṣṇa. Śrīla Sārvabhauma Bhaṭṭācārya explains this further.

TEXT 52

তেঁহ – প্রেমাধীন, তোমার প্রেম – গাঢ়তর ।
অবশ্য করিবেন কৃপা তোমার উপর ॥ ৫২ ॥

teṅha——premādhīna, tomāra prema——gāḍhatara
avaśya karibena kṛpā tomāra upara

SYNONYMS

teṅha—He (Śrī Caitanya Mahāprabhu); *prema-adhīna*—under the control of love; *tomāra prema*—your love; *gāḍha-tara*—very deep; *avaśya*—certainly; *karibena kṛpā*—He will bestow mercy; *tomāra upara*—upon you.

TRANSLATION

As soon as Bhaṭṭācārya saw the King's firm determination, he declared, "The Supreme Lord is approached only by pure love. Your love for Śrī Caitanya Mahāprabhu is very, very deep; therefore without a doubt He will be merciful upon you."

PURPORT

Such determination is the first qualification. As confirmed by Rūpa Gosvāmī (*Upadeśāmṛta,* 3): *utsāhān niścayād dhairyāt.* One must first have firm determination, firm faith. When one engages in devotional service, he must maintain this firm determination. Then Kṛṣṇa will be pleased with his service. The spiritual master can show the path of devotional service. If the disciple follows the principles rigidly and undeviatingly, he will certainly receive the mercy of Kṛṣṇa. This is confirmed by the *śāstras.*

TEXT 53

তথাপি কহিয়ে আমি এক উপায়।
এই উপায় কর' প্রভু দেখিবে যাহায় ॥ ৫৩ ॥

tathāpi kahiye āmi eka upāya
ei upāya kara' prabhu dekhibe yāhāya

SYNONYMS

tathāpi—still; *kahiye*—say; *āmi*—I; *eka upāya*—one means; *ei upāya*—this means; *kara'*—try to adopt; *prabhu*—Lord Śrī Caitanya Mahāprabhu; *dekhibe*—will see you; *yāhāya*—by that.

TRANSLATION

Sārvabhauma Bhaṭṭācārya then suggested, "There is one means by which you can directly see Him.

TEXT 54

রথযাত্রা-দিনে প্রভু সব ভক্ত লঞা ।
রথ-আগে নৃত্য করিবেন প্রেমাবিষ্ট হঞা ॥ ৫৪ ॥

ratha-yātrā-dine prabhu saba bhakta lañā
ratha-āge nṛtya karibena premāviṣṭa hañā

SYNONYMS

ratha-yātrā-dine—on the day of the car festival ceremony; *prabhu*—Śrī Caitanya Mahāprabhu; *saba*—all; *bhakta*—devotees; *lañā*—taking with Him; *ratha*—the chariot; *āge*—in front of; *nṛtya karibena*—will dance; *prema-āviṣṭa hañā*—in great ecstatic love.

TRANSLATION

"On the day of the car festival, Śrī Caitanya Mahāprabhu will dance before the Deity in great ecstatic love.

TEXT 55

প্রেমাবেশে পুষ্পোদ্যানে করিবেন প্রবেশ ।
সেইকালে একলে তুমি ছাড়ি' রাজবেশ ॥ ৫৫ ॥

premāveśe puṣpodyāne karibena praveśa
sei-kāle ekale tumi chāḍi' rāja-veśa

SYNONYMS

prema-āveśe—in ecstatic love; *puṣpa-udyāne*—into the garden at Guṇḍicā where the Lord stays; *karibena praveśa*—will enter; *sei-kāle*—at that time; *ekale*—alone; *tumi*—you; *chāḍi'*—giving up; *rāja-veśa*—the royal dress.

TRANSLATION

"On that Ratha-yātrā festival day, after dancing before the Lord, Śrī Caitanya Mahāprabhu will enter the Guṇḍicā garden. At that time you should go there alone, stripped of your royal dress.

TEXT 56

'কৃষ্ণ-রাসপঞ্চাধ্যায়' করিতে পঠন ।
একলে যাই' মহাপ্রভুর ধরিবে চরণ ॥ ৫৬ ॥

'kṛṣṇa-rāsa-pañcādhyāya' karite paṭhana
ekale yāi' mahāprabhura dharibe caraṇa

SYNONYMS

kṛṣṇa-rāsa-pañca-adhyāya—the five chapters in the Tenth Canto of *Śrīmad-Bhāgavatam* in which Lord Kṛṣṇa's pastimes of the *rāsa* dance are described; *karite paṭhana*—to recite; *ekale yāi'*—going alone; *mahāprabhura*—of Lord Śrī Caitanya Mahāprabhu; *dharibe caraṇa*—catch hold of the lotus feet.

TRANSLATION

"When Śrī Caitanya Mahāprabhu enters the Guṇḍicā, you should also go there and read five chapters about Lord Kṛṣṇa's dancing with the gopīs. In this way you can catch hold of the Lord's lotus feet.

TEXT 57

বাহ্যজ্ঞান নাহি, সে-কালে কৃষ্ণনাম শুনি' ।
আলিঙ্গন করিবেন তোমায় 'বৈষ্ণব' জানি' ॥ ৫৭ ॥

bāhya-jñāna nāhi, se-kāle kṛṣṇa-nāma śuni'
āliṅgana karibena tomāya 'vaiṣṇava' jāni'

SYNONYMS

bāhya-jñāna nāhi—without external consciousness; *se-kāle*—at that time; *kṛṣṇa-nāma śuni'*—by hearing the holy name of Lord Kṛṣṇa; *āliṅgana karibena*—He will embrace; *tomāya*—you; *vaiṣṇava jāni'*—taking you to be a Vaiṣṇava.

TRANSLATION

"Lord Śrī Caitanya Mahāprabhu will be in a mood of ecstatic love without external consciousness. At that time you should begin to recite those chapters from Śrīmad-Bhāgavatam. Then He will embrace you, knowing you to be a pure Vaiṣṇava.

PURPORT

A Vaiṣṇava is always ready to help another Vaiṣṇava progress toward realization of the Absolute Truth. Sārvabhauma Bhaṭṭācārya could understand the King's position as a pure Vaiṣṇava. The King was always thinking of Śrī Caitanya Mahāprabhu, and Bhaṭṭācārya wanted to help him approach the Lord. A Vaiṣṇava is always compassionate, especially when he sees a prospective devotee very determined (*dṛḍha-vrata*). Consequently Bhaṭṭācārya was ready to help the King.

TEXT 58

রামানন্দ রায়, আজি তোমার প্রেম-গুণ ।
প্রভু-আগে কহিতে প্রভুর ফিরি' গেল মন ॥ ৫৮ ॥

rāmānanda rāya, āji tomāra prema-guṇa
prabhu-āge kahite prabhura phiri' gela mana

SYNONYMS

rāmānanda rāya—Rāmānanda Rāya; *āji*—today; *tomāra*—your; *prema-guṇa*—quality of love; *prabhu-āge*—in front of the Lord; *kahite*—when he described; *prabhura*—of Lord Śrī Caitanya Mahāprabhu; *phiri' gela*—became changed; *mana*—the mind.

TRANSLATION

"The Lord has already changed His mind due to Rāmānanda Rāya's description of your pure love for Him."

PURPORT

At first the Lord did not want to see the King, but due to Bhaṭṭācārya's and Rāmānanda Rāya's earnest endeavors, the Lord's mind was changed. The Lord already declared that Kṛṣṇa would be merciful upon the King due to the King's service to the devotees. This is the process by which one can advance in Kṛṣṇa consciousness. First there must be the devotee's mercy; then Kṛṣṇa's mercy will descend. *Yasya prasādād bhagavat-prasādo/ yasyāprasādān na gatiḥ kuto 'pi.* Our first duty, therefore, is to satisfy the spiritual master, who can arrange for the Lord's mercy. A common man must first begin to serve the spiritual master or the devotee. Then, through the mercy of the devotee, the Lord will be satisfied. Unless one receives the dust of a devotee's lotus feet on one's head, there is no possibility of advancement. This is also confirmed by a statement of Prahlāda Mahārāja in *Śrīmad-Bhāgavatam* (7.5.32):

naiṣāṁ matis tāvad urukramāṅghriṁ
spṛśaty anarthāpagamo yad-arthaḥ
mahīyasāṁ pāda-rajo 'bhiṣekaṁ
niṣkiñcanānāṁ na vṛṇīta yāvat

Unless one approaches a pure devotee, he cannot understand the Supreme Personality of Godhead. Mahārāja Pratāparudra worshiped both Rāmānanda Rāya and Sārvabhauma Bhaṭṭācārya. Thus he touched the lotus feet of pure devotees and was able thereby to approach Śrī Caitanya Mahāprabhu.

TEXT 59

শুনি' গজপতির মনে সুখ উপজিল ।
প্রভুরে মিলিতে এই মন্ত্রণা দৃঢ় কৈল ॥ ৫৯ ॥

śuni' gajapatira mane sukha upajila
prabhure milite ei mantraṇā dṛḍha kaila

SYNONYMS

śuni'—hearing; *gaja-patira*—of King Pratāparudra; *mane*—in the mind; *sukha*—happiness; *upajila*—awakened; *prabhure*—Śrī Caitanya Mahāprabhu; *milite*—to meet; *ei*—this; *mantraṇā*—instruction; *dṛḍha kaila*—decided to accept rigidly.

TRANSLATION

Mahārāja Pratāparudra took Bhaṭṭācārya's advice and firmly decided to follow his instructions. Thus he felt transcendental happiness.

TEXT 60

স্নানযাত্রা কবে হবে পুছিল ভট্টেরে ।
ভট্ট কহে,—তিন দিন আছয়ে যাত্রারে ॥ ৬০ ॥

snāna-yātrā kabe habe puchila bhaṭṭere
bhaṭṭa kahe, ——tina dina āchaye yātrāre

SYNONYMS

snāna-yātrā—the bathing ceremony of Lord Jagannātha; *kabe*—when; *habe*—will be; *puchila*—he inquired; *bhaṭṭere*—from Bhaṭṭācārya; *bhaṭṭa kahe*—Bhaṭṭācārya said; *tina dina*—three days; *āchaye*—there are still; *yātrāre*—until the festival.

TRANSLATION

When the King asked Bhaṭṭācārya when the bathing ceremony [Snāna-yātrā] of Lord Jagannātha would take place, Bhaṭṭācārya replied that there were only three days left before the ceremony.

TEXT 61

রাজারে প্রবোধিয়া ভট্ট গেলা নিজালয় ।
স্নানযাত্রা-দিনে প্রভুর আনন্দ হৃদয় ॥ ৬১ ॥

rājāre prabodhiyā bhaṭṭa gelā nijālaya
snāna-yātrā-dine prabhura ānanda hṛdaya

SYNONYMS

rājāre—the King; *prabodhiyā*—encouraging; *bhaṭṭa*—Sārvabhauma Bhaṭṭācārya; *gelā*—departed; *nija-ālaya*—to his own home; *snāna-yātrā-dine*—on the day of the bathing ceremony of Lord Jagannātha; *prabhura*—of Śrī Caitanya Mahāprabhu; *ānanda*—full of happiness; *hṛdaya*—heart.

TRANSLATION

After thus encouraging the King, Sārvabhauma Bhaṭṭācārya returned home. On the day of Lord Jagannātha's bathing ceremony, Śrī Caitanya Mahāprabhu was very happy at heart.

TEXT 62

স্নানযাত্রা দেখি' প্রভুর হৈল বড় সুখ ।
ঈশ্বরের 'অনবসরে' পাইল বড় দুঃখ ॥ ৬২ ॥

snāna-yātrā dekhi' prabhura haila baḍa sukha
īśvarera 'anavasare' pāila baḍa duḥkha

SYNONYMS

snāna-yātrā—the bathing ceremony of Lord Jagannātha; *dekhi'*—seeing; *prabhura*—of Lord Śrī Caitanya Mahāprabhu; *haila*—became; *baḍa*—very much; *sukha*—happiness; *īśvarera*—of the Lord; *anavasare*—during the pastime of retirement; *pāila*—got; *baḍa*—very much; *duḥkha*—unhappiness.

TRANSLATION

After seeing the bathing ceremony of Lord Jagannātha, Śrī Caitanya Mahāprabhu became very happy. But when Lord Jagannātha retired after the ceremony, Lord Caitanya became very unhappy because He could not see Him.

PURPORT

After the bathing ceremony of Śrī Jagannātha, which takes place just a fortnight before the Ratha-yātrā ceremony, the body of the Lord Jagannātha Deity is repainted, and this takes just about a fortnight to complete. This period is called Anavasara. There are many who visit the temple to see Lord Jagannātha regularly every day, and for them His retirement after the bathing ceremony is unbearable.

Śrī Caitanya Mahāprabhu felt Lord Jagannātha's absence from the temple very much.

TEXT 63

গোপীভাবে বিরহে প্রভু ব্যাকুল হঞা।
আলালনাথে গেলা প্রভু সবারে ছাড়িয়া ॥ ৬৩ ॥

gopī-bhāve virahe prabhu vyākula hañā
ālālanāthe gelā prabhu sabāre chāḍiyā

SYNONYMS

gopī-bhāve—in the mood of the *gopīs; virahe*—in separation; *prabhu*—Lord Śrī Caitanya Mahāprabhu; *vyākula*—agitated; *hañā*—being; *ālālanāthe*—to Ālālanātha; *gelā*—went; *prabhu*—Lord Śrī Caitanya Mahāprabhu; *sabāre*—all; *chāḍiyā*—having given up.

TRANSLATION

Due to the separation of Lord Jagannātha, Śrī Caitanya Mahāprabhu felt great anxiety such as the gopīs feel in separation from Kṛṣṇa. In this condition He gave up all association and went to Ālālanātha.

TEXT 64

পাছে প্রভুর নিকট আইলা ভক্তগণ।
গৌড় হৈতে ভক্ত আইসে,— কৈল নিবেদন ॥ ৬৪ ॥

pāche prabhura nikaṭa āilā bhakta-gaṇa
gauḍa haite bhakta āise, —kaila nivedana

SYNONYMS

pāche—behind; *prabhura*—of Śrī Caitanya Mahāprabhu; *nikaṭa*—in the presence; *āilā*—came; *bhakta-gaṇa*—the devotees; *gauḍa haite*—from Bengal; *bhakta*—devotees; *āise*—come; *kaila nivedana*—submitted.

TRANSLATION

The devotees following the Lord came into His presence and requested Him to return to Purī. They submitted that the devotees from Bengal were coming to Puruṣottama-kṣetra.

TEXT 65

সার্বভৌম নীলাচলে আইলা প্রভু লঞা ।
প্রভু আইলা,– রাজা-ঠাঞি কহিলেন গিয়া ॥ ৬৫ ॥

sārvabhauma nīlācale āilā prabhu lañā
prabhu āilā, ——rājā-ṭhāñi kahilena giyā

SYNONYMS

sārvabhauma—Sārvabhauma Bhaṭṭācārya; *nīlācale*—to Jagannātha Purī; *āilā*—came; *prabhu*—Śrī Caitanya Mahāprabhu; *lañā*—taking; *prabhu*—Śrī Caitanya Mahāprabhu; *āilā*—arrived; *rājā-ṭhāñi*—to the King; *kahilena*—said; *giyā*—after going.

TRANSLATION

In this way Sārvabhauma Bhaṭṭācārya brought Lord Caitanya back to Jagannātha Purī. He then went to King Pratāparudra and informed him of the Lord's arrival.

TEXT 66

হেনকালে আইলা তথা গোপীনাথাচার্য ।
রাজাকে আশীর্বাদ করি' কহে,– শুন ভট্টাচার্য ॥ ৬৬॥

hena-kāle āilā tathā gopīnāthācārya
rājāke āśīrvāda kari' kahe, ——śuna bhaṭṭācārya

SYNONYMS

hena-kāle—during this time; *āilā*—came; *tathā*—there; *gopīnātha-ācārya*—Gopīnātha Ācārya; *rājāke*—unto the King; *āśīrvāda kari'*—offering a benediction; *kahe*—said; *śuna bhaṭṭācārya*—my dear Bhaṭṭācārya, kindly listen.

TRANSLATION

At this time, Gopīnātha Ācārya came there while Sārvabhauma Bhaṭṭācārya was with King Pratāparudra. Being a brāhmaṇa, he offered his benediction to the King and addressed Sārvabhauma Bhaṭṭācārya as follows.

TEXT 67

গৌড় হৈতে বৈষ্ণব আসিতেছেন দুইশত ।
মহাপ্রভুর ভক্ত সব – মহাভাগবত ॥ ৬৭ ॥

gauḍa haite vaiṣṇava āsitechena dui-śata
mahāprabhura bhakta saba——mahā-bhāgavata

SYNONYMS

gauḍa haite—from Bengal; *vaiṣṇava*—devotees; *āsitechena*—are coming; *dui-śata*—numbering about two hundred; *mahāprabhura*—of Lord Śrī Caitanya Mahāprabhu; *bhakta*—the devotees; *saba*—all; *mahā-bhāgavata*—greatly advanced devotees.

TRANSLATION

"About two hundred devotees are coming from Bengal. All of them are greatly advanced devotees and specifically devoted to Śrī Caitanya Mahāprabhu.

TEXT 68

নরেন্দ্রে আসিয়া সবে হৈল বিদ্যমান।
তাঁ-সবারে চাহি বাসা প্রসাদ-সমাধান ॥ ৬৮ ॥

narendre āsiyā sabe haila vidyamāna
tāṅ-sabāre cāhi vāsā prasāda-samādhāna

SYNONYMS

narendre—on the bank of Lake Narendra; *āsiyā*—coming; *sabe*—all of them; *haila vidyamāna*—staying; *tāṅ-sabāre*—for all of them; *cāhi*—I want; *vāsā*—residential quarters; *prasāda*—for distributing *prasāda; samādhāna*—arrangement.

TRANSLATION

"All of them have already arrived on the bank of Lake Narendra and are waiting there. I desire residential quarters and prasāda arrangements for them."

PURPORT

Narendra is a small lake still existing in Jagannātha Purī, where the Candana-yātrā festival takes place. Up to the present date, all the Bengali devotees who visit the Jagannātha temple first take their bath in the lake. There they wash their hands and feet before entering the temple.

TEXT 69

রাজা কহে,—পড়িছাকে আমি আজ্ঞা দিব।
বাসা আদি যে চাহিয়ে,—পড়িছা সব দিব ॥ ৬৯ ॥

rājā kahe, —paḍichāke āmi ājñā diba
vāsā ādi ye cāhiye, —paḍichā saba diba

SYNONYMS

rājā kahe—the King said; *paḍichāke*—unto the attendant; *āmi*—I; *ājñā diba*—shall give orders; *vāsā*—residential quarters; *ādi*—and other arrangements; *ye cāhiye*—whatever you want; *paḍichā*—the attendant; *saba*—everything; *diba*—will supply.

TRANSLATION

The King replied, "I shall give orders to the attendant in the temple. He will arrange for everyone's residential quarters and prasāda, as you desire.

TEXT 70

মহাপ্রভুর গণ যত আইল গৌড় হৈতে।
ভট্টাচার্য, একে একে দেখাহ আমাতে ॥ ৭০ ॥

mahāprabhura gaṇa yata āila gauḍa haite
bhaṭṭācārya, eke eke dekhāha āmāte

SYNONYMS

mahāprabhura—of Śrī Caitanya Mahāprabhu; *gaṇa*—associates; *yata*—all; *āila*—who have come; *gauḍa haite*—from Bengal; *bhaṭṭācārya*—Sārvabhauma Bhaṭṭācārya; *eke eke*—one after another; *dekhāha*—please show; *āmāte*—to me.

TRANSLATION

"Sārvabhauma Bhaṭṭācārya, please show me, one after another, all of Śrī Caitanya Mahāprabhu's devotees who are coming from Bengal."

TEXT 71

ভট্ট কহে,—অট্টালিকায় কর আরোহণ।
গোপীনাথ চিনে সবারে, করাবে দরশন ॥ ৭১ ॥

bhaṭṭa kahe, —aṭṭālikāya kara ārohaṇa
gopīnātha cine sabāre, karābe daraśana

SYNONYMS

bhaṭṭa kahe—Bhaṭṭācārya said; *aṭṭālikāya*—on the roof of the palace; *kara ārohaṇa*—just get up; *gopīnātha*—Gopīnātha Ācārya; *cine*—knows; *sabāre*—everyone; *karābe daraśana*—he will show.

TRANSLATION

Sārvabhauma Bhaṭṭācārya requested the King, "Go up on the roof of the palace. Gopīnātha Ācārya knows every one of the devotees. He will identify them for you.

TEXT 72

আমি কাহো নাহি চিনি, চিনিতে মন হয়।
গোপীনাথাচার্য'সবারে করা'বে পরিচয় ॥ ৭২ ॥

āmi kāho nāhi cini, cinite mana haya
gopīnāthācārya sabāre karā'be paricaya

SYNONYMS

āmi—I; *kāho*—anyone; *nāhi*—do not; *cini*—know; *cinite mana haya*—I desire to know; *gopīnātha-ācārya*—Gopīnātha Ācārya; *sabāre*—all of them; *karā'be paricaya*—will identify.

TRANSLATION

"Actually I do not know any of them, although I have a desire to know them. Since Gopīnātha Ācārya knows them all, he will give you their names."

TEXT 73

এত বলি' তিন জন অট্টালিকায় চড়িল।
হেনকালে বৈষ্ণব সব নিকটে আইল ॥ ৭৩ ॥

eta bali' tina jana aṭṭālikāya caḍila
hena-kāle vaiṣṇava saba nikaṭe āila

SYNONYMS

eta bali'—saying this; *tina jana*—the three persons (namely, the King, Gopīnātha Ācārya and Sārvabhauma Bhaṭṭācārya); *aṭṭālikāya*—on the roof of the palace; *caḍila*—got up; *hena-kāle*—at this time; *vaiṣṇava*—the Vaiṣṇava devotees; *saba*—all; *nikaṭe*—nearby; *āila*—came.

TRANSLATION

After Sārvabhauma said this, he went up to the top of the palace with the King and Gopīnātha Ācārya. At this time all the Vaiṣṇava devotees from Bengal drew closer to the palace.

TEXT 74

দামোদর-স্বরূপ, গোবিন্দ,—দুই জন।
মালা-প্রসাদ লঞা যায়, যাহাঁ বৈষ্ণবগণ ॥ ৭৪ ॥

dāmodara-svarūpa, govinda, —dui jana
mālā-prasāda lañā yāya, yāhāṅ vaiṣṇava-gaṇa

SYNONYMS

dāmodara-svarūpa—Svarūpa Dāmodara; *govinda*—Govinda; *dui jana*—two persons; *mālā-prasāda*—flower garlands and remnants of Lord Jagannātha's food; *lañā*—taking; *yāya*—went; *yāhāṅ*—where; *vaiṣṇava-gaṇa*—the Vaiṣṇavas.

TRANSLATION

Svarūpa Dāmodara and Govinda, taking the flower garlands and prasāda of Lord Jagannātha, proceeded to where all the Vaiṣṇavas were standing.

TEXT 75

প্রথমেতে মহাপ্রভু পাঠাইলা দুঁহারে।
রাজা কহে, এই দুই কোন্ চিনাহ আমারে ॥ ৭৫ ॥

prathamete mahāprabhu pāṭhāilā duṅhāre
rājā kahe, ei dui kon cināha āmāre

SYNONYMS

prathamete—at first; *mahāprabhu*—Śrī Caitanya Mahāprabhu; *pāṭhāilā*—sent; *duṅhāre*—two persons; *rājā kahe*—the King said; *ei dui*—these two; *kon*—who are they; *cināha*—kindly identify; *āmāre*—to me.

TRANSLATION

Lord Śrī Caitanya Mahāprabhu first sent them both in advance. The King inquired, "Who are these two? Please let me know their identity."

TEXT 76

ভট্টাচার্য কহে,—এই স্বরূপ-দামোদর।
মহাপ্রভুর হয় ইঁহ দ্বিতীয় কলেবর ॥ ৭৬ ॥

bhaṭṭācārya kahe, —ei svarūpa-dāmodara
mahāprabhura haya iṅha dvitīya kalevara

SYNONYMS

bhaṭṭācārya kahe—Bhaṭṭācārya said; *ei*—this gentleman; *svarūpa-dāmodara*—his name is Svarūpa Dāmodara; *mahāprabhura*—of Śrī Caitanya Mahāprabhu; *haya*—is; *iṅha*—he; *dvitīya*—the second; *kalevara*—expansion of the body.

TRANSLATION

Śrī Sārvabhauma Bhaṭṭācārya replied, "Here is Svarūpa Dāmodara, who is practically the second expansion of the body of Śrī Caitanya Mahāprabhu.

TEXT 77

দ্বিতীয়, গোবিন্দ—ভৃত্য, ইহাঁ দোঁহা দিয়া।
মালা পাঠাঞাছেন প্রভু গৌরব করিয়া॥ ৭৭ ॥

dvitīya, govinda——bhṛtya, ihāṅ doṅhā diyā
mālā pāṭhāñāchena prabhu gaurava kariyā

SYNONYMS

dvitīya—the second; *govinda*—Govinda; *bhṛtya*—personal servant; *ihāṅ*—here; *doṅhā diyā*—through these two persons; *mālā*—flower garlands; *pāṭhāñāchena*—has sent; *prabhu*—Śrī Caitanya Mahāprabhu; *gaurava kariyā*—giving much honor.

TRANSLATION

"The second person is Govinda, Lord Caitanya's personal servant. The Lord has sent garlands and remnants of Lord Jagannātha's food with these two persons simply to honor the devotees from Bengal."

TEXT 78

আদৌ মালা অদ্বৈতেরে স্বরূপ পরাইল।
পাছে গোবিন্দ দ্বিতীয় মালা আনি' তাঁরে দিল ॥৭৮॥

ādau mālā advaitere svarūpa parāila
pāche govinda dvitīya mālā āni' tāṅre dila

SYNONYMS

ādau—in the beginning; *mālā*—a garland; *advaitere*—unto Advaita Ācārya; *svarūpa*—Svarūpa Dāmodara; *parāila*—offered; *pāche*—after that; *govinda*—the Lord's personal servant named Govinda; *dvitīya*—a second; *mālā*—garland; *āni'*—bringing; *tāṅre dila*—delivered to him.

TRANSLATION

At the beginning, Svarūpa Dāmodara came forward and garlanded Advaita Ācārya. Govinda next came and offered a second garland to Advaita Ācārya.

TEXT 79

তবে গোবিন্দ দণ্ডবৎ কৈল আচার্যেরে ।
তাঁরে নাহি চিনে আচার্য, পুছিল দামোদরে ॥ ৭৯ ॥

tabe govinda daṇḍavat kaila ācāryere
tāṅre nāhi cine ācārya, puchila dāmodare

SYNONYMS

tabe—at that time; *govinda*—Govinda; *daṇḍavat*—falling flat to offer obeisances; *kaila*—did; *ācāryere*—unto Advaita Ācārya; *tāṅre*—him; *nāhi*—not; *cine*—recognized; *ācārya*—Advaita Ācārya; *puchila*—inquired; *dāmodare*—to Svarūpa Dāmodara.

TRANSLATION

After Govinda offered his obeisances by falling down flat before Advaita Ācārya, Advaita Ācārya asked Svarūpa Dāmodara about his identity, for He did not know Govinda at that time.

TEXT 80

দামোদর কহে,—ইহার 'গোবিন্দ' নাম ।
ঈশ্বর-পুরীর সেবক অতি গুণবান্ ॥ ৮০ ॥

dāmodara kahe, —ihāra 'govinda' nāma
īśvara-purīra sevaka ati guṇavān

SYNONYMS

dāmodara kahe—Dāmodara said; *ihāra*—of him; *govinda*—Govinda; *nāma*—the name; *īśvara-purīra sevaka*—servant of Īśvara Purī; *ati guṇavān*—very qualified.

TRANSLATION

Svarūpa Dāmodara informed Him, "Govinda was the servant of Īśvara Purī. He is very highly qualified.

TEXT 81

প্রভুর সেবা করিতে পুরী আজ্ঞা দিল।
অতএব প্রভু ইঁহাকে নিকটে রাখিল ॥ ৮১ ॥

prabhura sevā karite purī ājñā dila
ataeva prabhu iṅhāke nikaṭe rākhila

SYNONYMS

prabhura—of Śrī Caitanya Mahāprabhu; *sevā*—the service; *karite*—to perform; *purī*—Īśvara Purī; *ājñā dila*—ordered; *ataeva*—therefore; *prabhu*—Śrī Caitanya Mahāprabhu; *iṅhāke*—him; *nikaṭe*—by His side; *rākhila*—kept.

TRANSLATION

"Īśvara Purī ordered Govinda to serve Śrī Caitanya Mahāprabhu. Thus the Lord keeps him by His side."

TEXT 82

রাজা কহে,—যাঁরে মালা দিল দুইজন।
আশ্চর্য তেজ, বড় মহান্ত,— কহ কোন্ জন? ৮২ ॥

rājā kahe, ——yāṅre mālā dila dui-jana
āścarya teja, baḍa mahānta, ——kaha kon jana?

SYNONYMS

rājā kahe—the King inquired; *yāṅre*—unto which person; *mālā*—garlands; *dila*—offered; *dui-jana*—Svarūpa Dāmodara and Govinda; *āścarya teja*—wonderfully effulgent; *baḍa mahānta*—a very great devotee; *kaha kon jana*—kindly let me know who He is.

TRANSLATION

The King inquired, "To whom did Svarūpa Dāmodara and Govinda offer the two garlands? His bodily effulgence is so great that He must be a very great devotee. Please let me know who He is."

TEXT 83

আচার্য কহে,— ইঁহার নাম অদ্বৈত আচার্য।
মহাপ্রভুর মান্যপাত্র, সর্ব-শিরোধার্য ॥ ৮৩ ॥

ācārya kahe, ——iṅhāra nāma advaita ācārya
mahāprabhura mānya-pātra, sarva-śirodhārya

SYNONYMS

ācārya kahe—Gopīnātha Ācārya said; *iṅhāra nāma*—His name; *advaita ācārya*—Advaita Ācārya; *mahāprabhura*—of Śrī Caitanya Mahāprabhu; *mānya-pātra*—honorable; *sarva-śirodhārya*—the topmost devotee.

TRANSLATION

Gopīnātha Ācārya replied, "His name is Advaita Ācārya. He is honored even by Śrī Caitanya Mahāprabhu, and He is therefore the topmost devotee.

TEXT 84

শ্রীবাস-পণ্ডিত ইঁহ, পণ্ডিত-বক্রেশ্বর ।
বিদ্যানিধি-আচার্য, ইঁহ পণ্ডিত-গদাধর ॥ ৮৪ ॥

śrīvāsa-paṇḍita iṅha, paṇḍita-vakreśvara
vidyānidhi-ācārya, iṅha paṇḍita-gadādhara

SYNONYMS

śrīvāsa-paṇḍita—Śrīvāsa Paṇḍita; *iṅha*—here; *paṇḍita-vakreśvara*—Vakreśvara Paṇḍita; *vidyānidhi-ācārya*—Vidyānidhi Ācārya; *iṅha*—here; *paṇḍita-gadādhara*—Gadādhara Paṇḍita.

TRANSLATION

"Here are Śrīvāsa Paṇḍita, Vakreśvara Paṇḍita, Vidyānidhi Ācārya and Gadādhara Paṇḍita.

TEXT 85

আচার্যরত্ন ইঁহ, পণ্ডিত-পুরন্দর ।
গঙ্গাদাস পণ্ডিত ইঁহ, পণ্ডিত-শঙ্কর ॥ ৮৫ ॥

ācāryaratna iṅha, paṇḍita-purandara
gaṅgādāsa paṇḍita iṅha, paṇḍita-śaṅkara

SYNONYMS

ācāryaratna—Candraśekhara; *iṅha*—here; *paṇḍita-purandara*—Purandara Paṇḍita; *gaṅgādāsa paṇḍita*—Gaṅgādāsa Paṇḍita; *iṅha*—here; *paṇḍita-śaṅkara*—Śaṅkara Paṇḍita.

TRANSLATION

"Here are Ācāryaratna, Purandara Paṇḍita, Gaṅgādāsa Paṇḍita and Śaṅkara Paṇḍita.

TEXT 86

এই মুরারি গুপ্ত, ইঁহ পণ্ডিত নারায়ণ ।
হরিদাস ঠাকুর ইঁহ ভুবনপাবন ॥ ৮৬ ॥

ei murāri gupta, iṅha paṇḍita nārāyaṇa
haridāsa ṭhākura iṅha bhuvana-pāvana

SYNONYMS

ei—this; *murāri gupta*—Murāri Gupta; *iṅha*—here; *paṇḍita nārāyaṇa*—Nārāyaṇa Paṇḍita; *haridāsa ṭhākura*—Haridāsa Ṭhākura; *iṅha*—here; *bhuvana-pāvana*—deliverer of the whole universe.

TRANSLATION

"Here are Murāri Gupta, Paṇḍita Nārāyaṇa and Haridāsa Ṭhākura, the deliverer of the whole universe.

TEXT 87

এই হরি-ভট্ট, এই শ্রীনৃসিংহানন্দ ।
এই বাসুদেব দত্ত, এই শিবানন্দ ॥ ৮৭ ॥

ei hari-bhaṭṭa, ei śrī-nṛsiṁhānanda
ei vāsudeva datta, ei śivānanda

SYNONYMS

ei—this; *hari-bhaṭṭa*—Hari Bhaṭṭa; *ei*—this; *śrī-nṛsiṁhānanda*—Śrī Nṛsiṁhānanda; *ei*—this; *vāsudeva datta*—Vāsudeva Datta; *ei*—this; *śivānanda*—Śivānanda.

TRANSLATION

"Here is Hari Bhaṭṭa, and there is Nṛsiṁhānanda. Here are Vāsudeva Datta and Śivānanda Sena.

TEXT 88

গোবিন্দ, মাধব ঘোষ, এই বাসুঘোষ ।
তিন ভাইর কীর্তনে প্রভু পায়েন সন্তোষ ॥ ৮৮ ॥

govinda, mādhava ghoṣa, ei vāsu-ghoṣa
tina bhāira kīrtane prabhu pāyena santoṣa

SYNONYMS

govinda—Govinda Ghosh; *mādhava ghoṣa*—Mādhava Ghosh; *ei*—this; *vāsu-ghoṣa*—Vāsudeva Ghosh; *tina bhāira*—of the three brothers; *kīrtane*—in the *saṅkīrtana; prabhu*—the Lord; *pāyena santoṣa*—gets very much pleasure.

TRANSLATION

"Here also are Govinda Ghosh, Mādhava Ghosh and Vāsudeva Ghosh. They are three brothers, and their saṅkīrtana, congregational chanting, pleases the Lord very much.

PURPORT

Govinda Ghosh belonged to the *kāyastha* dynasty of the Uttara-rāḍhīya section, and he was known as Ghosh Ṭhākura. Even to the present day there is a place named Agradvīpa, near Katwa, where a fair takes place and is named after Ghosh Ṭhākura. As far as Vāsudeva Ghosh is concerned, he composed many nice songs about Lord Śrī Caitanya Mahāprabhu, and these are all authorized Vaiṣṇava songs, like the songs of Narottama dāsa Ṭhākura, Bhaktivinoda Ṭhākura, Locana dāsa Ṭhākura, Govinda dāsa Ṭhākura and other great Vaiṣṇavas.

TEXT 89

রাঘব পণ্ডিত, ইঁহ আচার্য নন্দন ।
শ্রীমান্ পণ্ডিত এই, শ্রীকান্ত, নারায়ণ ॥ ৮৯ ॥

rāghava paṇḍita, iṅha ācārya nandana
śrīmān paṇḍita ei, śrīkānta, nārāyaṇa

SYNONYMS

rāghava paṇḍita—Rāghava Paṇḍita; *iṅha*—here; *ācārya nandana*—Ācārya Nandana; *śrīmān paṇḍita*—Śrīmān Paṇḍita; *ei*—this; *śrī-kānta*—Śrīkānta; *nārāyaṇa*—and also Nārāyaṇa.

TRANSLATION

"Here is Rāghava Paṇḍita, here is Ācārya Nandana, there is Śrīmān Paṇḍita, and here are Śrīkānta and Nārāyaṇa."

PURPORT

Narottama dāsa Ṭhākura, honoring the personal associates of Lord Śrī Caitanya Mahāprabhu, has sung as follows (*Prārthanā* 13):

gaurāṅgera saṅgi-gaṇe nitya-siddha kari' māne
se yāya vrajendra-suta-pāśa

One who is intelligent understands that all the personal associates and devotees of Lord Śrī Caitanya Mahāprabhu are ever liberated. This means that they do not belong to this material world because they are always engaged in the devotional service of the Lord. One who is engaged in the Lord's devotional service twenty-four hours daily and never forgets the Lord is called *nitya-siddha.* Śrīla Rūpa Gosvāmī also confirms this statement:

īhā yasya harer dāsye
karmaṇā manasā girā
nikhilāsv apy avasthāsu
jīvan-muktaḥ sa ucyate

"A person acting in the service of Kṛṣṇa with body, mind, intelligence and words is a liberated person even within the material world, although he may be engaged in many so-called material activites." (*Bhakti-rasāmṛta-sindhu,* 1.2.187)

A devotee is always thinking of how better to serve Lord Kṛṣṇa, the Supreme Personality of Godhead, and how to broadcast His name, fame and qualities throughout the world. One who is *nitya-siddha* has no business other than broadcasting the glories of the Lord all over the world according to his ability. Such people are already associates of Lord Caitanya Mahāprabhu. Therefore Narottama dāsa Ṭhākura says, *nitya-siddha kari' māne.* One should not think that because Śrī Caitanya Mahāprabhu was personally present five hundred years ago, only His associates were liberated. Rather, Śrīla Narottama dāsa Ṭhākura says that anyone is a *nitya-siddha* if he acts on behalf of Śrī Caitanya Mahāprabhu by spreading the glories of the holy name of the Lord. We should respect those devotees preaching the glories of the Lord as *nitya-siddha* and should not consider them conditioned.

māṁ ca yo 'vyabhicāreṇa
bhakti-yogena sevate
sa guṇān samatītyaitān
brahma-bhūyāya kalpate
(Bg. 14.26)

One who has transcended the material modes of nature is supposed to be on the Brahman platform. That is also the platform of *nitya-siddha.* The *nitya-siddha* not only stays on the Brahman platform but also works on that platform. Simply by accepting the associates of Lord Caitanya Mahāprabhu as *nitya-siddha,* one can very easily go back home, back to Godhead.

TEXT 90

শুক্লাম্বর দেখ, এই শ্রীধর, বিজয় ।
বল্লভ-সেন, এই পুরুষোত্তম, সঞ্জয় ॥ ৯০ ॥

śuklāmbara dekha, ei śrīdhara, vijaya
vallabha-sena, ei puruṣottama, sañjaya

SYNONYMS

śuklāmbara—Śuklāmbara; *dekha*—see; *ei*—this; *śrīdhara*—Śrīdhara; *vijaya*—Vijaya; *vallabha-sena*—Vallabha Sena; *ei*—this; *puruṣottama*—Puruṣottama; *sañjaya*—Sañjaya.

TRANSLATION

Gopīnātha Ācārya continued to point out the devotees. "Here is Śuklāmbara. See, there is Śrīdhara. Here is Vijaya, and there is Vallabha Sena. Here is Puruṣottama, and there is Sañjaya.

TEXT 91

কুলীন-গ্রামবাসী এই সত্যরাজ-খান ।
রামানন্দ-আদি সবে দেখ বিদ্যমান ॥ ৯১ ॥

kulīna-grāma-vāsī ei satyarāja-khāna
rāmānanda-ādi sabe dekha vidyamāna

SYNONYMS

kulīna-grāma-vāsī—residents of the village known as Kulīna-grāma; *ei*—these; *satyarāja-khāna*—Satyarāja Khān; *rāmānanda-ādi*—headed by Rāmānanda; *sabe*—everyone; *dekha*—you see; *vidyamāna*—present.

TRANSLATION

"And here are all the residents of Kulīna-grāma, such as Satyarāja Khān and Rāmānanda. Indeed, all of them are present here. Please see.

TEXT 92

মুকুন্দদাস, নরহরি, শ্রীরঘুনন্দন ।
খণ্ডবাসী চিরঞ্জীব, আর সুলোচন ॥ ৯২ ॥

mukunda-dāsa, narahari, śrī-raghunandana
khaṇḍa-vāsī ciranjīva, āra sulocana

SYNONYMS

mukunda-dāsa—Mukunda dāsa; *narahari*—Narahari; *śrī-raghunandana*—Śrī Raghunandana; *khaṇḍa-vāsī*—residents of Khaṇḍa; *ciranjīva*—Cirañjīva; *āra*—and; *sulocana*—Sulocana.

TRANSLATION

"Here are Mukunda dāsa, Narahari, Śrī Raghunandana, Cirañjīva and Sulocana, all residents of Khaṇḍa.

TEXT 93

কতেক কহিব, এই দেখ যত জন।
চৈতন্যের গণ, সব—চৈতন্যজীবন॥ ৯৩॥

kateka kahiba, ei dekha yata jana
caitanyera gaṇa, saba——caitanya-jīvana

SYNONYMS

kateka kahiba—how many I shall speak; *ei*—these; *dekha*—see; *yata jana*—all the persons; *caitanyera gaṇa*—associates of Śrī Caitanya Mahāprabhu; *saba*—all of them; *caitanya-jīvana*—consider Śrī Caitanya Mahāprabhu their life and soul.

TRANSLATION

"How many names shall I speak to you? All the devotees you see here are associates of Śrī Caitanya Mahāprabhu, who is their life and soul."

TEXT 94

রাজা কহে—দেখি' মোর হৈল চমৎকার।
বৈষ্ণবের ঐছে তেজ দেখি নাহি আর॥ ৯৪॥

rājā kahe——dekhi' mora haila camatkāra
vaiṣṇavera aiche teja dekhi nāhi āra

SYNONYMS

rājā kahe—the King said; *dekhi'*—after seeing; *mora*—my; *haila*—there is; *camatkāra*—astonishment; *vaiṣṇavera*—of the devotees of the Lord; *aiche*—such; *teja*—effulgence; *dekhi*—I see; *nāhi*—not; *āra*—anyone else.

TRANSLATION

The King said, "Upon seeing all these devotees, I am much astonished, for I have never seen such an effulgence.

TEXT 95

কোটিসূর্য-সম সব—উজ্জ্বল-বরণ।
কভু নাহি শুনি এই মধুর কীর্তন॥ ৯৫॥

koṭi-sūrya-sama saba——ujjvala-varaṇa
kabhu nāhi śuni ei madhura kīrtana

SYNONYMS

koṭi-sūrya-sama—equal to the shining of millions of suns; *saba*—all of them; *ujjvala-varaṇa*—very bright luster; *kabhu nāhi śuni*—I have never heard; *ei*—this; *madhura kīrtana*—such melodious performance of congregational chanting.

TRANSLATION

"Indeed, their effulgence is like the brilliance of a million suns. Nor have I ever heard the Lord's names chanted so melodiously.

PURPORT

Such are the symptoms of pure devotees when they are chanting. All the pure devotees are as bright as sunshine, and their bodily luster is very effulgent. In addition, their performance of *saṅkīrtana* is unparalleled. There are many professional chanters who can perform congregational chanting with various musical instruments in an artistic and musical way, but their chanting cannot be as attractive as the congregational chanting of pure devotees. If a devotee sticks strictly to the principles governing Vaiṣṇava behavior, his bodily luster will naturally be attractive, and his singing and chanting of the holy names of the Lord will be effective. People will appreciate such *kīrtana* without hesitation. Even dramas about the pastimes of Lord Caitanya or Śrī Kṛṣṇa should be played by devotees. Such dramas will immediately interest an audience and be full of potency. The students of the International Society for Krishna Consciousness should note these two points and try to apply these principles in their spreading of the Lord's glories.

TEXT 96

ঐছে প্রেম, ঐছে নৃত্য, ঐছে হরিধ্বনি।
কাহাঁ নাহি দেখি, ঐছে কাহাঁ নাহি শুনি॥ ৯৬॥

aiche prema, aiche nṛtya, aiche hari-dhvani
kāhāṅ nāhi dekhi, aiche kāhāṅ nāhi śuni

SYNONYMS

aiche—such; *prema*—ecstatic love; *aiche nṛtya*—such dancing; *aiche hari-dhvani*—such vibration of the chanting of the holy name; *kāhāṅ*—anywhere; *nāhi dekhi*—I have never seen; *aiche*—such; *kāhāṅ*—anywhere; *nāhi śuni*—I never heard.

TRANSLATION

"I have never before seen such ecstatic love, nor heard the vibration of the holy name of the Lord chanted in such a way, nor seen such dancing during saṅkīrtana."

PURPORT

Because the temple of Lord Jagannātha is situated at Jagannātha Purī, many devotees from all parts of the world came to perform *saṅkīrtana* in glorification of the Lord. All these devotees were certainly seen and heard by Mahārāja Pratāparudra, but he herein admits that the *kīrtana* performed by the associates of the Lord was unique. He had never before heard such *saṅkīrtana* nor seen such attractive features manifest by the devotees. The members of the International Society for Krishna Consciousness should go to India during the birthday ceremony of Lord Caitanya Mahāprabhu at Māyāpur and perform *saṅkīrtana* congregationally. This will attract the attention of all the important personalities in India, just as the beauty, bodily luster and *saṅkīrtana* performance by the associates of Śrī Caitanya Mahāprabhu attracted the attention of Mahārāja Pratāparudra. The associates of Śrī Caitanya Mahāprabhu were unlimited during the Lord's presence on this planet, but anyone who is pure in life and devoted to the mission of Śrī Caitanya Mahāprabhu is to be understood as a *nitya-siddha* associate of the Lord.

TEXT 97

ভট্টাচার্য কহে এই মধুর বচন ।
চৈতন্যের সৃষ্টি – এই প্রেম-সংকীর্তন ॥ ৯৭ ॥

bhaṭṭācārya kahe ei madhura vacana
caitanyera sṛṣṭi——ei prema-saṅkīrtana

SYNONYMS

bhaṭṭācārya—Sārvabhauma Bhaṭṭācārya; *kahe*—replied; *ei*—this; *madhura vacana*—transcendental sweetness of the voice; *caitanyera sṛṣṭi*—the creation of

Lord Śrī Caitanya Mahāprabhu; *ei*—this; *prema-saṅkīrtana*—chanting in the ecstasy of love of Godhead.

TRANSLATION

Sārvabhauma Bhaṭṭācārya replied, "This sweet transcendental sound is a special creation of the Lord known as prema-saṅkīrtana, congregational chanting in love of Godhead.

TEXT 98

অবতরি' চৈতন্য কৈল ধর্মপ্রচারণ ।
কলিকালে ধর্ম– কৃষ্ণনাম-সংকীর্তন ॥ ৯৮ ॥

avatari' caitanya kaila dharma-pracāraṇa
kali-kāle dharma——kṛṣṇa-nāma-saṅkīrtana

SYNONYMS

avatari'—descending; *caitanya*—Śrī Caitanya Mahāprabhu; *kaila*—did; *dharma-pracāraṇa*—preaching of real religion; *kali-kāle*—in this age of Kali; *dharma*—religious principle; *kṛṣṇa-nāma*—of the holy name of Lord Kṛṣṇa; *saṅkīrtana*—chanting.

TRANSLATION

"In this age of Kali, Śrī Caitanya Mahāprabhu has descended to preach the religion of Kṛṣṇa consciousness. Therefore the chanting of the holy names of Lord Kṛṣṇa is the religious principle for this age.

TEXT 99

সংকীর্তন-যজ্ঞে তাঁরে করে আরাধন ।
সেই ত' সুমেধা, আর—কলিহতজন ॥ ৯৯ ॥

saṅkīrtana-yajñe tāṅre kare ārādhana
sei ta' sumedhā, āra——kali-hata-jana

SYNONYMS

saṅkīrtana-yajñe—in the performance of congregational chanting; *tāṅre*—unto Śrī Caitanya Mahāprabhu; *kare*—does; *ārādhana*—worship; *sei ta'*—such a person; *su-medhā*—sharply intelligent; *āra*—others; *kali-hata-jana*—victims of this age of Kali.

TRANSLATION

"Anyone who worships Lord Caitanya Mahāprabhu by congregational chanting should be understood to be very intelligent. One who does not do so must be considered a victim of this age and bereft of all intelligence.

PURPORT

Rascals propose that anyone can invent his own religious process, and this proposition is condemned herein. If one actually wants to become religious, he must take up the chanting of the Hare Kṛṣṇa *mahā-mantra.* The real meaning of religion is stated in *Śrīmad-Bhāgavatam* (6.3.19-22).

dharmaṁ tu sākṣād-bhagavat-praṇītaṁ
na vai vidur ṛṣayo nāpi devāḥ
na siddha-mukhyā asurā manuṣyāḥ
kutaś ca vidyādhara-cāraṇādayaḥ

svayambhūr nāradaḥ śambhuḥ
kumāraḥ kapilo manuḥ
prahlādo janako bhīṣmo
balir vaiyāsakir vayam

dvādaśaite vijānīmo
dharmaṁ bhāgavataṁ bhaṭāḥ
guhyaṁ viśuddhaṁ durbodhaṁ
yaṁ jñātvāmṛtam aśnute

etāvān eva loke 'smin
puṁsāṁ dharmaḥ paraḥ smṛtaḥ
bhakti-yogo bhagavati
tan-nāma-grahaṇādibhiḥ

The purport of these verses is that *dharma,* or religion, cannot be manufactured by a human being. Religion is the law or code of the Lord. Consequently religion cannot be manufactured even by great saintly persons, demigods or *siddha-mukhyas,* and what to speak of *asuras,* human beings, Vidyādharas, Cāraṇas, and so on. The principles of *dharma,* religion, come down in the *paramparā* system beginning with twelve personalities—namely, Lord Brahmā; the great saint Nārada; Lord Śiva; the four Kumāras; Kapila, the son of Devahūti; Svāyambhuva Manu; Prahlāda Mahārāja; King Janaka; grandfather Bhīṣma; Bali Mahārāja; Śukadeva Gosvāmī; and Yamarāja. The principles of religion are known to these twelve personalities. *Dharma* refers to the religious principles by which one can understand the Supreme Personality of Godhead. *Dharma* is very confidential, uncontaminated by all material influence, and very difficult for ordinary men to understand. However, if one actually understands *dharma,* he immediately becomes liberated and is transferred to the kingdom of God. *Bhāgavata-dharma,* or the principle of religion enunciated by the *paramparā* system, is the supreme principle of religion. In other words, *dharma* refers to the science of *bhakti-yoga,* which begins by the novice's chanting the holy name of the Lord (*tan-nāma-grahaṇādibhiḥ*).

In this age of Kali it is recommended in *Caitanya-caritāmṛta, kali-kāle dharma—kṛṣṇa-nāma-saṅkīrtana.* In the age of Kali the chanting of the holy name of the Lord is the method of religion approved by all Vedic scriptures. In the next text of this *Caitanya-caritāmṛta,* from *Śrīmad-Bhāgavatam* (11.5.32), it is further stressed.

TEXT 100

কৃষ্ণবর্ণং ত্বিষাঽকৃষ্ণং সাঙ্গোপাঙ্গাস্ত্রপার্ষদম্ ।
যজ্ঞৈঃ সংকীর্তনপ্রায়ৈর্যজন্তি হি সুমেধসঃ ॥ ১০০ ॥

kṛṣṇa-varṇaṁ tviṣākṛṣṇaṁ
sāṅgopāṅgāstra-pārṣadam
yajñaiḥ saṅkīrtana-prāyair
yajanti hi sumedhasaḥ

SYNONYMS

kṛṣṇa-varṇam—repeating the syllables *kṛṣ-ṇa; tviṣā*—with a luster; *akṛṣṇam*—not black (golden); *sa-aṅga*—along with associates; *upāṅga*—servitors; *astra*—weapons; *pārṣadam*—confidential companions; *yajñaiḥ*—by sacrifice; *saṅkīrtana-prāyaiḥ*—consisting chiefly of congregational chanting; *yajanti*—they worship; *hi*—certainly; *su-medhasaḥ*—intelligent persons.

TRANSLATION

" 'In the age of Kali, intelligent persons perform congregational chanting to worship the incarnation of Godhead who constantly sings the name of Kṛṣṇa. Although His complexion is not blackish, He is Kṛṣṇa Himself. He is accompanied by His associates, servants, weapons and confidential companions.' "

PURPORT

For an explanation of this verse, refer to *Ādi-līlā,* Chapter Three, verse 52.

TEXT 101

রাজা কহে,—শাস্ত্রপ্রমাণে চৈতন্য হন কৃষ্ণ।
তবে কেনে পণ্ডিত সব তাঁহাতে বিতৃষ্ণ ? ১০১ ॥

rājā kahe, ——śāstra-pramāṇe caitanya hana kṛṣṇa
tabe kene paṇḍita saba tāṅhāte vitṛṣṇa?

SYNONYMS

rājā kahe—the King said; *śāstra-pramāṇe*—by the evidence of revealed scripture; *caitanya*—Śrī Caitanya Mahāprabhu; *hana*—is; *kṛṣṇa*—the Supreme Personality of Godhead, Lord Kṛṣṇa; *tabe*—therefore; *kene*—why; *paṇḍita*—so-called learned scholars; *saba*—all; *tāṅhāte*—unto Him; *vitṛṣṇa*—indifferent.

TRANSLATION

The King said, "According to evidence given in revealed scriptures, it is concluded that Lord Śrī Caitanya Mahāprabhu is Lord Kṛṣṇa Himself. Why, then, are learned scholars sometimes indifferent to Him?"

TEXT 102

ভট্ট কহে,—তাঁর কৃপা-লেশ হয় যাঁরে।
সেই সে তাঁহারে 'কৃষ্ণ' করি' লইতে পারে ॥ ১০২ ॥

bhaṭṭa kahe, ——tāṅra kṛpā-leśa haya yāṅre
sei se tāṅhāre 'kṛṣṇa' kari' la-ite pāre

SYNONYMS

bhaṭṭa kahe—Sārvabhauma Bhaṭṭācārya said; *tāṅra kṛpā*—of Lord Kṛṣṇa's mercy; *leśa*—even a fraction; *haya*—there is; *yāṅre*—unto whom; *sei se*—that person only; *tāṅhāre*—Lord Śrī Caitanya Mahāprabhu; *kṛṣṇa kari'*—accepting as Kṛṣṇa; *la-ite pāre*—can take up.

TRANSLATION

Bhaṭṭācārya replied, "Only a person who has received but a small fraction of mercy from the Lord can understand that Lord Śrī Caitanya Mahāprabhu is Kṛṣṇa. No one else can.

PURPORT

The *saṅkīrtana* movement can be spread by a person who is especially favored by Lord Kṛṣṇa (*kṛṣṇa-śakti vinā nahe tāra pravartana*). Without first obtaining the mercy of the Lord, one cannot spread the holy name of the Lord. One who can spread the Lord's name is called *labdha-caitanya* in the words of Bhaktisiddhānta Sarasavtī. The *labdha-caitanya* is one who has actually awakened his original consciousness, Kṛṣṇa consciousness. The influence of the pure devotees in Kṛṣṇa consciousness is such that it can awaken others to become immediately Kṛṣṇa conscious and engage themselves in the transcendental loving service of Kṛṣṇa. In this way the descendants of pure devotees increase, and Lord Caitanya Mahāprabhu takes much pleasure in seeing the increase of His devotees. The word *sumedhasaḥ* means "sharply intelligent." When one's intelligence is sharp, he can increase the interests of common men in loving Caitanya Mahāprabhu and through Him in loving Rādhā-Kṛṣṇa. Those not interested in understanding Śrī Caitanya Mahāprabhu are simply material in their attempts at professional chanting and dancing for money, despite their supposed artistry. If one does not have full faith in Śrī Caitanya Mahāprabhu, he cannot properly chant and dance in the *saṅkīrtana* movement. Artificial chanting and dancing may be due to sentiments or sentimental agitation, but this cannot help one advance in Kṛṣṇa consciousness.

TEXT 103

তাঁর কৃপা নহে যারে, পণ্ডিত নহে কেনে ।
দেখিলে শুনিলেহ তাঁরে 'ঈশ্বর' না মানে ॥ ১০৩ ॥

tāṅra kṛpā nahe yāre, paṇḍita nahe kene
dekhile śunileha tāṅre 'īśvara' nā māne

SYNONYMS

tāṅra kṛpā—His mercy; *nahe*—there is not; *yāre*—unto whom; *paṇḍita*—learned scholar; *nahe*—even though; *kene*—nevertheless; *dekhile*—even by seeing; *śunileha*—even by listening; *tāṅre*—Him; *īśvara*—as the Supreme Personality of Godhead; *nā māne*—does not accept.

TRANSLATION

"If the mercy of Śrī Caitanya Mahāprabhu is not bestowed upon a person—regardless of how learned a scholar that person may be and regardless of his seeing or listening—he cannot accept the Lord as the Supreme Personality of Godhead.

PURPORT

The same principles can be applied to demoniac persons, even though they be in the *sampradāya* of Lord Śrī Caitanya Mahāprabhu. Without receiving the Lord's special power, one cannot preach His glories all over the world. Even though one may celebrate himself as a learned follower of Śrī Caitanya Mahāprabhu, and even though one may attempt to preach the holy name of the Lord all over the world, if he is not favored by Śrī Caitanya Mahāprabhu he will find fault with the pure devotee and will not be able to understand how a preacher is empowered by Lord Caitanya. One must be considered bereft of the mercy of Śrī Caitanya Mahāprabhu when he criticizes the Kṛṣṇa consciousness movement now spreading all over the world or finds fault with this movement or the leader of the movement.

TEXT 104

অথাপি তে দেব পদাম্বুজদ্বয়-
প্রসাদলেশানুগৃহীত এব হি ।
জানাতি তত্ত্বং ভগবন্মহিম্নো
ন চান্য একোঽপি চিরং বিচিন্বন্ ॥ ১০৪ ॥

athāpi te deva padāmbuja-dvaya-
prasāda-leśānugṛhīta eva hi
jānāti tattvaṁ bhagavan-mahimno
na cānya eko 'pi ciraṁ vicinvan

SYNONYMS

atha—therefore; *api*—indeed; *te*—Your; *deva*—my Lord; *pada-ambuja-dvaya*—of the two lotus feet; *prasāda*—of the mercy; *leśa*—by only a trace; *anugṛhītaḥ*—favored; *eva*—certainly; *hi*—indeed; *jānāti*—one knows; *tattvam*—the truth; *bhagavat*—of the Supreme Personality of Godhead; *mahimnaḥ*—of the greatness; *na*—never; *ca*—and; *anyaḥ*—another; *ekaḥ*—one; *api*—although; *ciram*—for a long period; *vicinvan*—speculating.

TRANSLATION

" 'My Lord, if one is favored by even a slight trace of the mercy of Your lotus feet, he can understand the greatness of Your personality. But those who speculate to understand the Supreme Personality of Godhead are unable to know You, even though they continue to study the Vedas for many years.' "

PURPORT

This verse is a quotation from the *Śrīmad-Bhāgavatam* (10.14.29). It is explained in the *Madhya-līlā,* in the Sixth Chapter, text 84.

TEXT 105

রাজা কহে,—সবে জগন্নাথ না দেখিয়া ।
চৈতন্যের বাসা-গৃহে চলিলা ধাঞা ॥ ১০৫ ॥

rājā kahe, —sabe jagannātha nā dekhiyā
caitanyera vāsā-gṛhe calilā dhāñā

SYNONYMS

rājā kahe—the King said; *sabe*—all of them; *jagannātha*—Lord Jagannātha; *nā dekhiyā*—without visiting; *caitanyera*—of Lord Śrī Caitanya Mahāprabhu; *vāsā-gṛhe*—to the residential place; *calilā*—they went; *dhāñā*—running.

TRANSLATION

The King said, "Instead of visiting the temple of Lord Jagannātha, all the devotees are running toward the residence of Śrī Caitanya Mahāprabhu."

TEXT 106

ভট্ট কহে,— এই ত' স্বাভাবিক প্রেম-রীত ।
মহাপ্রভু মিলিবারে উৎকণ্ঠিত চিত ॥ ১০৬ ॥

bhaṭṭa kahe, —ei ta' svābhāvika prema-rīta
mahāprabhu milibāre utkaṇṭhita cita

SYNONYMS

bhaṭṭa kahe—Bhaṭṭācārya replied; *ei ta'*—this is; *svābhāvika*—spontaneous; *prema-rīta*—attraction of love; *mahāprabhu*—Śrī Caitanya Mahāprabhu; *milibāre*—for meeting; *utkaṇṭhita*—anxious; *cita*—mind.

TRANSLATION

Sārvabhauma Bhaṭṭācārya replied, "This is spontaneous love. All the devotees are very anxious to meet Śrī Caitanya Mahāprabhu.

TEXT 107

আগে তাঁরে মিলি' সবে তাঁরে সঙ্গে লঞা ।
তাঁর সঙ্গে জগন্নাথ দেখিবেন গিয়া ॥ ১০৭ ॥

āge tāṅre mili' sabe tāṅre saṅge lañā
tāṅra saṅge jagannātha dekhibena giyā

SYNONYMS

āge—first; *tāṅre*—Śrī Caitanya Mahāprabhu; *mili'*—meeting; *sabe*—all the devotees; *tāṅre*—Him; *saṅge*—with them; *lañā*—taking; *tāṅra saṅge*—with Him; *jagannātha*—Lord Jagannātha; *dekhibena*—they will see; *giyā*—going.

TRANSLATION

"First the devotees will meet Śrī Caitanya Mahāprabhu and then take Him with them to the temple to see Lord Jagannātha."

TEXT 108

রাজা কহে,—ভবানন্দের পুত্র বাণীনাথ।
প্রসাদ লঞা সঙ্গে চলে পাঁচ-সাত ॥ ১০৮ ॥

rājā kahe,——bhavānandera putra vāṇīnātha
prasāda lañā saṅge cale pāṅca-sāta

SYNONYMS

rājā kahe—the King said; *bhavānandera putra*—the son of Bhavānanda; *vāṇīnātha*—Vāṇīnātha; *prasāda lañā*—taking *mahā-prasāda; saṅge*—along; *cale*—goes; *pāṅca-sāta*—five or seven men.

TRANSLATION

The King said, "The son of Bhavānanda Rāya named Vāṇīnātha, along with five or seven other men, is going there to take the remnants of Lord Jagannātha's food.

TEXT 109

মহাপ্রভুর আলয়ে করিল গমন।
এত মহাপ্রসাদ চাহি'—কহ কি কারণ ॥ ১০৯ ॥

mahāprabhura ālaye karila gamana
eta mahā-prasāda cāhi'——kaha ki kāraṇa

SYNONYMS

mahāprabhura—of Śrī Caitanya Mahāprabhu; *ālaye*—the residential place; *karila gamana*—he has already gone; *eta*—so much; *mahā-prasāda*—*mahā-prasāda; cāhi'*—requiring; *kaha*—please tell; *ki kāraṇa*—what is the reason.

TRANSLATION

"Indeed, Vāṇīnātha has already gone to the residence of Lord Śrī Caitanya Mahāprabhu and has taken a huge quantity of mahā-prasāda. Please let me know the reason for this."

TEXT 110

ভট্ট কহে,—ভক্তগণ আইল জানিঞা।
প্রভুর ইঙ্গিতে প্রসাদ যায় তাঁরা লঞা ॥ ১১০ ॥

bhaṭṭa kahe,——bhakta-gaṇa āila jāniñā
prabhura iṅgite prasāda yāya tāṅrā lañā

SYNONYMS

bhaṭṭa kahe—Sārvabhauma Bhaṭṭācārya said; *bhakta-gaṇa*—all the devotees; *āila*—have come; *jāniñā*—knowing; *prabhura*—of Lord Śrī Caitanya Mahāprabhu; *iṅgite*—by the indication; *prasāda*—remnants of the food of Jagannātha; *yāya*—go; *tāṅrā*—all of them; *lañā*—taking.

TRANSLATION

Sārvabhauma Bhaṭṭācārya said, "Understanding that all the devotees have come, Lord Caitanya gave the sign, and therefore they have brought such great quantities of mahā-prasāda."

TEXT 111

রাজা কহে,—উপবাস, ক্ষৌর—তীর্থের বিধান।
তাহা না করিয়া কেনে খাইব অন্ন-পান ॥ ১১১ ॥

rājā kahe,——upavāsa, kṣaura——tīrthera vidhāna
tāhā nā kariyā kene khāiba anna-pāna

SYNONYMS

rājā kahe—the King said; *upavāsa*—fasting; *kṣaura*—shaving; *tīrthera vidhāna*—this is the regulation for visiting a holy place; *tāhā*—that; *nā kariyā*—without performing; *kene*—why; *khāiba*—they shall eat; *anna-pāna*—solid and liquid food.

TRANSLATION

The King then asked Bhaṭṭācārya, "Why have they not observed the regulations for visiting the pilgrimage place, such as fasting, shaving and so on? Why have they first eaten prasāda?"

TEXT 112

ভট্ট কহে,—তুমি যেই কহ, সেই বিধি-ধর্ম ।
এই রাগমার্গে আছে সূক্ষ্মধর্ম-মর্ম ॥ ১১২ ॥

bhaṭṭa kahe,——tumi yei kaha, sei vidhi-dharma
ei rāga-mārge āche sūkṣma-dharma-marma

SYNONYMS

bhaṭṭa kahe—Bhaṭṭācārya said; *tumi yei kaha*—whatever you say; *sei vidhi-dharma*—that is a regulative principle; *ei rāga-mārge*—in this spontaneous love; *āche*—there are; *sūkṣma-dharma-marma*—subtle intricacies of the religious system.

TRANSLATION

Bhaṭṭācārya told the King, "What you have said is right according to the regulative principles governing the visiting of holy places, but there is another path, which is the path of spontaneous love. According to those principles, there are subtle intricacies involved in the execution of religious principles.

PURPORT

According to the Vedic regulative principles, one has to be celibate before entering a holy place of pilgrimage. Generally people are very much addicted to sense gratification, and unless they have sex at night, they cannot sleep. The regulative principles therefore enjoin that before a common man goes to a holy place of pilgrimage, he should observe complete celibacy. As soon as one enters a holy place, he must observe fasting for the day, and after shaving his head clean, he must take a bath in a river or ocean near the holy place. These methods are adopted to neutralize the effects of sinful activities. Visiting a holy place of pilgrimage means neutralizing the reactions of a sinful life. Those who go to holy places of pilgrimage actually unload the reactions of their sinful lives, and consequently holy places are overloaded with sinful activities left there by visitors.

When a saintly person or pure devotee visits such a holy place, he absorbs the sinful effects left by the common man and again purifies the holy place. *Tīrthī-kurvanti tīrthāni* (*Bhāg.* 1.13.10). Therefore a common man's visit to a holy place and an exalted saintly person's visit there are different. The common man leaves his sins in the holy place, and a saintly person or devotee cleanses these sins simply by his presence. The devotees of Lord Caitanya Mahāprabhu were not common men, and they could not be subjected to the rules and regulations governing the visiting of holy places. Rather, they exhibited their spontaneous love for Śrī Caitanya Mahāprabhu. Immediately upon arrival at the holy place, they went to see Lord Caitanya, and by His order they took *mahā-prasāda* without following the regulations governing holy places.

TEXT 113

ঈশ্বরের পরোক্ষ আজ্ঞা—ক্ষৌর, উপোষণ।
প্রভুর সাক্ষাৎ আজ্ঞা—প্রসাদ-ভোজন॥ ১১৩॥

īśvarera parokṣa ājñā——kṣaura, upoṣaṇa
prabhura sākṣāt ājñā——prasāda-bhojana

SYNONYMS

īśvarera—of the Supreme Personality of Godhead; *parokṣa*—indirect; *ājñā*—order; *kṣaura*—shaving; *upoṣaṇa*—fasting; *prabhura*—of the Lord; *sākṣāt*—direct; *ājñā*—order; *prasāda-bhojana*—to take the *prasāda.*

TRANSLATION

"The scriptural injunctions for shaving and fasting are indirect orders of the Supreme Personality of Godhead. However, when there is a direct order from the Lord to take prasāda, naturally the devotees take prasāda as their first duty.

TEXT 114

তাহাঁ উপবাস, যাহাঁ নাহি মহাপ্রসাদ।
প্রভু-আজ্ঞা-প্রসাদ-ত্যাগে হয় অপরাধ॥ ১১৪॥

tāhāṅ upavāsa, yāhāṅ nāhi mahā-prasāda
prabhu-ājñā-prasāda-tyāge haya aparādha

SYNONYMS

tāhāṅ—there; *upavāsa*—fasting; *yāhāṅ*—where; *nāhi*—there is not; *mahā-prasāda*—remnants of foodstuffs of the Lord; *prabhu-ājñā*—direct order of Śrī Caitanya Mahāprabhu; *prasāda*—remnants of foodstuffs; *tyāge*—giving up; *haya*—there is; *aparādha*—offense.

TRANSLATION

"When mahā-prasāda is not available, there must be fasting, but when the Supreme Personality of Godhead orders one directly to take prasāda, neglecting such an opportunity is offensive.

TEXT 115

বিশেষে শ্রীহস্তে প্রভু করে পরিবেশন ।
এত লাভ ছাড়ি' কোন্ করে উপোষণ ॥ ১১৫ ॥

viśeṣe śrī-haste prabhu kare pariveśana
eta lābha chāḍi' kon kare upoṣaṇa

SYNONYMS

viśeṣe—especially; *śrī-haste*—with His transcendental hands; *prabhu*—Śrī Caitanya Mahāprabhu; *kare*—does; *pariveśana*—distribution; *eta*—so much; *lābha*—profit; *chāḍi'*—giving up; *kon*—who; *kare*—does; *upoṣaṇa*—fasting.

TRANSLATION

"When Śrī Caitanya Mahāprabhu is distributing prasāda with His transcendental hand, who will neglect such an opportunity and accept the regulative principles of fasting?

TEXT 116

পূর্বে প্রভু মোরে প্রসাদ-অন্ন আনি' দিল ।
প্রাতে শয্যায় বসি' আমি সে অন্ন খাইল ॥ ১১৬ ॥

pūrve prabhu more prasāda-anna āni' dila
prāte śayyāya vasi' āmi se anna khāila

SYNONYMS

pūrve—before this; *prabhu*—Śrī Caitanya Mahāprabhu; *more*—unto me; *prasāda-anna*—rice *mahā-prasāda; āni'*—bringing; *dila*—delivered; *prāte*—early in the morning; *śayyāya*—on my bed; *vasi'*—sitting; *āmi*—I; *se*—that; *anna*—rice; *khāila*—ate.

TRANSLATION

"Previously the Lord gave me mahā-prasāda rice one morning, and I ate that just sitting on my bed, without having even washed out my mouth.

TEXT 117

যাঁরে কৃপা করি' করেন হৃদয়ে প্রেরণ ।
কৃষ্ণাশ্রয় হয়, ছাড়ে বেদ-লোক-ধর্ম ॥ ১১৭ ॥

yāṅre kṛpā kari' karena hṛdaye preraṇa
kṛṣṇāśraya haya, chāḍe veda-loka-dharma

SYNONYMS

yāṅre—in whomever; *kṛpā*—mercy; *kari'*—bestowing; *karena*—does; *hṛdaye*—in the heart; *preraṇa*—inspiration; *kṛṣṇa-āśraya*—shelter of Lord Kṛṣṇa; *haya*—there is; *chāḍe*—he gives up; *veda*—Vedic principles; *loka-dharma*—social etiquette.

TRANSLATION

"The man to whom the Lord shows His mercy by inspiring him within the heart takes shelter only of Lord Kṛṣṇa and abandons all Vedic and social customs.

PURPORT

This is also the teaching of *Bhagavad-gītā:*

sarva-dharmān parityajya
mām ekaṁ śaraṇaṁ vraja
ahaṁ tvāṁ sarva-pāpebhyo
mokṣayiṣyāmi mā śucaḥ

"Abandon all varieties of religion and just surrender unto Me. I shall deliver you from all sinful reaction. Do not fear." (Bg. 18.66) Such firm faith in the Supreme Personality of Godhead is possible only by the mercy of the Lord. The Lord is sitting within everyone's heart, and when He personally inspires His devotee, the devotee does not stick to the Vedic principles or social customs but rather devotes himself to the transcendental loving service of the Lord. This is confirmed in the following verse from *Śrīmad-Bhāgavatam* (4.29.47).

TEXT 118

যদা যমনুগৃহ্ণাতি ভগবানাত্মভাবিতঃ ।
স জহাতি মতিং লোকে বেদে চ পরিনিষ্ঠিতাম্ ॥ ১১৮ ॥

yadā yam anugṛhṇāti
bhagavān ātma-bhāvitaḥ
sa jahāti matiṁ loke
vede ca pariniṣṭhitām

SYNONYMS

yadā—when; *yam*—to whom; *anugṛhṇāti*—shows special favor; *bhagavān*—the Supreme Personality of Godhead; *ātma-bhāvitaḥ*—who is seated in everyone's heart; *saḥ*—that person; *jahāti*—gives up; *matim*—attention; *loke*—to social behavior; *vede*—to Vedic injunctions; *ca*—also; *pariniṣṭhitām*—attached.

TRANSLATION

" 'When one is inspired by the Lord, who is sitting in everyone's heart, he does not care for social custom or Vedic regulative principles.' "

PURPORT

This instruction was given by Nārada Gosvāmī to King Prācīnabarhi in connection with the story of Purañjana. Without the mercy of the Supreme Personality of Godhead, one cannot extricate himself from the fruitive activities that are under the jurisdiction of the *Vedas.* Even personalities like Lord Brahmā, Lord Śiva, Manu, the Prajāpatis headed by Dakṣa, the four Kumāras, Marīci and even Nārada himself could not properly receive the causeless mercy of the Lord.

TEXT 119

তবে রাজা অট্টালিকা হৈতে তলেতে আইলা ।
কাশীমিশ্র, পড়িছা-পাত্র, দুঁহে আনাইলা ॥ ১১৯ ॥

tabe rājā aṭṭālikā haite talete āilā
kāśī-miśra, paḍichā-pātra, duṅhe ānāilā

SYNONYMS

tabe—thereafter; *rājā*—the King; *aṭṭālikā haite*—from the top of the palace; *talete*—to the ground; *āilā*—came down; *kāśī-miśra*—of the name Kāśī Miśra; *paḍichā-pātra*—the inspector of the temple; *duṅhe*—both of them; *ānāilā*—called for.

TRANSLATION

After this, King Pratāparudra came down from the top of his palace to the ground and called for Kāśī Miśra and the inspector in the temple.

TEXTS 120-121

প্রতাপরুদ্র আজ্ঞা দিল সেই দুই জনে ।
প্রভু-স্থানে আসিয়াছেন যত প্রভুর গণে ॥ ১২০ ॥

সবারে স্বচ্ছন্দ বাসা, স্বচ্ছন্দ প্রসাদ ।
স্বচ্ছন্দ দর্শন করাইহ, নহে যেন বাধ ॥ ১২১ ॥

pratāparudra ājñā dila sei dui jane
prabhu-sthāne āsiyāchena yata prabhura gaṇe

sabāre svacchanda vāsā, svacchanda prasāda
svacchanda darśana karāiha, nahe yena bādha

SYNONYMS

pratāparudra—King Pratāparudra; *ājñā dila*—ordered; *sei dui jane*—to those two persons; *prabhu-sthāne*—at the place of Śrī Caitanya Mahāprabhu; *āsiyāchena*—have arrived; *yata*—all the devotees who; *prabhura gaṇe*—associates of the Lord; *sabāre*—to all of them; *svacchanda*—convenient; *vāsā*—residential place; *svacchanda*—convenient; *prasāda*—remnants of the food of Jagannātha; *svacchanda darśana*—convenient visit; *karāiha*—arrange for; *nahe yena bādha*—so that there will not be any difficulties.

TRANSLATION

Mahārāja Pratāparudra then told both Kāśī Miśra and the temple inspector, "Provide all the devotees and associates of Śrī Caitanya Mahāprabhu with comfortable residences, convenient eating facilities for prasāda and convenient visiting arrangements at the temple so that there will not be any difficulty.

TEXT 122

প্রভুর আজ্ঞা পালিহ দুঁহে সাবধান হঞা ।
আজ্ঞা নহে, তবু করিহ, ইঙ্গিত বুঝিয়া ॥ ১২২ ॥

prabhura ājñā pāliha duṅhe sāvadhāna hañā
ājñā nahe, tabu kariha, iṅgita bujhiyā

SYNONYMS

prabhura—of Lord Śrī Caitanya Mahāprabhu; *ājñā*—the order; *pāliha*—carry out; *duṅhe*—both of you; *sāvadhāna*—careful; *hañā*—becoming; *ājñā nahe*—although there is no direct order; *tabu*—still; *kariha*—do; *iṅgita*—indication; *bujhiyā*—understanding.

TRANSLATION

"The orders of Śrī Caitanya Mahāprabhu must be carefully carried out. Although the Lord may not give direct orders, you are still to carry out His desires simply by understanding His indications."

TEXT 123

এত বলি' বিদায় দিল সেই দুই-জনে।
সার্বভৌম দেখিতে আইল বৈষ্ণব-মিলনে ॥ ১২৩ ॥

eta bali' vidāya dila sei dui-jane
sārvabhauma dekhite āila vaiṣṇava-milane

SYNONYMS

eta bali'—saying this; *vidāya dila*—granted permission to go; *sei dui-jane*—to those two persons; *sārvabhauma*—Sārvabhauma Bhaṭṭācārya; *dekhite*—to see; *āila*—came; *vaiṣṇava-milane*—in the meeting of all the Vaiṣṇavas.

TRANSLATION

Saying this, the King gave permission to them to leave. Sārvabhauma Bhaṭṭācārya also went to see the assembly of all the Vaiṣṇavas.

TEXT 124

গোপীনাথাচার্য ভট্টাচার্য সার্বভৌম।
দূরে রহি' দেখে প্রভুর বৈষ্ণব-মিলন ॥ ১২৪ ॥

gopīnāthācārya bhaṭṭācārya sārvabhauma
dūre rahi' dekhe prabhura vaiṣṇava-milana

SYNONYMS

gopīnātha-ācārya—Gopīnātha Ācārya; *bhaṭṭācārya sārvabhauma*—Sārvabhauma Bhaṭṭācārya; *dūre rahi'*—standing a little off; *dekhe*—see; *prabhura*—of Śrī Caitanya Mahāprabhu; *vaiṣṇava-milana*—meeting with the Vaiṣṇavas.

TRANSLATION

From a distant place both Gopīnātha Ācārya and Sārvabhauma Bhaṭṭācārya watched the meeting of all the Vaiṣṇavas with Śrī Caitanya Mahāprabhu.

TEXT 125

সিংহদ্বার ডাহিনে ছাড়ি' সব বৈষ্ণবগণ ।
কাশীমিশ্র-গৃহ-পথে করিলা গমন ॥ ১২৫ ॥

siṁha-dvāra ḍāhine chāḍi' saba vaiṣṇava-gaṇa
kāśī-miśra-gṛha-pathe karilā gamana

SYNONYMS

siṁha-dvāra ḍāhine—on the right side of the lion gate; *chāḍi'*—leaving aside; *saba*—all; *vaiṣṇava-gaṇa*—devotees of Lord Śrī Caitanya Mahāprabhu; *kāśī-miśra-gṛha*—to the house of Kāśī Miśra; *pathe*—on the way; *karilā gamana*—began to proceed.

TRANSLATION

Beginning from the right side of the lion gate, or the main gate of the temple, all the Vaiṣṇavas began to proceed toward the house of Kāśī Miśra.

TEXT 126

হেনকালে মহাপ্রভু নিজগণ-সঙ্গে ।
বৈষ্ণবে মিলিলা আসি' পথে বহুরঙ্গে ॥ ১২৬ ॥

hena-kāle mahāprabhu nija-gaṇa-saṅge
vaiṣṇave mililā āsi' pathe bahu-raṅge

SYNONYMS

hena-kāle—at this time; *mahāprabhu*—Śrī Caitanya Mahāprabhu; *nija-gaṇa-saṅge*—in the association of His personal assistants; *vaiṣṇave*—all the Vaiṣṇavas; *mililā*—met; *āsi'*—coming; *pathe*—on the road; *bahu-raṅge*—in great jubilation.

TRANSLATION

In the meantime, Śrī Caitanya Mahāprabhu, accompanied by His personal associates, met all the Vaiṣṇavas on the road with great jubilation.

TEXT 127

অদ্বৈত করিল প্রভুর চরণ বন্দন ।
আচার্যেরে কৈল প্রভু প্রেম-আলিঙ্গন ॥ ১২৭ ॥

advaita karila prabhura caraṇa vandana
ācāryere kaila prabhu prema-āliṅgana

SYNONYMS

advaita—Advaita Ācārya; *karila*—did; *prabhura*—of Lord Śrī Caitanya Mahāprabhu; *caraṇa*—of the lotus feet; *vandana*—worship; *ācāryere*—unto Advaita Ācārya; *kaila*—did; *prabhu*—Śrī Caitanya Mahāprabhu; *prema-āliṅgana*—embracing in ecstatic love.

TRANSLATION

First Advaita Ācārya offered prayers to the lotus feet of the Lord, and the Lord immediately embraced Him in ecstatic love.

TEXT 128

প্রেমানন্দে হৈলা দুঁহে পরম অস্থির ।
সময় দেখিয়া প্রভু হৈলা কিছু ধীর ॥ ১২৮ ॥

premānande hailā duṅhe parama asthira
samaya dekhiyā prabhu hailā kichu dhīra

SYNONYMS

prema-ānande—in ecstatic love; *hailā*—became; *duṅhe*—both of them; *parama asthira*—greatly agitated; *samaya*—the time; *dekhiyā*—seeing; *prabhu*—the Lord; *hailā*—became; *kichu*—a little; *dhīra*—patient.

TRANSLATION

Indeed, Śrī Caitanya Mahāprabhu and Advaita Ācārya displayed agitation due to ecstatic love. Seeing the time and circumstance, however, Lord Caitanya Mahāprabhu remained patient.

TEXT 129

শ্রীবাসাদি করিল প্রভুর চরণ বন্দন ।
প্রত্যেকে করিল প্রভু প্রেম-আলিঙ্গন ॥ ১২৯ ॥

śrīvāsādi karila prabhura caraṇa vandana
pratyeke karila prabhu prema-āliṅgana

SYNONYMS

śrīvāsa-ādi—devotees headed by Śrīvāsa Ṭhākura; *karila*—did; *prabhura*—of Śrī Caitanya Mahāprabhu; *caraṇa vandana*—worshiping the lotus feet; *pratyeke*—to everyone; *karila*—did; *prabhu*—Śrī Caitanya Mahāprabhu; *prema-āliṅgana*—embracing in love.

TRANSLATION

After this, all the devotees, headed by Śrīvāsa Ṭhākura, offered prayers to the lotus feet of the Lord, and the Lord embraced each and every one of them in great love and ecstasy.

TEXT 130

একে একে সর্বভক্তে কৈল সম্ভাষণ ।
সবা লঞা অভ্যন্তরে করিলা গমন ॥ ১৩০ ॥

eke eke sarva-bhakte kaila sambhāṣaṇa
sabā lañā abhyantare karilā gamana

SYNONYMS

eke eke—one after another; *sarva-bhakte*—to every devotee; *kaila*—did; *sambhāṣaṇa*—address; *sabā lañā*—taking all of them; *abhyantare*—inside; *karilā gamana*—entered.

TRANSLATION

The Lord addressed all the devotees one after another and took all of them with Him into the house.

TEXT 131

মিশ্রের আবাস সেই হয় অল্প স্থান ।
অসংখ্য বৈষ্ণব তাহাঁ হৈল পরিমাণ ॥ ১৩১ ॥

miśrera āvāsa sei haya alpa sthāna
asaṅkhya vaiṣṇava tāhāṅ haila parimāṇa

SYNONYMS

miśrera āvāsa—the residence of Kāśī Miśra; *sei*—that; *haya*—is; *alpa sthāna*—insufficient place; *asaṅkhya*—unlimited; *vaiṣṇava*—devotees; *tāhāṅ*—there; *haila*—were; *parimāṇa*—overcrowded.

TRANSLATION

Since the residence of Kāśī Miśra was insufficient, all the assembled devotees were very overcrowded.

TEXT 132

আপন-নিকটে প্রভু সবা বসাইলা ।
আপনি শ্রীহস্তে সবারে মাল্য-গন্ধ দিলা ॥ ১৩২ ॥

āpana-nikaṭe prabhu sabā vasāilā
āpani śrī-haste sabāre mālya-gandha dilā

SYNONYMS

āpana-nikaṭe—by His own side; *prabhu*—Śrī Caitanya Mahāprabhu; *sabā*—all of them; *vasāilā*—made sit; *āpani*—personally Himself; *śrī-haste*—with His hand; *sabāre*—unto everyone; *mālya*—garland; *gandha*—sandalwood pulp; *dilā*—offered.

TRANSLATION

Śrī Caitanya Mahāprabhu made all the devotees sit at His side, and with His own hand He offered them garlands and sandalwood pulp.

TEXT 133

ভট্টাচার্য, আচার্য তবে মহাপ্রভুর স্থানে ।
যথাযোগ্য মিলিলা সবাকার সনে ॥ ১৩৩ ॥

bhaṭṭācārya, ācārya tabe mahāprabhura sthāne
yathā-yogya mililā sabākāra sane

SYNONYMS

bhaṭṭācārya—Sārvabhauma Bhaṭṭācārya; *ācārya*—Gopīnātha Ācārya; *tabe*—thereafter; *mahāprabhura sthāne*—at the place of Śrī Caitanya Mahāprabhu; *yathā-yogya*—as it is befitting; *mililā*—met; *sabākāra sane*—with all the Vaiṣṇavas assembled there.

TRANSLATION

After this, Gopīnātha Ācārya and Sārvabhauma Bhaṭṭācārya met all the Vaiṣṇavas at the place of Śrī Caitanya Mahāprabhu in a befitting manner.

TEXT 134

অদ্বৈতেরে কহেন প্রভু মধুর বচনে ।
আজি আমি পূর্ণ হইলাঙ তোমার আগমনে ॥১৩৪॥

advaitere kahena prabhu madhura vacane
āji āmi pūrṇa ha-ilāṅa tomāra āgamane

SYNONYMS

advaitere—unto Advaita Ācārya Prabhu; *kahena*—says; *prabhu*—Śrī Caitanya Mahāprabhu; *madhura vacane*—in sweet language; *āji*—today; *āmi*—I; *pūrṇa*—perfect; *ha-ilāṅa*—became; *tomāra*—Your; *āgamane*—on arrival.

TRANSLATION

Śrī Caitanya Mahāprabhu addressed Advaita Ācārya Prabhu, saying sweetly, "My dear sir, today I have become perfect because of Your arrival."

TEXTS 135-136

অদ্বৈত কহে,—ঈশ্বরের এই স্বভাব হয় ।
যদ্যপি আপনে পূর্ণ, সর্বৈশ্বর্যময় ॥ ১৩৫ ॥
তথাপি ভক্তসঙ্গে হয় সুখোল্লাস ।
ভক্ত-সঙ্গে করে নিত্য বিবিধ বিলাস ॥ ১৩৬ ॥

advaita kahe, ——īśvarera ei svabhāva haya
yadyapi āpane pūrṇa, sarvaiśvarya-maya

tathāpi bhakta-saṅge haya sukhollāsa
bhakta-saṅge kare nitya vividha vilāsa

SYNONYMS

advaita kahe—Advaita Ācārya Prabhu said; *īśvarera*—of the Lord; *ei*—this; *sva-bhāva*—feature; *haya*—becomes; *yadyapi*—although; *āpane*—Himself; *pūrṇa*—all-perfect; *sarva-aiśvarya-maya*—full of all opulences; *tathāpi*—still; *bhakta-saṅge*—in the association of devotees; *haya*—there is; *sukha-ullāsa*—great jubilation; *bhakta-saṅge*—with devotees; *kare*—does; *nitya*—eternally; *vividha*—various; *vilāsa*—pastimes.

TRANSLATION

Advaita Ācārya Prabhu replied, "This is a natural characteristic of the Supreme Personality of Godhead. Although He is personally complete and full of all opulences, He takes transcendental pleasure in the association of His devotees, with whom He has a variety of eternal pastimes."

TEXT 137

বাসুদেব দেখি' প্রভু আনন্দিত হঞা ।
তাঁরে কিছু কহে তাঁর অঙ্গে হস্ত দিয়া ॥ ১৩৭ ॥

vāsudeva dekhi' prabhu ānandita hañā
tāṅre kichu kahe tāṅra aṅge hasta diyā

SYNONYMS

vāsudeva—Vāsudeva; *dekhi'*—seeing; *prabhu*—Lord Śrī Caitanya Mahāprabhu; *ānandita hañā*—becoming very much pleased; *tāṅre*—unto him; *kichu kahe*—says something; *tāṅra aṅge*—on his body; *hasta diyā*—placing His hand.

TRANSLATION

As soon as Śrī Caitanya Mahāprabhu saw Vāsudeva Datta, the father of Mukunda Datta, He immediately became very happy and, placing His hand on his body, began to speak.

TEXT 138

যদ্যপি মুকুন্দ—আমা-সঙ্গে শিশু হৈতে ।
তাঁহা হৈতে অধিক সুখ তোমারে দেখিতে ॥১৩৮॥

yadyapi mukunda——āmā-saṅge śiśu haite
tāṅhā haite adhika sukha tomāre dekhite

SYNONYMS

yadyapi—although; *mukunda*—Mukunda; *āmā-saṅge*—with me; *śiśu haite*—from childhood; *tāṅhā haite*—than him; *adhika*—still more; *sukha*—happiness; *tomāre dekhite*—to see you.

TRANSLATION

Śrī Caitanya Mahāprabhu said, "Although Mukunda is My friend from childhood, I nonetheless take greater pleasure in seeing you than in seeing him."

PURPORT

Vāsudeva Datta was the father of Mukunda Datta, who was the childhood friend of Śrī Caitanya Mahāprabhu. It is naturally a great pleasure to see a friend, but Śrī Caitanya Mahāprabhu informed the father that although it was His pleasure to see His friend, His pleasure was increased by seeing the father.

TEXT 139

বাসু কহে,—মুকুন্দ আদৌ পাইল তোমার সঙ্গ।
তোমার চরণ পাইল সেই পুনর্জন্ম ॥ ১৩৯ ॥

vāsu kahe, —mukunda ādau pāila tomāra saṅga
tomāra caraṇa pāila sei punar-janma

SYNONYMS

vāsu kahe—Vāsudeva Datta said; *mukunda*—Mukunda; *ādau*—in the beginning; *pāila*—got; *tomāra saṅga*—Your association; *tomāra caraṇa*—Your lotus feet; *pāila*—got; *sei*—that; *punaḥ-janma*—transcendental rebirth.

TRANSLATION

Vāsudeva replied, "Mukunda got Your association in the beginning. As such, he has taken shelter at Your lotus feet. That is his transcendental rebirth."

TEXT 140

ছোট হঞা মুকুন্দ এবে হৈল আমার জ্যেষ্ঠ।
তোমার কৃপাপাত্র তাতে সর্বগুণে শ্রেষ্ঠ ॥ ১৪০ ॥

choṭa hañā mukunda ebe haila āmāra jyeṣṭha
tomāra kṛpā-pātra tāte sarva-guṇe śreṣṭha

SYNONYMS

choṭa hañā—being junior; *mukunda*—Mukunda; *ebe*—now; *haila*—has become; *āmāra*—my; *jyeṣṭha*—senior; *tomāra*—Your; *kṛpā-pātra*—favorite; *tāte*—therefore; *sarva-guṇe*—in all good qualities; *śreṣṭha*—superior.

TRANSLATION

Thus Vāsudeva Datta admitted his inferiority to Mukunda, his son. "Although Mukunda is my junior," he said, "he first received Your favor. Consequently he became transcendentally senior to me. Besides that, You very much favored Mukunda. Thus he is superior in all good qualities."

TEXT 141

পুনঃ প্রভু কহে—আমি তোমার নিমিত্তে।
দুই পুস্তক আনিয়াছি 'দক্ষিণ' হইতে ॥ ১৪১ ॥

punaḥ prabhu kahe——āmi tomāra nimitte
dui pustaka āniyāchi 'dakṣiṇa' ha-ite

SYNONYMS

punaḥ—again; *prabhu kahe*—the Lord said; *āmi*—I; *tomāra nimitte*—for your sake; *dui*—two; *pustaka*—books; *āniyāchi*—have brought; *dakṣiṇa ha-ite*—from South India.

TRANSLATION

The Lord said, "For your sake only, I have brought two books from South India.

TEXT 142

স্বরূপের ঠাঁই আছে, লহ তা লিখিয়া।
বাসুদেব আনন্দিত পুস্তক পাঞা॥ ১৪২॥

svarūpera ṭhāñi āche, laha tā likhiyā
vāsudeva ānandita pustaka pāñā

SYNONYMS

svarūpera ṭhāñi—in the possession of Svarūpa Dāmodara; *āche*—they are; *laha*—you take; *tā*—them; *likhiyā*—copying; *vāsudeva*—Vāsudeva; *ānandita*—very glad; *pustaka*—the books; *pāñā*—getting.

TRANSLATION

"The books are kept with Svarūpa Dāmodara, and you can get them copied." Hearing this, Vāsudeva became very glad.

TEXT 143

প্রত্যেক বৈষ্ণব সবে লিখিয়া লইল।
ক্রমে ক্রমে দুই গ্রন্থ সর্বত্র ব্যাপিল॥ ১৪৩॥

pratyeka vaiṣṇava sabe likhiyā la-ila
krame krame dui grantha sarvatra vyāpila

SYNONYMS

pratyeka—each and every; *vaiṣṇava*—devotee; *sabe*—all; *likhiyā*—copying; *la-ila*—took; *krame krame*—by and by; *dui grantha*—the two books; *sarvatra*—everywhere; *vyāpila*—become broadcast.

TRANSLATION

Indeed, each and every Vaiṣṇava copied the two books. By and by, the two books [Brahma-saṁhitā and Śrī Kṛṣṇa-karṇāmṛta] were broadcast all over India.

TEXT 144

শ্রীবাসাদ্যে কহে প্রভু করি' মহাপ্রীত ।
তোমার চারি-ভাইর আমি হইনু বিক্রীত ॥ ১৪৪ ॥

śrīvāsādye kahe prabhu kari' mahā-prīta
tomāra cāri-bhāira āmi ha-inu vikrīta

SYNONYMS

śrīvāsa-ādye—unto the Śrīvāsa and his three brothers; *kahe*—says; *prabhu*—the Lord; *kari'*—giving; *mahā-prīta*—great love; *tomāra*—of you; *cāri-bhāira*—of four brothers; *āmi*—I; *ha-inu*—became; *vikrīta*—purchased.

TRANSLATION

The Lord addressed Śrīvāsa and his brothers with great love and affection, saying, "I am so obliged that I am purchased by you four brothers."

TEXT 145

শ্রীবাস কহেন,—কেনে কহ বিপরীত ।
কৃপা-মূল্যে চারি ভাই হই তোমার ক্রীত ॥ ১৪৫ ॥

śrīvāsa kahena, ——kene kaha viparīta
kṛpā-mūlye cāri bhāi ha-i tomāra krīta

SYNONYMS

śrīvāsa kahena—Śrīvāsa Ṭhākura replied; *kene*—why; *kaha viparīta*—do You speak just the opposite; *kṛpā-mūlye*—by the price of Your mercy; *cāri bhāi*—we four brothers; *ha-i*—become; *tomāra*—of You; *krīta*—purchased.

TRANSLATION

Śrīvāsa then replied to the Lord, "Why are You speaking in a contradictory way? Rather, we four brothers have been purchased by Your mercy."

TEXT 146

শঙ্করে দেখিয়া প্রভু কহে দামোদরে ।
সগৌরব-প্রীতি আমার তোমার উপরে ॥ ১৪৬ ॥

śaṅkare dekhiyā prabhu kahe dāmodare
sagaurava-prīti āmāra tomāra upare

SYNONYMS

śaṅkare dekhiyā—seeing Śaṅkara; *prabhu*—the Lord; *kahe*—says; *dāmodare*—unto Dāmodara; *sa-gaurava-prīti*—affection with awe and reverence; *āmāra*—My; *tomāra upare*—upon you.

TRANSLATION

After seeing Śaṅkara, Lord Śrī Caitanya Mahāprabhu told Dāmodara, "My affection for you is on the platform of affection with awe and reverence.

PURPORT

Here the Lord is addressing Dāmodara Paṇḍita, who is different from Svarūpa Dāmodara. Dāmodara Paṇḍita is the elder brother of Śaṅkara. Thus the Lord informed Dāmodara that His affection toward him was on the platform of awe and reverence. However, the Lord's affection toward his younger brother, Śaṅkara, was on the platform of pure love.

TEXT 147

শুদ্ধ কেবল-প্রেম শঙ্কর-উপরে ।
অতএব তোমার সঙ্গে রাখহ শঙ্করে ॥ ১৪৭ ॥

śuddha kevala-prema śaṅkara-upare
ataeva tomāra saṅge rākhaha śaṅkare

SYNONYMS

śuddha kevala-prema—pure unalloyed affection; *śaṅkara-upare*—upon Śaṅkara; *ataeva*—therefore; *tomāra saṅge*—along with you; *rākhaha*—keep; *śaṅkare*—Śaṅkara.

TRANSLATION

"Therefore keep your younger brother Śaṅkara with you because he is connected to Me by pure unalloyed love."

TEXT 148

দামোদর কহে,—শঙ্কর ছোট আমা হৈতে।
এবে আমার বড় ভাই তোমার কৃপাতে ॥ ১৪৮ ॥

dāmodara kahe, —śaṅkara choṭa āmā haite
ebe āmāra baḍa bhāi tomāra kṛpāte

SYNONYMS

dāmodara kahe—Dāmodara Paṇḍita replied; *śaṅkara*—Śaṅkara; *choṭa*—younger; *āmā haite*—than me; *ebe*—now; *āmāra*—my; *baḍa bhāi*—elder brother; *tomāra*—of You; *kṛpāte*—by the mercy.

TRANSLATION

Dāmodara Paṇḍita replied, "Śaṅkara is my younger brother, but from today he becomes my elder brother because of Your special mercy upon him."

TEXT 149

শিবানন্দে কহে প্রভু,—তোমার আমাতে।
গাঢ় অনুরাগ হয়, জানি আগে হৈতে ॥ ১৪৯ ॥

śivānande kahe prabhu, —tomāra āmāte
gāḍha anurāga haya, jāni āge haite

SYNONYMS

śivānande—unto Śivānanda Sena; *kahe*—says; *prabhu*—the Lord; *tomāra*—your; *āmāte*—upon Me; *gāḍha anurāga*—deep affection; *haya*—there is; *jāni*—I know; *āge haite*—from the very beginning.

TRANSLATION

Then turning toward Śivānanda Sena, the Lord said, "I know that from the very beginning your affection for Me has been very great."

TEXT 150

শুনি' শিবানন্দ-সেন প্রেমাবিষ্ট হঞা।
দণ্ডবৎ হঞা পড়ে শ্লোক পড়িয়া ॥ ১৫০ ॥

śuni' śivānanda-sena premāviṣṭa hañā
daṇḍavat hañā paḍe śloka paḍiyā

SYNONYMS

śuni'—hearing; *śivānanda-sena*—Śivānanda Sena; *prema-āviṣṭa hañā*—becoming absorbed in pure love; *daṇḍavat hañā*—offering obeisances; *paḍe*—falls down; *śloka*—a verse; *paḍiyā*—reciting.

TRANSLATION

Immediately upon hearing this, Śivānanda Sena became absorbed in ecstatic love and fell down on the ground, offering obeisances to the Lord. He then began to recite the following verse.

TEXT 151

নিমজ্জতোঽনন্ত ভবার্ণবান্তশ্চিরায় মে কূলমিবাসি লব্ধঃ ।
ত্বয়াপি লব্ধং ভগবন্নিদানীমনুত্তমং পাত্রমিদং দয়ায়াঃ ॥১৫১॥

nimajjato 'nanta bhavārṇavāntaś
cirāya me kūlam ivāsi labdhaḥ
tvayāpi labdhaṁ bhagavann idānīm
anuttamaṁ pātram idaṁ dayāyāḥ

SYNONYMS

nimajjataḥ—being immersed; *ananta*—O unlimited one; *bhava-arṇava-antaḥ*—within the ocean of nescience; *cirāya*—after a long time; *me*—of me; *kūlam*—the shore; *iva*—like; *asi*—You are; *labdhaḥ*—obtained; *tvayā*—by You; *api*—also; *labdham*—has been gained; *bhagavan*—O my Lord; *idānīm*—now; *anuttamam*—the best; *pātram*—candidate; *idam*—this; *dayāyāḥ*—for showing Your mercy.

TRANSLATION

"O my Lord! O unlimited one! Although I was merged in the ocean of nescience, I have now, after a long time, attained You, just as one may attain the seashore. My dear Lord, by getting me, You have obtained the right person upon whom to bestow Your causeless mercy."

PURPORT

This is a verse composed by Ālabandāru Yamunācārya. One's relationship with the Supreme Personality of Godhead may be reestablished even after one has fallen into the ocean of nescience, which is the ocean of material existence involving the repetition of birth, death, old age and disease, all arising out of the acceptance of the material body. There are 8,400,000 species of material life, but in the human body one attains a chance to get release from the repetition of birth and death. When one becomes the Lord's devotee, he is rescued from this dangerous ocean of birth and death. The Lord is always prepared to show His mercy upon fallen souls struggling against miserable material conditions. As stated in *Bhagavad-gītā:*

mamaivāṁśo jīva-loke
jīva-bhūtaḥ sanātanaḥ
manaḥ-ṣaṣṭhānīndriyāṇi
prakṛti-sthāni karṣati

"The living entities in this conditioned world are My eternal, fragmental parts. Due to conditioned life, they are struggling very hard with the six senses, which include the mind." (Bg. 15.7)

Thus every living being is struggling hard in this material nature. Actually the living entity is part and parcel of the Supreme Lord, and when he surrenders unto the Supreme Personality of Godhead, he attains release from the ocean of birth and death. The Lord, being very kind to fallen souls, is always anxious to get the living entity out of the ocean of nescience. If the living entity understands his position and surrenders to the Lord, his life becomes successful.

TEXT 152

প্রথমে মুরারি-গুপ্ত প্রভুরে না মিলিয়া।
বাহিরেতে পড়ি' আছে দণ্ডবৎ হঞা॥ ১৫২॥

prathame murāri-gupta prabhure nā miliyā
bāhirete paḍi' āche daṇḍavat hañā

SYNONYMS

prathame—at first; *murāri-gupta*—Murāri Gupta; *prabhure*—to Śrī Caitanya Mahāprabhu; *nā*—without; *miliyā*—meeting; *bāhirete*—outside; *paḍi'*—falling down; *āche*—was there; *daṇḍavat*—falling flat like a stick; *hañā*—becoming so.

TRANSLATION

Murāri Gupta at first did not meet the Lord but rather remained outside the door, falling down like a stick to offer obeisances.

TEXT 153

মুরারি না দেখিয়া প্রভু করে অন্বেষণ।
মুরারি লইতে ধাঞা আইলা বহুজন॥ ১৫৩॥

murāri nā dekhiyā prabhu kare anveṣaṇa
murāri la-ite dhāñā āilā bahu-jana

SYNONYMS

murāri—Murāri; *nā*—without; *dekhiyā*—seeing; *prabhu*—the Lord; *kare*—does; *anveṣaṇa*—inquiry; *murāri*—Murāri Gupta; *la-ite*—to take; *dhāñā*—running; *āilā*—came; *bahu-jana*—many persons.

TRANSLATION

When Lord Śrī Caitanya Mahāprabhu could not see Murāri amongst the devotees, He inquired about him. Thereupon many people immediately went to Murāri, running to take him to the Lord.

TEXT 154

তৃণ দুইগুচ্ছ মুরারি দশনে ধরিয়া ।
মহাপ্রভু আগে গেলা দৈন্যাধীন হঞা ॥ ১৫৪ ॥

tṛṇa dui-guccha murāri daśane dhariyā
mahāprabhu āge gelā dainyādhīna hañā

SYNONYMS

tṛṇa—of straw; *dui*—two; *guccha*—bunches; *murāri*—Murāri; *daśane*—in his teeth; *dhariyā*—catching; *mahāprabhu*—of Śrī Caitanya Mahāprabhu; *āge*—in front; *gelā*—went; *dainya-adhīna*—under obligation of meekness; *hañā*—becoming.

TRANSLATION

Thus Murāri Gupta, catching two bunches of straw in his teeth, went before Śrī Caitanya Mahāprabhu with humility and meekness.

TEXT 155

মুরারি দেখিয়া প্রভু আইলা মিলিতে ।
পাছে ভাগে মুরারি, লাগিলা কহিতে ॥ ১৫৫ ॥

murāri dekhiyā prabhu āilā milite
pāche bhāge murāri, lāgilā kahite

SYNONYMS

murāri—Murāri; *dekhiyā*—seeing; *prabhu*—Lord Caitanya Mahāprabhu; *āilā*—came out; *milite*—to meet; *pāche*—thereafter; *bhāge*—runs away; *murāri*—Murāri; *lāgilā*—began; *kahite*—to speak.

TRANSLATION

Upon seeing Murāri come to meet Him, Lord Śrī Caitanya Mahāprabhu went up to him, but Murāri began to run away and speak as follows.

TEXT 156

মোরে না ছুঁইহ, প্রভু, মুঞি ত' পামর ।
তোমার স্পর্শযোগ্য নহে পাপ কলেবর ॥ ১৫৬ ॥

more nā chuṅiha, prabhu, muñi ta' pāmara
tomāra sparśa-yogya nahe pāpa kalevara

SYNONYMS

more—me; *nā chuṅiha*—do not touch; *prabhu*—my Lord; *muñi*—I; *ta'*—certainly; *pāmara*—most abominable; *tomāra*—of You; *sparśa-yogya*—fit to be touched; *nahe*—not; *pāpa*—sinful; *kalevara*—body.

TRANSLATION

"My Lord, please do not touch me. I am most abominable and am not fit for You to touch because my body is sinful."

TEXT 157

প্রভু কহে,—মুরারি, কর দৈন্য সম্বরণ ।
তোমার দৈন্য দেখি' মোর বিদীর্ণ হয় মন ॥ ১৫৭ ॥

prabhu kahe, —murāri, kara dainya saṁvaraṇa
tomāra dainya dekhi' mora vidīrṇa haya mana

SYNONYMS

prabhu kahe—the Lord said; *murāri*—My dear Murāri; *kara dainya saṁvaraṇa*—please restrain your great humility; *tomāra*—your; *dainya*—humility; *dekhi'*—seeing; *mora*—My; *vidīrṇa haya mana*—mind becomes distorted.

TRANSLATION

The Lord said, "My dear Murāri, please restrain your unnecessary humility. My mind is disturbed to see your meekness."

TEXT 158

এত বলি' প্রভু তাঁরে কৈল আলিঙ্গন।
নিকটে বসাঞা করে অঙ্গ সম্মার্জন ॥ ১৫৮ ॥

eta bali' prabhu tāṅre kaila āliṅgana
nikaṭe vasāñā kare aṅga sammārjana

SYNONYMS

eta bali'—saying this; *prabhu*—the Lord; *tāṅre*—him; *kaila*—did; *āliṅgana*—embrace; *nikaṭe*—nearby; *vasāñā*—making sit down; *kare*—does; *aṅga*—of his body; *sammārjana*—cleansing.

TRANSLATION

Saying this, the Lord embraced Murāri and had him sit down by His side. The Lord then began to cleanse his body with His own hands.

TEXT 159-160

আচার্যরত্ন, বিদ্যানিধি, পণ্ডিত গদাধর।
গঙ্গাদাস, হরিভট্ট, আচার্য পুরন্দর ॥ ১৫৯ ॥
প্রত্যেকে সবার প্রভু করি' গুণ গান।
পুনঃ পুনঃ আলিঙ্গিয়া করিল সম্মান ॥ ১৬০ ॥

ācāryaratna, vidyānidhi, paṇḍita gadādhara
gaṅgādāsa, hari-bhaṭṭa, ācārya purandara

pratyeke sabāra prabhu kari' guṇa gāna
punaḥ punaḥ āliṅgiyā karila sammāna

SYNONYMS

ācāryaratna—Ācāryaratna; *vidyānidhi*—Vidyānidhi; *paṇḍita gadādhara*—Paṇḍita Gadādhara; *gaṅgādāsa*—Gaṅgādāsa; *hari-bhaṭṭa*—Hari Bhaṭṭa; *ācārya purandara*—Ācārya Purandara; *pratyeke*—each and every one of them; *sabāra*—of all of them; *prabhu*—the Lord; *kari' guṇa gāna*—glorifying the qualities; *punaḥ punaḥ*—again and again; *āliṅgiyā*—embracing; *karila*—did; *sammāna*—honor.

TRANSLATION

Lord Śrī Caitanya Mahāprabhu then again and again embraced all the devotees, including Ācāryaratna, Vidyānidhi, Paṇḍita Gadādhara, Gaṅgādāsa, Hari Bhaṭṭa and Ācārya Purandara. The Lord described their good qualities and glorified them again and again.

TEXT 161

সবারে সম্মানি' প্রভুর হইল উল্লাস ।
হরিদাসে না দেখিয়া কহে,—কাহাঁ হরিদাস ॥ ১৬১ ॥

sabāre sammāni' prabhura ha-ila ullāsa
haridāse nā dekhiyā kahe, ——kāhāṅ haridāsa

SYNONYMS

sabāre sammāni'—respecting everyone; *prabhura*—of the Lord; *ha-ila*—there was; *ullāsa*—jubilation; *haridāse*—Haridāsa Ṭhākura; *nā dekhiyā*—without seeing; *kahe*—says; *kāhāṅ haridāsa*—where is Haridāsa.

TRANSLATION

After thus offering respect to each and every devotee, Lord Śrī Caitanya Mahāprabhu became very jubilant. However, not seeing Haridāsa Ṭhākura, He inquired, "Where is Haridāsa?"

TEXT 162

দূর হৈতে হরিদাস গোসাঞে দেখিয়া ।
রাজপথ-প্রান্তে পড়ি' আছে দণ্ডবৎ হঞা ॥ ১৬২ ॥

dūra haite haridāsa gosāñe dekhiyā
rājapatha-prānte paḍi' āche daṇḍavat hañā

SYNONYMS

dūra haite—from a distance; *haridāsa gosāñe*—Haridāsa Ṭhākura; *dekhiyā*—seeing; *rājapatha-prānte*—at the side of the common road; *paḍi'*—falling down; *āche*—he was; *daṇḍavat hañā*—offering obeisances.

TRANSLATION

Śrī Caitanya Mahāprabhu then saw in the distance that Haridāsa Ṭhākura was lying down flat on the road offering obeisances.

TEXT 163

মিলন-স্থানে আসি' প্রভুরে না মিলিলা ।
রাজপথ-প্রান্তে দূরে পড়িয়া রহিলা ॥ ১৬৩ ॥

milana-sthāne āsi' prabhure nā mililā
rājapatha-prānte dūre paḍiyā rahilā

SYNONYMS

milana-sthāne—in the meeting place; *āsi'*—coming; *prabhure*—unto Lord Śrī Caitanya Mahāprabhu; *nā*—not; *mililā*—did meet; *rājapatha-prānte*—on the side of the common road; *dūre*—at a distant place; *paḍiyā*—falling flat; *rahilā*—remained.

TRANSLATION

Haridāsa Ṭhākura did not come to the Lord's meeting place but remained fallen flat on the common road at a distance.

TEXT 164

ভক্ত সব ধাঞা আইল হরিদাসে নিতে ।
প্রভু তোমায় মিলিতে চাহে, চলহ ত্বরিতে ॥ ১৬৪ ॥

bhakta saba dhāñā āila haridāse nite
prabhu tomāya milite cāhe, calaha tvarite

SYNONYMS

bhakta—devotees; *saba*—all; *dhāñā*—running; *āila*—came; *haridāse*—Haridāsa; *nite*—to take; *prabhu*—Lord Śrī Caitanya Mahāprabhu; *tomāya*—you; *milite*—to meet; *cāhe*—wants; *calaha*—just come; *tvarite*—very soon.

TRANSLATION

All the devotees then went to Haridāsa Ṭhākura, saying, "The Lord wants to meet you. Please come immediately."

TEXT 165

হরিদাস কহে,—মুঞি নীচ-জাতি ছার ।
মন্দির-নিকটে যাইতে মোর নাহি আধিকার ॥১৬৫॥

haridāsa kahe, —muñi nīca-jāti chāra
mandira-nikaṭe yāite mora nāhi ādhikāra

SYNONYMS

haridāsa kahe—Haridāsa Ṭhākura said; *muñi*—I; *nīca-jāti*—low caste; *chāra*—abominable; *mandira-nikaṭe*—near the temple; *yāite*—to go; *mora*—my; *nāhi*—there is not; *ādhikāra*—authority.

TRANSLATION

Haridāsa Ṭhākura replied, "I cannot go near the temple because I am a low-caste abominable person. I have no authority to go there."

PURPORT

Although Haridāsa Ṭhākura was such a highly exalted Vaiṣṇava that he was addressed as Haridāsa Gosvāmī, he still did not like to disturb the common sense of the general populace. Haridāsa Ṭhākura was so exalted that he was addressed as *ṭhākura* and *gosāñi,* and these titles are offered to the most advanced Vaiṣṇavas. The spiritual master is generally called *gosāñi,* and *ṭhākura* is used to address the *paramahaṁsas,* those in the topmost rank of spirituality. Nonetheless Haridāsa Ṭhākura did not want to go near the temple, although he was called there by Śrī Caitanya Mahāprabhu Himself. The Jagannātha temple still accepts only those Hindus who are in the *varṇāśrama* order. Other castes, especially those who are not Hindu, are not allowed to enter the temple. This is a long-standing regulation and thus Haridāsa Ṭhākura, although certainly competent and qualified to enter the temple, did not want even to go near it. This is called Vaiṣṇava humility.

TEXT 166

নিভৃতে টোটা-মধ্যে স্থান যদি পাঙ ।
তাহাঁ পড়ি' রহো, একলে কাল গোঙাঙ ॥ ১৬৬ ॥

nibhṛte ṭoṭā-madhye sthāna yadi pāṅa
tāhāṅ paḍi' raho, ekale kāla goṅāṅa

SYNONYMS

nibhṛte—in a solitary place; *ṭoṭā-madhye*—within the gardens; *sthāna*—place; *yadi*—if; *pāṅa*—I get; *tāhāṅ*—there; *paḍi' raho*—I shall stay; *ekale*—alone; *kāla*—time; *goṅāṅa*—I shall pass.

TRANSLATION

Haridāsa Ṭhākura then expressed his desire: "If I could just get to a solitary place near the temple, I could stay there alone and pass my time.

TEXT 167

জগন্নাথ-সেবকের মোর স্পর্শ নাহি হয়।
তাহাঁ পড়ি' রহোঁ,—মোর এই বাঞ্ছা হয় ॥ ১৬৭ ॥

jagannātha-sevakera mora sparśa nāhi haya
tāhāṅ paḍi' rahoṅ, ——mora ei vāñchā haya

SYNONYMS

jagannātha-sevakera—of the servants of Lord Jagannātha; *mora*—my; *sparśa*—touching; *nāhi*—not; *haya*—takes place; *tāhāṅ*—there; *paḍi' rahoṅ*—I stay; *mora*—my; *ei*—this; *vāñchā*—desire; *haya*—is.

TRANSLATION

"I do not wish the servants of Lord Jagannātha to touch me. I would remain there in the garden alone. That is my desire."

TEXT 168

এই কথা লোক গিয়া প্রভুরে কহিল।
শুনিয়া প্রভুর মনে বড় সুখ হইল ॥ ১৬৮ ॥

ei kathā loka giyā prabhure kahila
śuniyā prabhura mane baḍa sukha ha-ila

SYNONYMS

ei kathā—this message; *loka*—people; *giyā*—going; *prabhure*—unto Lord Śrī Caitanya Mahāprabhu; *kahila*—informed; *śuniyā*—hearing; *prabhura mane*—in the mind of the Lord; *baḍa*—very much; *sukha*—happiness; *ha-ila*—became.

TRANSLATION

When this message was relayed to Śrī Caitanya Mahāprabhu by the people, the Lord became very happy to hear it.

TEXT 169

হেনকালে কাশীমিশ্র, পড়িছা,—তুই জন।
আসিয়া করিল প্রভুর চরণ বন্দন ॥ ১৬৯ ॥

hena-kāle kāśī-miśra, paḍichā, ——dui jana
āsiyā karila prabhura caraṇa vandana

SYNONYMS

hena-kāle—at this time; *kāśī-miśra*—Kāśī Miśra; *paḍichā*—the superintendent; *dui jana*—two persons; *āsiyā*—coming; *karila*—did; *prabhura*—of Lord Śrī Caitanya Mahāprabhu; *caraṇa vandana*—worshiping the lotus feet.

TRANSLATION

At this time, Kāśī Miśra, along with the superintendent of the temple, came and offered his respects unto the lotus feet of Lord Śrī Caitanya Mahāprabhu.

TEXT 170

সর্ব বৈষ্ণব দেখি' সুখ বড় পাইলা ।
যথাযোগ্য সবা-সনে আনন্দে মিলিলা ॥ ১৭০ ॥

sarva vaiṣṇava dekhi' sukha baḍa pāilā
yathā-yogya sabā-sane ānande mililā

SYNONYMS

sarva vaiṣṇava—all the Vaiṣṇavas; *dekhi'*—seeing; *sukha*—happiness; *baḍa*—very much; *pāilā*—got; *yathā-yogya*—as is befitting; *sabā-sane*—along with everyone; *ānande*—in happiness; *mililā*—met.

TRANSLATION

Upon seeing all the Vaiṣṇavas together, both Kāśī Miśra and the superintendent became very happy. With great happiness they met with them in a befitting manner.

TEXT 171

প্রভুপদে দুই জনে কৈল নিবেদনে ।
আজ্ঞা দেহ',—বৈষ্ণবের করি সমাধানে ॥ ১৭১ ॥

prabhu-pade dui jane kaila nivedane
ājñā deha', —vaiṣṇavera kari samādhāne

SYNONYMS

prabhu-pade—unto the lotus feet of Śrī Caitanya Mahāprabhu; *dui jane*—both of them; *kaila*—did; *nivedane*—submission; *ājñā deha'*—please order; *vaiṣṇavera*—of all the Vaiṣṇavas; *kari*—let us do; *samādhāne*—accommodation.

TRANSLATION

Both submitted to Lord Śrī Caitanya Mahāprabhu: "Please give us orders so that we may make proper arrangements to accommodate all the Vaiṣṇavas.

TEXT 172

সবার করিয়াছি বাসা-গৃহ-স্থান ।
মহাপ্রসাদ সবাকারে করি সমাধান ॥ ১৭২ ॥

sabāra kariyāchi vāsā-gṛha-sthāna
mahā-prasāda sabākāre kari samādhāna

SYNONYMS

sabāra—for all of them; *kariyāchi*—we have arranged; *vāsā-gṛha-sthāna*—residential place for staying; *mahā-prasāda*—remnants of foodstuff of Jagannātha; *sabākāre*—to all of them; *kari*—let us do; *samādhāna*—distribution.

TRANSLATION

"Accommodations have been arranged for all the Vaiṣṇavas. Now let us distribute mahā-prasāda to all of them."

TEXT 173

প্রভু কহে,—গোপীনাথ, যাহ' বৈষ্ণব লঞা ।
যাহাঁ যাহাঁ কহে বাসা, তাহাঁ দেহ' লঞা ॥ ১৭৩ ॥

prabhu kahe, —gopīnātha, yāha' vaiṣṇava lañā
yāhāṅ yāhāṅ kahe vāsā, tāhāṅ deha' lañā

SYNONYMS

prabhu kahe—the Lord Caitanya Mahāprabhu said; *gopīnātha*—My dear Gopīnātha; *yāha'*—please go; *vaiṣṇava lañā*—taking all the Vaiṣṇavas; *yāhāṅ yāhāṅ*—wherever; *kahe*—they say; *vāsā*—staying place; *tāhāṅ*—there; *deha'*—give; *lañā*—accepting.

TRANSLATION

Śrī Caitanya Mahāprabhu immediately told Gopīnātha Ācārya, "Please go with the Vaiṣṇavas and accommodate them in whatever residence Kāśī Miśra and the temple superintendent offer."

TEXT 174

মহাপ্রসাদান্ন দেহ বাণীনাথ-স্থানে ।
সর্ব বৈষ্ণবের ইঁহো করিবে সমাধানে ॥ ১৭৪ ॥

mahā-prasādānna deha vāṇīnātha-sthāne
sarva-vaiṣṇavera iṅho karibe samādhāne

SYNONYMS

mahā-prasāda-anna—the remnants of food; *deha*—deliver; *vāṇīnātha-sthāne*—unto Vāṇīnātha; *sarva-vaiṣṇavera*—unto all the Vaiṣṇavas; *iṅho*—he; *karibe*—will do; *samādhāne*—distribution.

TRANSLATION

Then the Lord told Kāśī Miśra and the temple superintendent, "As for the remnants of food left by Jagannātha, let them be delivered to Vāṇīnātha Rāya's charge, for he can take care of all the Vaiṣṇavas and distribute mahā-prasāda to them."

TEXT 175

আমার নিকটে এই পুষ্পের উদ্যানে ।
একখানি ঘর আছে পরম-নির্জনে ॥ ১৭৫ ॥

āmāra nikaṭe ei puṣpera udyāne
eka-khāni ghara āche parama-nirjane

SYNONYMS

āmāra nikaṭe—nearby My place; *ei*—this; *puṣpera udyāne*—in a garden of flowers; *eka-khāni*—one; *ghara*—room; *āche*—there is; *parama-nirjane*—in a very solitary place.

TRANSLATION

Śrī Caitanya Mahāprabhu then said, "Nearby My place in this garden of flowers is one single room that is very solitary.

TEXT 176

সেই ঘর আমাকে দেহ'—আছে প্রয়োজন ।
নিভৃতে বসিয়া তাহাঁ করিব স্মরণ ॥ ১৭৬ ॥

sei ghara āmāke deha'——āche prayojana
nibhṛte vasiyā tāhāṅ kariba smaraṇa

SYNONYMS

sei ghara—that room; *āmāke deha'*—please give to Me; *āche prayojana*—there is necessity; *nibhṛte*—in the solitary place; *vasiyā*—sitting; *tāhāṅ*—there; *kariba smaraṇa*—I shall remember the lotus feet of the Lord.

TRANSLATION

"Please give that room to Me, for I have need for it. Indeed, I shall remember the lotus feet of the Lord sitting in that solitary place."

PURPORT

This statement of Śrī Caitanya Mahāprabhu is significant. *Nibhṛte vasiyā tāhāṅ kariba smaraṇa:* "I shall sit down there in that solitary place and remember the lotus feet of the Lord." Neophyte students are not to imitate sitting in a solitary place and remembering the lotus feet of the Lord by chanting the Hare Kṛṣṇa *mahā-mantra.* We should always remember that it was Śrī Caitanya Mahāprabhu Himself who wanted such a place, either for Himself or Haridāsa Ṭhākura. No one can suddenly attain the level of Haridāsa Ṭhākura and sit down in a solitary place to chant the Hare Kṛṣṇa *mahā-mantra* and remember the lotus feet of the Lord. Only an exalted person like Haridāsa Ṭhākura or Śrī Caitanya Mahāprabhu, who is personally exhibiting the proper behavior for an *ācārya,* can engage in such a practice.

At the present moment we see that some of the members of the International Society for Krishna Consciousness are tending to leave their preaching activities in order to sit in a solitary place. This is not a very good sign. It is a fact that Śrīla Bhaktisiddhānta Sarasvatī Ṭhākura has condemned this process for neophytes. He has even stated in a song: *pratiṣṭhāra tare, nirjanera ghare, tava hari-nāma kevala kaitava.* Sitting in a solitary place intending to chant the Hare Kṛṣṇa *mahā-mantra* is considered a cheating process. This practice is not possible for neophytes at all. The neophyte devotee must act and work very laboriously under the direction of the spiritual master, and he must thus preach the cult of Śrī Caitanya Mahāprabhu. Only after maturing in devotion can he sit down in a solitary place to chant the Hare Kṛṣṇa *mahā-mantra* as Śrī Caitanya Mahāprabhu Himself did. Although Śrī Caitanya Mahāprabhu is the Supreme Personality of Godhead, He nonetheless traveled all over India continuously for six years and then retired at Jagannātha Purī to teach us a lesson. Even at Jagannātha Purī the Lord chanted the Hare Kṛṣṇa *mahā-mantra* in a great meeting at the Jagannātha temple. The point is that one should not try to imitate Haridāsa Ṭhākura at the beginning of one's transcendental life. One must first become very mature in devotion and thus receive the approval of Śrī Caitanya Mahāprabhu. Only at such a time may one actually sit down peacefully in a solitary place to chant the Hare Kṛṣṇa *mahā-mantra* and remember the lotus feet of the Lord. The senses are very strong, and if a neophyte devotee imitates Haridāsa Ṭhākura, his enemies (*kāma, krodha, lobha, moha, mada* and *mātsarya)* will disturb and fatigue him. Instead of chanting the Hare Kṛṣṇa *mahā-mantra,* the neophyte will simply sleep soundly. Preaching work is meant for advanced devotees, and when an advanced devotee is further elevated on the devotional scale, he may retire to chant the Hare Kṛṣṇa *mantra* in a solitary place. However, if one simply imitates advanced spiritual life, he will fall down, just like the *sahajiyās* in Vṛndāvana.

TEXT 177

মিশ্র কহে,—সব তোমার, চাহ কি কারণে ?
আপন-ইচ্ছায় লহ, যেই তোমার মনে ॥ ১৭৭ ॥

miśra kahe, ——saba tomāra, cāha ki kāraṇe?
āpana-icchāya laha, yei tomāra mane

SYNONYMS

miśra kahe—Kāśī Miśra said; *saba*—everything; *tomāra*—Yours; *cāha ki kāraṇe*—why do You beg; *āpana-icchāya*—by Your own will; *laha*—You take; *yei*—whatever; *tomāra mane*—is in Your mind.

TRANSLATION

Kāśī Miśra then told Śrī Caitanya Mahāprabhu: "Everything belongs to You. What is the use of Your begging? By Your own will You can take whatever You like.

TEXT 178

আমি-দুই হই তোমার দাস আজ্ঞাকারী।
যে চাহ, সেই আজ্ঞা দেহ' কৃপা করি' ॥ ১৭৮ ॥

āmi-dui ha-i tomāra dāsa ājñākārī
ye cāha, sei ājñā deha' kṛpā kari'

SYNONYMS

āmi—we; *dui*—two; *ha-i*—are; *tomāra*—Your; *dāsa*—servants; *ājñā-kārī*—order-carriers; *ye cāha*—whatever you want; *sei ājñā*—that order; *deha'*—give; *kṛpā kari'*—being merciful.

TRANSLATION

"My Lord, we are Your two servants and are here just to carry out Your orders. By Your mercy, please tell us to do whatever You want."

TEXT 179

এত কহি' দুই জনে বিদায় লইল ।
গোপীনাথ, বাণীনাথ—দুঁহে সঙ্গে নিল ॥ ১৭৯ ॥

eta kahi' dui jane vidāya la-ila
gopīnātha, vāṇīnātha——duṅhe saṅge nila

SYNONYMS

eta kahi'—saying this; *dui jane*—both of them; *vidāya la-ila*—took departure; *gopīnātha*—Gopīnātha Ācārya; *vāṇīnātha*—Vāṇīnātha Rāya; *duṅhe saṅge nila*—took both of them with them.

TRANSLATION

Saying this, Kāśī Miśra and the temple inspector took their departure, and Gopīnātha and Vāṇīnātha went with them.

TEXT 180

গোপীনাথে দেখাইল সব বাসা-ঘর ।
বাণীনাথ-ঠাঞি দিল প্রসাদ বিস্তর ॥ ১৮০ ॥

gopīnāthe dekhāila saba vāsā-ghara
vāṇīnātha-ṭhāñi dila prasāda vistara

SYNONYMS

gopīnāthe—unto Gopīnātha Ācārya; *dekhāila*—showed; *saba*—all; *vāsā-ghara*—residential places; *vāṇīnātha-ṭhāñi*—unto Vāṇīnātha Rāya; *dila*—delivered; *prasāda vistara*—remnants of food in large quantity.

TRANSLATION

Gopīnātha was then shown all the residential places, and Vāṇīnātha was given large quantities of food [mahā-prasāda] left by Lord Jagannātha.

TEXT 181

বাণীনাথ আইলা বহু প্রসাদ পিঠা লঞা ।
গোপীনাথ আইলা বাসা সংস্কার করিয়া ॥ ১৮১ ॥

vāṇīnātha āilā bahu prasāda piṭhā lañā
gopīnātha āilā vāsā saṁskāra kariyā

SYNONYMS

vāṇīnātha—Vāṇīnātha; *āilā*—returned; *bahu*—a very large quantity of; *prasāda*—remnants of food; *piṭhā lañā*—also taking cakes with them; *gopīnātha*—Gopīnātha Ācārya; *āilā*—returned; *vāsā*—residential places; *saṁskāra kariyā*—cleansing.

TRANSLATION

Thus Vāṇīnātha Rāya returned with large quantities of Lord Jagannātha's food remnants, along with cakes and other good eatables. Gopīnātha Ācārya also returned after cleansing all the residential quarters.

TEXT 182

মহাপ্রভু কহে,—শুন, সর্ব বৈষ্ণবগণ ।
নিজ-নিজ-বাসা সবে করহ গমন ॥ ১৮২ ॥

mahāprabhu kahe, ——śuna, sarva vaiṣṇava-gaṇa
nija-nija-vāsā sabe karaha gamana

SYNONYMS

mahāprabhu kahe—Lord Śrī Caitanya Mahāprabhu said; *śuna*—kindly listen; *sarva vaiṣṇava-gaṇa*—all Vaiṣṇavas; *nija-nija-vāsā*—to the respective residential quarters; *sabe*—all of you; *karaha*—make; *gamana*—departure.

TRANSLATION

Śrī Caitanya Mahāprabhu then addressed all the Vaiṣṇavas and requested that they listen to Him. He said, "Now you can go to your respective residential quarters.

TEXT 183

সমুদ্রস্নান করি' কর চূড়া দরশন ।
তবে আজি ইহঁ আসি' করিবে ভোজন ॥ ১৮৩ ॥

samudra-snāna kari' kara cūḍā daraśana
tabe āji ihaṅ āsi' karibe bhojana

SYNONYMS

samudra-snāna—bathing in the sea; *kari'*—finishing; *kara*—just do; *cūḍā darasana*—observing the top of the temple; *tabe*—thereafter; *āji*—today; *ihaṅ*—here; *āsi'*—coming back; *karibe bhojana*—take your lunch.

TRANSLATION

"Go to the sea and bathe and look at the top of the temple. After so doing, please come back here and take your lunch."

TEXT 184

প্রভু নমস্করি' সবে বাসাতে চলিলা।
গোপীনাথাচার্য সবে বাসা-স্থান দিলা॥ ১৮৪ ॥

prabhu namaskari' sabe vāsāte calilā
gopīnāthācārya sabe vāsā-sthāna dilā

SYNONYMS

prabhu namaskari'—after offering obeisances to Lord Śrī Caitanya Mahāprabhu; *sabe*—all the devotees; *vāsāte calilā*—departed for their residential quarters; *gopīnātha-ācārya*—Gopīnātha Ācārya; *sabe*—to everyone; *vāsā*—residential quarters; *sthāna*—place; *dilā*—delivered.

TRANSLATION

After offering obeisances to Śrī Caitanya Mahāprabhu, all the devotees departed for their residences, and Gopīnātha Ācārya showed them their respective quarters.

TEXT 185

মহাপ্রভু আইলা তবে হরিদাস-মিলনে।
হরিদাস করে প্রেমে নাম-সংকীর্তনে॥ ১৮৫ ॥

mahāprabhu āilā tabe haridāsa-milane
haridāsa kare preme nāma-saṅkīrtane

SYNONYMS

mahāprabhu—Śrī Caitanya Mahāprabhu; *āilā*—came; *tabe*—thereafter; *haridāsa-milane*—to meet Ṭhākura Haridāsa; *haridāsa*—Ṭhākura Haridāsa; *kare*—does; *preme*—in ecstatic love; *nāma-saṅkīrtane*—chanting of the holy name.

TRANSLATION

After this, Śrī Caitanya Mahāprabhu went to meet Haridāsa Ṭhākura, and He saw him engaged in chanting the mahā-mantra with ecstatic love. Haridāsa chanted, "Hare Kṛṣṇa, Hare Kṛṣṇa, Kṛṣṇa Kṛṣṇa, Hare Hare/ Hare Rāma, Hare Rāma, Rāma Rāma, Hare Hare."

TEXT 186

প্রভু দেখি' পড়ে আগে দণ্ডবৎ হঞা।
প্রভু আলিঙ্গন কৈল তাঁরে উঠাঞা॥ ১৮৬॥

prabhu dekhi' paḍe āge daṇḍavat hañā
prabhu āliṅgana kaila tāṅre uṭhāñā

SYNONYMS

prabhu dekhi'—after seeing the Lord; *paḍe*—fell down; *āge*—in front of Him; *daṇḍavat*—flat like a stick; *hañā*—becoming; *prabhu*—Lord Śrī Caitanya Mahāprabhu; *āliṅgana kaila*—embraced; *tāṅre*—him; *uṭhāñā*—raising him up.

TRANSLATION

As soon as Haridāsa Ṭhākura saw Śrī Caitanya Mahāprabhu, he immediately fell down like a stick to offer Him obeisances, and Lord Śrī Caitanya Mahāprabhu raised him up and embraced him.

TEXT 187

দুইজনে প্রেমাবেশে করেন ক্রন্দনে।
প্রভু-গুণে ভৃত্য বিকল, প্রভু ভৃত্য-গুণে॥ ১৮৭॥

dui-jane premāveśe karena krandane
prabhu-guṇe bhṛtya vikala, prabhu bhṛtya-guṇe

SYNONYMS

dui-jane—both of them; *prema-āveśe*—in loving ecstasy; *karena krandane*—were crying; *prabhu-guṇe*—by the quality of the Lord; *bhṛtya*—servant; *vikala*—transformed; *prabhu*—the Lord; *bhṛtya-guṇe*—by the quality of the servant.

TRANSLATION

Then both the Lord and His servant began to cry in ecstatic love. Indeed, the Lord was transformed by the quality of His servant, and the servant was transformed by the quality of his master.

PURPORT

The Māyāvādī philosophers say that the living entity and the Supreme Lord are nondifferent, and therefore they equate the transformation of the living entity with the transformation of the Lord. In other words, Māyāvādīs say that if the living entity is pleased, the Lord is also pleased, and if the living entity is displeased, the Lord is also displeased. By juggling words in this way, Māyāvādīs try to prove that there is no difference between the living entity and the Lord. This, however, is not a fact. In this verse Kṛṣṇadāsa Kavirāja Gosvāmī explains: *prabhu-guṇe bhṛtya vikala, prabhu bhṛtya-guṇe.* The Lord and the living entity are not equal, for the Lord is always the master, and the living entity is always the servant. Transformation takes place due to transcendental qualities, and it is thus said that the servant of the Lord is the heart of the Lord, and the Lord is the heart of the servant. This is also explained in *Bhagavad-gītā:*

ye yathā māṁ prapadyante
tāṁs tathaiva bhajāmy aham
mama vartmānuvartante
manuṣyāḥ pārtha sarvaśaḥ

"All of them—as they surrender unto Me—I reward accordingly. Everyone follows My path in all respects, O son of Pṛthā." (Bg. 4.11)

The Lord is always eager to congratulate the servant because of the servant's transcendental quality. The servant pleasingly renders service unto the Lord, and the Lord also very pleasingly reciprocates, rendering even more than the servant.

TEXT 188

হরিদাস কহে,—প্রভু, না ছুঁইও মোরে ।
মুঞি—নীচ, অস্পৃশ্য, পরম পামরে ॥ ১৮৮ ॥

haridāsa kahe, ——prabhu, nā chuṅio more
muñi——nīca, aspṛśya, parama pāmare

SYNONYMS

haridāsa kahe—Haridāsa Ṭhākura said; *prabhu*—my dear Lord; *nā chuṅio more*—please do not touch me; *muñi*—I; *nīca*—most fallen; *aspṛśya*—untouchable; *parama pāmare*—the lowest of mankind.

TRANSLATION

Haridāsa Ṭhākura said, "My dear Lord, please do not touch me, for I am most fallen and untouchable and am lowest among men."

TEXT 189

প্রভু কহে,—তোমা স্পর্শি পবিত্র হইতে।
তোমার পবিত্র ধর্ম নাহিক আমাতে ॥ ১৮৯ ॥

prabhu kahe, ——tomā sparśi pavitra ha-ite
tomāra pavitra dharma nāhika āmāte

SYNONYMS

prabhu kahe—the Lord said; *tomā sparśi*—I touch you; *pavitra ha-ite*—just to become purified; *tomāra*—your; *pavitra*—purified; *dharma*—occupation; *nāhika*—is not; *āmāte*—in Me.

TRANSLATION

The Lord said, "I wish to touch you just to be purified, for your purified activities do not exist in Me."

PURPORT

This is an example of the reciprocation of feelings between master and servant. The servant thinks that he is most impure and that the master should not touch him, and the master thinks that because He has become impure by associating with so many impure living entities, He should touch a pure devotee like Haridāsa Ṭhākura just to purify Himself. Actually both the servant and the master are already purified because neither of them is in touch with the impurities of material existence. They are already equal in quality because both of them are the purest. There is a difference in quantity, however, because the master is unlimited and the servant is limited. Consequently the servant always remains subordinate to the master, and this relationship is eternal and undisturbed. As soon as the servant feels like becoming the master, he falls into *māyā*. Thus it is by misuse of free will that one falls under the influence of *māyā*.

The Māyāvādī philosophers try to explain the equality of master and servant in terms of quantity, but they fail to explain why, if the master and servant are equal, the servant falls victim of *māyā*. They try to explain that when the servant, the living entity, is out of the clutches of *māyā*, he immediately becomes the so-called master again. Such an explanation is never satisfactory. Being unlimited, the master cannot become a victim of *māyā*, for in such a case His unlimitedness is crippled or limited. Thus the Māyāvāda explanation is not correct. The fact is that the master is always master and unlimited, and the servant, being limited, is sometimes curtailed by the influence of *māyā*. *Māyā* is also the master's energy and is also unlimited; therefore the limited servant or limited living entity is forced to remain under the master or the master's potency, *māyā*. Being freed from *māyā's* influence, one can again become a pure servant and equal qualitatively to the Lord. The relationship between master and servant continues due to their being unlimited and limited respectively.

TEXT 190

ক্ষণে ক্ষণে কর তুমি সর্বতীর্থে স্নান ।
ক্ষণে ক্ষণে কর তুমি যজ্ঞ-তপো-দান ॥ ১৯০ ॥

kṣaṇe kṣaṇe kara tumi sarva-tīrthe snāna
kṣaṇe kṣaṇe kara tumi yajña-tapo-dāna

SYNONYMS

kṣaṇe kṣaṇe—at every moment; *kara*—do; *tumi*—you; *sarva-tīrthe snāna*—bathing in all the holy places of pilgrimage; *kṣaṇe kṣaṇe*—at every moment; *kara*—perform; *tumi*—you; *yajña*—sacrifices; *tapaḥ*—austerities; *dāna*—charity.

TRANSLATION

Śrī Caitanya Mahāprabhu exalted Haridāsa Ṭhākura, stating, "At every moment you take your bath in all the holy places of pilgrimage, and at every moment you perform great sacrifices, austerity and charity.

TEXT 191

নিরন্তর কর চারি বেদ অধ্যয়ন ।
দ্বিজ-ন্যাসী হৈতে তুমি পরম-পাবন ॥ ১৯১ ॥

nirantara kara cāri veda adhyayana
dvija-nyāsī haite tumi parama-pāvana

SYNONYMS

nirantara—constantly; *kara*—you do; *cāri*—four; *veda*—of the *Vedas; adhyayana*—study; *dvija—brāhmaṇa; nyāsī—sannyāsī; haite*—than; *tumi*—you; *parama-pāvana*—supremely pure.

TRANSLATION

"You are constantly studying the four Vedas, and you are far better than any brāhmaṇa or sannyāsī."

TEXT 192

অহো বত শ্বপচোঽতো গরীয়ান্
যজ্জিহ্বাগ্রে বর্ত্ততে নাম তুভ্যম্ ।
তেপুস্তপস্তে জুহুবুঃ সস্নুরার্যা
ব্রহ্মানূচুর্নাম গৃণন্তি যে তে ॥ ১৯২ ॥

aho bata śva-paco 'to garīyān
yaj-jihvāgre vartate nāma tubhyam
tepus tapas te juhuvuḥ sasnur āryā
brahmānūcur nāma gṛṇanti ye te

SYNONYMS

aho bata—how wonderful it is; *śva-pacaḥ*—dog-eaters; *ataḥ*—than the initiated *brāhmaṇa; garīyān*—more glorious; *yat*—of whom; *jihvā-agre*—on the tongue; *vartate*—remains; *nāma*—holy name; *tubhyam*—of You, my Lord; *tepuḥ*—have performed; *tapaḥ*—austerity; *te*—they; *juhuvuḥ*—have performed sacrifices; *sasnuḥ*—have bathed in all holy places; *āryāḥ*—really belonging to the Āryan race; *brahma*—all the *Vedas; anūcuḥ*—have studied; *nāma*—holy name; *gṛṇanti*—chant; *ye*—who; *te*—they.

TRANSLATION

Śrī Caitanya Mahāprabhu then recited the following verse: " 'My dear Lord, one who always keeps Your holy name on his tongue becomes greater than an initiated brāhmaṇa. Although he may be born in a family of dog-eaters and therefore by material calculation may be the lowest among men, he is still glorious. This is the wonderful effect of chanting the holy name of the Lord. It is therefore concluded that one who chants the holy name of the Lord should be understood to have performed all kinds of austerities and great sacrifices mentioned in the Vedas. He has already taken his bath in all the holy places of pilgrimage. He has studied all the Vedas, and he is actually an Āryan.' "

PURPORT

The word Āryan means advanced. Unless one is spiritually advanced, he cannot be called an Āryan, and this is the difference between Āryan and non-Āryan. Non-Āryans are those who are not spiritually advanced. By following the Vedic culture, by performing great sacrifices and by becoming a strict follower of the Vedic instructions, one may become a *brāhmaṇa,* a *sannyāsī* or an Āryan. It is not possible to become a *brāhmaṇa, sannyāsī* or Āryan without being properly qualified.

Bhāgavata-dharma never allows one to become a cheap *brāhmaṇa, sannyāsī* or Āryan. The qualities or qualifications described herein are quoted from *Śrīmad-Bhāgavatam* (3.33.7) and were spoken by Devahūti, the mother of Kapiladeva, when she understood the influence of devotional service (*bhakti-yoga*). In this way Devahūti praised the devotee, pointing out his greatness in all respects.

TEXT 193

এত বলি তাঁরে লঞা গেলা পুষ্পোদ্যানে ।
অতি নিভৃতে তাঁরে দিলা বাসা-স্থানে ॥ ১৯৩ ॥

eta bali tāṅre lañā gelā puṣpodyāne
ati nibhṛte tāṅre dilā vāsā-sthāne

SYNONYMS

eta bali—saying this; *tāṅre lañā*—taking him; *gelā*—went; *puṣpa-udyāne*—in the flower garden; *ati nibhṛte*—in a very secluded place; *tāṅre*—unto him; *dilā*—delivered; *vāsā-sthāne*—a place to remain.

TRANSLATION

Saying this, Śrī Caitanya Mahāprabhu took Haridāsa Ṭhākura within the flower garden, and there, in a very secluded place, He showed him his residence.

TEXT 194

এইস্থানে রহি' কর নাম সংকীর্তন ।
প্রতিদিন আসি' আমি করিব মিলন ॥ ১৯৪ ॥

ei-sthāne rahi' kara nāma saṅkīrtana
prati-dina āsi' āmi kariba milana

SYNONYMS

ei-sthāne—in this place; *rahi'*—remaining; *kara*—perform; *nāma saṅkīrtana*—chanting of the holy name; *prati-dina*—every day; *āsi'*—coming; *āmi*—I; *kariba*—shall do; *milana*—meeting.

TRANSLATION

Śrī Caitanya Mahāprabhu requested Haridāsa Ṭhākura: "Remain here and chant the Hare Kṛṣṇa mahā-mantra. I shall personally come here to meet you daily.

TEXT 195

মন্দিরের চক্র দেখি' করিহ প্রণাম ।
এই ঠাঞি তোমার আসিবে প্রসাদান্ন ॥ ১৯৫ ॥

mandirera cakra dekhi' kariha praṇāma
ei ṭhāñi tomāra āsibe prasādānna

SYNONYMS

mandirera—of the temple of Jagannātha; *cakra*—the wheel on the top; *dekhi'*—seeing; *kariha praṇāma*—offer your obeisances; *ei ṭhāñi*—in this place; *tomāra*—your; *āsibe*—will come; *prasāda-anna*—remnants of foodstuff of Jagannātha.

TRANSLATION

"Remain here peacefully and look at the cakra on the top of the temple and offer obeisances. As far as your prasāda is concerned, I shall arrange to have that sent here."

PURPORT

Since he was born in a Mohammedan family, Śrīla Haridāsa Ṭhākura could not enter the temple of Jagannātha due to temple restrictions. Nonetheless, he was recognized by Śrī Caitanya Mahāprabhu as Nāmācārya Haridāsa Ṭhākura. Haridāsa Ṭhākura, however, considered himself unfit to enter the Jagannātha temple. Śrī Caitanya Mahāprabhu could have personally taken Haridāsa Ṭhākura in the Jagannātha temple if He wished, but the Lord did not like to disturb a popular custom. Consequently the Lord asked His servant simply to look at the Viṣṇu wheel on top of the temple and offer obeisances (*namaskāra*). This means that if one is not allowed to enter the temple, or if he thinks himself unfit to enter the temple, he can look at the wheel from outside the temple, and that is as good as seeing the Deity within.

Śrī Caitanya Mahāprabhu promised to come daily to see Śrīla Haridāsa Ṭhākura, and this indicates that Śrīla Haridāsa Ṭhākura was so advanced in spiritual life that, although considered unfit to enter the temple, he was being personally visited by the Lord every day. Nor was there any need for his going outside his residence to collect food. Śrī Caitanya Mahāprabhu assured Haridāsa Ṭhākura that the remnants of His foodstuffs would be sent there. *Yoga-kṣemaṁ vahāmy aham* (Bg. 9.22). As stated in *Bhagavad-gītā,* the Lord arranges all life's necessities for His devotees.

One reference is made here for those who are very anxious to imitate the behavior of Ṭhākura Haridāsa in an unnatural way. One must receive the order of

Śrī Caitanya Mahāprabhu or His representative before adopting such a way of life. The duty of a pure devotee or a servant of the Lord is to carry out the order of the Lord. Śrī Caitanya Mahāprabhu asked Nityānanda Prabhu to go to Bengal and preach, and He asked the Gosvāmīs, Rūpa and Sanātana, to go to Vṛndāvana and excavate the lost places of pilgrimage. In this case the Lord asked Haridāsa Ṭhākura to remain there at Jagannātha Purī and constantly chant the holy names of the Lord. Thus Śrī Caitanya Mahāprabhu gave different persons different orders, and consequently one should not try to imitate the behavior of Haridāsa Ṭhākura without being ordered by Śrī Caitanya Mahāprabhu or His representative. Śrīla Bhaktisiddhānta Sarasvatī Ṭhākura condemns such imitations in this way:

duṣṭa mana! tumi kisera vaiṣṇava?
pratiṣṭhāra tare, nirjanera ghare,
tava hari-nāma kevala kaitava

"My dear mind, you are trying to imitate Haridāsa Ṭhākura and chant the Hare Kṛṣṇa *mantra* in a secluded place, but you are not worth being called a Vaiṣṇava because what you want is cheap popularity and not the actual qualifications of Haridāsa Ṭhākura. If you try to imitate him you will fall down, for your neophyte position will cause you to think of women and money. Thus you will fall into the clutches of *māyā,* and your so-called chanting in a secluded place will bring about your downfall."

TEXT 196

নিত্যানন্দ, জগদানন্দ, দামোদর, মুকুন্দ ।
হরিদাসে মিলি' সবে পাইল আনন্দ ॥ ১৯৬ ॥

nityānanda, jagadānanda, dāmodara, mukunda
haridāse mili' sabe pāila ānanda

SYNONYMS

nityānanda—Nityānanda; *jagadānanda*—Jagadānanda; *dāmodara*—Dāmodara; *mukunda*—Mukunda; *haridāse*—Haridāsa; *mili'*—meeting; *sabe*—all of them; *pāila*—got; *ānanda*—great pleasure.

TRANSLATION

When Nityānanda Prabhu, Jagadānanda Prabhu, Dāmodara Prabhu and Mukunda Prabhu met Haridāsa Ṭhākura, they all became very much pleased.

TEXT 197

সমুদ্রস্নান করি' প্রভু আইলা নিজ স্থানে।
অদ্বৈতাদি গেলা সিন্ধু করিবারে স্নানে ॥ ১৯৭ ॥

samudra-snāna kari' prabhu āilā nija sthāne
advaitādi gelā sindhu karibāre snāne

SYNONYMS

samudra-snāna kari'—after bathing in the sea; *prabhu*—Śrī Caitanya Mahāprabhu; *āilā*—came; *nija sthāne*—to His own place; *advaita-ādi*—devotees, headed by Advaita Prabhu; *gelā*—went; *sindhu*—to the ocean; *karibāre*—just to take; *snāne*—bath.

TRANSLATION

When Śrī Caitanya Mahāprabhu returned to His residence after taking a bath in the sea, all the devotees, headed by Advaita Prabhu, went to bathe in the sea.

TEXT 198

আসি' জগন্নাথের কৈল চূড়া দরশন।
প্রভুর আবাসে আইলা করিতে ভোজন ॥ ১৯৮ ॥

āsi' jagannāthera kaila cūḍā daraśana
prabhura āvāse āilā karite bhojana

SYNONYMS

āsi'—coming back; *jagannāthera*—of Lord Jagannātha; *kaila*—did; *cūḍā daraśana*—looking at the top of the temple; *prabhura*—of Lord Caitanya Mahāprabhu; *āvāse*—at the residence; *āilā*—came; *karite bhojana*—to take their luncheon.

TRANSLATION

After bathing in the sea, all the devotees, headed by Advaita Prabhu, returned, and on their return they saw the top of the Jagannātha temple. They then went to the residence of Śrī Caitanya Mahāprabhu to take their luncheon.

TEXT 199

সবারে বসাইলা প্রভু যোগ্য ক্রম করি'।
শ্রীহস্তে পরিবেশন কৈল গৌরহরি ॥ ১৯৯ ॥

sabāre vasāilā prabhu yogya krama kari'
śrī-haste pariveśana kaila gaurahari

SYNONYMS

sabāre—all the devotees; *vasāilā*—made to sit; *prabhu*—Śrī Caitanya Mahāprabhu; *yogya*—befitting; *krama*—in order, one after another; *kari'*—setting; *śrī-haste*—by His own transcendental hand; *pariveśana*—distribution; *kaila*—did; *gaurahari*—Lord Śrī Caitanya Mahāprabhu.

TRANSLATION

One after the other, Śrī Caitanya Mahāprabhu made all the devotees sit in their proper places. He then began to distribute prasāda with His own transcendental hand.

TEXT 200

অল্প অন্ন নাহি আইসে দিতে প্রভুর হাতে ।
দুই-তিনের অন্ন দেন এক এক পাতে ॥ ২০০ ॥

alpa anna nāhi āise dite prabhura hāte
dui-tinera anna dena eka eka pāte

SYNONYMS

alpa anna—a small quantity of *prasāda; nāhi*—does not; *āise*—come; *dite*—to give; *prabhura*—of Śrī Caitanya Mahāprabhu; *hāte*—in the hand; *dui*—two; *tinera*—or of three; *anna*—food; *dena*—He delivers; *eka eka pāte*—on each and every plantain leaf.

TRANSLATION

All the devotees were served prasāda on plantain leaves, and Śrī Caitanya Mahāprabhu distributed on each leaf a quantity suitable for two or three men to eat, for His hand could not distribute less than that.

TEXT 201

প্রভু না খাইলে কেহ না করে ভোজন ।
ঊর্ধ্ব-হস্তে বসি' রহে সর্ব ভক্তগণ ॥ ২০১ ॥

prabhu nā khāile keha nā kare bhojana
ūrdhva-haste vasi' rahe sarva bhakta-gaṇa

SYNONYMS

prabhu—Śrī Caitanya Mahāprabhu; *nā khāile*—without eating; *keha*—anyone; *nā*—not; *kare*—does; *bhojana*—eating; *ūrdhva-haste*—raising the hand; *vasi'*—sitting; *rahe*—remain; *sarva*—all; *bhakta-gaṇa*—devotees.

TRANSLATION

All the devotees kept their hands raised over the prasāda distributed to them, for they did not want to eat without seeing the Lord eat first.

TEXT 202

স্বরূপ-গোসাঞি প্রভুকে কৈল নিবেদন ।
তুমি না বসিলে কেহ না করে ভোজন ॥ ২০২ ॥

svarūpa-gosāñi prabhuke kaila nivedana
tumi nā vasile keha nā kare bhojana

SYNONYMS

svarūpa-gosāñi—Svarūpa Dāmodara Gosāñi; *prabhuke*—unto Śrī Caitanya Mahāprabhu; *kaila*—did; *nivedana*—submission; *tumi*—You; *nā vasile*—if not sitting; *keha*—anyone; *nā*—not; *kare*—does; *bhojana*—eating.

TRANSLATION

Svarūpa Dāmodara Gosvāmī then informed Śrī Caitanya Mahāprabhu: "Unless You sit and take prasāda, no one will accept it.

TEXT 203

তোমা-সঙ্গে রহে যত সন্ন্যাসীর গণ ।
গোপীনাথাচার্য তাঁরে করিয়াছে নিমন্ত্রণ ॥ ২০৩ ॥

tomā-saṅge rahe yata sannyāsīra gaṇa
gopīnāthācārya tāṅre kariyāche nimantraṇa

SYNONYMS

tomā-saṅge—along with You; *rahe*—remain; *yata*—as many as; *sannyāsīra gaṇa*—rank of *sannyāsīs; gopīnātha-ācārya*—Gopīnātha Ācārya; *tāṅre*—all of them; *kariyāche*—has done; *nimantraṇa*—invitation.

TRANSLATION

"Gopīnātha Ācārya has invited all the sannyāsīs who remained with You to come and take prasāda.

TEXT 204

আচার্য আসিয়াছেন ভিক্ষার প্রসাদান্ন লঞা।
পুরী, ভারতী আছেন তোমার অপেক্ষা করিয়া ॥২০৪

ācārya āsiyāchena bhikṣāra prasādānna lañā
purī, bhāratī āchena tomāra apekṣā kariyā

SYNONYMS

ācārya—Gopīnātha Ācārya; *āsiyāchena*—has come; *bhikṣāra*—for eating; *prasāda-anna lañā*—taking the remnants of all kinds of food; *purī*—Paramānanda Purī; *bhāratī*—Brahmānanda Bhāratī; *āchena*—are; *tomāra*—for You; *apekṣā kariyā*—waiting.

TRANSLATION

"Gopīnātha Ācārya has already come bringing sufficient remnants of food to distribute to all the sannyāsīs, and sannyāsīs like Paramānanda Purī and Brahmānanda Bhāratī are waiting for You.

TEXT 205

নিত্যানন্দ লঞা ভিক্ষা করিতে বৈস তুমি।
বৈষ্ণবের পরিবেশন করিতেছি আমি ॥ ২০৫ ॥

nityānanda lañā bhikṣā karite vaisa tumi
vaiṣṇavera pariveśana karitechi āmi

SYNONYMS

nityānanda lañā—taking along Śrī Nityānanda Prabhu; *bhikṣā*—luncheon; *karite*—to take; *vaisa*—sit down; *tumi*—You; *vaiṣṇavera*—to all the devotees; *pariveśana*—distribution of *prasāda; karitechi*—am doing; *āmi*—I.

TRANSLATION

"You may sit down and accept the luncheon with Nityānanda Prabhu, and I shall distribute the prasāda to all the Vaiṣṇavas."

TEXT 206

তবে প্রভু প্রসাদান্ন গোবিন্দ-হাতে দিলা।
যত্ন করি' হরিদাস-ঠাকুরে পাঠাইলা ॥ ২০৬ ॥

tabe prabhu prasādānna govinda-hāte dilā
yatna kari' haridāsa-ṭhākure pāṭhāilā

SYNONYMS

tabe—thereafter; *prabhu*—Śrī Caitanya Mahāprabhu; *prasāda-anna*—remnants of Jagannātha's food; *govinda-hāte*—in the hand of Govinda; *dilā*—delivered; *yatna kari'*—with great attention; *haridāsa-ṭhākure*—unto Haridāsa Ṭhākura; *pāṭhāilā*—sent.

TRANSLATION

After this, Śrī Caitanya Mahāprabhu carefully delivered some prasāda into the hands of Govinda to be given to Haridāsa Ṭhākura.

TEXT 207

আপনে বসিলা সব সন্ন্যাসীরে লঞা।
পরিবেশন করে আচার্য হরষিত হঞা ॥ ২০৭ ॥

āpane vasilā saba sannyāsīre lañā
pariveśana kare ācārya haraṣita hañā

SYNONYMS

āpane—personally; *vasilā*—sat down; *saba*—all; *sannyāsīre lañā*—taking with Him the *sannyāsīs; pariveśana kare*—distributes; *ācārya*—Gopīnātha Ācārya; *haraṣita hañā*—with great pleasure.

TRANSLATION

Then Śrī Caitanya Mahāprabhu personally sat down to accept lunch with the other sannyāsīs, and Gopīnātha Ācārya began to distribute the prasāda with great pleasure.

TEXT 208

স্বরূপ গোসাঞি, দামোদর, জগদানন্দ।
বৈষ্ণবেরে পরিবেশে তিন জনে—আনন্দ ॥ ২০৮ ॥

svarūpa gosāñi, dāmodara, jagadānanda
vaiṣṇavere pariveśe tina jane——ānanda

SYNONYMS

svarūpa gosāñi—Svarūpa Gosāñi; *dāmodara*—Dāmodara; *jagadānanda*—Jagadānanda; *vaiṣṇavere pariveśe*—distributed to the Vaiṣṇavas; *tina jane*—the three persons; *ānanda*—very jubilant.

TRANSLATION

Then Svarūpa Dāmodara Gosvāmī, Dāmodara Paṇḍita and Jagadānanda all began to distribute prasāda to the devotees with great pleasure.

TEXT 209

নানা পিঠাপানা খায় আকণ্ঠ পূরিয়া।
মধ্যে মধ্যে 'হরি' কহে আনন্দিত হঞা ॥ ২০৯ ॥

nānā piṭhā-pānā khāya ākaṇṭha pūriyā
madhye madhye 'hari' kahe ānandita hañā

SYNONYMS

nānā—various; *piṭhā-pānā*—cakes and sweet rice; *khāya*—eat; *ākaṇṭha pūriyā*—filling up to the throat; *madhye madhye*—occasionally; *hari*—the holy name of Kṛṣṇa; *kahe*—they speak; *ānandita hañā*—in great jubilation.

TRANSLATION

They ate all kinds of cakes and sweet rice, filling themselves up to their throats, and at intervals they vibrated the holy name of the Lord in great jubilation.

PURPORT

It is the practice of Vaiṣṇavas while taking *prasāda* to chant the holy name of Lord Hari at intervals and also sing various songs, such as *śarīra avidyā-jāla.* Those who are honoring *prasāda,* accepting the remnants of food offered to the Deity, must always remember that *prasāda* is not ordinary food. *Prasāda* is transcendental. We are therefore reminded:

mahā-prasāde govinde
nāma-brahmaṇi vaiṣṇave
svalpa-puṇya-vatām rājan
viśvāso naiva jāyate

Those who are not pious cannot understand the value of *mahā-prasāda* and the holy name of the Lord. Both *prasāda* and the Lord's name are on the Brahman or spiritual platform. One should never consider *prasāda* to be like ordinary hotel cooking. Nor should one touch any kind of food not offered to the Deity. Every Vaiṣṇava strictly follows this principle and does not accept any food that is not *prasāda*. One should take *prasāda* with great faith and should chant the holy name of the Lord and worship the Deity in the temple, always remembering that the Deity, *mahā-prasāda* and the holy name do not belong to the mundane platform. By worshiping the Deity, eating *prasāda* and chanting the Hare Kṛṣṇa *mahā-mantra,* one can always remain on the spiritual platform (*brahma-bhūyāya kalpate*).

TEXT 210

ভোজন সমাপ্ত হৈল, কৈল আচমন ।
সবারে পরাইল প্রভু মাল্য-চন্দন ॥ ২১০ ॥

bhojana samāpta haila, kaila ācamana
sabāre parāila prabhu mālya-candana

SYNONYMS

bhojana—lunch; *samāpta*—ending; *haila*—there was; *kaila*—did; *ācamana*—washing the mouth; *sabāre*—on everyone; *parāila*—put; *prabhu*—Śrī Caitanya Mahāprabhu; *mālya-candana*—a garland and sandalwood pulp.

TRANSLATION

After everyone had finished his lunch and washed his mouth and hands, Śrī Caitanya Mahāprabhu personally decorated everyone with flower garlands and sandalwood pulp.

TEXT 211

বিশ্রাম করিতে সবে নিজ বাসা গেলা ।
সন্ধ্যাকালে আসি' পুনঃ প্রভুকে মিলিলা ॥ ২১১॥

viśrāma karite sabe nija vāsā gelā
sandhyā-kāle āsi' punaḥ prabhuke mililā

SYNONYMS

viśrāma karite—going to take rest; *sabe*—all the Vaiṣṇavas; *nija*—to their own; *vāsā*—residential quarters; *gelā*—went; *sandhyā-kāle*—in the evening; *āsi'*—coming; *punaḥ*—again; *prabhuke mililā*—met Śrī Caitanya Mahāprabhu.

TRANSLATION

After thus accepting prasāda, they all went to take rest at their respective residences, and in the evening they again came to meet Śrī Caitanya Mahāprabhu.

TEXT 212

হেনকালে রামানন্দ আইলা প্রভু-স্থানে ।
প্রভু মিলাইল তাঁরে সব বৈষ্ণবগণে ॥ ২১২ ॥

hena-kāle rāmānanda āilā prabhu-sthāne
prabhu milāila tāṅre saba vaiṣṇava-gaṇe

SYNONYMS

hena-kāle—at this time; *rāmānanda*—Rāmānanda; *āilā*—came; *prabhu-sthāne*—at the place of Śrī Caitanya Mahāprabhu; *prabhu*—Śrī Caitanya Mahāprabhu; *milāila*—caused to meet; *tāṅre*—him (Śrī Rāmānanda Rāya); *saba*—all; *vaiṣṇava-gaṇe*—the devotees of the Lord.

TRANSLATION

At this time Rāmānanda Rāya also came to meet Śrī Caitanya Mahāprabhu, and the Lord took the opportunity to introduce all the Vaiṣṇavas to him.

TEXT 213

সবা লঞা গেলা প্রভু জগন্নাথালয় ।
কীর্তন আরম্ভ তথা কৈল মহাশয় ॥ ২১৩ ॥

sabā lañā gelā prabhu jagannāthālaya
kīrtana ārambha tathā kaila mahāśaya

SYNONYMS

sabā lañā—taking all of them; *gelā*—went; *prabhu*—Śrī Caitanya Mahāprabhu; *jagannātha-ālaya*—to the temple of Lord Jagannātha; *kīrtana*—congregational chanting; *ārambha*—beginning; *tathā*—there; *kaila*—did; *mahāśaya*—the great personality.

TRANSLATION

The great Personality of Godhead, Śrī Caitanya Mahāprabhu, then took all of them to the temple of Jagannātha and began the congregational chanting of the holy name there.

TEXT 214

**সন্ধ্যা-ধূপ দেখি' আরম্ভিলা সংকীর্তন ।
পড়িছা আসি' সবারে দিল মাল্য-চন্দন ॥ ২১৪ ॥**

sandhyā-dhūpa dekhi' ārambhilā saṅkīrtana
paḍichā āsi' sabāre dila mālya-candana

SYNONYMS

sandhyā-dhūpa—*dhūpa-ārati* just in the beginning of the evening; *dekhi'*—they all saw; *ārambhilā*—began; *saṅkīrtana*—congregational chanting; *paḍichā*—the inspector of the temple; *āsi'*—coming; *sabāre*—unto everyone; *dila*—offered; *mālya-candana*—flower garlands and sandalwood pulp.

TRANSLATION

After seeing the dhūpa-ārati of the Lord, they all began congregational chanting. Then the paḍichā, the superintendent of the temple, came and offered flower garlands and sandalwood pulp to everyone.

TEXT 215

**চারিদিকে চারি সম্প্রদায় করেন কীর্তন ।
মধ্যে নৃত্য করে প্রভু শচীর নন্দন ॥ ২১৫ ॥**

cāri-dike cāri sampradāya karena kīrtana
madhye nṛtya kare prabhu śacīra nandana

SYNONYMS

cāri-dike—in the four directions; *cāri*—four; *sampradāya*—groups; *karena*—performed; *kīrtana*—congregational chanting; *madhye*—in the middle; *nṛtya kare*—dances; *prabhu*—Śrī Caitanya Mahāprabhu; *śacīra nandana*—the son of mother Śacī.

TRANSLATION

Four parties were then distributed in four directions to perform saṅkīrtana, and in the middle of them the Lord Himself, known as the son of mother Śacī, began to dance.

TEXT 216

**অষ্ট মৃদঙ্গ বাজে, বত্রিশ করতাল ।
হরিধ্বনি করে সবে, বলে – ভাল, ভাল ॥ ২১৬ ॥**

aṣṭa mṛdaṅga bāje, batriśa karatāla
hari-dhvani kare sabe, bale——bhāla, bhāla

SYNONYMS

aṣṭa mṛdaṅga—eight *mṛdaṅgas; bāje*—sounded; *batriśa*—thirty-two; *karatāla*—cymbals; *hari-dhvani*—vibrating the transcendental sound; *kare*—does; *sabe*—every one of them; *bale*—says; *bhāla bhāla*—very good, very good.

TRANSLATION

In the four groups there were eight mṛdaṅgas and thirty-two cymbals. All together they began to vibrate the transcendental sound, and everyone said, "Very good! Very good!"

TEXT 217

কীর্ত্তনের ধ্বনি মহামঙ্গল উঠিল ।
চতুর্দ্দশ লোক ভরি' ব্রহ্মাণ্ড ভেদিল ॥ ২১৭ ॥

kīrtanera dhvani mahā-maṅgala uṭhila
caturdaśa loka bhari' brahmāṇḍa bhedila

SYNONYMS

kīrtanera dhvani—the vibration of the *saṅkīrtana; mahā-maṅgala uṭhila*—all good fortune awakened; *catuḥ-daśa*—fourteen; *loka*—planetary systems; *bhari'*—filling up; *brahmāṇḍa*—the whole universe; *bhedila*—penetrated.

TRANSLATION

When the tumultuous vibration of saṅkīrtana resounded, all good fortune immediately awakened, and the sound penetrated the whole universe through the fourteen planetary systems.

TEXT 218

কীর্ত্তন-আরম্ভে প্রেম উথলি' চলিল ।
নীলাচলবাসী লোক ধাঞা আইল ॥ ২১৮ ॥

kīrtana-ārambhe prema uthali' calila
nīlācala-vāsī loka dhāñā āila

SYNONYMS

kīrtana-ārambhe—in the beginning of the *saṅkīrtana; prema*—ecstasy of love; *uthali'*—overpowering; *calila*—began to proceed; *nīlācala-vāsī*—all the residents of Jagannātha Purī; *loka*—people; *dhāñā*—running; *āila*—came.

TRANSLATION

When the congregational chanting began, ecstatic love immediately overflooded everything, and all the residents of Jagannātha Purī came running.

TEXT 219

কীর্তন দেখি' সবার মনে হৈল চমৎকার ।
কভু নাহি দেখি ঐছে প্রেমের বিকার ॥ ২১৯ ॥

kīrtana dekhi' sabāra mane haila camatkāra
kabhu nāhi dekhi aiche premera vikāra

SYNONYMS

kīrtana dekhi'—seeing the performance of *saṅkīrtana; sabāra*—of all of them; *mane*—in the mind; *haila*—there was; *camatkāra*—astonishment; *kabhu*—at any time; *nāhi*—never; *dekhi*—see; *aiche*—such; *premera*—of ecstatic love; *vikāra*—transformation.

TRANSLATION

Everyone was astonished to see such a performance of saṅkīrtana, and they all agreed that never before had kīrtana been so performed and ecstatic love of God so exhibited.

TEXT 220

তবে প্রভু জগন্নাথের মন্দির বেড়িয়া ।
প্রদক্ষিণ করি' বুলেন নর্তন করিয়া ॥ ২২০ ॥

tabe prabhu jagannāthera mandira beḍiyā
pradakṣiṇa kari' bulena nartana kariyā

SYNONYMS

tabe—thereafter; *prabhu*—Śrī Caitanya Mahāprabhu; *jagannāthera*—of Lord Jagannātha; *mandira*—temple; *beḍiyā*—walking all around; *pradakṣiṇa*—circumambulation; *kari'*—doing; *bulena*—walks; *nartana kariyā*—dancing.

TRANSLATION

At this time Śrī Caitanya Mahāprabhu circumambulated the temple of Jagannātha and continuously danced about the whole area.

TEXT 221

আগে-পাছে গান করে চারি সম্প্রদায় ।
আছাড়ের কালে ধরে নিত্যানন্দ রায় ॥ ২২১ ॥

āge-pāche gāna kare cāri sampradāya
āchāḍera kāle dhare nityānanda rāya

SYNONYMS

āge-pāche—in front and in the rear; *gāna*—singing; *kare*—do; *cāri*—four; *sampradāya*—groups; *āchāḍera*—of falling down; *kāle*—at the time; *dhare*—captures; *nityānanda rāya*—Lord Śrī Nityānanda Prabhu.

TRANSLATION

As the circumambulation was performed, the four kīrtana parties sang in front and in the rear. When Śrī Caitanya Mahāprabhu fell down to the ground, Śrī Nityānanda Rāya Prabhu lifted Him up.

TEXT 222

অশ্রু, পুলক, কম্প, স্বেদ, গম্ভীর হুঙ্কার ।
প্রেমের বিকার দেখি' লোকে চমৎকার ॥ ২২২ ॥

aśru, pulaka, kampa, sveda, gambhīra huṅkāra
premera vikāra dekhi' loke camatkāra

SYNONYMS

aśru—tears; *pulaka*—jubilation; *kampa*—trembling; *sveda*—perspiration; *gambhīra huṅkāra*—deep resounding; *premera*—of ecstatic love; *vikāra*—transformation; *dekhi'*—seeing; *loke*—all the people; *camatkāra*—were astonished.

TRANSLATION

While kīrtana was going on, there was a transformation of ecstatic love and much tears, jubilation, trembling, perspiration and deep resounding in the body of Śrī Caitanya Mahāprabhu. Upon seeing this transformation, all the people present became very much astonished.

TEXT 223

পিচ্‌কারি-ধারা জিনি' অশ্রু নয়নে ।
চারিদিকের লোক সব করয়ে সিনানে ॥ ২২৩ ॥

pickāri-dhārā jini' aśru nayane
cāri-dikera loka saba karaye sināne

SYNONYMS

pickāri-dhārā—like water coming in force from a syringe; *jini'*—conquering; *aśru*—tears; *nayane*—in the eyes; *cāri-dikera*—in all four directions; *loka*—people; *saba*—all; *karaye sināne*—moistened.

TRANSLATION

The tears from the eyes of the Lord came out with great force, like water from a syringe. Indeed, all the people who surrounded Him were moistened by His tears.

TEXT 224

'বেড়ানৃত্য' মহাপ্রভু করি' কতক্ষণ ।
মন্দিরের পাছে রহি' করয়ে কীর্তন ॥ ২২৪ ॥

'beḍā-nṛtya' mahāprabhu kari' kata-kṣaṇa
mandirera pāche rahi' karaye kīrtana

SYNONYMS

beḍā-nṛtya—the dancing surrounding the temple; *mahāprabhu*—Śrī Caitanya Mahāprabhu; *kari'*—performing; *kata-kṣaṇa*—for some time; *mandirera pāche*—at the rear of the temple; *rahi'*—staying; *karaye*—performed; *kīrtana*—congregational chanting.

TRANSLATION

After circumambulating the temple, Śrī Caitanya Mahāprabhu for some time remained at the rear of the temple and continued His saṅkīrtana.

TEXT 225

চারিদিকে চারি সম্প্রদায় উচ্চৈঃস্বরে গায় ।
মধ্যে তাণ্ডব-নৃত্য করে গৌররায় ॥ ২২৫ ॥

cāri-dike cāri sampradāya uccaiḥsvare gāya
madhye tāṇḍava-nṛtya kare gaurarāya

SYNONYMS

cāri-dike—on four sides; *cāri sampradāya*—the four groups; *uccaiḥ-svare*—very loudly; *gāya*—chant; *madhye*—in the middle; *tāṇḍava-nṛtya*—jumping and dancing; *kare*—performs; *gaurarāya*—Śrī Caitanya Mahāprabhu.

TRANSLATION

On all four sides the four saṅkīrtana groups chanted very loudly, and in the middle Śrī Caitanya Mahāprabhu danced, jumping high.

TEXT 226

বহুক্ষণ নৃত্য করি' প্রভু স্থির হৈলা ।
চারি মহান্তেরে তবে নাচিতে আজ্ঞা দিলা ॥ ২২৬ ॥

bahu-kṣaṇa nṛtya kari' prabhu sthira hailā
cāri mahāntere tabe nācite ājñā dilā

SYNONYMS

bahu-kṣaṇa—for a long period; *nṛtya kari'*—dancing; *prabhu*—Śrī Caitanya Mahāprabhu; *sthira hailā*—became silent; *cāri mahāntere*—to four great personalities; *tabe*—then; *nācite*—to dance; *ājñā dilā*—ordered.

TRANSLATION

After dancing for a long time, Śrī Caitanya Mahāprabhu became still and ordered four great personalities to begin to dance.

TEXT 227

এক সম্প্রদায়ে নাচে নিত্যানন্দ-রায়ে ।
অদ্বৈত-আচার্য নাচে আর সম্প্রদায়ে ॥ ২২৭ ॥

eka sampradāye nāce nityānanda-rāye
advaita-ācārya nāce āra sampradāye

SYNONYMS

eka sampradāye—in one group; *nāce*—dances; *nityānanda-rāye*—Lord Nityānanda; *advaita-ācārya*—Advaita Ācārya Prabhu; *nāce*—dances; *āra*—another; *sampradāye*—in a group.

TRANSLATION

In one group Nityānanda Prabhu began to dance, and in another group Advaita Ācārya began to dance.

TEXT 228

আর সম্প্রদায়ে নাচে পণ্ডিত-বক্রেশ্বর ।
শ্রীবাস নাচে আর সম্প্রদায়-ভিতর ॥ ২২৮ ॥

āra sampradāye nāce paṇḍita-vakreśvara
śrīvāsa nāce āra sampradāya-bhitara

SYNONYMS

āra sampradāye—in another *sampradāya,* or group; *nāce*—dances; *paṇḍita-vakreśvara*—Vakreśvara Paṇḍita; *śrīvāsa*—Śrīvāsa Ṭhākura; *nāce*—dances; *āra*—another; *sampradāya-bhitara*—in the middle of a group.

TRANSLATION

In another group Vakreśvara Paṇḍita and in another group Śrīvāsa Ṭhākura began to dance.

TEXT 229

মধ্যে রহি' মহাপ্রভু করেন দরশন ।
তাহাঁ এক ঐশ্বর্য তাঁর হইল প্রকটন ॥ ২২৯ ॥

madhye rahi' mahāprabhu karena daraśana
tāhāṅ eka aiśvarya tāṅra ha-ila prakaṭana

SYNONYMS

madhye rahi'—keeping in the middle; *mahāprabhu*—Śrī Caitanya Mahāprabhu; *karena daraśana*—looks over; *tāhāṅ*—there; *eka*—one; *aiśvarya*—miracle; *tāṅra*—of Him; *ha-ila*—became; *prakaṭana*—exhibited.

TRANSLATION

While this dancing was going on, Śrī Caitanya Mahāprabhu watched them and performed a miracle.

TEXT 230

চারিদিকে নৃত্যগীত করে যত জন ।
সবে দেখে,—প্রভু করে আমারে দরশন ॥ ২৩০ ॥

cāri-dike nṛtya-gīta kare yata jana
sabe dekhe, —prabhu kare āmāre daraśana

SYNONYMS

cāri-dike—on four sides; *nṛtya-gīta*—chanting and dancing; *kare*—does; *yata jana*—all people; *sabe dekhe*—everyone sees; *prabhu*—Śrī Caitanya Mahāprabhu; *kare*—does; *āmāre daraśana*—looking at me.

TRANSLATION

Śrī Caitanya Mahāprabhu stood in the middle of the dancers, and all the dancers in all directions perceived that Śrī Caitanya Mahāprabhu was looking at them.

TEXT 231

চারি জনের নৃত্য দেখিতে প্রভুর অভিলাষ ।
সেই অভিলাষে করে ঐশ্বর্য প্রকাশ ॥ ২৩১ ॥

cāri janera nṛtya dekhite prabhura abhilāṣa
sei abhilāṣe kare aiśvarya prakāśa

SYNONYMS

cāri janera—of the four persons; *nṛtya*—dancing; *dekhite*—to see; *prabhura*—of Śrī Caitanya Mahāprabhu; *abhilāṣa*—desire; *sei abhilāṣe*—for that purpose; *kare*—does; *aiśvarya prakāśa*—exhibition of a miracle.

TRANSLATION

Wanting to see the dancing of the four great personalities, Śrī Caitanya Mahāprabhu exhibited Himself in such a way to appear as if He were seeing everyone.

TEXT 232

দর্শনে আবেশ তাঁর দেখি' মাত্র জানে ।
কেমনে চৌদিকে দেখে,—ইহা নাহি জানে ॥ ২৩২ ॥

darśane āveśa tāṅra dekhi' mātra jāne
kemane caudike dekhe, —ihā nāhi jāne

SYNONYMS

darśane—while looking over; *āveśa*—emotional ecstasy; *tāṅra*—His; *dekhi'*—seeing; *mātra jāne*—only knows; *kemane*—how; *cau-dike*—on four sides; *dekhe*—He sees; *ihā nāhi jāne*—one does not know.

TRANSLATION

Everyone who saw Śrī Caitanya Mahāprabhu could understand that He was performing a miracle, but they did not know how it was that He could see from all four sides.

TEXT 233

পুলিন-ভোজনে যেন কৃষ্ণ মধ্য-স্থানে ।
চৌদিকের সখা কহে,—আমারে নেহানে ॥ ২৩৩ ॥

pulina-bhojane yena kṛṣṇa madhya-sthāne
caudikera sakhā kahe, —āmāre nehāne

SYNONYMS

pulina-bhojane—eating on the bank of Yamunā; *yena*—as; *kṛṣṇa*—Lord Kṛṣṇa; *madhya-sthāne*—sitting in the middle; *cau-dikera*—on four sides; *sakhā*—cowherd boy friends; *kahe*—say; *āmāre nehāne*—just seeing me.

TRANSLATION

In His own pastimes in Vṛndāvana, when Kṛṣṇa used to eat on the bank of the Yamunā and sit in the center of His friends, every one of the cowherd boys would perceive that Kṛṣṇa was looking at him. In the same way, when Caitanya Mahāprabhu was dancing, everyone saw that Caitanya Mahāprabhu was facing him.

TEXT 234

নৃত্য করিতে যেই আইসে সন্নিধানে ।
মহাপ্রভু করে তাঁরে দৃঢ় আলিঙ্গনে ॥ ২৩৪ ॥

nṛtya karite yei āise sannidhāne
mahāprabhu kare tāṅre dṛḍha āliṅgane

SYNONYMS

nṛtya karite—dancing; *yei*—anyone who; *āise*—comes; *sannidhāne*—nearby; *mahāprabhu*—Śrī Caitanya Mahāprabhu; *kare*—does; *tāṅre*—unto him; *dṛḍha*—tight; *āliṅgane*—embracing.

TRANSLATION

When someone came nearby while dancing, Śrī Caitanya Mahāprabhu would tightly embrace him.

TEXT 235

মহানৃত্য, মহাপ্রেম, মহাসংকীর্তন ।
দেখি' প্রেমাবেশে ভাসে নীলাচল-জন ॥ ২৩৫ ॥

mahā-nṛtya, mahā-prema, mahā-saṅkīrtana
dekhi' premāveśe bhāse nīlācala-jana

SYNONYMS

mahā-nṛtya—great dancing; *mahā-prema*—great love; *mahā-saṅkīrtana*—great congregational chanting; *dekhi'*—seeing; *prema-āveśe*—in ecstatic love; *bhāse*—flow; *nīlācala-jana*—all the residents of Jagannātha Purī.

TRANSLATION

Upon seeing the great dancing, great love and great saṅkīrtana, all the people of Jagannātha Purī floated in an ecstatic ocean of love.

TEXT 236

গজপতি রাজা শুনি' কীর্তন-মহত্ত্ব ।
অট্টালিকা চড়ি' দেখে স্বগণ-সহিত ॥ ২৩৬ ॥

gajapati rājā śuni' kīrtana-mahattva
aṭṭālikā caḍi' dekhe svagaṇa-sahita

SYNONYMS

gajapati rājā—the King of Orissa; *śuni'*—hearing; *kīrtana-mahattva*—the greatness of *saṅkīrtana; aṭṭālikā caḍi'*—ascending to the top of the palace; *dekhe*—sees; *svagaṇa-sahita*—along with his personal associates.

TRANSLATION

Hearing the greatness of the saṅkīrtana, King Pratāparudra went up to the top of his palace and watched the performance with his personal associates.

TEXT 237

কীর্তন দেখিয়া রাজার হৈল চমৎকার ।
প্রভুকে মিলিতে উৎকণ্ঠা বাড়িল অপার ॥ ২৩৭ ॥

kīrtana dekhiyā rājāra haila camatkāra
prabhuke milite utkaṇṭhā bāḍila apāra

SYNONYMS

kīrtana dekhiyā—seeing the performance of *kīrtana; rājāra*—of the King; *haila*—there was; *camatkāra*—astonishment; *prabhuke*—Śrī Caitanya Mahāprabhu; *milite*—to meet; *utkaṇṭhā*—anxiety; *bāḍila*—increased; *apāra*—unlimitedly.

TRANSLATION

The King was very astonished to see Śrī Caitanya Mahāprabhu's kīrtana, and the King's anxiety to meet Him increased unlimitedly.

TEXT 238

কীর্তন-সমাপ্ত্যে প্রভু দেখি' পুষ্পাঞ্জলি ।
সর্ব বৈষ্ণব লঞা প্রভু আইলা বাসা চলি' ॥ ২৩৮ ॥

kīrtana-samāptye prabhu dekhi' puṣpāñjali
sarva vaiṣṇava lañā prabhu āilā vāsā cali'

SYNONYMS

kīrtana-samāptye—at the end of the performance of *kīrtana; prabhu*—Śrī Caitanya Mahāprabhu; *dekhi'*—after seeing; *puṣpāñjali*—offering flowers to the Lord Jagannātha Deity; *sarva vaiṣṇava*—all the devotees; *lañā*—accompanying; *prabhu*—Śrī Caitanya Mahāprabhu; *āilā*—returned; *vāsā*—to His residential place; *cali'*—going.

TRANSLATION

After the saṅkīrtana ended, Śrī Caitanya Mahāprabhu watched the offering of flowers to the Lord Jagannātha Deity. Then He and all the Vaiṣṇavas returned to His residence.

TEXT 239

পড়িছা আনিয়া দিল প্রসাদ বিস্তর ।
সবারে বাঁটিয়া তাহা দিলেন ঈশ্বর ॥ ২৩৯ ॥

paḍichā āniyā dila prasāda vistara
sabāre bāṅṭiyā tāhā dilena īśvara

SYNONYMS

paḍichā—the superintendent of the temple; *āniyā*—bringing; *dila*—delivered; *prasāda*—of remnants of Jagannātha's food; *vistara*—a large quantity; *sabāre*—

unto everyone; *bāṅṭiyā*—distributing; *tāhā*—that; *dilena*—gave; *īśvara*—the Lord.

TRANSLATION

The superintendent of the temple then brought large quantities of prasāda, which Śrī Caitanya Mahāprabhu personally distributed to all the devotees.

TEXT 240

সবারে বিদায় দিল করিতে শয়ন।
এইমত লীলা করে শচীর নন্দন ॥ ২৪০ ॥

sabāre vidāya dila karite śayana
ei-mata līlā kare śacīra nandana

SYNONYMS

sabāre—unto everyone; *vidāya*—bidding farewell; *dila*—gave; *karite śayana*—to take rest; *ei-mata*—in this way; *līlā*—pastimes; *kare*—performed; *śacīra nandana*—the son of Śacī.

TRANSLATION

Finally they all departed to rest in bed. In this way Śrī Caitanya Mahāprabhu, the son of Śacīmātā, performed His pastimes.

TEXT 241

যাবৎ আছিলা সবে মহাপ্রভু-সঙ্গে।
প্রতিদিন এইমত করে কীর্তন-রঙ্গে ॥ ২৪১ ॥

yāvat āchilā sabe mahāprabhu-saṅge
prati-dina ei-mata kare kīrtana-raṅge

SYNONYMS

yāvat—so long; *āchilā*—remained; *sabe*—all the devotees; *mahāprabhu-saṅge*—along with Śrī Caitanya Mahāprabhu; *prati-dina*—every day; *ei-mata*—in this way; *kare*—performed; *kīrtana-raṅge*—*saṅkīrtana* in great pleasure.

TRANSLATION

As long as the devotees remained at Jagannātha Purī with Śrī Caitanya Mahāprabhu, the pastime of saṅkīrtana was performed with great jubilation every day.

TEXT 242

**এই ত' কহিলুঁ প্রভুর কীর্তন-বিলাস।
যেবা ইহা শুনে, হয় চৈতন্যের দাস ॥ ২৪২ ॥**

*ei ta' kahiluṅ prabhura kīrtana-vilāsa
yebā ihā śune, haya caitanyera dāsa*

SYNONYMS

ei ta' kahiluṅ—thus I have explained; *prabhura*—of the Lord; *kīrtana-vilāsa*—pastimes in *saṅkīrtana; yebā*—anyone who; *ihā*—this; *śune*—listens to; *haya*—becomes; *caitanyera dāsa*—a servant of Śrī Caitanya Mahāprabhu.

TRANSLATION

In this way I have explained the Lord's pastime of saṅkīrtana, and I bless everyone with this benediction: By listening to this description, one will surely become a servant of Śrī Caitanya Mahāprabhu.

TEXT 243

**শ্রীরূপ-রঘুনাথ-পদে যার আশ।
চৈতন্যচরিতামৃত কহে কৃষ্ণদাস ॥ ২৪৩ ॥**

*śrī-rūpa-raghunātha-pade yāra āśa
caitanya-caritāmṛta kahe kṛṣṇadāsa*

SYNONYMS

śrī-rūpa—Śrīla Rūpa Gosvāmī; *raghunātha*—Śrīla Raghunātha dāsa Gosvāmī; *pade*—at the lotus feet; *yāra*—whose; *āśa*—expectation; *caitanya-caritāmṛta*—the book named *Caitanya-caritāmṛta; kahe*—describes; *kṛṣṇadāsa*—Śrīla Kṛṣṇadāsa Kavirāja Gosvāmī.

TRANSLATION

Praying at the lotus feet of Śrī Rūpa and Śrī Raghunātha, always desiring their mercy, I, Kṛṣṇadāsa, narrate Śrī Caitanya-caritāmṛta, following in their footsteps.

Thus end the Bhaktivedanta purports to the Śrī Caitanya-caritāmṛta, Madhya-līlā, *Eleventh Chapter, describing the* beḍā-kīrtana *pastimes of Śrī Caitanya Mahāprabhu.*

References

The statements of *Śrī Caitanya-caritāmṛta* are all confirmed by standard Vedic authorities. The following authentic scriptures are quoted in this book on the pages listed. Numerals in bold type refer the reader to *Śrī Caitanya-caritāmṛta's* translations. Numerals in regular type are references to its purports.

Ādī Purāṇa, **223**

Bhagavad-gītā, 03, 135, 136, 166, 192

Bhakti-rasāmṛta-sindhu (Rūpa Gosvāmī), 197, **199**

Brahma-saṁhitā, 37, **87,** 103, 192, 200-201

Caitanya-bhāgavata (Vṛndāvana dāsa Ṭhākura), 121

Caitanya-candrāmṛta (Prabhodhānanda Sarasvatī), 197, 198

Caitanya-candrodaya-nāṭaka (Kavi Karṇapura), 101, 212, **214-215, 234**

Hari-bhakti-vilāsa (Sanātana Gosvāmī), 178

Kaṭha Upaniṣad, 14, 228-229

Kurma Purāṇa, **19, 23**

Laghu-bhāgavatāmṛta (Rūpa Gosvāmī), **223, 224**

Mahābhārata, 65, 80, **193**

Manu-saṁhitā, 185

Padma Purāṇa, 224

Rāmāyana, 16, 81, **181**

Śrīmad-Bhāgavatam, 14, 18, 52, **53,** 58, 59, 105, 115, 135-6, 196, **224,** 241, 262, 263, **273-274**

Śvetāśvatara Upaniṣad, 237

Upadeśāmṛta (Rūpa Gosvāmī), 238

Vidagdha-mādhava (Rūpa Gosvāmī), 225

Glossary

A

Ācārya—spiritual master who teaches by his example.
Acintya-bhedābheda-tattva—simultaneous oneness and difference.
Agni—the fire-god.
Anavasara—period of a fortnight between bathing ceremony and Ratha-yātrā when the body of Jagannātha Deity is repainted.
Apsarās—beautiful dancing girls on heavenly planets.
Arcā-vigraha—the worshipable Deity.
Āryan—a person who believes in advancing in spiritual life.
Aśramas—four orders of spiritual life—*brahmacārya, gṛhastha, vānaprastha* and *sannyāsa.*
Asuras—demons.

B

Bāula community—one of the *apa-sampradāyas,* or unauthorized devotional groups.
Bhakti-siddhānta-viruddha—that which is against the philosophy of *acintya-bhedābheda.*
Bhāgavata-dharma—the transcendental religion that is the eternal function of the living being.
Bhakti—devotional service.
Bhava-sāgara—the ocean of repeated birth and death.
Brahmā—the first living being in and the creator of this universe.
Brahmacārī—celibate student.
Brahman—the Lord's all-pervading feature.
Brāhmaṇa—the intelligent class of men.
Bhaya—fear.

C

Cakra—wheel of Viṣṇu on top of temples.

D

Dāsa—servant.
Dharma—religious principles by which one can understand the Supreme Personality of Godhead.
Dāsya-rasa—relationship with Kṛṣṇa in servitude.
Devahūti—mother of Kapiladeva.

Dhūpa-ārati—ceremony of offering incense and a flower to the Deity.
Dṛḍha-vrata—firm determination.

G

Gopī-candana—type of clay used for *tilaka.*
Gosāñi—*See:* Gosvāmī.
Gosvāmī—Master of the senses.
Govinda—the name of Kṛṣṇa which means "He who pleases the senses and the cows".
Guru—the spiritual master.

I

Indra—the King of the heavenly planets.

J

Jīva—the spirit soul.
Jñāna-kāṇḍa—the section of the *Vedas* which deals with empiric philosophical speculation.

K

Kaivalya—oneness in the effulgence of Brahman.
Kāma—lust.
Kāṇḍas—three divisions of the *Vedas.*
Karatālas—hand cymbals.
Karma—material activities subject to reaction.
Karma-kāṇḍa—the section of the *Vedas* which deals with fruitive activites.
Krodha—anger.
Kṣatriya—the administrative and warrior class of men.

L

Lobha—greed.

M

Māda—intoxication.
Mādhurya-rasa—relationship with Kṛṣṇa in conjugal love.

Mahā-bhāgavata—a devotee in the highest stage of devotional life.
Mahā-mantra—the great chanting for deliverance: Hare Kṛṣṇa, Hare Kṛṣṇa, Kṛṣṇa Kṛṣṇa, Hare Hare/ Hare Rāma, Hare Rāma, Rāma Rāma, Hare Hare.
Mātsarya—enviousness.
Moha—illusion.
Mokṣa—liberation.
Mṛdaṅga—a double-headed drum.

N

Nitya-siddha—eternal perfection attained by never forgetting Kṛṣṇa.

P

Paḍichā—superintendent of the temple.
Pālas—attendants who look after a temple's external affairs.
Pañcopāsanā—worship of the five deities (Viṣṇu, Śiva, Durgā, Ganeśa and Sūrya) which is performed by Māyāvādīs.
Pāṇḍās—See: Paṇḍitas.
Paṇḍita—a learned scholar.
Pāṇḍya—title of kings who ruled over Mādurā and Rāmeśvara.
Paramahaṁsa—the topmost class of God-realized devotees.
Paraṁ Brahman—the Supreme Lord, the chief of all living entities.
Paramparā—disciplic succession.
Prabhu—master.
Prabhupāda—master at whose feet all other masters surrender.
Praharāja—a designation given to *brāhmaṇas* who represent the king when the throne is vacant.
Prajāpatis— progenitors of mankind.
Prākṛta-sahajiyā—a materialistic devotee.
Prema-saṅkīrtana—a special creation of the Lord of congregational chanting in love of Godhead.

R

Rasa—mellow, or the sweet taste of a relationship.
Rasābhāsa—incompatible overlapping of transcendental mellows.

S

Śabda-pramāṇa—the evidence of transcendental sound.

Sakhya-rasa—relationship with Kṛṣṇa in friendship.
Śālagrāma-śilā—a Deity of Nārāyaṇa in the form of a small stone.
Sampradāya—a line of disciplic succession.
Sanātana—eternal, having no beginning or end.
Sanātana-dharma—eternal religion, the sum and substance of which is chanting the *mahā-mantra.*
Saṅkīrtana—congregational chanting of the Lord's holy names.
Sannyāsa—the renounced order of spiritual life.
Śānta-rasa—relationship with Kṛṣṇa in neutral appreciation.
Saptatāla—the seven palm trees in Rāmacandra's forest.
Śāstras—the revealed scriptures.
Snāna-yātra—the bathing ceremony of Lord Jagannātha.
Śruti—the *Vedas.*
Śūdra—the working or servant class of men.

T

Tattvavādīs—the followers of Madhvācārya's *śuddha-dvaita* philosophy.
Tīrtha—holy place of pilgrimage.

U

Upāsanā-kāṇḍa—section of the *Vedas* dealing with processes of worship.

V

Vaikuṇṭha—the place without anxiety—the spiritual world.
Vaiśya—the mercantile and farming class of men.
Varṇas—the four social orders of society—*brāhmaṇas, kṣatriyas, vaiśyas, śūdras.*
Varṇāśrama-dharma—the four castes and four orders of spiritual life.
Vātsalya-rasa—relationship with Kṛṣṇa in the mood of parenthood.
Vidyādharas—attendants of Lord Śiva.
Viṣṇu-tattva—a primary expansion of Kṛṣṇa having full status as Godhead.

Y

Yajña—sacrifice.
Yoga-nidrā—mystic slumber in which Mahā-Viṣṇu creates universes.

Bengali Pronunciation Guide

BENGALI DIACRITICAL EQUIVALENTS AND PRONUNCIATION

Vowels

অ a আ ā ই i ঈ ī উ u ঊ ū ঋ ṛ

ৠ ṝ এ e ঐ ai ও o ঔ au

ং ṁ *(anusvāra)* ঁ ṅ *(candra-bindu)* ঃ ḥ *(visarga)*

Consonants

Gutterals:	ক ka	খ kha	গ ga	ঘ gha	ঙ ṅa
Palatals:	চ ca	ছ cha	জ ja	ঝ jha	ঞ ña
Cerebrals:	ট ṭa	ঠ ṭha	ড ḍa	ঢ ḍha	ণ ṇa
Dentals:	ত ta	থ tha	দ da	ধ dha	ন na
Labials:	প pa	ফ pha	ব ba	ভ bha	ম ma
Semivowels:	য ya	র ra	ল la	ব va	
Sibilants:	শ śa	ষ ṣa	স sa	হ ha	

Vowel Symbols

The vowels are written as follows after a consonant:

া ā ি i ী ī ু u ূ ū ৃ ṛ ৄ ṝ ে e ৈ ai ো o ৌ au

For example: কা kā কি ki কী kī কু ku কূ kū কৃ kṛ

কৄ kṝ কে ke কৈ kai কো ko কৌ kau

The letter *a* is implied after a consonant with no vowel symbol.

The symbol *virāma* (্) indicates that there is no final vowel. ক্ k

The letters above should be pronounced as follows:

a –like the *o* in h*o*t; sometimes like the *o* in go; final *a* is usually silent.
ā –like the *a* in f*a*r.
i, ī –like the *ee* in m*ee*t.
u, ū –like the *u* in r*u*le.
ṛ –like the *ri* in *ri*m.
ṝ –like the *ree* in *ree*d.
e –like the *ai* in p*ai*n; rarely like *e* in b*e*t.
ai –like the *oi* in b*oi*l.
o –like the *o* in g*o*.
au –like the *ow* in *ow*l.
ṁ –*(anusvāra)* like the *ng* in so*ng*.
ḥ –*(visarga)* a final *h* sound like in Ah.
ṅ –*(candra-bindu)* a nasal *n* sound like in the French word *bon*.
k –like the *k* in *k*ite.
kh –like the *kh* in Ec*kh*art.
g –like the *g* in *g*ot.
gh –like the *gh* in bi*g-h*ouse.
ṅ –like the *n* in ba*n*k.
c –like the *ch* in *ch*alk.
ch –like the *chh* in mu*ch-h*aste.
j –like the *j* in *j*oy.
jh –like the *geh* in colle*ge-h*all.
ñ –like the *n* in bu*n*ch.
ṭ –like the *t* in *t*alk.
ṭh –like the *th* in ho*t-h*ouse.
ḍ –like the *d* in *d*awn.
ḍh –like the *dh* in goo*d-h*ouse.
ṇ –like the *n* in g*n*aw.
t–as in *t*alk but with the tongue against the the teeth.
th–as in ho*t-h*ouse but with the tongue against the teeth.
d–as in *d*awn but with the tongue against the teeth.
dh–as in goo*d-h*ouse but with the tongue against the teeth.
n–as in *n*or but with the tongue against the teeth.
p –like the *p* in *p*ine.
ph –like the *ph* in *ph*ilosopher.
b –like the *b* in *b*ird.
bh –like the *bh* in ru*b-h*ard.
m –like the *m* in *m*other.
y –like the *j* in *j*aw. য
y –like the *y* in *y*ear. য়
r –like the *r* in *r*un.
l –like the *l* in *l*aw.
v –like the *b* in *b*ird or like the *w* in d*w*arf.
ś, ṣ –like the *sh* in *sh*op.
s –like the *s* in *s*un.
h–like the *h* in *h*ome.

This is a general guide to Bengali pronunciation. The Bengali transliterations in this book accurately show the original Bengali spelling of the text. One should note, however, that in Bengali, as in English, spelling is not always a true indication of how a word is pronounced. Tape recordings of His Divine Grace A.C. Bhaktivedanta Swami Prabhupāda chanting the original Bengali verses are available from the International Society for Krishna Consciousness, 3959 Landmark St., Culver City, California 90230.

Index of Bengali and Sanskrit Verses

This index constitutes a complete alphabetical listing of the first and third line of each four-line verse and both lines of each two-line verse in *Śrī Caitanya-caritāmṛta*. In the first column the transliteration is given, and in the second and third columns respectively the chapter-verse references and page number for each verse are to be found.

A

B

J

K

R

S

T

General Index

Numerals in bold type indicate references to *Śrī Caitanya-caritāmṛta's* verses. Numerals in regular type are references to its purports.

A

C

D

E

Envy
- of bona fide spiritual master by *sahajiyās,* 121

F

Faith
- in scriptures necessary, 105
- hearing Caitanya's pastimes with, 104-105
- in Caitanya required for *saṅkīrtana,* 265
- in Caitanya saves life of *brāhmaṇa,* **15**
- in words of *ācārya,* 15
- possible through mercy of Lord, 273

Fasting
- as indirect order of Supreme, **271**
- as regulation for pilgrimage, **269**-270
- performed by Rāmacandra's devotee *brāhmaṇa,* **10-15**
- required in absence of *mahā-prasāda,* **271**

Father
- order of to be executed without consideration, **181**

Fear
- as enemy of mind, 214
- devotee accepts any position withou, 59
- of losing post by Indra, 64
- surrender without, **56**

Fire, god of
- Agni as, **18**
- *brāhmaṇa* to give up life by, **11**
- Sītā brought before, **20, 23**

Food
- Caitanya receives remnants of Jagannātha's, **124**
- Caitanya's unprepared, **8**
- cooked for Caitanya, **25**
- offered by *brāhmaṇa* to Caitanya, **67**
- *See also: Prasāda*

Form of Lord
- Caitanya reveals four-armed to Kāśī Miśra, **125**
- rejected by Māyāvāda *sampradāya,* 63

Fruitive activities
- as painful and transient by nature, 55
- condemned in all scripture, **53,** 55
- contamination associated with, 63
- dedicated to Lord, 54
- execution of stressed in *karma-kāṇḍa,* 54
- favored by Madhvācārya-*sampradāya,* **62**-63
- knowledge superior to, 55
- mercy needed for extrication from, 274
- must be utilized for devotional service, 55
- rejected by devotees, **60**

Fruitive workers
- realization of as waste of time, 103

G

Gadādhara Paṇḍita
- embraced and glorified by Caitanya, **293**
- identified by Gopīnātha Ācārya, **253**
- pleased to hear of Caitanya's return, **149**

Gajendra-mokṣaṇa
- Caitanya visits Viṣṇu temple at, **27**

Gandharvas
- Svarūpa Dāmodara as expert a musician as, **165**

Gaṇeśa
- explained in *Brahma-saṁhitā,* 37

Gaṅgādāsa Paṇḍita
- embraced and glorified by Caitanya, **293**
- identified by Gopīnātha Ācārya, **254**

Ganges
- Paramānanda plans to bathe in, **3**

Garbhodakaśāyī Viṣṇu
- explained in *Brahma-saṁhitā,* 37

Gauḍīya-Vaiṣṇava
- *saṅkīrtana* parties of, 66

Gaurāṅgera saṅgi-gaṇe
- quoted, 256

Gaurahari
- as name of Caitanya, **190**

Gāyatrī *mantra*
- origin of explained in *Brahma-saṁhitā,* 37

H

Kṛṣṇa-karṇāmṛta
studying of elevates one to knowledge of pure devotional service, **78**
supports devotional service, **87**
Kṛṣṇadāsa Kavirāja Gosvāmī
calls himself greedy and shameless, **102**
wrote commentary on Bilvamaṅgala's book, 78
Kṛṣṇa-veṇvā River
Lord Caitanya visits holy places of, **77**
Kṛṣṇa
as spiritual master of everyone, 178
Caitanya and Śrī Raṅga Purī discuss, **72**
Caitanya as, **116,** 196, **197, 221, 263-264**
chanting fixed mind on, 214
complexion of, **263**
Deity of at Uḍupī, **41**
Deity of holds lump of food, 42
dependent on His affection, **177**-178
gives direct audience through His mercy, **200**
Madhvācārya's meditation on, 42
mercy of gotten by mercy of devotee, 241
quoted on qualities of devotees, **224**
statement of to Arjuna, **223**
worshiped alone, 70
worshiped by Caitanya in *mādhurya-rasa,* 225
Kṛṣṇa-śakti vinā nahe tāra
quoted, 176
Kṛtamālā River
Caitanya bathes in, **8, 15**
Kṣatriya
as one of four *varṇas,* 50
can't be disciple of *brāhmaṇa,* 175-176
Pratāparudra as, 117
follows orders of saintly persons, 117-118
Kṣetrajñaṁ cāpi māṁ viddhi
verses quoted, 192
Kṣīra-bhagavatī
temple of visited by Caitanya, **65**
Kulaśekhara
as ruler of Mādurā, 7
Kulīna-grāma
Gopīnātha Ācārya identifies residents of, **257**
Kulīna-grāma
inhabitants of join Advaita, **152**
Kumāras
as part of *paramparā,* 262
unable to receive the Lord's mercy, 274
Kuntī
as wife of Bhavānanda Rāya, **134**
Kūrma Purāṇa
contains chaste woman's narration, **17**
Caitanya receives old manuscripts of, **21**
cited on Rāvaṇa kidnapping Sītā, **19**
quoted on deliverance of Sītā to Rāmacandra, **23**
Kurukṣetra, Battle of
Kṛṣṇa broke promise not to fight in, 196
Kuśāvarta
visited by Caitanya, **83**
Kutakācala
as forest where Ṛṣabhadeva burned, 1

L

Laghu-bhāgavatāmṛta
quoted on devotees of Kṛṣṇa's servant, **223**
quoted on service to Vaiṣṇavas, **224**
Lakṣmaṇa
accepted orders of Rāmacandra, **181**
brought food from forest for Caitanya, **9**
Deity of at Cāmātpura, **27, 28**
Lamentation
accompanying material desire also vanishes, 168
Lāṅga-gaṇeśa
seen by Caitanya, **65**
Leaders
take instruction from saintly persons, 117-118
Liberation
by understanding *dharma,* 263
dedication of duties to Kṛṣṇa makes one eligible for, **49**
devotee always on platform of, 52
five kinds described, **57-58**
insignificant to pure devotee, **58, 60**
of associates of Caitanya, 256

Liberation
same as hell and heaven to devotee, **57, 59**
Lion gate
as main gate of Jagannātha temple, **277**
Living entities
as localized, **191**-192
as predominated, 192
attain release upon surrender to Supreme Lord, 289
Caitanya is not one of, **115**
compared to charioteers, 228-229
described in *Brahma-saṁhitā,* 37
size of, 192
struggling hard in material nature, 167, 289
Locana dāsa Ṭhākura
as Vaiṣṇava song writer, 255
Lotus feet of Kṛṣṇa
chanting engages mind at, 214
mind cleansed by connection with, 167
Love of God
as highest goal according to Caitanya, 50
Caitanya's dancing merged world in, **208**
Caitanya inundated by ecstasy of, **71**
described in *Brahma-saṁhitā,* 37
devotees exhibit spontaneous, **267**
distributed by Caitanya, 225
Kṛṣṇa seen directly by, **200**-201
Mādhavendra Purī as root of worship in ecstatic, **69**-70
not attained by *karma-kāṇḍa* or *jñāna-kāṇḍa,* 54
prema-saṅkīrtana as chanting in, **261**
Śrī Raṅga Purī inundated by ecstasy of, **71**
symptoms of displayed by King Pratāparudra, **219**
vision of divine described in *Brahma-saṁhitā,* 37
Lust
as enemy of mind, 214

M

Mādhava Ghosh
identified by Gopīnātha Ācārya, **255**
Mādhavendra Purī
accepted Madvhācārya-sampradāya, 63
as root of worship in ecstatic love, **69**-70
as spiritual master of Śrī Raṅga Purī, **68**
visited house of Jagannātha Miśra, **73**
Mādhurya-rasa
as supreme spiritual activity, 225
Madhvācārya
as authority on party policy, **61**
Caitanya visits place of, **41**
dreams of Deity, **44**
life history of summarized, 41-44
Madhvācārya-sampradāya
accepted by Mādhavendra Purī, 63
accepts transcendental form of God, 63
Madhva-vijaya
as reference on Madhvācārya, 43
Mādurā
See: Mathurā
Mahā-baleśvara
as famous temple of Śiva, 65
Mahābhārata
cited on Sūrpāraka, 65
quoted on qualities of Caitanya, **193**
quoted on Sahadeva's victory, 80
summarized by Madhvācārya, 43
Mahājano yena gataḥ sa
cited on accepting authority, 15
Mahā-mantra
chanted by Haridāsa Ṭhākura, **305**
Mahā-prasāda
impious cannot understand value of holy name and, 319
Mahā-prasāde govinde
verse quoted, 318
Mahārāṣṭra
saṅkīrtana spread in province of, 66
Mahātmā
symptoms of, 235
See also: Devotee, Pure devotees
Mahā-Viṣṇu
the original presented in *Brahma-saṁhitā,* 37
Mahendra-śaila
Caitanya saw Paraśurāma at, **16**
Māhiṣmatī-pura
visited by Caitanya, **80**

Paramahaṁsas
addressed by title *Ṭhākura,* 295
free from sense gratification, 70
Paramātmā
is expanded everywhere, 192
Pratāparudra arranges for devotees', **246-247**
served on plantain leaves, **314**
taken by Vāṇīnātha, **268-269**
the Lord orders devotees to take, **271**
transcendental, not ordinary food, 318
Pratāparudra
arranges for devotees' *prasāda,* **246-247**
as fully surrendered soul, 233
as *kṣatriya,* 117
as servant of Jagannātha, **213**
benedicted by Gopīnātha Ācārya, **245**
desires audience with Caitanya, **112**
determination of, **234-**238
follows instruction of Sārvabhauma, **242**
inquires about bathing of Jagannātha, **242**
meets Sārvabhauma, **111-119**
released Rāmānanda Rāya from service, **218-220**
Ṣārvabhauma requested Caitanya to meet, **210-213**
visits temple of Jagannātha, **216**
watched *saṅkīrtana* from top of palace, **330**
Prayers
composed by Madhvācārya, 42
discussed in *Brahma-saṁhitā,* 37
offered to Agastya Muni, **29**
offered to Caitanya by Advaita first, **278**
offered to Caitanya by Śrīvāsa Ṭhākura and other Vaiṣṇavas, **279**
offered to Paramānanda Purī by Svarūpa Dāmodara, **172**
offering as process of devotional service, **51**
Premāñjana-cchurita-bhakti
verses quoted, 200
Prema-saṅkīrtana
as chanting in love of God, 261
Purāṇas
cited on spiritual substance, **13**
Purāṇas
quoted on orders of spiritual master, **181**
Purandara Ācārya
embraced and glorified by Caitanya, **293**
identified by Gopīnātha Ācārya, **253**
Pure devotees
do not accept impure principles, 164
free from all desire, 63
mind of fixed in service, **58**
no relief from *māyā* without service of, 142
obtaining service of, **225-226**
perform unparalleled *saṅkīrtana,* 259
purify holy places, 270
reject five kinds of liberation, **57**
serve as ornaments to Jagannātha Purī, **131**
study *Kṛṣṇa-karṇāmṛta,* **77**
Purification
association of devotees necessary for, 54
of places of pilgrimage by saints, **115**
of those addicted to sinful acts, 136
Paramparā
personalities of named, 262
principles of religion handed down in, 262
See also: Disciplic succession
Paras tasmāt tu bhāvo 'nyo
verses quoted, 212
Paraśurāma
killed his mother, **181**
Parīkṣit
Śukadeva described King Bharata to, 58
Pārvatī
as goddess Durgā, **19**
curses Citraketu, 59
Pastimes of Caitanya
as unlimited, **102**
not properly describable, **102**
result of analytical study of, **106**
Pastimes of Kṛṣṇa
can be seen everywhere, 168
discussed by Sārvabhauma and Caitanya, **173**
the Lord takes pleasure in, **281**

R

S

T

U

V